Charlemagne

The publisher gratefully acknowledges the generous contribution to this book provided by the General Endowment Fund of the University of California Press Associates.

The translation of this work has been funded by SEPS
Segretariato Europeo per le Pubblicazioni Scientifiche
Via Val d'Aposa 7 · 40123 Bologna · Italy
tel +39 051 271992 · fax +39 051 265983
seps@alma.unibo.it · www.seps.it

Charlemagne

Father of a Continent

Alessandro Barbero

Translated by Allan Cameron

UNIVERSITY OF CALIFORNIA PRESS

Berkeley   Los Angeles   London

University of California Press
Berkeley and Los Angeles, California

University of California Press, Ltd.
London, England

© Guis. Laterza & Figli SpA, 2000. This translation of *Carlo Magno, Un Padre dell'Europa* is published by arrangement with Guis. Laterza & Figli SpA, Roma-Bari.

Library of Congress Cataloging-in-Publication Data

Barbero, Alessandro.
  [Carlo Magno. English]
  Charlemagne : father of a continent / Alessandro Barbero ; translated by Allan Cameron.
      p.   cm.
  Includes bibliographical references and index.
  ISBN 0–520–23943–1 (alk. paper)
  1. Charlemagne, Emperor, 742–814. 2. France—Kings and rulers—Biography. 3. France—History—To 987.
4. Europe—History—392–814. I. Title.

DC73.B3613   2004
944'.0142'092—dc22   2003017208

Manufactured in the United States of America

13   12   11   10   09   08   07   06   05
11   10   9   8   7   6   5   4   3   2

CONTENTS

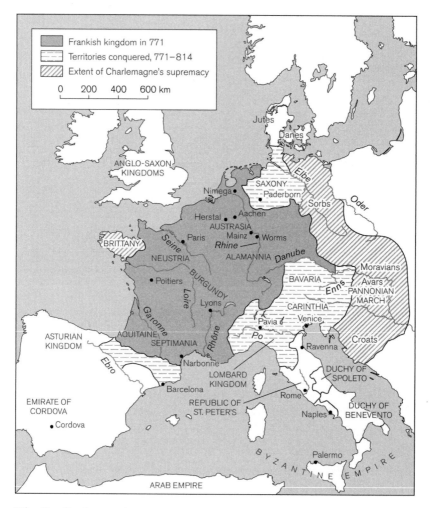

The Carolingian empire.

Introduction

Paderborn, Summer of 799

In July 799 Charles, king of the Franks, had set up camp at Paderborn, in the heart of vanquished Saxony, and it was bustling with bricklayers and carpenters. Convoys of carts loaded with bricks and mortar were arriving every day along dirt tracks. Other materials were brought by waterways on barges and scows. The king was building a city in the forest and marshland, which was to be Christendom's bridgehead among the newly converted pagans. Its palace and a basilica were to rival those of Aachen. But at this particular moment, the king had little time to think about his building plans or even his military ambitions. He was anxiously waiting for the return of his son Charles, who had pressed on as far as the Elbe to negotiate with the Slavic tribes that had settled on the banks of that great river, and then to add to his troubles, Pope Leo III suddenly arrived in Paderborn. Leo's arrival had been preceded by news of the insurrection in Rome, during which his enemies had captured him, gouged out his eyes, and cut off his tongue. Then Providence had miraculously intervened to assist his escape.[1]

When he did arrive, the pope turned out to be something of a disappointment, because it was immediately obvious that he was still in possession of his eyes and his tongue. Leo III explained that they had miraculously grown back again, and out of politeness his listeners showed no sign of disbelief. King Charles found it difficult to give much credence to this man who had too often been the subject of scandal. Charles had sent him an odd letter at the time of his election to the papal throne, exhorting him to behave well and not to give grounds for suspicion.[2] Nevertheless, Leo III was the pope, and the king of the Franks, whom everyone considered the true protector of the Church in the West, had to do everything he could to ensure that the papacy received the respect it deserved. Although he had little desire to do so, he was obliged to go to Rome, quell the revolt, and reestablish the pope's authority in the eyes of the world, as long as there was not too much evidence to prove the rumors about the pope.

During talks between the pope and the king in that hot and dusty Paderborn summer, an exciting idea was first suggested or at least fully fleshed out: when Charles reached Rome, the inhabitants, who in spite of everything were still the people of the Eternal City, were to acclaim him as emperor, just as in previous times they had acclaimed Augustus and Constantine. Thus the Frankish king would become the successor to the Roman emperors on a par with the *basileus* who ruled in Constantinople, and no one could object to his meddling in the affairs of the Eternal City or indeed of Christendom as a whole. It is possible that the prospect of such a scenario had been circulating for some time both at the royal court in Aachen and at the papal court, which at the time resided at the palace and church of St. John Lateran. But it wasn't discussed seriously until the Paderborn meeting in the summer of 799, although the matter was still so delicate that no written record of the discussions survives.

In the same brief period a poet who remains anonymous, in spite of repeated efforts by historians to identify him as one or other of the men of learning at the court, undertook the composition of a short poem in Latin hexameters, which copyists were to call *Karolus Magnus et Leo Papa*.[3] The poetry is perfectly adequate, but we are not so interested here in its literary merits as in the anonymous writer's political intent. In this contemporary account, the pope clearly asserts that he must be defended from his enemies and that Charles is the only sovereign in the world capable of reestablishing the majesty of the Church. Precisely for this reason, it is right that Christians all over Western Europe should acknowledge him as their leader to an extent that is not justified by his kingly title alone. The poet, who was evidently privy to the negotiations that were taking place, perceived the Frankish king as the successor to the Roman emperors, ruling in Aachen as though it were a second Rome. He hailed Charles as *rex pater Europae*, "the king and father of Europe."

Now that the peoples of our continent have found a way out from the dead end into which they had been driven by nationalist ideologies and seem to be moving toward an integrated and supranational Europe, the image conjured up by the Paderborn poet appears surprisingly topical. After all, it was Charlemagne who first created a single political structure in Europe that stretched from Hamburg to Benevento, and from Vienna to Barcelona, with its trade centered on the Rhine and the seaports of the North Sea. It was profoundly different from the Roman Empire, which had been centered on the Mediterranean, and whose richest and most civilized regions had been in the Middle East. To quote perhaps the greatest historians of the century that has just come to a close, while "Europe appeared when the Roman Empire fell" (Marc Bloch), it was "the empire of Charlemagne that first gave it the form that we call Europe" (Lucien Febvre).[4]

Of course, every generation of historians constructs its own image of the past, and there was not always so much agreement on the parallel between Charlemagne's empire and the birth of a European entity. A quarter of a century ago an important conference in Spoleto, attended by leading specialists on the early Middle Ages, posed the question in its title: "The Birth of Europe and Carolingian Europe: A Link Yet to Be Demonstrated." Opinions differed a great deal, and some were diametrically opposed, but on the whole the case for Charlemagne as the father of Europe emerged somewhat the worse for wear or, at the very least, less indisputable than it had seemed a generation earlier to Bloch and Febvre.[5]

Today the pendulum has swung back in the other direction, and there is again wide support for this interpretation, thanks in part to a veritable revolution in research fields, particularly the economic one. Until a few years ago the military victories achieved on all horizons and the program of cultural renewal promoted by Charlemagne seemed like the glittering surface of a profoundly backward society and a stagnant economy. Today a wide variety of indicators lead us to perceive the Carolingian age as the basis for the demographic and economic recovery that became clear around 1000 A.D. and from which modern Europe was born with all its overwhelming vitality. The current state of academic research, irrespective of the superficial enthusiasm for everything European in the year 2000, allows us to revive the term used twelve centuries ago by the anonymous poet and speak of Charlemagne as a father of Europe.

ONE

The Frankish Tradition

THE SETTLEMENT OF THE FRANKS IN GAUL

Charlemagne is firmly identified in the European imagination with the title of emperor that was conferred on him at St. Peter's on Christmas morning of 800. In reality, he only carried this title for the last fourteen years of his long life. Thirty-two years earlier he had become the king of the Franks, a title he kept even after gaining the imperial one, which, as we shall see, was intrinsically different and did not cancel out the kingship he inherited from his father, Pepin the Short, in September 768. The poet who many years after his death was to write the *Chanson de Roland* would refer to him as "Carles li reis, nostre emperere magnes" and was clearly still well aware of this twin identity.[1]

What did it mean to be king of the Franks toward the end of the eighth century? From the very beginning the Franks occupied an important position among the Germanic people who three or four centuries before Charles crossed the Rhine in small groups and settled there, first as allies and then as overlords in the territory of the Roman Empire of the West. Strictly speaking, they were not even a people but a confederation of tribes from the Rhine basin—Bructerii, Cattuarii, and Camavi—who spoke the same Germanic dialect, practiced the same religious cults, and followed the same warrior leaders. Thus they ended up adopting a collective name but one that initially constituted an extremely weak form of identity. Originally Frank simply meant "courageous person" and later "free man."

Sidonius Apollinaris, a Roman, a Christian bishop, and a classical poet, describes the Franks he came to know in Gaul during the fifth century. His words evoke a physical type that must have appeared decidedly exotic to a Mediterranean reader, but he did not hide his admiration for the courage of these barbarians:

> Their red hair falls from the top of their heads, while their necks are shaved at the back. Their eyes are clear, transparent, and of a grayish blue color. Instead of a beard, they have narrow mustaches which they curl with a comb. Their preferred amusements are throwing axes at targets, spinning their shields, and running and catching their spears after having thrown them. From childhood they have an intense passion for warfare. If they are overcome by superior enemy numbers or adverse terrain, they yield only to death and never to fear.[2]

Sidonius concludes, "They could even have tamed monsters." While waiting for the monsters, these barbarians took control of Gaul, which in the impoverished Western Europe of the late imperial period was perhaps the most prosperous and populous province—probably more than Spain and certainly more than Italy. They immediately demonstrated that they had no intention of sharing it with anyone else: the Visigoths, who had previously settled in the south of the country—in the current Provence and Languedoc—were defeated and driven over the Pyrenees, and the Burgundians, who had settled in the Rhône Valley, had to acknowledge the superiority of the Franks and submit to their king. Moreover, it was only with great difficulty that first Byzantine generals and then Lombard kings managed to prevent the new lords of Gaul from spreading over the Alps into Italy.

The Romans, or rather the Romano-Gauls of Celtic or Italic blood who populated the Gallic provinces and were by then all Latin speakers, were allowed to stay as long as they acknowledged the supremacy of the Frankish king. This was true not only of peasants and slaves but also of rich land-owning and senatorial families and the Catholic clergy. In any case, the Franks could never have populated the whole of Gaul and replaced the many millions of Romans who lived there, given that there were no more than two hundred thousand of them, including women and children, and possibly even fewer. These warriors, whose superhuman stature contemporaries found so striking, only settled in great numbers with their families in the northern part of the country along the course of the Rhine, the Meuse, and the Moselle. That was the only region in which they outnumbered the Romans, and indeed, the linguistic border between Latin and Germanic Europe passes through that region to this day.

To the south, in the land where wine, corn, and oil replaced beer, meat, and butter, the Frankish presence gradually grew less marked, and the Romano-Gallic population more easily absorbed the conquerors. The former imposed their customs and dialect on the latter, leading to the birth of modern French. Around Paris, already one of the favorite residences of Frankish kings, no Germanic dialect ever replaced the Romance tongue. The Franks were almost never seen south of the Loire, and there the Romano-Gallic population continued to live as in the past, although they obeyed the barbarian kings in the north and paid their taxes to them.

THE FRANKISH MONARCHY
The Merovingian Kingdoms

The Frankish kingdom in Gaul was in reality a collection of kingdoms. Although the various tribes that made up the Frankish people did briefly submit to one king, the cruel and energetic Clovis, with whom they converted to Christianity, that unity did not last very long. The custom of subdividing the king's inheritance among all the male sons led to the formation of many kingdoms that rejoined and divided again according to circumstance. The most easterly kingdom between the Moselle and the Rhine, the only one in which the Franks were the majority and the language in general use was of Germanic origin, was called the "kingdom of the East," Austrasia or Austria. Because of its geographic position, it was able to impose its authority on the peoples of southern Germany, and it incorporated the duchies of the Thuringians, *Alamanni*, and Bavarians into the Frankish area of influence.

Further west, beyond the immense forest of Ardennes that covered part of modern Belgium, the kingdoms of Paris, Orléans, and Soissons came together over time to form a single kingdom, whose main language was Romance and whose southern border was marked by the Loire. The Franks called this Neustria, which probably meant the "kingdom of the West." Beyond the Vosges to the southeast and between the Rhône and the Alps, the kingdom of Burgundy formed a separate political entity, although the Burgundians were soon to be forced to renounce their own king and acknowledge the overlordship of the Frankish king of Neustria. Further south where few ethnic Franks were to be found, Provence continued to be ruled by a Roman official with the title of patrician, even though he was now accountable to one or other of the Frankish kings and no longer to Constantinople. Finally, in the southwest where the Romano-Gaulish population lived alongside a restive Basque minority, Aquitaine tended to slip out of Frankish control, in spite of being governed by a duke rather than an independent king.

The most energetic monarchs in the Frankish ruling family, which was called the Merovingian dynasty after their ancestor Merovech (or Merovaeus), occasionally managed to reunite the different kingdoms, only to have them divided up again on their death. The majority of these kings, who initially governed Gaul as supposed appointees of the distant Byzantine emperor, had more of a priestly than a warrior role. The symbol of their kingship was their long hair, hence the term *reges criniti* (long-haired kings). According to ancient beliefs, these flowing, almost unmanly, locks represented the king's magical powers and his ability to guarantee prosperity for his people and fertility for women and the land. Following their conversion to Christianity, this pagan belief in the sacredness of kingly office gradually began to dissolve, and the priest-kings of the Merovingian dynasty found that their authority was disintegrating.

Mayors of the Palace

The real power in the two principal kingdoms of Austrasia and Neustria passed into the hands of men who could not boast sacred charisma but knew how to lead the Franks to victory in war. These mayors of the palace were effectively ministers or even viceroys, who governed officially on behalf of the kings, while tending to supplant them and drive them into a purely ceremonial role. Originally there was a mayor in each kingdom, but in 688 Pepin, who had grown extremely powerful and held the office in Austrasia, managed to impose his authority on Neustria as well, after he defeated the Neustrian magnates in battle. From that time on, even when there were still two kings, the Frankish people were effectively ruled by a single mayor of the palace. This Pepin of Herstal, as historians refer to him, was the great-grandfather of Charlemagne.

At this stage, the family later known as Carolingian was referred to as Pepinids or Arnulfings, descended from the alliance between two prominent landowners in Austrasia, Pepin the Old and Arnulf, who both died in 640. To be more precise, Pepin's daughter married Arnulf's son before Arnulf, who was eventually to be venerated as a saint, became the bishop of Metz. This union produced Pepin of Herstal, the sole mayor for the Frankish kingdoms. On his death in 714, the office was passed on to his son Charles, known as Martel after Mars because of his fame as a warrior. The position initially inherited by Charles Martel, Charlemagne's grandfather, was far from stable. He was forced to defend it by force of arms against several rebellions. He was able to strengthen it by leading the Franks to victory over the most terrible threat they had ever confronted in their history, that of the Muslims who had just destroyed the

Visigothic kingdom of Spain and were attempting to establish themselves north of the Pyrenees in southern Gaul.

In 732 at Poitiers, Charles Martel defeated an Arab force that had
pushed forward as far as the Loire, spreading terror as it went. In the
years that followed, the Franks reconquered southern France by the
sword and took their revenge on any local leaders in Aquitaine and
Burgundy who were suspected of having welcomed the Muslims in
order to free themselves from the hated Frankish yoke. Today, historians
tend to play down the significance of the battle of Poitiers, pointing out
that the purpose of the Arab force defeated by Charles Martel was not to
conquer the Frankish kingdom but simply to pillage the wealthy
monastery of St-Martin of Tours. However, the Franks and Christendom in general believed that the expulsion of the Moors from Gaul had
earned lasting glory for the mayor of the palace. He was proclaimed a
new Joshua, after the king of Israel who reconquered the Promised Land
for his people.

On his death in 741, Charles Martel left his sons, Pepin the Short
and Carloman, complete and uncontested authority over a kingdom
that was now well established. Childeric III was still formally king, but
this puppet, who was appointed by the mayor of the palace, no longer
had any role at all, not even a ceremonial one. Contemporary chroniclers regularly referred to Charles as a prince (*princeps*) who reigned
over the Frankish people. His sons were even more assertive, and
Carloman spoke of "his kingdom" (*regno meo*) in the first of his edicts.[3]
It is not surprising then that when he abdicated his powers in order to
withdraw to a monastery, his brother, Pepin, who now found himself
alone in the government of the kingdom, decided that the time had
come formally to claim the title of king of the Franks that in practice
was already his.

Before giving an account of the anointment of Pepin in 751, which
sanctioned the dynastic change in the leadership of the Frankish people,
we need to consider an event that occurred in the preceding year and
passed almost unnoticed by people at the time. Indeed no chronicler

took the trouble to record it, but it represents the real starting point for our story.

THE BIRTH OF CHARLEMAGNE

Shortly after Charles Martel's death, Pepin's wife, Bertrada, who came from one of the powerful land-owning families of Austrasia that were traditionally allied to the Pepinids, gave birth to their first child, a boy who took the name of the grandfather who had just died. The name Charles signified masculinity and virility in the Frankish tongue, and the boy was also destined to take his grandfather's place. We do not know where he was born, and it would in any case be an entirely meaningless piece of information. For the delivery, Bertrada could have been installed in any of the many residences that Pepin owned in the countryside between the Loire and the Rhine, and only nationalist obtuseness can explain the tremendous efforts made by French and German scholars to demonstrate that Charles was born within the current borders of either France or Germany. It would be more important for our purposes to know exactly when the future emperor was born, but strangely we cannot even establish this question with any certainty.

Charles's biographer, Einhard, wrote that Charles died in January 814 "in the seventy-second year of his life and the forty-seventh of his reign."[4] If we subtract these figures, we come up with the date of 742. The Royal Annals, the most official source we have, are somewhat less precise, although they attempt to provide further reference points. They date Charles's death as "in about the seventy-first year of his life, the forty-third from the conquest of Italy, the forty-seventh of his reign and fourteenth from when he was called emperor and Augustus."[5] The chronicler must have suspected that his figures did not agree, particularly in relation to the conquest of Italy, and so he put in the "about" to advise us not to expect anything too accurate. The inscription on his tomb at Aachen is even vaguer and simply defines him as *septuagenarius* (i.e., a seventy-year-old).[6] This doesn't mean that he was exactly seventy, and it seems to have been sufficient to know that he had reached that threshold, give or take a year or two. No one cared about the precise figure.

This is a fine example of what Marc Bloch has defined as the "supreme indifference to time" that is to be found in the medieval mindset. Perhaps it was not so much indifference to time as an extreme difficulty in measuring it and mastering it, even when there was a clear desire to do so. No less noteworthy is the fact that none of the three sources just mentioned bothered to provide the date of birth, an item of information that today we would consider essential. We are assisted here by another contemporary manuscript, containing a calendar that identifies the emperor's birthday as 2 April. If we put this conflicting information together and decide to place more trust in Einhard than the muddleheaded keeper of the Royal Annals, we come up with 2 April 742, which is generally considered in textbooks to be Charlemagne's date of birth. I will also use this point of reference, even though some German historians have suggested a much later date, albeit without too much evidence.[7]

A precise date is not that important, just as it wasn't important for the people of the time, who rarely kept a record of their own ages and, unlike us, were not in the habit of celebrating their birthdays. Time, then, was measured out by the circular rhythm of the agrarian and liturgical year. The habit of numbering years from the birth of Christ had only recently spread to the West, but it was a calculation exclusively used by chroniclers and notaries, and, as we have just seen, even they had difficulty in keeping track of the years with any precision. With so many children being born and so many dying, parents did not take the trouble to record the exact year of birth, and so adults had only an approximate idea of their own age. This is demonstrated by trial records in which witnesses always declare their age in round and approximate figures, such as fifty years old or sixty-five years old. In order to understand them, we will have to start to think like them; so let us forget any idea of establishing Charles's exact date of birth and be content with knowing that he was born around 742 and died at just over seventy years of age.

TRADITION AND PROPAGANDA
The Trojan Origins

So far we have concerned ourselves with events preceding the birth of Charlemagne in terms of what we have been able to establish from today's viewpoint. The history taught to the son of the mayor of the palace was certainly very different. At the time, people interpreted the history of the Franks through a worldview that we would consider mythical, but one that to them undoubtedly appeared as perfectly authentic and credible. Charlemagne's contemporaries, who knew less about the origins of their own people than modern historians do, were convinced that the Franks descended from none other than the Trojans. This legend was written down for the first time in a chronicle attributed to Fredegarius and written around 660, almost a century before the birth of Charlemagne.[8] After that, we find it circulating in such varying forms that it seems likely to have been not a scholarly invention but a popular tradition that spread among the barbarian warriors as soon as they came into contact with the Roman world.

The Trojan origin had a precise comparative or even competitive significance in relation to Rome. While the Romans descended from Priam through Aeneas, who according to Virgil fled to Latium, the Franks were convinced that they descended from another Trojan prince, Francio, who gave them his name and led them through lengthy migrations to Europe, where they settled along the banks of the Rhine. They were therefore blood relations of the Romans, and this kinship gave them the authority to rule over Gaul and perhaps further afield, given that their relations, the sons of Aeneas, had grown soft and were no longer capable of commanding respect. This idea probably had more currency among the clergy than the ordinary people, but it was without doubt instilled in Charlemagne from a very early age, and we should remember that this child was later to wear the imperial crown.

Paradoxically, the idea of ancestral kinship between Franks and Romans was not so far from the truth. The high degree of integration between the two peoples during the period of the Roman Empire had been forgotten by the time of Charlemagne and is only now being redis-covered by historians and archaeologists. The settlement of Franks in Gaul did not occur through the mass migration of a barbarian horde that fought its way through the *limes* or fortified frontier along the Rhine. Back in the third and fourth centuries, groups of Frankish warriors at the service of the empire were peacefully settled in Roman territory. Indeed, the national identity was formed during this phase under the profound influence of Roman culture. The funeral stele of a legionary who died in the eastern province of Pannonia in the third century bears this inscription, "Francus ego cives, romanus miles in armis," which we could translate as "I belong to the Frankish people, but under arms I am a Roman soldier."[9] That man very probably didn't know about his sup-posed Trojan origins, but he would not have been surprised at the idea.

The Chosen People

The history of the Franks contained another dimension that strength-ened their claim to be successors to the Romans. This was their privi-leged relationship with the Church of Rome. The alliance dated back to the conversion of King Clovis, who was baptized in Gaul on Christmas Day. We are not entirely certain of the year, but it might have been 496. The other Germanic peoples had been converted to Christianity by mis-sionaries trained under Greek influence and embraced the new religion in its Arian form, which at the time was widespread in the eastern Roman Empire but almost completely unknown in the western empire. Unlike Catholics, Arians believed in a Christ who was more human than divine and inferior in nature to the Father. By avoiding the complica-tions of the dogma of the Trinity, this interpretation of Christianity was perhaps easier to assimilate for peoples who lacked any theological or philosophical tradition. The result was that, following conversion, Goths, Vandals, and Lombards had trouble in coming to an under-standing with the Roman Catholics, from whom they were divided not only by doctrine but also by rival ecclesiastical hierarchies. In the eyes of the Roman world, these barbarians were Christians, but heretical ones, and therefore little better than pagans, or possibly even worse.

When the Franks reached Gaul, they were polytheists and their conversion to Christianity took place under the supervision of the local bishopric. They therefore accepted the new religion in accordance with the Catholic confession from the very beginning. This accident of history was to produce beneficial results for the future of the Frankish kingdom: Romano-Gaulish bishops and senators found it easier to cooperate with the Frankish kings, as they considered them protectors and not tyrants. Hence these kings were able to establish relatively efficient administrative and fiscal regimes, at least in relation to the other Romano-barbarian kingdoms. In the eyes of the Roman population, theirs was a legitimate power. They had not usurped but governed by the grace of God, in the same manner as the Roman emperors before them, since the times of Constantine.

Above all, the Catholicism of the Franks allowed them to form good relations with the pope, the spiritual head of the Catholic Church. The successors to Saint Peter were in theory subjects of the Roman emperor who continued to rule from distant Byzantium, and they were supposed to rely on him for defense from their enemies, such as the Lombards, savage barbarians of the Arian faith, who in 568 moved into Italy and for some time posed a real threat to Rome. Yet the emperor was far away, and, what is more, he prayed in Greek and followed a liturgy that with the passing generations had become increasingly alien to the Latin Church.

For all these reasons, the popes soon realized the usefulness of securing a protector who was less distant and more familiar. Given that the only real candidate was the king of the Franks, at the papal court they started to proclaim that his was the new chosen people. In a letter written by Pope Stephen II to Pepin in 756, Saint Peter himself addresses the Franks, assuring them that the Creator considers them a most special people destined for a mission that would be as great as that of the

Romans.[10] A few years later, the newly elected pope Paul I did not notify the emperor of the East of this election in accordance with tradition from time immemorial but instead informed Pepin. To the Franks he said, "now has the name of your people been raised up above all the other nations, and the kingdom of the Franks shines brightly before the Lord." He went on to quote the New Testament: "a chosen generation, a royal priesthood, a holy nation, a peculiar people."[11]

The message did not fall on deaf ears: the most important legislative text of the Frankish people, the law of the Salian Franks (Salic law or *lex Salica*), was drawn up on the instructions of King Pepin in 763–64, when Charlemagne was twenty, and its prologue spoke of the "illustrious people of the Franks, founded by God, courageous in war and constant in peace, converted to the Catholic faith and untouched by any heresy even when still barbarian." The Franks here considered themselves not only on a par with but manifestly superior to the Romans whom they defeated by feat of arms and who were after all the descendants of Nero and Diocletian, persecutors of the true faith: "This is the people who overthrew by force the heavy yoke imposed by the Romans, and, having undergone baptism, they covered with gold and jewels the bodies of the martyred saints that the Romans had burned, decapitated, and had torn apart by beasts."[12]

The child who learned about the history of his people in his father's palace could not have perceived the Franks as a collection of tribes without any original cohesiveness, gradually transformed into a nation through the activities of some enterprising warrior leaders in the service of the Roman rulers, as is argued by historians today. For him they were the glorious progeny of the Trojans, as noble as the Romans and, like them, destined one day to govern the world because they were the people chosen by God to defend the Christian faith. In all their undertakings, the hand of Providence would be upon them and protect them because they were Christ's people, just as the Jews had been God's people in the times of the Old Testament: "Glory to Christ, who loves the Franks," proclaims the prologue to the Salic law. The sovereign of this new Israel was no longer just a new Joshua as Charles Martel had been, but a new Moses, a new David, and a new Solomon. This understanding was reflected in the official declarations of the pope in Rome and not only in the flattery of fawning Gaulish bishops. If we are to understand the course of Charles's life once he took over the leadership of the Franks from his father, we should remember that at Pepin's court these were not opinions but incontrovertible facts.

The Family Tradition

For Pepin's son, the history of his own family was also something very different from the dry genealogy of potentates that I have just outlined in the preceding pages. Paul the Deacon (Paulus diaconus), the Lombard intellectual who lived at the court of Charlemagne, recalled Charles telling an extraordinary story of one of the founders of his dynasty, Saint Arnulf, the bishop of Metz. According to the emperor, Arnulf had thrown a ring into the Moselle as a sign of penitence, and when he asked for forgiveness of his sins, he declared that he would not consider himself to have been absolved until the ring was returned to his possession. Many years later, a cook found the ring in the stomach of a fish he was cooking for the bishop, thus demonstrating that God had forgiven Arnulf's sins and returned his pledge.

The story of the ring thrown into the water and found again in a fish's belly is clearly a folkloric motif that appears in many fairy tales. For anyone who believes in the extremely ancient origins of fables, it is fascinating to discover that Charlemagne would tell a story of this kind not as a fairy tale but as a true story relating to a member of his own family. Yet we should not overlook the ideological implications of the story, which in all probability was handed down orally in the home of the mayors of the palace, so that Charles must have heard it during his childhood. The saintliness of Arnulf, extolled by the miracle, was destined to reverberate down the generations to his great-grandchildren, convincing them that they belonged to a charismatic line. It is no surprise that

Paul the Deacon told this story in his *History of the Bishops of Metz*, and that he added that the benediction of Arnulf entitled his descendants to reign over the Franks.[13] After all, the work had been commissioned by Charles himself for political reasons.

By the time of Charles's childhood, official propaganda was already stressing that the Pepinid line was destined by the will of God to reign over the Franks. Pepin's uncle Childebrand and later his son Nibelung, who continued the work of Fredegarius's chronicle, implied in their writings that the victories of Charles Martel and his son conformed to the plans of Providence.[14] In other words, the chosen people were led by a chosen dynasty, and it was appropriate that at the very time that Charles was listening at the age of seven or eight to the story of the ring, which he was to remember in his old age, his father, Pepin, had decided that it was no longer sufficient to rule the Franks as the mayor of the palace and the time had come to proclaim himself king.

THE PEPINIDS IN POWER
Pepin's Coup d'État

Pepin's plan was founded on the pope, who since the time of Clovis's baptism was the natural ally of the Franks. Although at that time the bishop of Rome did not enjoy the absolute power that he now wields within the Catholic Church, his political and moral authority was widely recognized throughout Latin Christendom, and he was best placed to legitimize what, if we were to be uncharitable, was ultimately the usurpation of a Christian king. Before explicitly putting forward his claim to the throne, Pepin therefore wrote to Pope Zacharias asking whether it was right that in the case of the Franks the name of king should apply to someone who had no effective power. The pope, basing himself on the authority of Saint Augustine and Gregory the Great, replied that the title of king should be held by the person who actually exercised power.[15]

Strengthened by this opinion and by the approval that his family had enjoyed among Frankish nobles for more than a century, Pepin had himself proclaimed king in November 751 by an assembly of magnates of the kingdom, and he was anointed with holy oil by the bishops of Gaul, while the legitimate king was sent off to finish his days in the silence of a monastery. Pope Zacharias died shortly afterward, and his successor, Stephen, who was threatened by the Lombards bearing down on Rome, got the new king of the Franks to promise that he would intervene militarily in Italy to put an end to that threat once and for all. In exchange, Stephen went to Gaul in 754 to repeat the ceremony of anointing the king. This was the first time that a pope had traveled to that distant country, and it made an enormous impression. It provided the final seal of approval for the new dynasty, particularly as the pope wished personally to anoint not only Pepin, but also his sons, who by then were Charles and his younger brother, Carloman.

At this meeting, a solemn pact of friendship was sworn between the king and the pope, which their successors renewed to establish a lasting alliance between Rome and the kingdom of the Franks. On this occasion, the pope gave Pepin and his sons the title of patrician of the Romans, whose exact legal significance remains somewhat obscure but was supposed in some way to persuade the Frankish king that he had become the protector of the papal see. The title of patrician, without any geographic specification, had been traditionally conferred by the emperor of the East and belonged to the Byzantine exarch of Ravenna, but by that time Ravenna had fallen to the Lombards and there were no more exarchs in Italy. Even though the title of patrician of the Romans would probably have sounded barbaric to Byzantine ears, by conferring it on the king of the Franks, the pope undoubtedly intended to encourage him to take up the defense of the Eternal City in place of the emperor of the East.

In order to strengthen the alliance between Stephen and Pepin, a relationship of spiritual guardianship was established. It is not clear exactly why the pope referred to the king after 754 as the father of his godchildren and to Charles and Carloman as his spiritual children, given that both were too old to be baptized then. It is more probable that the pope was their godfather at confirmation. This relationship between parent and godparent was considered so important that successive popes did everything they could to renew it. When Charlemagne's sister, Gisla, was born in 757, King Pepin sent the new pope, Paul I, the sheet in which the baby had been wrapped for her baptism. The pope received it in a solemn ritual and immediately wrote to the king that from then on he considered himself to be the girl's godfather, just as though he had held her personally at the baptismal font.[16] Clearly the Pepinids, who after the triumphs of Charles Martel we can start to call Carolingians, enjoyed a privileged position in their relationship with the pope and therefore an unchallenged preeminence in the Frankish world and in the whole of western Christendom.

The Sacred Royal Line

The ritual anointment introduced by Pepin in 751 represented an extraordinary ideological innovation, given that until that time the Frankish kings had risen to the throne by acclamation, and if consensus was also accompanied by mystical charisma, this was generally due to the royal blood flowing in their veins. By having himself anointed with holy oil, Pepin brought into use the ritual recorded in the Old Testament, in which it is told that Saul took control of the kingdom by being anointed by the prophet Samuel. After him, David and Solomon took the throne by being anointed. In the Christian world, a ritual of this kind had already been introduced by the Visigothic kings of Spain, but by this time their kingdom had fallen to the Arabs. Pepin was not just the first Frankish king but also the only Christian king of his times to introduce this sacred symbolism into his coronation, although the kings of England lost little time in following his example.

Anointment was not simply a matter of attributing an air of holiness to the king, it also conferred upon him an almost priestly quality, as with the kings of Israel. Pepin could therefore rightfully claim to have been "anointed by the Lord" and assert his own authority over the Church as well as his kingdom, in a manner that he could not have done as a temporal lord who had only been crowned. For his part, Pope Paul I did not hesitate to speak of him as a new David chosen by God to protect the Christian people, and he applied to him the words of the psalmist, "I have found David my servant; with my holy oil I have anointed him."[17] Thus the Franks were again ruled by a priest-king, as in the time of the *reges criniti* or long-haired kings, but this time the sacred charisma was wholly Christian and not pagan as in the case of the Merovingians. It did not preclude the use of the sword, which the king girded by divine will, and which he was required to draw in defense of the faith. Charlemagne was soon to demonstrate the immense advantage that the king of the Franks could gain from this kind of religious legitimacy.

TWO

The War against the Lombards

A DIFFICULT DIVISION OF INHERITANCE

In September 768 King Pepin died in Paris, probably from dropsy. His two sons, Charles and Carloman, had to share their father's kingdom. At that time, it was not yet the practice to give precedence to the eldest son, and even in the case of a kingdom, property was shared between the male children. When deciding the criteria for the division of his lands, the dying king preferred not to follow the borders between the old Frankish kingdoms and, just as his father, Charles Martel, had done before him, he cut out substantially new territories. Charles took the outer region of the Frankish dominions, a vast crescent that stretched from the Atlantic coast of Aquitaine northward beyond the Loire to occupy part of Neustria and the greater part of Austrasia, and then further along the coast to Frisia before turning to the southeast to take in most of the German provinces down to Thuringia. Carloman, on the other hand, took the inner territories, which covered a small part of Austrasia, the southern German provinces of Alamannia, most of Neustria, including the Seine basin, the Burgundian kingdom along the valley of the Rhône from the Vosges to the Mediterranean, the southern part of Gaul in general, and the Aquitaine interior.

The logic behind these new entities that disregarded the existence of past kingdoms was to emphasize the effective unity of the Frankish people. There were two kings, but only one kingdom. It was no coincidence that the two brothers had themselves anointed in Noyon and Soissons, two cities that are close to each other, in an area where King Pepin had resided most often and where their mother, Bertrada, had settled as the guest of a monastery. Relations between them very soon became tense, possibly because the geopolitical conditions created by the division forced them to direct their policies in opposite directions. Charles had the opportunity of unrestricted expansion into pagan Germany, whereas Carloman was confronted with the most dangerous border, the Pyrenean one with Arab Spain, and the most sensitive border, the one with the Lombard kingdom of Italy. There was probably a certain diffidence between the two brothers and their temporal and ecclesiastical magnates, as could be seen when Charles, in only the second year of his reign, had to suppress a revolt in Aquitaine, and Carloman's followers advised their king not to intervene on Charles's side. Of course, it should be remembered that this version of events, the only one that survived, was written at Charles's court, and a chronicler in Carloman's retinue may have given a very different account.[1]

The mutual distrust appears to be responsible for the fact that while Carloman lived, neither brother conducted a military campaign, other than Charles's punitive expedition against the Aquitanian rebels. This is quite startling if we consider that once he had his hands free, Charles hardly let a year pass without making war against one or other of the surrounding peoples. In short, the division of the kingdom created an unstable situation, and it was only their mother's intercession that kept peace between the brothers. The balance would not have lasted very long, but fate arranged things differently. In the first days of December 771 Carloman died after many months of illness. Although barely twenty years old, the unfortunate king already had two sons who under the regency of their mother, Gerberga, and the magnates of the kingdom could have succeeded to his throne. Charles acted promptly to take advantage of the situation, had himself proclaimed the sole king of the Franks, and seized his brother's territories. Many of the bishops, abbots, and counts who had served Carloman submitted to their new lord, but others preferred to follow the dead king's widow and sons to seek refuge in Italy.

This flight itself demonstrates that the brothers did not see eye to eye. The entry in the Royal Annals claiming that "the king was not angered by this departure for Italy, considering it to be without importance" has all the air of an apocryphal flourish typical of the partisan manner in which history was written at Charlemagne's court.[2] Some time later, the Irishman Catwulf wrote a letter overflowing with praise to Charles, and he did not hesitate to congratulate him on having conquered his brother's kingdom without spilling any blood.[3] This compliment would appear a little strange if reunification had been simply an automatic and universally desired event. The king, having ensured the obedience of the entire Frankish people, was no longer concerned about his sister-in-law and the other exiles who had accompanied her to Italy, and he now felt free to turn his ambitions in another direction. A few months after Carloman's death and as though he had just been waiting for that moment, he crossed the Rhine with his army to fight the pagans of the north.

The campaign against the Saxons, which was carried out in the summer of 772, was short and apparently decisive. The Franks penetrated deep into the enemy country, imposing their authority by the sword and forcing the Saxons to hand over twelve hostages from princely families to guarantee their submission. When he returned to celebrate Christmas at the ancestral palace of Herstal near Liège, Charles, the sole and victorious king of the Franks, could not have suspected that in order to subjugate the Saxons definitively he would have to wage war against them for the rest of his life. But before he could undertake that enterprise, he would first have to turn his attention back to Italy, where the family of Carloman had taken refuge.

FRANKS AND LOMBARDS: AN ANCIENT ENMITY

Relations between the Franks and their Lombard neighbors had often been poor, particularly since the popes had given up any hope of assistance from Byzantium and turned to the Catholic kings of Gaul and their mayors of the palace for protection. In 739 Gregory III wrote to Charles Martel in the most flattering terms, making it plain that though not the king, he was the true leader of the Franks in the eyes of Saint Peter. He implored him to intervene militarily against King Liutprand, who was threatening Rome. In exchange for his assistance, which was not however forthcoming, the pope even sent him the keys to the sepulcher of Saint Peter, implying that he had been appointed the protector of the Roman church. He wrote that, after God, only Charles could save the Church from the barbarians.[4]

In 754 the anointment of Pepin by Pope Stephen and the granting of the title of patrician of the Romans were met with the promise of military intervention in the peninsula, and this time the king of the Franks acted upon his words. In the summer of the same year, he laid siege to King Aistulf in Pavia, forcing him to renounce all the Lombard conquests in central Italy in favor of the pope and to acknowledge the supremacy of the Franks. Just two years later, in 756, Aistulf went back on his word and took his army to the gates of Rome, forcing Pope Stephen to send a desperate appeal to Pepin, which purported to have been written in the first person by Peter the apostle, "Come quickly, come quickly and help us."[5] Frankish military power temporarily put things back as they had been, by compelling Aistulf to hand over the keys of twenty-two fortified cities in central Italy, which Pepin ceremonially placed on the altar in St. Peter's.

Following this victory, the policy of Frankish kings in Italy changed. Having been so completely humiliated, the Lombard king acknowledged the supremacy of the Franks and became a client rather than an adversary. Unsurprisingly Pepin avoided using the title of patrician of the Romans in his edicts, given that the degree of involvement in Italy it might entail would not have been in his interests. The succession of Charles and Carloman did not change the situation: the Lombard kingdom was a potentially useful ally for both of them, so both brothers were keen to maintain good relations with King Desiderius, who succeeded to Aistulf's throne in 756. The Royal Annals refer to a successful mission to Italy conducted by Queen Mother Bertrada in 770,[6] and although we know little else, it seems logical that in her peacemaking role Bertrada sought a three-way agreement so that neither of the rival brothers could use an alliance with the Lombards against the other.

Carloman's good relations with Desiderius are demonstrated by the fact that following the former's death, his widow, sons, and many followers took refuge in Italy. Yet Charles entered into equally good relations with the court in Pavia, and it was in this period that he married Desiderius's daughter whom Manzoni with poetic license called Ermengarda, though in reality no contemporary chronicler ever recorded her name.[7] That this alliance was supposed to bury the pro-papal policy of the Franks and seal the coexistence with the Lombards can be seen from the extremely bitter letter Pope Stephen III wrote to the Frankish kings to complain of their decision: "What folly is this: your noble Frankish people, the light of all other peoples, and your illustrious and noble line sullied by the foul-smelling and treacherous Lombards, who are not even entitled to be called a nation and who, as is well known, are the cause of leprosy?"[8] But the aging Bertrada was able to overcome these objections and the Lombard princess traveled over the Alps to join her husband-to-be.

Why then did Charlemagne invade Italy no more than two years after this marriage? As often happens, it is not easy to apportion blame in any reliable manner. This is not only because all contemporary accounts are brazenly one-sided, but also because the exact sequence of events is not always clear and it is therefore very difficult for us to sort out cause and effect. What is certain is that between 771 and 772 three significant events took place, although we do not know in what order. Desiderius encouraged Carloman's widow to claim the dead king's inheritance for her son and to request that the child be anointed by the pope. The Lombard was thinking of a way to cover his back by paralyzing the Frankish power divided between two rival courts, with the intention of fighting another war to occupy Rome, this time for good.

For his part, Charles rejected his Lombard wife, who had not yet provided a son, and returned her to her father. This could be construed as a legitimate act, because the king needed a wife who could produce an heir, but it violently undid the diplomatic balance patiently engineered by Bertrada. Lastly, recently elected Pope Adrian I wrote to Charles to inform him that Rome was under a greater threat from the Lombards than ever before. He invited him to follow his father's example by bringing his army to defend the holy city, of which he was after all the patrician.[9]

Clearly, any one of these three events could have provoked a crisis, and given the impossibility of establishing the exact sequence, we must refrain from attributing what we would now call political responsibility for the war. It seems certain that up until the last moment, Charles left the door open for a diplomatic solution, in contrast to the brutal manner in which he often rushed to war against other enemies, particularly pagan ones, at times without any provocation. It does not appear then that on this occasion the war was coldly sought after by the king of the Franks, who had just demonstrated his preference for expansion into the pagan north and did not rush into an attack on Italy, even though the international situation had been turning in his favor. The claim to the throne by Carloman's son was not followed up, although this might have happened if Desiderius had managed to enter Rome and force the pope to anoint him. The Lombard king's campaign ended in the winter of 772–73 at the gates of the Eternal City, partly because of Adrian's threat of excommunication.

At this stage, war between the Franks and Lombards could still have been avoided. Moreover, the Frankish magnates were reluctant to get involved, and indeed they had not been enamored of Pepin's Italian expeditions. Charles therefore attempted to reach an agreement with his former father-in-law and the pope, by suggesting that the latter should pay an exorbitant indemnity of 14,000 gold pieces in exchange for the withdrawal of the Lombards from the occupied territories. However, the negotiations collapsed, and at the insistence of the pope, who saw an opportunity to free himself of the Lombard threat once and for all, Charles started to plan his Italian campaign.

THE WAR OF 773–74
War Plans

In strategic terms, the problem was simple but not at all easy to resolve: it was the problem of taking an army over the Alps. Although there were many passes that a good walker could easily cross in summer, there were only two Roman roads that would allow an army to get through with its horses and baggage. The most direct was the Via Francigena that traveled from Lyons along the Arc Valley, over Mont Cenis, and down into the Susa Valley toward Turin. Pilgrims on their way to Rome used to take the same road, which was also known as the Via Romea. But at the entrance to the valley the Lombards had restored the system of fortifications that from the time of the late Roman Empire had barred access to the Italian plain. They were known as *clusae* or fortifications closing off the exit to the pass, often now referred to as the Chiuse di San Michele, after the name of the abbey that stands on a rocky promontory and dominates the narrow valley.

The other Roman road to reach Italy, also much used throughout the Middle Ages by pilgrims and merchants, was the Great St. Bernard Pass, at that time called Mons Jovis. Here again the frontier of the Lombard kingdom was defended by *clusae*, where the road reached the plain and the fortress of Bard is currently to be found. It seems surprising that the border between the two kingdoms ran along the entrance to the plain and not along the Alpine watershed, as it now does between France and Italy. The fact is that the Franks, more powerful and more aggressive than their neighbors, had long since taken possession of the Susa Valley and Val d'Aosta, and they jealously guarded their control over these two important passes. To this day, the linguistic border between the Piedmontese dialects of Italy and the Franco-Provençal dialects of the Gallo-Romance area passes along the entrance to the two valleys.

The existence of the *clusae*, particularly those in the Susa Valley, made a strong impression on medieval chroniclers and nineteenth-century scholars. In *Adelchi*, Manzoni attributed a critical role to these fortifications and imagined that Charles, unable to pass by and on the point of renouncing the entire undertaking, was shown another path around the obstacle by Martin the Deacon, who had been sent by God for that purpose. Shortly after 1000 A.D. the *Novalesa Chronicle* described the *clusae* as a massive and compact barrier, an ancient wall of stone and mortar erected from one side of the valley to the other, and asserted that its ruins were still visible on the valley floor.[10] In more recent times, historians have been rather skeptical about this account and have objected that the *clusae* must have been a series of provisional fortifications, watchtowers, and customs barriers, rather than a single, enormous rampart of stone. It seemed that historical and archaeological research would destroy the perhaps overly romantic image handed down by the collective imagination. However, even more recent research has shown that the last Lombard kings, following their disastrous experience during the wars against Pepin, invested considerable resources in strengthening the *clusae*, and unlike their predecessors, who were accustomed to a more flexible form of defense, they deceived themselves that they could block the invader's way by entrenching themselves behind these preparations. It seems possible that, after all, there was a massive wall that closed off the valley floor, at least at the time of Desiderius.

As soon as he had decided to invade Italy, Charlemagne started to gather his army at Geneva. A glance at the map is sufficient to understand that from there he could take either the road for the Susa Valley along the course of the Rhône, or the road for San Bernardo by skirting the lake and then moving up the Rhône toward Martigny. The choice of Geneva made sense strategically, given that bringing together armed men from all the provinces of the vast Frankish kingdom took several months and clearly the enemy would have been informed in time of where the gathering was taking place. His choice meant that they would be unable to guess from which direction the blow would come.

Even if they had guessed it, the Lombards would not have gained much of an advantage, as Charlemagne struck from both directions. He decided to organize two separate expeditions: one through the Great St. Bernard under the command of his uncle, coincidentally called Bernard, and the other through Mont Cenis under his own command. This was the first demonstration of his personal strategic preference: throughout his career as a military commander, Charlemagne was to make systematic use of the pincer movement, displaying his particular skill in planning and coordinating the actions of separate bodies of armed men. Obviously, this tactic was only possible for someone who found himself at the head of a large army that was generally superior to that of his enemy. Thus we can assert that Charlemagne was a great general but not in the sense of a brilliant tactician capable of making up for his lack of resources. He was more in the mold of a modern commander, whose talent is above all organizational and logistic.

The Invasion

The Franks' crossing of the Alps in the summer of 773 was in its own way an epic undertaking, comparable to that of Hannibal, barring the elephants. Charles's biographer, Einhard, stresses "how difficult it was to cross the Alps, and what an enormous exertion it was for the Franks to pass that chain of inaccessible mountains with their peaks reaching to the heavens and their impassable rocks."[11] But still more memorable is the sudden defeat that Charlemagne inflicted on the enemy who awaited him at the end of the valley. This event has remained alive in the popular imagination to this day, partly because of Manzoni, it is true, but not entirely because of him. Chroniclers of the time are agreed that Charles did not attack the Lombards frontally while they held their well-established position in the *clusae* but managed somehow to get round them. They attribute this success either to the Frankish king's skill in maneuvering his men or to a divine miracle, without giving further details.[12] Only in the next millennium did the *Novalesa Chronicle* invent a fictional narration around this event by introducing a Lombard minstrel who showed Charles the road around the *clusae* in exchange for money.[13] The anonymous chronicler directly inspired Manzoni, who wanted to blend his version with the more ancient tradition of a miraculous intervention. He therefore replaced the treacherous minstrel with Martin the Deacon, an instrument of God's will.

There is still the question of the exact route taken by the Franks. In the lower Susa Valley, there is a path known in the local tradition as the "Franks' Path." It has been recently assessed for its tourist potential with the suggestion that it was in fact the route taken by Charlemagne. In reality, it is simply one of the tracks that during the Middle Ages constituted the Via Francigena. A medieval road was not in fact necessarily identified with a linear and well-paved route, as with an ancient Roman road. According to the environmental conditions, it could split into a series of tracks, which modern historians define as a road area. The most credible version of the route taken by Charlemagne to get round the *clusae* is in strategic terms the one provided by the monk of Novalesa, according to whom the Franks turned right down Val Sangone, went down to Giaveno, and then climbed back up to Avigliana, thus finding themselves at the enemy's rear. Taken by surprise, the Lombards fell back in a disorderly manner as far as Pavia, where King Desiderius shut himself up with most of his remaining warriors, while his wife and son Adelchis fled even further back to Verona.

Up until this point, Charles's expedition had not obtained very different results from those of his father. Even Pepin, having defeated King Aistulf, lay siege to Pavia, where he had retreated. A few days later, having obtained the return of the lands claimed by the pope and the handover of hostages, he returned to his homeland. Here we encounter Charlemagne's political strategy and its much wider vision, which we could rightly define as imperialist. The Frankish king besieged Pavia for more than a year until June 774, when Desiderius having no further resources had to capitulate unconditionally. The victor installed himself in the royal palace and had his father-in-law's treasure distributed to his warriors, while Desiderius was obliged to become a monk and was enclosed in the distant monastery of Corbie. As for Adelchis, in whom the Lombards placed their last hopes, he was driven from Verona and had to take refuge outside Italy in Constantinople, where he lived into old age maintained by the Byzantine emperor, awaiting a reconquest that never materialized. The king of the Franks did not abolish the conquered kingdom, nor did he incorporate it into his own kingdom. He decided to maintain its governmental structures and administrative autonomy, and he assumed from that time the title of *rex Langobardorum*.

THE CONSEQUENCES OF THE FRANKISH CONQUEST
The Birth of the Papal State

Even before Desiderius surrendered, Charles felt so confident about his situation that he left the siege of Pavia to go and celebrate Easter of 774 in Rome, which he visited for the first time. He was greeted by Pope Adrian with the honors due to the exarch of Ravenna or the patrician of the Romans, which were in fact fairly modest. Charles climbed the steps of St. Peter's on his knees, kissing each one to demonstrate the immense religious power that in his eyes resided in that place, of which he had made himself the protector. The most important moment of his stay in Rome came with the negotiations between the king and the pope, although we still cannot be sure about how they progressed, because of the discrepancies between the chroniclers on the Frankish side and those on the side of the pope. Undoubtedly, the two renewed the pact of friendship entered into twenty years before between Pepin and Stephen II. Furthermore, Adrian asked Charles to confirm a written promise that his father had signed on the previous occasion. This document was read to the king, who according to the papal chroniclers agreed to sign it. It massively expanded the territories governed by the pope, creating the so-called Republic of Saint Peter's, while the Franks were to remain close to the Alps and in the Po Valley as far south as Pavia, and Byzantium was to have Calabria, Sicily, and Sardinia.[14]

This version has raised some doubts among historians, who were not convinced that Charles and Pepin before him would have taken on such an onerous commitment. But even if we accept the papal version, it has to be remembered that the meeting between Charles and Adrian occurred while the war against the Lombards was still going on, Desiderius was resisting in the besieged city of Pavia, and the future makeup of the Italian peninsula was yet to be decided. It should not surprise us, then, that when Charles had personally assumed the crown of the king of the Lombards, he preferred to think again. Clearly, he decided not to implement a commitment that, if taken literally, would have meant the breakup of his new kingdom. Only the pope's authority over the ancient duchy of Rome was acknowledged, with the addition of Sabina, the former Byzantine territories of the exarchate, and the Pentapolis, linked by a strip of territory in the Apennines. The Republic of Saint Peter's, whose creation had been the ambition of popes since the beginning of the eighth century, thus took on the more or less definitive shape of the papal state whose last remnants only fell more than a thousand years later under the cannon fire that breached the walls of Rome at Porta Pia.

The Revolt of 776

The fall of the Lombard kingdom undoubtedly provoked consternation and disbelief. A private document written in May 774, just one month before Desiderius's surrender, in a fortress in the Emilian section of the Apennine range not yet occupied by the Franks, starts with an unprecedented formula that testifies to the catastrophe that had struck the kingdom: "In the name of Christ, charter written in a period of barbarous events."[15] At the same time, it is undeniable that many Lombard dukes had been unenthusiastic in the defense of the kingdom and had promptly submitted to their new lord, and this explains the relative ease with which the conquest had taken place. Internal dissent had always been the weakness of the Lombard kingdom, and the election in 756 of Desiderius, then duke of Tuscia, had only aggravated matters, given that it was perceived as a humiliating blow to the rival duke of Friuli. The Italian nobles were therefore split, and some of them looked unsympathetically on their king and were not willing to give him unconditional loyalty. It is not surprising then that Charles did not consider it necessary to replace them following the conquest of the kingdom and kept them in their positions of power in their own provinces.

It was the duke of Friuli, called Rothgaud, who quickly started to organize an uprising, in which all the dukes who had remained in office were supposed to take part. When they had witnessed the downfall of Desiderius without too much concern, they probably did not realize that this would lead to an end of Lombard independence, and now they were willing to recommence the struggle. In Constantinople, the emperor of the East and his protégé, Adelchis, were observing developments with interest, ready to take advantage of any opportunity that presented itself. While returning from an expedition against the Saxons in the autumn of 775, Charles received a letter from Pope Adrian, in which he informed the king that Rothgaud had met up with Duke Arechis of Benevento and was preparing an insurrection in the following spring. Charlemagne reacted promptly: instead of returning home for the winter and remaining there until Easter, as was his habit, he wintered at the foot of the Alps and as soon as weather permitted, he crossed the mountains and appeared in Friuli in February or March 776.

There the rebellious Lombard dukes awaited him, although there were in the end only three of them: the dukes of Friuli, Treviso, and Vicenza. The outcome of the engagement is told in very different ways by the Frankish and Lombard chroniclers: according to the Royal Annals, Rothgaud died in battle, and Charles retook one rebellious city after the other, replacing the Lombard dukes with Frankish counts. He then celebrated Easter in Treviso, before returning to the frontier on the Rhine, which was threatened by the Saxons.[16] On the other hand, the Lombard chronicler Andrea da Bergamo, writing a century later, claims that the rebel dukes confronted the Franks at the bridge of Livenza where they were advancing amid much destruction and pillage. They stopped the

Franks there in a bloody clash, and he added that afterward Charles agreed to let the dukes retain their positions, albeit in return for an oath of loyalty that they did not dare to break.[17]

Andrea's account could be interpreted as the wishful ramblings of a Lombard who, even after so much time, found it difficult to accept the defeat of his people at the hands of the Franks. The existence of such sentiments for a long time afterward is demonstrated by the chronicle tradition in the south of Italy where the duchy of Benevento retained its independence into the next millennium. Today, the majority of historians prefer to accept the account in the Frankish annals and believe that only after the revolt of the dukes did Charles start to distrust the Lombard nobility. Their systematic replacement with Frankish and Alamannian bishops, counts, and vassals led to the drastic changeover in the Italian aristocracy that had not occurred immediately after the surrender of Pavia.

FROM THE *REGNUM LANGOBARDORUM* TO THE ITALIC KINGDOM
The Laws of 776

Whatever its outcome, there can be no doubt that the revolt of 776 frightened Charles and induced him to seek out the consensus of his new subjects through legislative measures. The conquest of Lombard Italy had provoked devastation and poverty throughout the country, although there was probably a certain amount of exaggeration in Andrea da Bergamo's report of "a great desolation throughout Italy; many were put to the sword, many died of hunger, many fell prey to wild animals, so that few remained to populate the countryside and the cities."[18] Pope Adrian spoke of the famine and its tragic consequences in a letter written in 776 and condemned the increasing traffic in Christian slaves run by unscrupulous Greek merchants. In order to escape the famine, Lombards were selling their slaves or embarking on the Greek ships themselves in order to escape at least with their own lives.[19] In February of that same year, as he was preparing to do battle with the rebels, Charlemagne issued his first Italian capitulary or, in other words, his first law expressly intended for the conquered kingdom, whose purpose was to alleviate the sufferings caused by the invasion.

This legislation was completely unprecedented. The king was informed that where his army had passed, the resulting devastation had caused many to sell themselves, their wives, and their children into slavery, while others had been "obliged by hunger" to donate or sell their property to the Church or sell their land at much reduced prices. The king ordered that all these transfers of property should be declared void and the related deeds of sale torn up, when it could be demonstrated that the vendor had been driven by hunger. In any event, all these transactions were to be assessed by a tribunal that would consider their equity by calculating the value of the possessions sold at their price before the war and judging whether a fair price had been paid. All the transferals into slavery were automatically nullified and even the donations to ecclesiastical bodies were suspended pending an assessment of the circumstances in which they occurred.[20]

This extraordinary decision confirms the account of Andrea da Bergamo: the Frankish invasion caused such catastrophic results that the king could not ignore them and had to take action to alleviate the misery of his new subjects. Not without reason, Charles's legislation concludes by specifying that these measures would only come into force "where we or our army has passed" and would not affect sales that occurred previously "in the time of Desiderius." Of course, if we consider that it was mainly the Lombard landowners—both temporal and ecclesiastical—who were profiting from the poverty of the peasantry, this legislation could be interpreted as a direct attack on their interest at the very time that Charlemagne was preparing to meet the rebels in the field of battle. Whatever the case, the promulgation of this law on the eve of the battle of Livenza was a deliberate act aimed at gaining the support of the common people and dividing them from their leaders. It marked a turning point in his policy toward Italy. From that time, this was to be the line adopted by Charles: his message to the great majority of Lombards was that they were fully subjects of their king on a par with the Franks, with all the rights and duties that parity implied. At the same time, he proceeded with the systematic appointment of Franks and trustworthy foreigners to positions in the administration and the clergy in order to weaken the indigenous ruling group that had proved so disloyal.

The Government of the Kingdom

The intention of maintaining the autonomy of the Lombard kingdom under Frankish dominion was confirmed at Easter 781, when Charles's second son by Hildegard, until then known as Carloman, was baptized in Rome by the pope with the new name of Pepin and anointed the king of the Lombards.[21] From then on there were two kings, the father, who mostly resided north of the Alps, and the son, who took up residence in Pavia, the kingdom's ancient capital. Pepin was barely four years old, and the actual government of the country was managed by Charles through trusted officials, the most important of whom was Waldo, the abbot of Reichenau, whom the king unsuccessfully attempted to have appointed bishop of Pavia by the pope. Later, the young king grew up and was capable of personally commanding the army of his kingdom, largely made up of Lombards, in the campaign against the Avars in 796, the repeated punitive expeditions against the duke of Benevento, and the prolonged war against the Byzantines on the eastern border, which concluded with the capture of Venice in 810. When he died in that very year, the youthful Pepin was no longer a puppet ruler but a real king who had learned to govern, and court poets celebrated his victories.[22]

In spite of the appointment of a number of Frankish bishops, abbots, and counts, government of the kingdom kept many of its own characteristics, which no one consciously wanted to destroy. Thus, local officials with Lombard titles, such as *gastaldio*, *sculdahis*, and *locopositus*, continued to carry out their duties under the direction of counts imported

from the Frankish or Alamannian lands. In peripheral areas of the kingdom, government continued for a long time to be entrusted to dukes, in
accordance with the Lombard tradition, although the original Lombard
incumbent was everywhere replaced by a Frank, starting in Friuli and
finishing in Spoleto. Even after the rebellion of 776, these measures
were introduced gradually, almost as though Charles preferred in each
case to await the death of a duke before appointing a more trusted successor. The result was a smoother and gentler transition from the old to
the new regime.

Another aspect of the autonomy intended for the kingdom was the
regular publication by Charles or Pepin of capitularies explicitly directed
at Italy. While it is true that the intention of these Italian laws was often
to extend to the new kingdom institutions and rules of behavior (for
instance for the clergy) that were already common practice in the
Frankish kingdom, it is no less the case that the existence of a body of
law expressly restricted to Italy helped considerably to maintain the
identity of the Lombard kingdom and prevented it from dissolving into
the empire. Indeed it was to reemerge from the imperial context with all
its vigor following the death of Charlemagne. One change did occur: as
time passed the name "kingdom of the Lombards" would fall out of use
and be replaced by *regnum Italiae* or kingdom of Italy, although historians prefer to call it the Italic kingdom in order to distinguish it from the
one created in 1861.

HISTORY AND MYTH
The Legends of the Iron King and the Eater of Bones

Charlemagne's war against the Lombards left a profound impression on
the collective memory and produced a vast collection of widely circulated tales of a more or less fanciful nature. The siege of Pavia inspired
a later writer, who lived at the time of Charlemagne's great-grandchildren, to provide one of the most memorable descriptions of the Frankish
king at the head of his army. It was of course a legendary description,

mainly useful for understanding the image of Charlemagne that had been retained and handed down to later generations. It was such an extraordinary account that it is worth reproducing here in full. The author was Notker Balbulus (meaning the stutterer), a monk of St-Gall. His *Gesta Karoli Magni*, written around 886–87 and dedicated to the emperor Charles the Fat, are a fantastic collection of true and invented anecdotes. He tells us that when Desiderius was trapped in Pavia, he was accompanied by a Frankish noble called Otkerus, who following a violent quarrel with Charles had sought refuge with the Lombards. Incidentally, we come across this figure as Ogier in the chansons de geste and again as Uggieri il Danese (the Dane) in Italian versions.

On hearing of the approach of Charles's army, Desiderius and Otkerus climbed the highest tower in Pavia.

> Baggage trains appeared that would have been worthy of the campaigns of Darius or Caesar, and Desiderius said to Otkerus, "Is Charles in that vast army?" He replied, "Not yet." Seeing then the army of simple soldiers gathered by the immense empire, he said confidently to Otkerus, "Clearly Charles must be standing proudly among these troops." Otkerus replied, "But not yet, not yet." Then he started to become agitated and said, "What will we do, if he is to come with even greater forces?" Otkerus said, "You will see when he comes. As for us, I do not know what our fate will be." His bodyguards, always ready for action, then appeared, and on seeing them Desiderius said in stunned voice, "This must be Charles." And Otkerus, "Not yet, not yet."
>
> Then the bishops, abbots, and chaplains appeared with their retinue, and on seeing them Desiderius, who by now was terrified by the light and longed only for death, stammered with difficulty through his sobs, "Let us go down and hide ourselves underground to avoid seeing the anger of such a formidable adversary!" At this stage, the frightened Otkerus, who in the past had known the behavior and resources of the incomparable Charles and in better times had been a member of his court: "When you see a crop of iron shoot up in the fields, and black rivers of iron come flooding round the city walls like the surging waves of the ocean, then perhaps you can say that

Charles is arriving." He did not have time to finish, when a storm like a black cloud appeared in the west and turned the light of day into a fearful gloom. With the approach of the emperor, the day became darker than any night for the besieged, because of the splendor of the arms displayed before them.

Then they saw the iron-willed Charles, crested with an iron helmet, iron sleeves on his arms, the iron breast and shoulders protected by an iron breastplate, an iron lance lifted high with the left hand, while the right was always outstretched with the unconquered sword. The outer part of the thighs, which others leave without armor in order to mount their horses more easily, were in his case protected by sheets of iron. As for greaves, the entire army wore them made of iron. On his shield you could see only iron. Even his horse, because of its courage and color, shined like iron. All those who preceded him, flanked him, or followed him imitated this armament according to their means. Iron filled the fields and the plains. The rays of the sun reflected in the serried ranks of iron. The people chilled by fear bowed to the chill iron. The flashing iron lit up the darkness of the cellars and echoed the confused clamor of the citizens, "Oh, the iron! Alas, the iron!"[23]

Albeit filtered through the monk's literary style, this passage clearly reveals the military pride of the Franks, for whom Charles would always remain an unforgettable symbol, while the Lombard king and his besieged people cut a miserable figure. But it should be remembered that the collective memory also preserved or invented tales of the opposite sign, whose hero was Prince Adelchis, who was unjustly disinherited by the invader. Even in the next millennium, the author of the *Novalesa Chronicle*, who wrote at the monastery of Breme in Lomellina in modern Lombardy, recounts that one day Adelchis entered Pavia undetected while it was occupied by the Franks and managed to get into the main hall where Charles was banqueting. There, lost among the multitude of fellow diners, he devoured an unimaginable quantity of game, breaking the bones and sucking the marrow like a lion with its prey. He then vanished, leaving a huge pile of broken bones under the table. When

Charles saw the pile of bones, he knew that only a prince of royal blood could have eaten in that manner and that Adelchis had been there and had mocked him.[24]

Manzoni and Adelchi

If we are considering the grip that the figure of Adelchis held on the imagination of successive generations, it is only right to conclude with Manzoni's play of that name, particularly as it is the reason why the majority of Italians remember the events from their schooldays. From a historical point of view, this previous knowledge is not necessarily a bad thing. Manzoni researched his writing rather accurately, and the material he gathered for the tragedy was in fact used for his historical essay on the Lombard presence in Italy.[25] As far as political and military events are concerned, *Adelchi* is fairly faithful to history, although there is the occasional license, the most obvious of which is the death of the protagonist at the end of the play, while in reality we know Adelchis survived the catastrophic end of the Lombard kingdom and went to seek out his fortune in Constantinople. There was also poetic license in the name of Ermengarda attributed to the female role, because no reliable source provides the name of Desiderius's daughter. A hagiography of the following century calls her Desiderata, which was probably just a confusion with the father's name. Amusingly the name of Ermengarda, which Manzoni put into circulation, has in some cases sneaked its way into scholarly use, ending up in an entry in the authoritative *Dictionnaire de biographie française*.[26]

Above all, historians do not find the psychology of the characters very believable, particularly in the case of Ermengarda and Adelchis, who are quintessential products of romantic literature, although it would be absurd to blame the author who was following contemporary taste. There is a case for criticizing Manzoni's adherence to the historiographic theories of Augustin Thierry, which induced him to see the Lombards simply as foreign overlords, entirely separated from the Latin "scattered people" who had been reduced to servitude. Here the author's ideological concerns with depicting the state of Italy in his own time under a historical mask considerably hinder historical understanding, given that at the time of Charlemagne the Lombard kingdom no longer had any ethnic basis. It was a territorial entity, and the distinction between Lombards and Romans was on the point of disappearing. Moreover apologists for Manzoni cannot on this point plead the objective limitations of nineteenth-century historiography, because Sismondi, a contemporary of the Milanese writer, had understood the rapid assimilation of the two peoples and arrived at the conclusion that the Frankish conquest sought after by the Church interrupted a promising process of unification. In the context of the restless Italy of the post-Napoleonic restoration and the first Carbonari uprisings, Sismondi's position plainly implied a strong attack on papal policy, and it is not difficult to understand that a fervent Catholic like Manzoni could not accept such an interpretation of his country's ancient history.

THREE

Wars against the Pagans

Following his victory over the Lombards, Charlemagne was for all practical purposes the only Christian king in the West. The small Anglo-Saxon and Spanish kings only exerted power locally, in spite of the title they gave themselves, whereas Charles was the lord of two large kingdoms. His dominions stretched from the North Sea to the Adriatic, comprising the overwhelming majority of Christians of the Latin rite. He was surrounded by the enemies of God: the Saxons, who were pagans living in the interminable forests of northern Germany, and beyond them the Danes and the Slavs, who were also idolaters; the Muslim Arabs, who had been repulsed earlier by Charles Martel and lived on the other side of the Pyrenees; and finally the Avars, the cruel descendants of Attila the Hun, who lived in the Pannonian plain. The Franks were a warrior people, eager to attack and subjugate their neighbors. Charles Martel and later Pepin had earned their support precisely by leading them every year on victorious expeditions of conquest, from which everyone returned loaded with glory and booty. But now, more than ever in the past, these wars of aggression took on an unequivocal religious legitimacy. Every time Charles raised his sword against his neighbors, the pope's benediction would accompany him, and the God of armies, from up high in his heaven, could only look on his enterprises with gratification. How could he fail in such conditions?

THE WAR AGAINST THE SAXONS
The Atrocities of a Religious War

In fact he very rarely failed, but the price the king paid was a high one. "You love the lilies of peace and the roses of war; thus you are resplendent in white and scarlet." These were the flowery words that court poets used to flatter Charles, but the truth was that the color of roses and blood prevailed by far over the whiteness of lilies, because warfare accompanied him throughout almost every year of his life. The harshest war, and the one most fraught with complications, was the war against the Saxons, which lasted for more than twenty years, took the borders of Christendom to the banks of the Elbe, and incorporated the entire breadth of the German regions within the Frankish kingdom. Back in 772 Charles had already gathered his warriors and led them against the pagans of the north to achieve a spectacular victory: they took the principal Saxon sanctuary, the Irminsul, where the sacred tree stood. The tree that according to the Saxons held up the heavens had been burned, and Saxon idols destroyed. But these punitive expeditions had to be repeated every year, because the Saxons resisted with all their force a subjugation that implied both the loss of all their tribal independence and the abandonment of their ancestral beliefs.

Charles had not set himself the declared aim of converting the Saxons to Christianity right from the very beginning. Before him, his father and his grandfather had fought against them, and on each occasion, after having defeated them, they were satisfied with the payment of a tribute. Einhard, who was writing when the wounds had had time to heal and could have easily attributed Charles's campaigns beyond the Rhine to reassuring religious predestination, actually asserts in very pragmatic terms that "there were too many reasons for disturbing the peace, for example the border between us and them crossed an open plain, except in a few places where great forests or mountain chains more clearly divided the two countries. Thus murders, raids, and arson were continuously committed by one side or the other." In the chronicler's opinion, this insecurity of the frontier with the barbarians inevitably meant that "in the end the exasperated Franks could no longer be contented with returning each blow with another and decided to wage a full-scale war against them."[1]

It is clear that religious motivations were inextricably bound up with political ones, as since the time of Charles Martel, Frankish swords had sustained missionary work beyond the Rhine. One of the conditions that Pepin imposed on the defeated Saxons was the guarantee that the Frankish and Anglo-Saxon clergy working in the area would be free to continue their apostolic tasks without hindrance. It must have appeared obvious to some of these missionaries that Charles's war had a religious justification. "If you will not accept belief in God," Saint Lebuin told the Saxons, "there is a king in the next country who will enter your land, conquer it, and lay it waste."[2] But the Saxons obstinately refused to believe, so in the end that king had to make his move.

It was a ferocious war in a country with little or no civilization, with neither roads nor cities, and entirely covered with forests and marshland. The Saxons sacrificed prisoners of war to their gods, as Germans had always done before converting to Christianity, and the Franks did not hesitate to put to death anyone who refused to be baptized. Time and again the Saxon chiefs, worn down by war with no quarter, sued for peace, offered hostages, accepted baptism, and undertook to allow missionaries to go about their work. But every time that vigilance slackened and Charles was engaged on some other front, rebellions broke out, Frankish garrisons were attacked and massacred, and monasteries were pillaged. Even the border regions of the Frankish kingdom were not safe. In 778, when the Saxons found out that the king and his army were engaged on the other side of the Pyrenees and would not be able to return before many weeks of forced marches, they appeared in the Rhine Valley. Local commanders had great difficulty in containing them, and then only after much devastation and plunder.

During the period of these rebellions, the figure of a single leader emerged from the Saxon ranks. His name was Prince Widukind, and his authority was acknowledged by all the tribes. Just at the time when Charles felt confident that he had pacified the region and gained the loyalty of the Saxon nobles, it was this leader who triggered the most spectacular rebellion by wiping out the Frankish forces hurriedly sent to confront him on the Süntel Mountains in 782. Beside himself with anger at the treachery that had also cost him the lives of two of his closest aides, his chamberlain Adalgisile and his constable Geilo, Charles brought in a new army and forced the rebels to capitulate, with the exception of Widukind, who took refuge with the Danes. The Saxons had to hand over their arms and then, when he had them in his power, he had 4,500 of them decapitated in a single day at Verden on the Aller, a tributary of the Weser. This episode produced perhaps the greatest stain on his reputation.

Several historians have attempted to lessen Charles's responsibility for the massacre, by stressing that until a few months earlier the king thought he had pacified the country, the Saxon nobles had sworn allegiance, and many of them had been appointed counts. Thus the rebellion constituted an act of treason punishable with death, the same penalty that the extremely harsh Saxon law imposed with great facility, even for the most insignificant crimes. Others have attempted to twist the accounts provided by sources, arguing that the Saxons were killed in battle and not massacred in cold blood, or even that the verb *decollare* (to decapitate) was a copyist's error in place of *delocare* (to relocate), so the prisoners were simply deported. None of these attempts has proved credible. There would in fact be little point in digging up this controversy, if it were not for the fact that the era in which it reached its climax, the 1930s, gave it a particularly sinister tone. At the time Nazi historians, in whose eyes Widukind was a hero of the German race and Charles a *halbwelsch* and Latinized conqueror, attacked their colleagues who tried to negate the reality of the massacre, accusing them of creating a "degenerate historiography" (*entartete Geschichtsschreibung*), using the same language adopted by Goebbels to demonize avant-garde art.[3]

In reality, the most likely inspiration for the mass execution of Verden was the Bible. Exasperated by the continual rebellions, Charlemagne wanted to act like a true king of Israel. The Amalekites had dared raise their hand to betray God's people, and it was therefore right that every last one of them should be exterminated. Jericho was taken and all those inside had to be put to the sword, including men, women, old people, and children, even the oxen, sheep, and donkeys, so that no trace would be left of them. After defeating the Moabites, David, with whom Charles liked to compare himself, had the prisoners stretch out on the ground, and two out of three were killed. This, too, was part of the Old Testament from which the king drew constant inspiration, and it is difficult not to discern a practical and cruelly coherent application of that model in the massacre of Verden. Besides, the royal chronicler wrote a few years later, the war against the Saxons had to be conducted in such a manner that "either they were defeated and subjugated to the Christian religion or completely swept away."[4]

In the years that followed 782, Charles conducted a war of unparalleled ruthlessness. For the first time he wintered in enemy territory and systematically laid the country waste to starve the rebels. At the same time, he had published the most ferocious of all the laws enacted during his life, the *Capitulare de partibus Saxonie*, which imposed the death penalty on anyone who offended the Christian religion and its clergy, and in reality it constituted a program for the forced conversion of the Saxons.[5] We can only shudder as we read the sections of this law that condemn to death those who fail to observe fasting on Friday, thus reflecting a harsh Christianity far removed from the original message of the New Testament. Yet we should be careful not to put the blame for this barbarity onto the times in general. The *Capitulare de partibus Saxonie* is one of those provisions by which an infuriated general attempts to break the resistance of an entire people through terror, and Charles must bear the moral responsibility, like the many twentieth-century generals responsible for equally inhuman measures. It is more important to emphasize that the edict provoked criticisms among Charles's entourage precisely because of its ruthlessness. Particularly severe criticism came from Alcuin, the spiritual adviser he most listened to.[6]

The policy of terror and scorched earth initially appeared to pay off. In 785, after the Franks had ravaged the country as far as the Elbe, Widukind was obliged to capitulate, and he presented himself at the palace of Attigny in France to be baptized. The king acted as godfather. Pope Adrian congratulated the victor and ordered thanks to be given in all the churches of Christendom for the new and magnificent victory for the faith. But the baptism imposed by force did not prove very effective. In 793 the harshness of Frankish government that tended to repress any return to pagan rituals with the maximum ferocity provoked another mass insurrection in the northern regions of Saxony, which had been more superficially Christianized. "Once again breaking their faith," according to the royal chronicler, the Saxons burned churches, massacred clergymen, and prepared yet again to resist in their forests.[7]

Charles intervened with now customary ferocity, indeed with even more drastic and frighteningly modern measures. Rather than limit himself to devastating the rebel country and starving the population, he deported them en masse and planned the resettlement of those areas with Frankish and Slav colonists. However he was an able politician and soon understood the need to modify his approach to the problem. He intensified his contacts with the leading figures in the Saxon aristocracy and sought out their collaboration. At a large assembly in Aachen in 797, he issued on their advice a new version of the capitulary that was considerably more conciliatory than the previous one.[8] This twin policy proved immediately effective, because it guaranteed almost definitively the collaboration of the Saxon nobles with the new regime. Eigil, the monk at Fulda monastery who wrote the account of Abbot Sturmi's life, stated during those very years that Charles had imposed Christ's yoke on the Saxons "through war, persuasion, and also gifts,"[9] demonstrating that he well understood how a new flexibility had made it possible to integrate those obstinate pagans into the Christian empire.

The city that Charles had constructed at Paderborn in the heart of the conquered country was a symbol of this integration. It was erected on the drained marshland and included a royal palace and a magnificent cathedral. This was where the sovereign resided when operations against the rebels required his presence in Saxony, and in 799 it was here that he received Pope Leo III who had fled Rome to escape his enemies. It was also the departure point for missionary efforts that, following in the footsteps of Saint Boniface, managed in a short time to eradicate paganism much more effectively than did the Frankish swords. The spread of the faith was so successful that the first bishop appointed for Paderborn was a Saxon, Hathumar. The new province was rapidly integrated into the empire's political and military structure. This is demonstrated by the fact that a levy of Saxon troops started to be regularly assigned to imperial armies, especially in expeditions against Slav tribes, which became increasingly common and from which Saxons were most to benefit, as their peasants found new opportunities of colonizing land beyond the Elbe.

The front with northern Germany was thus definitively closed and another one was opened to the east, on which German rulers were to continue to fight for centuries. It was the *Drang nach Osten* front, by which the living space for Germanic peoples was to be enlarged to the detriment of the Slavs. Yet we must be careful not to confuse Charles with Frederick I "Barbarossa" or even Hitler, by forgetting the radically different perspective. The king certainly did not take into account any ethnic or racial principles when he made his policy decisions. For instance, he did not hesitate to use those Slav chiefs that accepted his authority against the Saxons. As far as the immense plains beyond the Elbe were concerned, the idea that it was the destiny of the German people to seek living space in that area would have been quite foreign to him, and throughout his entire life he always considered the great river to be the empire's natural border. His last measure against the Saxons, about which German historians have anguished, was the deportation of Saxons who lived beyond the Elbe as late as 804, and the granting of their land to the Obodrites, the neighboring Slavic tribes.

The Strategy of the Saxon War

So far we have considered the overview of a war that kept Charles occupied practically every year for over half of his reign. What do we know about how these campaigns were fought on the ground? From a military point of view, the principal feature of the war against the Saxons was the attempt to control a difficult terrain of forests and marshes by invaders who had a massive superiority in purely military terms but were fighting far from home and therefore depended entirely on their ability to build and defend advance positions. On the other hand, the inhabitants of the country as far as possible avoided engagements in the open field of battle and conducted a ruthless guerrilla war behind the invader's lines. When they managed a concerted action, they concentrated their efforts on besieging and destroying the more exposed of their enemy's bases.

It has been observed that while the strategic problem of Charlemagne's war against the Saxons was substantially the same as the campaigns of Drusus and Germanicus in the first century A.D., the solution adopted was radically different.[10] The Romans, who had control of the sea, were able to sail up rivers toward the interior and therefore conducted their campaigns not only from the west by sailing up the Lippe from its confluence with the Rhine, but also from the north by sailing up the Ems and its tributary, the Hase. Thus their legions could reach the Teutoburg Forest, the ancient battlefield of Varus. German archaeologists have found their principal fortified bases along these rivers. Instead, Charlemagne always entered the enemy's country by land, although he regularly used waterways for the transport of supplies. If the army gathered on the middle Rhine, it then moved to the east along the valleys of the Lippe and the Ruhr. If, on the other hand, it gathered at the upper Rhine, it went northward and forded the Main at the place that to this day is called Frankfurt, "the Franks' ford," and then continued directly north.

In both cases, the army entered enemy territory along the plateau to the west of the Weser, along the upper reaches of this river where the

Diemel and the Eder flow together. On the first of these two rivers the Saxons had built a fortress called Eresburg, which barred the invaders' way. From his first campaign in Saxony in 772, Charles took Eresburg and installed a garrison before moving on to fortify Büraburg on the Eder, which for some time constituted the main Frankish outpost in northern Germany. In all the subsequent campaigns, this area represented the operational base for the Frankish army, and here Charles went to great pains to transform the country. He erected one of the most important of Christendom's bridgeheads, the Corvey monastery, and here he would later build the new city of Paderborn, in the place where back in 777 he had held the annual gathering of Franks and where he built his favorite residence in the Saxon territories.

From a military point of view, the most important place for controlling the plateau was the fortress at Eresburg, as can be demonstrated by the Saxon persistence in capturing it. In 773, while the king was fighting the Lombards on the other side of the Alps, Eresburg was taken and destroyed for the first time. Charles rebuilt it during the 775 campaign, together with another more advanced fortress at Lübbecke, on the mountains facing the Weser. The Saxons decided to attack the latter and managed to enter it through deception, by mixing with the Frankish foragers who were reentering the encampment after having scoured the countryside for provisions. The garrison lost many men and had great difficulty in repelling the infiltrators, who then vanished into the forest without a trace. In 776, while Charles was fighting the Lombards on the Livenza, the Saxons turned up in force at Eresburg and persuaded the garrison to leave, and so the fort was again destroyed. But in that summer, the king returned to rebuild it. At the same time he built another fortress on the Lippe, which he called Karlsburg. This was destroyed in the 778 insurrection.

The Saxons also built wooden fortifications on a par with the Frankish ones, in order to withstand the advance of enemy bases. Thus in the majority of cases, the summer campaign planned by Charles had the purpose of capturing and destroying one or more of these fortresses, as well as reinforcing existing Frankish fortresses and, where possible, creating new ones. It was a laborious way to make war, and not likely to produce spectacular successes, but in the long run the vastly superior human and economic resources of the invader were bound to prevail. The Saxons' siege equipment, particularly their catapults (*petrariae*), was less effective than that of the Franks. Chroniclers put down their failure to divine intervention,[11] but it is more probable that Saxon engineers were not so skilled. The subjugation of Saxony was ultimately the result of its slow strangulation through the extension of a network of forts that were able to support each other and block all the rivers. They were able to send out bands of armed men to ravage enemy territory and reduce the inhabitants to submission by disseminating terror. At the same time, the corresponding enemy fortifications were slowly but surely taken and demolished one by one.

It is, however, possible to identify the moment during the dismal and monotonous unfolding of the Saxon war in which the degree of brutality suddenly accelerated and Charles clearly wished to force his enemy's hand. On the whole he succeeded. Having entered Saxony in the summer of 782, after the Saxon insurrection and the defeat at Süntel, Charles symbolically took revenge for his fallen soldiers at the massacre of Verden, but it was too late to conduct a large-scale campaign and the king returned to winter in Thionville. Immediately after Easter 783, he returned to Saxony with a large army, although it does appear that he had difficulties in coordinating its movements and had to engage the enemy for the first time with only part of his forces. In the end, he managed to bring his army together in force and crush the rebels. After that, he did not hesitate to follow through his victory by crossing the Weser and pushing on for the first time as far as the Elbe. For family reasons, he was persuaded to return home to winter in Worms, since Queen Hildegard had died in April and his mother, Bertrada, in July. It was not therefore appropriate for the king to remain outside his kingdom, particularly in view of his forthcoming marriage to Fastrada, which took place immediately on his return.

By then it was clear that Charles intended to conduct the war to the bitter end, with an overall strategic vision. The 784 campaign was commenced in more or less the usual manner with a long march along the Lippe as far as the Weser, but when excessive rain provoked flooding and made the land impassable, the king decided not to return home as he might have done at another time but to leave sufficient forces with his son Charles to keep the rebels at bay and march the majority of the army through Thuringia, laying waste the Saxon lands further to the east, between the Saale and the Elbe. Back in Worms before the autumn, he was still not happy with the results obtained and gathered more troops to replace those worn out by the long summer campaign. He then made another show of force on the Weser and, with the onset of winter, fell back to Eresburg to winter for the first time in enemy land. The firmness of his decision was demonstrated by the fact that he had his wife, Fastrada, and his children join him there. Rather than suspend operations during the winter months as was the custom, he continued personally to carry out punitive expeditions against the rebels.

Charles's strategic and logistical skills were even more clearly demonstrated in this winter campaign than his carefully planned and destructive blitzkrieg against the Lombards. It represented a new concept of inflicting an unbearable and continuous strain on the enemy in both material and moral terms. It was not simply a matter of disseminating indiscriminate terror in order to break the rebels' spirit of resistance but also of shrewdly destroying those enemy forts that in future could be an obstacle, maintaining control over the lines of communication, and meanwhile amassing provisions and materials in the forward base at Eresburg. The intention was that, once the good weather came, the 785 campaign would prove decisive. And so it was to be. That summer Widukind and the other rebel leaders found themselves without support in a devastated land, in which the Frankish cavalry was able to push forward wherever it wanted without resistance. When Charles promised to spare their lives, they preferred to give themselves up and accept baptism and deportation to France.

This same strategy, based on the control of fords and the building of fortified outposts, was then introduced into the campaigns against Slavs, which constituted a direct continuation of those against the Saxons. In 789 Frankish forces crossed the Elbe for the first time, and two wooden bridges were built across the river, one of which was defended by a wooden castle and earth fortifications. The local Slav chief, Dragawit, thought it best to surrender and hand over his fortified residence, submitting himself to the Frankish king. In 806 the emperor's son Charles led another large expedition, threw the Slavs back, and established one fort on the Elbe and another on the Saale. Two years later, another two forts were built on the Elbe, which was thus being more clearly transformed into the empire's frontier—a well-defended frontier from which it was possible to launch offensives when and as often as was wanted. Thus the policy of subjugating Slav lands through the construction of fortresses and the establishment of garrisons to protect German settlers and the encouragement of German migration first appeared in the days of Charlemagne. The policy was to be systematically pursued by the Teutonic knights in Prussia and was further theorized in more recent times in the deluded Nazi plans to occupy the Ukraine and Russia.

Pitched Battles

Charles's war against the Saxons was therefore a war of sieges, fortresses laboriously built in forest clearings, barges sent along rivers to supply besieged garrisons in enemy territory, crude war machines, and mountain ambushes. In such a war, pitched battles were a rarity. Einhard confirms that Charles personally only fought two battles, both within the same month in the summer of 783.[12] In them he crushed two concentrations of rebels, first on the Lippe and then on the Hase. There is reason to believe that the Frankish chroniclers embellished their version and that in the first of the two battles, which was fought near Detmold, Charles was in fact repelled. After the first encounter, fought with insufficient forces, the king apparently retreated to Paderborn and there rapidly collected reinforcements, while the Saxons, far from shaken, prepared for the next battle. In the second battle, the king was able to deploy the usual numerical superiority and was undoubtedly victorious. Afterward the Franks crossed the Weser and even pushed on as far as the Elbe, pillaging the enemy country as they went.

The battle about which we have most information was not a victory. The Franks were severely beaten, as occurred at Roncesvalles in similar circumstances. It is not altogether surprising that the worst defeats made the greatest impression on chroniclers, who were more accustomed to victories. The battle to which we have referred more than once occurred at the foot of a range called Süntel, close to the Weser River, and it is perhaps the only battle fought during Charlemagne's wars of which a fairly detailed account exists, allowing us to assess its strategic purpose and tactical development.[13]

It was the summer of 782, and news of Widukind's renewed rebellion had just begun to spread. The king sent an order to the army that at the time was in Saxony preparing a campaign against the Slavs under the command of his chamberlain Adalgisile, his constable Geilo, and the count palatine Worad, instructing it to turn around and attack the Saxons where they were gathering. This army was originally formed to intercept and destroy a band of raiders from a Slavic country between the Elbe and the Saale, and so it was mainly made up of cavalry. It does not appear that the frontier operations had already commenced, and the army was still in Saxon territory and almost certainly to the west of the Weser. The army soon reached the area in the Süntel range where the rebels were gathering, just on the other side of the great river. Here the column met up with another force that the king had hurriedly recruited in the Rhine area and sent as reinforcement under the command of one of his relations, Count Theodoric.

Frankish scouts discovered the Saxon encampment on the mountains beyond the Weser, and the commanders decided to maneuver so as to block any chance of escape. This was further evidence of how the Franks were so sure of their own superiority that they moved about in enemy territory in complete security, whereas the Saxons found themselves in a guerrilla or partisan situation, constantly pursued and threatened with annihilation. Theodoric approached the enemy encampment and set up his own camp opposite but still on the other side of the river. At the same time the second column circled round across the river and took up its position behind the enemy. The maneuver was a good one and we cannot help admiring commanders who were able to conceive and execute such a complex plan. But at this stage things must have started to go wrong. Perhaps the Franks, like innumerable other generals, were to experience to their cost how difficult it is to coordinate the movement of different formations and above all to launch their attack. Perhaps, as a royal chronicler prefers to argue, using a psychological explanation, the three generals of the second column wanted to claim all the glory for an easy victory without sharing it with Theodoric. In any case, they attacked on their own.

The Franks may well have underestimated the size of the enemy force or its morale, because it appears they charged with their heads down spurring their horses against the enemy camp, as though they were not expecting an enemy ready to do battle and saw their task as chasing a rout. The Saxons, who fought on foot in accordance with the ancient Germanic tradition, probably drew them into an area unsuited to horses, and after repelling the first charge, they gradually managed to get the upper hand to the point of being able to encircle and annihilate their enemies. We already know the outcome: Adalgisile and Geilo were killed, and with them four counts. Only a few fugitives managed to cross the mountain and the river to reach Count Theodoric's encampment. The count then had the task of breaking the news of the catastrophe to the king. (He was to continue to fight for many years on that front until the Saxons killed him in 793; by that time his son William had been appointed count of Toulouse and was to become the famous *Guillaume au cort nez* of the chansons de geste, but that is another story.)[14]

It is difficult to say what military lessons can be learned from the battle of Süntel. Some analysts have compared it to the initial stage of the battle of Hastings, in which the Norman heavy cavalry did not manage to breach the Saxon infantry's wall of shields in its well-established position on the hilltop, and thus conclude that the value of Charlemagne's cavalry was not necessarily in its ability to pierce enemy lines. In other ways, the circumstances remind us of the battle of Little Big Horn, where the unexpected number of Indians and their willingness to fight rather than flee made a disaster of the easy victory an experienced general like Custer felt he was certain of achieving. What is certain is that the battle of Süntel was an exception, as can be seen from the considerable attention paid to it in the annals. The general rule was that in pitched battles, Frankish armies were considerably superior to their adversaries.

THE WARS AGAINST THE ARABS
The 778 Campaign

Throughout most of his reign Charlemagne's attitude to the Arabs of Spain was on the whole a defensive one. The walls of the ancient Roman cities of Narbonne and Toulouse were fortified and the king was happy to defend Aquitaine against any incursions, as well as the insurrections by the region's inhabitants so frequent during Pepin's reign. In the spring of 778, however, the internal struggles that were undermining Muslim domination of Spain appeared to offer the golden opportunity to move onto the offensive. Charlemagne forewent a trip to Rome that he had already discussed with the pope, in order to organize a campaign beyond the Pyrenees to assist the governor of Barcelona, Sulaymān Yaqzan ibn al-ʿArabi, and other "Saracen princes" who had rebelled against the emir of Cordova and had come as far as Paderborn to request the assistance of the Franks.[15] The hope of an easy conquest was undoubtedly the principal reason for the campaign, but this did not stop Charles's writing to the pope that the Arabs were threatening to invade his kingdom and he was moving against them for preventive reasons. The pope replied in the manner that could be expected by beseeching an angel sent by God to precede the Frankish army in its campaign against the infidel and to allow the troops a victorious return to their home-land.[16] As can be seen, propaganda and the manipulation of information were already essential ingredients for imperialist policy.

The king planned one of his favorite pincer movements for his campaign beyond the Pyrenees. He personally was to lead an army through the Basque Country, which was Christian and nominally under his control, while a second army was to cross the mountains further to the east. The accounts provided by chroniclers demonstrate that logistical considerations were decisive in the adoption of this maneuver: the troops recruited in Neustria and Aquitaine gathered on the Atlantic side, while the troops from Austrasia, Provence, Germany, and Italy were more easily assembled on the Mediterranean side.[17] The two armies united under the walls of Saragossa, and when the local governor, contrary to what had been agreed, refused to surrender, Qârlo, as the Arab chroniclers called him, put the city under siege. However, he did not succeed in taking it, and after a month and half he decided to return home, as disturbing news of rebellion on the Saxon border had reached him. On 15 August 778, the retreating rearguard, caught in the Pyrenean ravines, suffered a surprise attack from the highland Basque tribes and was massacred. Einhard wrote that the seneschal Eggihard, the count palatine Anselm, and Roland or "Hruodlandus," the prefect of the march of Brittany, perished in the conflict.[18]

This Hruodlandus is mentioned in a few documents of doubtful authenticity as a close aide of the king, and we know nothing else about him, except that he was destined to become one of the most famous literary heroes of the West, the principal character in the *Chanson de Roland*, who fell at Roncesvalles after slaughtering innumerable heathens, because the Basques of history, who had long been Christians, were transformed into Muslims in popular memory. He was also the Orlando of Boiardo and Ariosto, the protagonist of the major works of Italian Renaissance literature. Yet we are not even certain that Hruodlandus was really killed in the ambush, as his name does not appear in some of the most important manuscripts of the *Vita Karoli*, and it may have been added to the other codices under the influence of the legend that was already widely known. As for Roncesvalles, the *Chanson de Roland*, written in the eleventh century, is the first text to identify this valley, so familiar to pilgrims on their way to Santiago de Compostela, as the battle site, whereas contemporary sources only speak of Pyrenean ravines.[19]

The Campaigns of Louis the Pious

Although the Roncesvalles episode makes us think of the Spanish campaign as a failure, the final balance sheet was not entirely negative, because the Christian populations on the other side of the Pyrenees had now identified the Frankish kingdom as their only available protector, and Charles had learned to his cost that greater planning was required for future expansion into the Iberian peninsula. The first step in that direction was the establishment of the independent kingdom of Aquitaine, of which Charlemagne's son Louis was anointed king in 781, at the same time that another son, Pepin, became king of the Lombards. The people of Aquitaine, so rebellious in the past, were pacified by this recognition of their identity. It was, of course, a purely symbolic recognition, given that the new King Louis was just three years old. The regency was run by a team of councillors who were directly responsible to Charles and put all their energies into defending the Pyrenean border and keeping an eye on events in Spain.

The Christian populations of the Iberian peninsula asked on several occasions for Frankish assistance, as occurred in 785 for the inhabitants of Gerona. But for the moment, the Muslims looked more threatening. In 793 they pushed on as far as the walls of Narbonne and Carcassonne, routing Count William of Toulouse, who attempted to intercept them, and then returned unmolested to Spain loaded with booty and Christian slaves. It was perhaps such episodes that persuaded Charles that the question of the Pyrenean frontier had to be resolved by drastic action, making the necessary resources available to Louis, when disagreements among the Arab princes again provided an opportunity to intervene. In 797, shortly after the death of the emir of Cordova, his brother 'Abd Allāh came to Aachen to ask the king's assistance in deposing his nephew, while another rebel, having taken control of Barcelona, offered to hand the city over to the Franks. On his father's orders, Louis crossed the Pyrenees and besieged Huesca, and although the enterprise proved beyond his power, a second campaign led by Count Borrell occupied the fortified city of Vich, as well as several less important fortified positions. He had thus established a permanent operational base on the other side of the mountains. The effects of this conquest did not take long to show themselves. In 799 the emir of Huesca wrote to Charles promising that the next time he would open the gates of his city to the Frankish army.

From this time on the king of Aquitaine, who was now an adolescent, felt strong enough to undertake a vast campaign of conquest. In 800 he returned to Spain at the head of an army and took Lérida. In 801 he laid siege to Barcelona, which fell after resisting for seven months, and he entrusted command of the city to Bera, a Gothic count. In the years that followed, Louis systematically enlarged his Iberian dominions, until in 810 the emir of Cordova sued for peace and acknowledged Frankish influence north of the Ebro River. The area taken from the Muslims was incorporated into the empire and organized militarily as a fortified frontier province, or march, to use the terminology of the imperial administration. This Spanish march (*limes Hispanicus*), which was recovered so early by Christendom and linked administratively to Aquitaine, gave rise to its own particular features that are today recognizable in Catalonia, such as the closeness of its language and customs to southern France. It was traditionally considered more European than the rest of Spain.

In strictly military terms, the Spanish wars do not teach us very much. Yet they hold one fundamental lesson: even though they were fighting in their own territory against an enemy that had considerable logistical problems, Arabs always avoided pitched battles and relied for their defense exclusively on their city walls. This reliance was by no means misplaced, because in such a highly urbanized region, the Franks found making progress an extremely slow business, particularly given the crudeness of their siege equipment.[20] The fact remains that their armies were clearly far too strong for the Arabs to meet on the field of battle, as had been the case with the Saxons, except for a few rare exceptions, and as was to be the case with the Avars.

THE WARS AGAINST THE AVARS
The Horsemen of the Steppes

According to Einhard, Charlemagne's war against the Avars was "the most important he ever fought, with the exception of the Saxons; and he committed himself to it with greater enthusiasm and with much greater resources."[21] Perhaps this is why the Avars are the least known of all the enemies who had the ill fortune to attract Charles's attention, for they paid a higher price than everyone else, and until not very long ago, it was believed that they disappeared from the face of the earth practically without leaving a trace of their past. Only recently have history and archaeology rescued them from the oblivion into which they were thrown by Frankish swords, but they have also shown that the merciless war Charles conducted against them was not entirely responsible for their decline.

Who, in fact, were they? A few centuries before, the name of the Avars had been used to describe not so much a people as a horde of nomads, raiders, and horse breeders, not too dissimilar to the Huns in their customs and Asian appearance. Indeed the Frankish sources called them precisely that: *Huni.* Besides, the horde formed about one century after Attila's death probably included some bands of real Huns. Under the leadership of a chief who bore the Turkish title of *khagan*, which Western chroniclers Latinized to *cacanus*, the Avars attacked the Byzantine Empire and settled as lords over the vast Danubian plains, which had just been left free by the migration of the Lombards to Italy. They

ruled over other populations of the same origins, known collectively as
the Bulgars, Germanic peoples such as the Gepids, and above all an
increasing number of Slav tribes.

The Avar khanate was therefore a very heterogeneous reality from an
ethnic and linguistic point of view, and by the time of Charlemagne, the
majority of its inhabitants had abandoned nomadism and lived by culti-
vating the land and rearing cattle in a manner not too dissimilar to the
Slavs of Eastern Europe. Its rulers formed an aristocracy of warrior
horsemen, who unlike the peasants had faithfully conserved their customs from the steppe, including their hair worn in two long pigtails,
which, all accounts agree, were the distinguishing mark of an Avar.
Archaeology suggests that those nobles were joined by other groups of
nomads from Asia and therefore at least the aristocracy continued to
speak languages of Turkic origin, rather than the Slav dialects that prevailed among their subjects. On the eve of their destruction, the Avars
were not so much a people as a collection of peoples who obeyed the
khagan, and more especially any of their number who owned arms,
horses, and jewels and exercised some form of authority. Even Turkish,
Bulgar, and Slav chiefs and nobles became Avars in the sense that they
acknowledged their vassalage to the *khagan.*

That is what we know about them, and what we do know has only
been discovered recently. The real question is how much did Charlemagne know? For him, the Avars probably seemed a contradictory people. On the one hand, everything that he could have read would have
associated them with the stereotype of the nomad from the steppes, such
as the Scythians described by Herodotus or the Huns described by Am-
mianus Marcellinus: bestial, cruel, and bloodthirsty savages who craved
pillage and raiding parties, clung obstinately to their pagan beliefs, and
were capable of any ungodly act. One of the men of learning at Charles's
court, Paul the Deacon, was a Lombard from Friuli, an area that in living memory had always been exposed to Avar raids, and was able to tell
bloodcurdling stories of their cruelty and lewdness. He would also have
been able to tell Charles that in earlier times those "Huns, now called

Avars," had clashed with the Franks in Danubian Germany and forced them to pay a tribute.[22]

On the other hand, the Avar khanate was a recognized power that entered into diplomatic relations with the Christian world. Even Paul the Deacon recalled that a century earlier *cacanus rex Hunnorum* (the *khagan* or king of the Huns) had sent ambassadors to Italy and Gaul and established peaceful agreements with the Lombard and Frankish kings.[23] The West would have known something, although a great deal less, about the long history of diplomatic relations between the Avars and Byzantium, dating back to the times of Justinian. In other words, the khanate was not a diabolic horde of the peoples of Gog and Magog descended from the mountains to murder and plunder wherever they went, but a kingdom with which Charles could maintain peaceful relations, although it was of course pagan and therefore to be treated with caution. Paradoxically, it was not the terrifying memory of Attila that drew the Avars into a war with the Franks, but rather the outcome of diplomatic negotiations in which the *khagan* proved to be a little too imprudent.

The Fall of Tassilo

The Germanic people who bordered with the Avars were the Bavarians, who were settled in the part of the Danubian plain now shared by Bavaria and Austria. The duke, Tassilo, had sworn fealty to Pepin and then Charles, but this did not stop him from seeking an ally to counterbalance Frankish supremacy in the Lombard king, Desiderius, one of whose daughters he had married. Having lost Lombard support with the fall of that kingdom in 774, Tassilo no longer had any hope of conducting an independent policy but, if we are to believe the chroniclers, he never lost the opportunity to provoke the king of the Franks, until the latter had no choice but to take drastic action against him. In truth, the story of his fall is a complicated one, which we will perhaps never fully understand.[24] The insistence of the Frankish writers on Tassilo's perfidy is not sufficient to remove the suspicion that the duke of the Bavarians was the victim of the cynical great power politics of his neighbor, and that Charles manipulated the situation until it grew intolerable and he had to be removed altogether.

We can be certain that in 787 their relations had deteriorated so far that the duke, knowing the king was in Rome, sent ambassadors to the pope to beseech his mediation. Adrian abruptly replied that, having sworn fealty to Charles, Tassilo could only obey or be excommunicated. On his return home, the Frankish king wrote to the duke in threatening tones, informing him that he should abide by the pope's order and immediately appear before him. The alarmed Tassilo did not obey, thus providing Charles with the pretext for accusing him of disloyalty and for intervening militarily in Bavaria, with the benediction of Adrian who declared the war to have a just cause. The invasion was planned as a large-scale military campaign, with three armies that were to converge on the enemy, one of which was to come from Italy under the nominal command of King Pepin and march on Trento and Bolzano. War was avoided at the last moment because the duke agreed to submit to Charles and hand over thirteen hostages, of whom one was his son.

It appeared that all had been forgiven, but Charles had not finished with Tassilo yet. The following year at the general assembly in Ingelheim, the duke's own bishops and vassals, the majority of whom now identified with the new regime, accused him of betraying his word and agreeing with the Avars to declare war against the Franks. It was implied that he had been put up to it by his wife, Liutperga, because as the daughter of Desiderius she had good reason to hate Charles. It is not easy to establish whether this was a trumped-up accusation to remove Tassilo permanently from the scene, or whether the duke, seeing that all was in any case lost, had turned to desperate means. For his part, the *khagan* may have been tempted to move against the Franks at a time when Tassilo had more need of him than ever. Even if Charles was not secretly pulling strings to manipulate events, he lost no time in taking the opportunity to rid himself of the last ethnic prince who resisted his authority.

Tassilo, who was virtually a prisoner from the moment the accusations were made against him, was condemned to death by the assembly for treason and desertion, but the king was content to have him shut up in a monastery, "where he lived in a manner as saintly as his willingness to enter it," as the royal chronicler records without a hint of irony.[25] In the meantime, as apparent confirmation of his guilt, Avar bands carried out raids in Bavaria and Friuli, but these could not have been large incursions, because the local commanders managed to repel them with their available forces. The force that entered Italy pushed into the Po Valley as far as Verona, where it burned down the church of San Zeno. Things went worse for the force that attacked Bavaria, which was pursued over the border and trapped against the Danube, where it was almost completely destroyed. Charlemagne was a methodical politician, and he had no intention of allowing the problem to continue without searching for a solution. Now that the duchy of Bavaria had lost its autonomy with the removal of Tassilo and had been incorporated into the Frankish kingdom, its border with the Avars had been added to the Lombard one in Friuli, but the new border was decidedly less peripheral than the previous one. Its security had to be guaranteed, and a demonstration of force would be a way of gaining lasting Bavarian loyalty.

Alcuin confirms that Charles was planning a war against the Avars in 789.[26] Military intervention was delayed by the arrival of the *khagan*'s ambassadors, to whom the Frankish king dictated his conditions. According to the Frankish chroniclers, he demanded the redrawing of the border between the two kingdoms.[27] The startling comparison with events in the twentieth century leads us to wonder whether Charles, knowing himself to be in the stronger position, put the *khagan* in the situation of having to choose between war, with all that would entail, or the acceptance of new borders that would have equaled capitulation. For more than a century the border between the Avars and the Bavarians had run along the River Enns, and the Avars had already shown their determination to defend it. (In 781, when Tassilo had sworn fealty to Charles, the *khagan*'s ambassadors went to Charles to reassure themselves of his peaceful intentions, and at the same time an Avar army had gathered on the Enns, but without crossing it, in order simply to provide a demonstration of force and to emphasize that the border would be defended.)

A few years later, after the Avar sovereign had heard from his ambassadors on their return from Worms and in turn discussed the matter with the Frankish ambassadors who came to his country, he unsurprisingly favored war over shameful capitulation and probable political suicide. Shifting the border eastward would have left the way open for the Franks to enter the Pannonian plain, guaranteeing protection for Germanic settlers who would not have taken long to move into the new country in force, as had already been occurring for some time along the border between the Germanic and Slav regions. What is certain is that the negotiations broke down after dragging on for more than a year, and in the summer of 791 the king of the Franks gathered his warriors in Bavaria and decided to attack first.

The War of 791 against the Avars

On paper, the challenge was worthy of Charles's military fame. Heavily armored Avar horsemen, with their 10-foot-long lances, bows, and arrows in the nomadic tradition and those stirrups that their enemies still did not understand, were an enemy that western and more particularly eastern Christians had learned to respect. Byzantine generals had been studying Avar weaponry and tactics for centuries, and even the Frankish chroniclers grudgingly praised the maneuverability of their cavalry, which was unsurpassed in its ability to feign a rout and then suddenly turn on its adversary with hidden reserves. Then there was the psychological effect of their war cries that resembled the howling of a pack of wolves, as they prepared for battle. Historians, faced with the unexpected ease with which Charles triumphed over the Avars, tend to believe that the khanate's power was merely a past memory, but these judgments are easy after the event, when we know how things turned out. In reality the uncertainty of war is such that we would do better to give credence to Einhard when he writes that Charles prepared for the war with unprecedented excitement and commitment.[28]

In military terms, the army that gathered at Ratisbon in the summer of 791 was perhaps the most numerous that Charles ever commanded, with contingents of Saxons and Frisians as well as Franks, Thuringians, and Bavarians. As the Danube was the natural route to enter the Avar lands, the king decided to divide his forces into two columns, which were to march along the opposite banks of the great river, the northern one under the command of Count Theodoric and the chamberlain Meginfredus, and the southern one under his personal command. A fleet of barges accompanied them along the course of the Danube, transporting supplies for both columns and allowing rapid communication between the two banks. At the same time, another force was to attack the Avars from behind, in accordance with Charles's well-established practice, which he had never had occasion to regret. This force was to come up from the border with Friuli under the command of his son King Pepin of Italy.

The campaign plan with its prolonged advance along the two banks of the Danube shows that Charles intended to seek a decisive encounter. The strategic problem posed by the invasion was that the Pannonian plain was everywhere divided in half by the Danube, which was not an easy river to cross. If the Franks had invaded as one unit, their operations would have been restricted to one side of the immense river basin. Charles's plan meant that the entire Avar lands were open to devastation on both sides of the Danube and if the *khagan* had gathered his forces and attacked one of the contingents, the fleet could have been used to bring the other contingent across the river to take part in the fighting.

As on previous occasions, the subdivision of the army was arranged according to logistical requirements, with the northern contingent mainly consisting of Saxons and Frisians who did not have to cross the Danube and could more easily maintain communications with their native land. Of course, the plan was intrinsically risky, as is always the case when the success of a campaign depends on the continuous coordination of the movements and timing of different contingents. The commanders chosen by Charles to lead the march must have been up to the task, because when the army he commanded reached the border with the Avar kingdom at Lorsch on the Enns, the other army arrived punctually at the appointment, and the chamberlain Meginfredus was able to cross the river in a boat to receive in person his instructions from the king.

Perhaps the most extraordinary event of the entire campaign occurred before the troops set foot on enemy territory, and it demonstrates the seriousness and anxiety with which the enterprise was undertaken. Priests imposed three days of fasting and prayers on the army to obtain God's favor. In a letter to Queen Fastrada, the king added that the ban on eating meat applied to everyone, while it was possible to obtain permission to drink wine by giving alms set at the considerable sum of one *solidus* in the case of the more wealthy, while everyone else had to pay in accordance with their conscience.[29] While priests said mass and clerics sang psalms and recited litanies, warriors fasted and gave alms so that they could be purified before going into battle against an enemy everyone still feared.

Bavarian noblemen made use of Charles's presence to submit their disputes to the king, and so he was also busy resolving these. Consequently, the army lingered at its encampment at Lorsch for longer than expected and only entered the enemy land toward the end of September. In the meantime, they had already received news that Pepin, on leaving Italy, had besieged and captured an Avar fortress that protected the border, taking many prisoners. Morale was therefore high and at least initially the outcome of the campaign looked promising. As the Franks advanced along the banks of the Danube, the population fled, abandoning houses and livestock and offering no resistance. The forts that defended the border were stormed and fell one after the other.

It soon became clear that the Avars were avoiding an engagement and preferred to oppose their enemy with a scorched-earth policy. The boundless Pannonian plain made it possible to withdraw before the enemy, evacuate the population, and take refuge in fortified sites capable of offering prolonged resistance. When Charles's army reached the River Raab, leaving behind it a trail of blazing ruins and devastation, autumn was well advanced. It was already the middle of October and provisions were getting scarce. Realizing that his horses were beginning to die from overwork and poor fodder, and that his men were also suffering from such a prolonged campaign in an unfavorable season and in an uninhabited country, Charles decided to suspend the operations and return home. He had ravaged a province that constituted only a tiny part of the Avar territory. He had not managed to force the enemy into a decisive battle, and almost without fighting, he had lost a large part of his horses as well as many men, including two bishops who had died of illness.

The Collapse of the Avar Khanate

Thus the 791 campaign ended with an outcome that did not match its expectations. Yet Charles had entered enemy territory without meeting resistance and had been able to lay waste the country and capture slaves wherever he managed to go. In other words, he had clearly demonstrated that the Avars were not capable of opposing the Franks, without the assistance of winter and a scorched-earth policy. Up to the end of 793 the king remained in Bavaria, mulling over the campaign for no less than two years and planning a resumption of hostilities, because he had decided that the Avar question had to be resolved once and for all. Here again, we find confirmation of Einhard's claim that Charles invested more enthusiasm and resources in the war against the Avars than he did in any other enterprise, with the exception of the submission of the Saxons. Indeed, the king devoted those two busy years to the development of infrastructures that were to facilitate the future invasion.

The work undertaken by Charles confirms that waterways were the indispensable key to a military campaign over long distances and also suggests that the fleet of boats on the Danube had proved insufficient to guarantee communications and supplies to the army. First of all, the king had a bridge of boats built across the great river, over which, we should not forget, no permanent bridge yet existed. He was then presented with a plan for a navigable canal joining the Rhine with the Danube. Immediately, the king moved in person to the chosen area, recruited a large number of laborers, and started work on what was to go down in history as the *fossa Karolina.* But the engineers who planned the work evidently were not up to the task: digging continued throughout the autumn of 793, but the ground did not hold up and the rains finished it off, so the canal was never operational. Finally, news of revolts in Saxony and on the Pyrenean border arrived toward the end of the year and Charles was obliged to give up on the enterprise for the moment and return to his homeland.

The Frankish cavalcade through Pannonia in the autumn of 791 was not without consequences. The *khagan*'s authority had been shaken and several Avar leaders started to assert political independence. One of them, who bore the Turkish title of *tudun*, sent ambassadors to Charles in 795, declaring his intention to submit himself to Charles and become a Christian. The year after this betrayal, the Avar khanate fell like a house of cards. The *khagan* was assassinated by his rivals, and Erich, the duke of Friuli, organized an expedition against the Avar capital, an immense fortified encampment on the left bank of the Danube, which was called the *ring* in the Frankish language. His forces sacked this capital without encountering resistance. Encouraged by this experience, King Pepin of Italy invaded the Avar lands with more powerful forces. The new *khagan* came out to meet him and make an act of submission but failed to prevent the Franks from sacking the *ring* for a second time and taking away all that remained of its treasures. For his part, the *tudun* turned up in Aachen as promised, was baptized, and returned to his country laden with rich gifts.

For a long time afterward, fabulous tales were told of the booty taken during the sacking of the *ring*. There the Avars kept the colossal tributes, or subsidies, according to the point of view, that in the past the Byzantine emperors had paid to the *khagan*, and that in some years had exceeded 200,000 gold coins. Einhard wrote dreamily that "all the money and treasure amassed over such a long period was pillaged, and human memory does not recall a war waged against the Franks in which they gained more wealth or filled their coffers with more riches."[30] There is no reason to doubt this account. Indeed, archaeology has confirmed that the Avars possessed vast quantities of gold. There is hardly a tomb of an Avar warrior or his woman that does not contain gold jewels, and *The Gold of the Avars* was the name of a recent and very successful archaeological exhibition.[31] It is therefore quite possible that the *khagan*'s treasure filled fifteen carts, each pulled by four oxen, as the chroniclers assure us. In Aachen part of the booty was shared out among counts, bishops, and abbots, which demonstrates that the Frankish king knew how to reward properly those who served him, while showing God his gratitude for the heavenly protection that accompanied him into battle. Another part of the booty was used to adorn the palace then under construction at Aachen, and yet another was sent as a gift to the pope.

The End of the Avars

The subjugation of the Avar khanate did not lead to its annexation to the Frankish kingdom, as had occurred with the Lombard kingdom. After all, the majority of the Avars were still pagans, even though serious planning toward the future conversion of those barbarians started as early as the summer of 796 in Pepin's encampment.[32] Charles could not, of course, entertain the idea of having himself crowned *khagan* as he had had himself crowned king of the Lombards. The border on the Enns was shifted eastward, opening new fertile lands to the advance of Germanic settlers. Up to the Danube, the converted *tudun* continued to govern as a vassal of the Frankish king, while beyond that point in the plains of the Tisza, other groups of Avars who had escaped Frankish steel were left to themselves and to their former subjects, the Bulgars, who lost no time in settling old scores.

As had occurred in Italy and Saxony, a relatively easy conquest was followed a few years later by a vast insurrection. In 799 Charles's two principal representatives on the eastern frontier were both assassinated. Duke Erich of Friuli was killed by the inhabitants of a city in Istria, possibly at the instigation of the Byzantines, and Gerold, the prefect of the Bavarian march, was killed as the result of a private vendetta. This all occurred at more or less the same time as the Avar insurrection against Frankish dominion under the leadership of the *tudun* himself. It was not a revolt of such dimensions as to seriously concern Charles, who did not return to that restless imperial border and shortly afterward left for Rome to be crowned emperor. However, the local commanders took a few years to break the revolt.

It was undoubtedly a dirty war, about which the chroniclers tell us little or nothing. The fact that as late as 802 the counts Cadalus and Gontramnus were killed fighting the Avars demonstrates that the conflict was prolonged. Only then, faced with the gravity of the situation, did Charles decide to return to his old base in Bavaria, and from there he sent an expedition, not however under his personal command, with the order to resolve the Avar question definitively. The order was followed to the letter and the Franks returned to their emperor with many prisoners: "multi Sclavi et Hunni."[33] These included the *tudun*, who made a further act of submission and was again pardoned. Clearly, by now it was merely a secondary irritation for Charles, although for the Avars the events must have presented themselves in much more dramatic terms. The years of ferocious guerrilla warfare and repression were undoubtedly more responsible than the almost bloodless campaigns of 791 and 796 for the situation described by Einhard: "the quantity of blood spilled at the time is demonstrated by Pannonia deserted of all inhabitants, the site where the *khagan*'s palace stood so abandoned that there is no sign of human habitation; all the Hun nobility perished in this war."[34]

The comment is symbolic of an attitude. The Franks felt a loathing for the Avars that it would be very difficult to find in relation to any of the other peoples against whom they fought. The war against the Avars became something of a holy war, as is clearly demonstrated by the fasting and prayers that preceded the 791 campaign. Recent historians have quite rightly attempted to show that the Frankish war did not in itself mean the annihilation of the Avar people and that the reasons for their disappearance from the European scene were more complex, as will shortly become clear, but the Frankish intentions to conduct a war of annihilation are confirmed by a great deal of evidence, not least of which is the joyous savagery with which a poem dedicated to Pepin's victory curtly addresses the defeated *khagan:*

> Tu cacane perdite!
> Regna vestra consumata,
> ultra non regnabitis!
> Adpropinquat rex Pippinus
> forti cum exercitu;
> fines tuos occupare,
> depopulare populum.[35]

Suppression of the revolt destroyed the military capacity of the Avars forever. What remained of the Avar nobility turned with increasing desperation to the Franks for protection from their former subjects, the Bulgars and the Slavs. In 805 an Avar prince who had converted to Christianity, the *kapkhan* Theodore, went to Aachen to implore Charles to grant him land to the west of the Raab, in a part of Pannonia that the Frankish king had earlier almost totally despoiled, so that he could transfer his people there away from the onslaught of the Slavs. A few months later another prince, who claimed the title of *khagan*, sent ambassadors to the emperor, requesting that his authority over the whole of the Avar people be confirmed in exchange for being baptized. This he did in great haste, taking the name of Abraham.

In the most westerly part of the ancient Avar country a khanate was thus reestablished, but it was only a shadow of its former glory, given that it acknowledged its subjugation to the emperor and paid him a tribute. This puppet state still existed when Charlemagne died, but the Franks grew tired of protecting it, and it did not take long to disintegrate in the face of Bulgar and Slav expansion. We know that the Avars were more of a confederation than a people, so with the collapse of the khanate the very idea of an Avar identity disappeared. Posterity would conclude that an entire people had disappeared without a trace, until the archaeologist's spade started to bring them back into the light of day. A Russian medieval chronicler wrote, "The Avars were large, heavily built, and of fierce temperament, and God wiped them out, they all died and not even one of them survived. To this day Russians have an expression: 'They have been scattered like the Avar, leaving neither descendants nor heirs.'"[36]

FOUR

The Rebirth of Empire

THE ALLIANCE BETWEEN THE PAPACY AND THE FRANKS
The Frankish King, Protector of Latin Christendom

As a result of the conquest of Lombards, Saxons, Arabs, and Avars, Charles's possessions bore no relation to the original kingdom of the Franks, even at its height. On a modern map of Europe, his lands would extend over the whole of France, Belgium, Holland, Switzerland, and Austria, Germany as far as the Elbe, northern and central Italy, Istria, Bohemia, Slovenia, and Hungary as far as the Danube, and finally Pyrenean Spain as far as the Ebro. Because the papal possessions and the duchies of Spoleto and Benevento came under Charles's area of influence, and southern Italy still under Byzantine rule predominantly used the Greek language and ritual, the king of the Franks now governed the totality of Christians of the Latin rite with the exception of Britain, Ireland, and the odd Iberian principality. Even in areas traditionally more linked to the Byzantine emperor, Charles's reputation now led the faithful to turn to him for protection. In 800 the patriarch of Jerusalem gave him the title of protector of the holy places and sent him the keys to the Holy Sepulchre.[1]

This explains how the idea of elevating the king of the Franks to the rank of emperor first developed in Rome and Aachen, where since 785 Charles had been building a magnificent complex of palaces, basilicas, and spa buildings. If Charles really was the new Constantine, as Pope Adrian I had called him just after his victory over the Lombards, it was only right that he should bear the title and crown. Thus the West would again have an emperor who prayed in accordance with the Latin rite, had his laws and correspondence written in Latin, and discussed politics and theology in Latin. The pope could far more easily reach an understanding with him than with his autocratic counterpart in the East. The fact that this new emperor would seem little more than a barbarian to the learned men of Rome and Byzantium was unfortunate but in no way represented an obstacle. Even back in the golden era of the empire, barbarian generals had often seized the imperial crown and no one had complained too much.

A more serious problem concerned the legitimate successor to the Roman emperors, the *basileus* who resided in Constantinople and who, as the direct and undisputed heir of Constantine, should have been the political leader of the entire Christian world. Practical experience suggested that the oriental and Greek part of the Roman Empire and the western and Latin part were difficult to govern together. Diocletian had realized this and had introduced the division between the empire of the East and the empire of the West. In spite of this, the oriental autocrat continued to bear the title (in Greek!) of *basileus ton Romaion*, emperor of the Romans, and the coronation of another sovereign as emperor in Rome would have been hard for him to accept. The same problem applied to religious affairs. The progressive estrangement between Latin and Greek theologians had almost destroyed the shared membership of the Christian faith, replacing the sense of community with an attitude of mutual suspicion. However the Christian religion was one, and there had to be one emperor called upon by God to lead the Christian people. Promoting a barbarian leader to the rank of emperor therefore represented a very grave decision, one that could be interpreted by the emperor of the East as a terrible insult. We need to go back to a period before Charlemagne was born to understand why the pope was willing to go so far.

The Conflict between the Papacy and Byzantium

The history of the alliance between the Church of Rome and the Franks, which culminated in the imperial coronation of 800, is closely related to the increasing disaffection of the pope and Italic peoples with the emperor of the East. For some considerable time, Byzantine rule had been perceived in most of Italy more as a foreign occupation than the legitimate Roman government. To Italians, the imperial envoys were foreign not only in language but also in religion. Given that the respective interpretations of Christianity tended increasingly to diverge, theological conflicts between Rome and Byzantium were the order of the day. Unlike the oriental patriarchs, the pope greeted the *basileus*'s meddling in religious controversies with visible irritation, which did not of course improve relations between the two churches.

From the end of the seventh century at the very latest, these doctrinal conflicts had given rise on more than one occasion to genuine confrontations that challenged the very political authority of the emperor and his military control in Italy. This attitude was strengthened by the imperial army's increasing inability to defend Italians from the Lombards. In these circumstances, it is hardly surprising that the pope started to behave as the legitimate representative of the Italic people and the authorized defender of their interests, by taking independent political initiatives in relation to the *basileus*. Around 706, Pope John VII actually planned to build a palace on the Palatine Hill, which until then had been reserved for the imperial residence. The idea was never realized but nobody failed to understand its symbolic value in an era in which the symbolism of power was enormously important. John's successors always acknowledged the emperor's authority but refused on several occasions to obey his orders and even denied his representatives the right to enter Rome. This effectively brought imperial authority over the Eternal City to an end and meant the pope now governed it from his Lateran Palace.

The mutual incomprehension was then exacerbated by an unusually serious religious dispute referred to as the iconoclastic controversy. Icons already enjoyed the prominent role in the religious life of Christians of the East that they do today, much more than in the West. At the beginning of the eighth century, some people in Constantinople began to be concerned that the excessive fervor with which the faithful prayed before icons could lead them to fall into idolatry. This fear was fueled by comparison with Judaism and Islam, both of which expressly prohibited any representation of God. Finally in 726 Emperor Leo III the Isaurian became persuaded of the need to fight the worship of images and started the *iconoclasm*, which in Greek means the destruction of icons, by having the icon of Christ removed from over the entrance to the imperial palace. The move was also aimed at diminishing the political power of the monasteries, which were the principal custodians of sacred images, and it triggered hysterical opposition among the faithful, who massacred the official charged with the task. The extremely violent conflict that followed set iconoclasts against iconolaters, or worshipers of images. Emperors persecuted the defenders of icons harshly.

In the West, the controversy was not an issue at the popular level but provoked irritation in the Church and definitively cooled relations with Byzantium, whose emperor could now even appear to be heretical. The reign of Leo the Isaurian (717–41) and his son Constantine V (741–75), called Copronymus or "the Shit" by his adversaries, coincided with the most acute phase of the iconoclastic persecution and the collapse of Byzantine domination in Italy, where it was under attack from the Lombards. The imperial armies no longer defended it effectively and the local population often resented it. In such circumstances, the pope had no choice but to seek the protection of the Franks and attempt with their assistance to rebuild his own political domination of Italy, by enlarging the dominion that he already exercised over Rome.

In chapter 2 we noted Gregory III's moves in 739 to establish an alliance with Charles Martel,[2] and even though this alliance did not lead to an actual military intervention, everything points to this being the moment when popes ceased to rely on the protection of the *basileus* and switched their allegiance entirely to the Franks. Indicative of this turning point is the fact that Gregory III was the last pope to notify the emperor of his election and to request its confirmation, as had been custom since time immemorial. His successor, Zacharias, who was elected in 741, broke with this tradition and, at a time when Rome was again threatened by the Lombards, he sent Pepin his famous ruling that it was right that he who exercised the powers of a king over the Franks should also bear the title.[3]

By attributing the kingly title to Pepin and personally traveling to Gaul to anoint him with holy oil, Zacharias' successor, Stephen II (752–57), had stressed his independence from the empire and had indeed challenged it, as only the *basileus* had the right to elevate a barbarian to the rank of king. The friendship between the new dynasty and the papacy was by this time the central axis of European politics, in relation to which the ancient rights of the empire were rapidly losing importance. With Charlemagne on the throne, things went much further. Adrian I (772–95) stopped dating his official documents by the years of the rule of the *basileus* and instead dated them by the years of his own papacy. He removed the emperor's head from the coins produced by the mint in Rome and replaced it with his own. Clearly the pope was working hard to assert his authority over those lands that the Lateran chancellery now called the *respublica Sancti Petri,* in line with the claims made in a famous document, the Donation of Constantine, which was perhaps composed precisely at that time by a Roman cleric.

It is less clear what the pope was offering in exchange for the protection of the Franks, the now dominant people in the West. Given that as far back as 778, twenty-two years before Charlemagne's coronation in St. Peter's, Adrian I had greeted him as the *novus Christianissimus Dei Constantinus imperator;*[4] and that in most of the western churches the ancient prayers in favor of the Roman Empire and its emperor were replaced with prayers for the Frankish kingdom and its sovereigns, we can conclude that in the eyes of the pope Charles had a role similar to that previously fulfilled by the emperor of the East. But this does not mean that the pope intended to declare himself a subject of the king of the Franks or renounce his control of central Italy, now abandoned to its destiny by the Greeks. The profound friendship between Charlemagne and Adrian I, so often confirmed personally or by letter during the course of their lives, hid an unresolved ambiguity, which was destined to weigh heavily on Western history for many centuries.

The Ambivalence of Leo III

Although many of Adrian's actions appear to us to be leading toward the imperial coronation of 800, we should not forget that this pope died five years before the event. The abandonment of collaboration with Byzantium and the warm acceptance of the power of the Frankish king, apparently leading irresistibly to the transfer of the empire from the Greeks to the Franks, was for the time being the most promising policy for Adrian, but he could have abandoned it if events had made it advisable. Even the language of the papal letters, which historians have carefully sifted through in search of some sign of Charles's coming closer to imperial status, demonstrates that the outcome was far from inevitable. When Empress Irene and her son Constantine VI made known their intention of bringing the iconoclastic persecution to an end, the pope who had a few years earlier greeted Charles as the new Constantine now wrote in a very similar fashion to the *basileus* and his mother, rejoicing at being able to perceive in them a new Constantine and a new Helen. He invited them to show themselves as generous toward the Church as the king of the Franks had been up until that time.[5]

The break with Byzantium and papal subordination to the Frankish court became a more immediate possibility only in 795, when Adrian I was succeeded by Leo III, a perhaps more ambiguous and certainly politically weaker pope. The new pope was a priest of modest origins, who came up through the Lateran bureaucracy and lacked support among the powerful Roman families. Moreover, there were serious accusations against him of embezzlement and immoral behavior, so he was willing to do anything in order to ensure the effective protection of the Frankish king, including concessions that might have been less acceptable to Adrian I. As soon as he rose to the papal throne, he sent Charles notification of his election, the keys to St. Peter's, and the standard of the city of Rome, traditionally used to greet emperors when they entered the Eternal City. The honorific prerogatives that Pope Adrian had taken away from the *basileus* were reintroduced but now attributed to the king of the Franks. For the first time, the papal chancellery started to date its documents by the number of years of the reign of Charles in Italy, as well as those of the current pope's rule.

The election of Leo III (795–816) therefore introduced a period in which the papacy put all its hopes on its alliance with the Franks, and this reliance was much more obvious than had been the case during the reign of his more energetic predecessor. Apart from the personalities of leading historical figures, political history is also influenced or indeed dominated by events, and in 797 a decisive event occurred that finally triggered the continuously postponed split between Rome and Constantinople. The Empress Irene, who until then had ruled in the name of her son Constantine VI, disinherited him and had him blinded and personally assumed the title of *basileus*, which never before had been borne by a woman. On hearing this news, Leo III decided that the time had come to resolve the situation. It was unheard of for a woman to govern the destiny of the empire on her own, so in symbolic terms, there had never been such a propitious moment for transferring the imperial title from East to West. His predecessor, Adrian, had flattered Charles by calling him the new Constantine; now Leo was to crown him emperor.

Suddenly Pope Leo was to manifest that contradictory side to his character. The early actions of his rule had shown him to limit his policies to obsequious deference to Charles, but once plans for a coronation in Rome by his hands were going ahead, he must have started to dream of inverting the relationship of power. The hopes entertained in Rome during that period were revealed by the iconography of a series of mosaics commissioned by the pope between 796 and 800 for the great reception hall of the Lateran Palace. In the center, Christ orders his apostles to spread the gospel around the world. On the left, Christ appears again handing over the pallium and standard to Pope Sylvester and Constantine, who are on their knees before him. On the right, Saint Peter entrusts the pallium to Leo III and the standard to Charles. The king of the Franks appears yet again as the new Constantine, but he is invested with temporal authority by Saint Peter and not directly by God. The emperor is therefore in some way diminished, and placed under the guardianship of the pope, who has the place of honor on the apostle's right-hand side.

THE IMPERIAL AMBITIONS OF THE FRANKISH COURT
The Conflict between Charlemagne and Byzantium

Up until now, we have examined the events leading up to Charles's coronation from the pope's point of view, and he was the main instigator. However, we should not perceive the Frankish king as passively involved in a project that was bigger than himself. At the Frankish court, Charles was often compared with the *basileus*, and the conclusion was that the latter was unfit and the king of the Franks more suited to the leadership of Christendom. Yet in the early years of his reign Charles had always intended to maintain good relations with Constantinople. In this he succeeded, in spite of the presence of Prince Adelchis in the eastern capital, where he was treated with full honors and even given the title of patrician. Adrian I, who aimed to enlarge the dominions of the Roman church in southern Italy at the cost of both the Lombards of Benevento and the remaining Byzantine presence, never tired of telling Charles of plots by supporters of Adelchis using Byzantine gold. But Charles does not appear to have been alarmed by the pope's assertions. Indeed, when in 781 Empress Irene officially requested the hand of his daughter

Rotrude for her son Constantine VI, he accepted her proposal. The eunuch Elissaios came from Byzantium to teach Greek to the princess and prepare her for her new life. The king instructed Paul the Deacon, an intellectual who had recently joined the court, to teach his clerics what he knew of Greek so that they did not make a bad impression on their Byzantine colleagues.

The peaceful coexistence of the two Christian powers of the West and the East seemed quite possible. Then in the spring of 787, when the Byzantine diplomatic mission arrived to take the princess away, Charlemagne refused to let her go, and the envoys returned to Constantinople empty-handed. In that crucial year the political situation suddenly changed, to the point of ruining relations between the two courts and postponing the marriage indefinitely. In the preceding winter, the Frankish king had led an expedition into southern Italy to subjugate Duke Arechis of Benevento, and he must have realized that the empress, whose representatives still ruled in Apulia, Calabria, and Sicily, would not have wanted a further strengthening of Frankish hegemony in Italy. Breaking off the engagement was probably not the best way to avert a crisis, but in this case Charles's well-known affection for his daughters and his strange reluctance, admitted even by loyal Einhard, to have them separated from him may have prevailed over rational political calculations.[6] The result was that Irene, with two reasons to take offense, offered her support to the duke of Benevento. After many false alarms, Adelchis finally landed in Calabria, with the intention of stirring up the Lombards against their usurper. The insurrection that was supposed to spread throughout the kingdom never took place, but the mutual distrust between the West and the East had been rekindled. For many years after these events, there was tension on the borders between these two powers in southern Italy and in the Balkans, and they became the theater of frequent military incidents.

The problematic balance of power in Italy was not the only reason why Charles preferred to break off the engagement and clash with the Byzantine Empire. Equally important was the sudden change of policy introduced by Irene in the theological controversy that was raging in the East. In that same 787 the empress, who for years had been negotiating at some risk to herself to restore the worship of images, decided to condemn the iconoclastic policy of her predecessors as heretical. The second Council of Nicaea, which the Orthodox Church recognizes as ecumenical, established that the faithful's veneration for icons was directed not at an image but at the being it represented, and in these terms the worship of images was the duty of every good Christian.

In general, there was nothing in the council's conclusions that could not be accepted in the West, particularly as representatives of Pope Adrian took part in the proceedings. Nevertheless Charlemagne greeted them with ill humor. He may not have understood them, and he could hardly be blamed for this, since he had little knowledge of Greek and the Latin translation that was read to him was full of errors. But in any case, he could not have been pleased that a theological question of such gravity should be resolved under the direction of the empress of the East rather than under his, or that a supposedly ecumenical council could be convened without bothering to inform Frankish bishops. Against the opinion of the pope, Charlemagne rejected the Nicene conclusions and gave orders to one of his councillors, probably Theodulf of Orléans, to confute them in writing. The resulting treatise, known as the *Libri Carolini*, is the most ambitious and original theological work produced at the time of Charles.[7] It formed the basis for the Council of Frankfurt, personally presided over by Charles in 794, where the theses approved by Greek bishops in Nicaea were formally condemned.

Theologically, the *Libri Carolini* argues that although the destruction of icons was wrong, so was the imposition of their veneration, in spite of the sophisticated arguments used by Greek theologians to justify it. But the most important response was political. The bishops gathered in Frankfurt explicitly stated that the Nicene conclusions were null and void for the simple reason that the council was presided over by a woman, while Saint Paul wrote, "But I suffer not a woman to teach, nor to usurp authority over man." More generally, it was declared that the

Greek emperors had deviated even before Irene by having themselves worshiped in a ceremony that bordered on the idolatrous, so they appeared to be heirs only to the Roman Empire of the pagan times before Constantine. The message was clear: the king of the Franks, patrician of the Romans and the protector of the bishop of Rome, no longer acknowledged that the empire of the East enjoyed any supremacy over matters of faith. He presented himself to the Catholic West as the "only leader of the Christian people," to use Alcuin's words.[8]

In this already heated climate, there came news of disagreements between the empress and her son, which shortly afterward led Irene to usurp the throne. Constantine VI was distancing himself from his mother's policies and had gathered the supporters of iconoclasm around him. It is probable that in this situation the conclusions of the Council of Frankfurt were greeted favorably and some people thought of seeking support from Charles to challenge Irene. In 797 the Byzantine governor of Sicily had a letter from Constantine VI sent to Aachen, about whose content the chroniclers are strangely reticent, but it was well received by the king.[9] This legation or perhaps another that followed shortly afterward is supposed to have actually offered Charles the eastern imperial crown. Although such a step may appear unprecedented, it is not impossible that, given the consternation following Irene's coup d'état, some people in Constantinople were willing to consider such a drastic move. These events were not followed up and when in 798 an imperial diplomatic mission visited the Frankish king to notify him officially that Irene had taken power, the Royal Annals assure us that the envoys only spoke of peace.[10] While Charles had no intention of going to war on behalf of blind Constantine and the iconoclasts, politically it was clear that respect for the government of Constantinople had fallen to its lowest point.

Imitatio Imperii

In the meantime Charlemagne's power was taking on increasingly explicit imperial connotations, in the Christian sense of the term and not just the Roman one, which after the *Libri Carolini* could in some ways appear discredited. Alcuin's correspondence between the years of 796 and 800 reveals growing concerns about the scandals that threatened to overtake the papacy under the rule of Leo III.[11] In such circumstances, it was reassuring to perceive Christendom as a kind of empire—*imperium Christianum*—whose leader was the king of the Franks rather than the pope. We should not take these expressions lightly or think that in the end they are only words. These were men in the habit of reflecting on the meaning of words and selecting them one by one, fully aware of their political effects as well as their literary ones. So when Alcuin, a little before 800, began to speak regularly of the "Christian empire" whose government God had bestowed upon Charles and his sons, we can be certain that he knew very well what he was saying.[12]

No less significant was the frequent reference to Charlemagne as the new David by literary figures in his service. Since 796, Alcuin had been in the habit of addressing his letters to Charles as "To the King David," specifying that "it is precisely with this name, inspired by the same virtue and the same faith, that our leader and guide reigns today: a chief in whose shadow the Christian people repose in peace and who on all sides strikes terror into the pagan nations, a chief whose devotion never ceases to fortify the Catholic faith with evangelical firmness against the followers of heresy."[13] Already used by Stephen II for Pepin, the name of David implied that the king was leader of the chosen people, inspired by God, and called upon to govern with wisdom the community of believers. By rights, this should have been the role of the Byzantine emperor, and now the king of the Franks was demanding it for himself. Pepin, who had made the leap from mayor of the palace to king, could not have aimed higher, but Charles had no such qualms. Long before 800, his chancellery had started to use for Charles epithets normally reserved for the *basileus*, such as "most serene" and "orthodox," and to place formal elements such as the monogram and seal typical of imperial custom in his edicts.

The Palace of Aachen

The elevation of the king of the Franks to emperor was not then a new idea in the final years of the eighth century, either in Rome or Aachen. With the events unfolding in Constantinople following the usurpation by Irene, the councillors who surrounded the Frankish king must have felt the time could not be more propitious for assigning the rank of emperor to their leader. Charles's commitment to this prospect, which historians have called *imitatio Imperii* or emulation of empire, appears to have been demonstrated by the symbolic connotations he wished to apply to the building of his palace in Aachen. He personally oversaw the works, whose essentials were completed by 798. The architects who undertook the building of the imposing new residence had clear instructions: Aachen had to compete with Rome and Constantinople, as well as Ravenna, whose significance we risk overlooking today, but which after being the fifth-century residence of the emperor of the West had become Theodoric's capital and latterly the residence of the Byzantine exarch. In the West, Ravenna came second only to Rome.

The king of the Franks was therefore declaring his intention to emulate the ancient Roman emperors, the Gothic kings of Italy, the contemporary Byzantine sovereigns, and even the popes, by building a residential complex capable of rivaling both the imperial palace of Byzantium and the pope's Lateran Palace in Rome. The main architect, a Frank called Odo of Metz, relied principally on the classical treatise by Vitruvius, but he also took advice from scholars of the palatine academy, whose international origins and mathematical knowledge proved particularly useful in this case. The Lombard Paul the Deacon, for example, was able to provide his direct knowledge of Byzantine architecture in Italy. The main buildings in the palatine complex were the throne room and the chapel, linked by a wooden portico, where they erected the equestrian statue of Theodoric that had been removed from Ravenna. The symbolic force was mainly concentrated in the octagonal chapel, dominated by a mosaic of Christ the Pantocrator. Below this mosaic in a raised position illuminated by the sun's rays stood the sovereign's throne. It clearly placed him in everyone's eyes in the position of mediator between God and the community of the faithful.

In commissioning the chapel, Charlemagne was probably inspired by the Lateran baptistery in Rome. One of the Aachen buildings, about which we unfortunately know very little, was known at the time as the Lateran. But the most important and politically significant inspiration was the *Chrysotriclinos*, the golden triclinium standing at the center of the imperial palace in Constantinople. This building was both church and throne room. As Fichtenau wrote, "it serves for the worship of God and his earthly trustee, the *basileus* and image of Christ."[14] Charles had never been to Constantinople, even though he avidly sought information from his ambassadors about the churches of that city, but it was known that the *Chrysotriclinos* was similar to the one in the church of San Vitale in Ravenna, and an architect sent to study this building returned to Aachen with plans and measurements sufficient for constructing a similar one. In it, Charles introduced a change that was full of political significance. He had his throne installed with calculated modesty in the west, opposite the altar, while the arrogant Byzantine emperors, descendants of Roman emperors who had dared to deify themselves, had it positioned in the east actually in place of the altar. Even when he was imitating their architecture, the Frankish king was denouncing the impiety of the emperors of the East in exactly the same terms as the *Libri Carolini*, and putting himself forward in their place as the authentic representative of the Christian God.

Naturally, we could go too far in perceiving this imitation of Roman and Byzantine models as simply a policy statement. In their ignorance, some contemporaries may well have believed that the bronze statue of Theodoric erected in the palace portico in 801 was a portrait of Constantine, and it is quite possible that Charles wanted it there to compete with the famous equestrian statue of Marcus Aurelius, which was at the pope's Lateran Palace (and not at the Campidoglio as it is today), since that statue really was thought to represent Constantine. But it could also be that possession of the ancient masterpiece was in itself considered appropriate to the magnificence of a great sovereign, without any further symbolic or political implications, rather like the elephant that was sent a year later as a gift from the caliph of Baghdad and that Charles took along everywhere he went until the animal died in 810.

In some cases, it was not so much emulation of the past as the desire to recycle ancient materials, whose quality could not be matched by contemporary artisans. Einhard wrote that Charles had columns and marble sent from Rome and Ravenna, because he could not procure them anywhere else.[15] We should also not forget that almost everything that we now see in Aachen has been reworked since Charlemagne's time. For a long time it was thought that the imperial throne was built purposefully to imitate the throne of Solomon as it is described in the Bible, but then some newly discovered drawings showed that it had been remodeled in that shape in the nineteenth century. And yet Alcuin compared the chapel to the Temple of Solomon and Aachen to a new Jerusalem, "a Jerusalem in our own land."[16] In one way or another, Roman history and the Old Testament, the memory of Constantine, David, and Solomon converged to designate the king of the Franks as the man of Providence.

THE CORONATION IN 800
The Roman Crisis of 799–800

We have seen that since the election of Pope Leo III in 795, his manner of addressing Charles increasingly took on explicitly imperial connotations, and this leads us to believe that the plan to crown Charles emperor began to take shape from that time. However, circumstances prevented the pope from carrying out his plan over the expected time period, forcing him to offer the crown in an emergency situation. In 799 there was an actual uprising against Leo III, led by two of the highest officials at the Roman court, the *primicerius* Pasquale and the *sacellarius* Campolo, both nephews of Adrian I. Leo fell into his enemies' hands, and they intended to pull out his eyes and cut off his tongue, as was the custom in the Byzantine Empire when an important functionary needed to be permanently removed from office. It kept him from ever returning to his position without requiring his enemies to answer to God for his death. But the pope managed to escape before they could implement their pious intentions and took refuge with the duke of Spoleto, who had him escorted to Charles in Paderborn. Initially the fugitive appears to have convinced the king that his eyes and tongue had been cut out and that he had been miraculously healed by Saint Peter. Shortly afterward a delegation of the Roman plotters came to Paderborn, where they restated the accusations of fornication and perjury that had already been made against Leo, meanwhile clarifying that the mutilations and therefore the miracle had not actually taken place.

It was up to the king to sort the muddle out. It was not clear that his title of patrician of the Romans allowed him to stand in judgment over the pope, and Charles felt he had to ask Alcuin for his opinion. The latter replied that three persons stood above all others, the pope, the emperor of Constantinople, and the king of the Franks, but since everyone knew what had happened to the pope and to the emperor, both deposed and mutilated by their own people, the king was now superior to the others, and the Church's only hope. In case this was not enough, Alcuin added, "We have seen what happened to the pope in his very see, in the Eternal City. Now it is up to you alone to pass judgment over all that."[17] Reassured by this ruling, Charles decided that he had to get to the bottom of why such a stench of corruption was coming from Rome, which in Alcuin's words was supposed to be a clear spring of equity and justice. He ordered an enquiry into the accusations against Leo III. Strictly speaking, it could have been argued that the pope enjoyed complete immunity and could not be judged by anyone, a position that even Alcuin had acknowledged as formally unassailable, but politically speaking it was not advisable to hide behind this claim and Leo thought it better to confront the enquiry. Some people discreetly suggested that it might be better to abandon the case, relinquish the papacy, and retire to grow old peacefully in a monastery,[18] but Leo held firm. The king therefore decided to send him back to Rome with an escort and accompanied by the commissioners who had to conduct the enquiry.

The long interval between the return of the pope to Rome in the autumn of 799 and the arrival of the king more than a year later suggests that Charles would have preferred not to make that journey. If the accusations against Leo proved to be manifestly groundless, the commission of enquiry made up of two archbishops, five bishops, and three counts would immediately proceed with his reinstatement. But to the consternation of Alcuin, who had hoped for a rapid settlement of the affair, things turned out to be more serious than expected. All the accusations could not be set aside, and not simply because, according to rumor, some of the commissioners had been bribed by the other side. The most prestigious of the ten and a man above all suspicion, Archbishop Arno of Salzburg, wrote a letter in which he detailed the findings. We do not know its tone, since Alcuin preferred to burn it, but it is easy to imagine it on the basis of Alcuin's own response, whose principal argument is "let him who is without sin cast the first stone."[19] Although Charles had made up his mind to absolve Leo of every accusation and reinstate him with all his powers, it was now clear that he would have to do it personally.

It was therefore as the supreme leader of Christendom and the protector of the Roman church that Charlemagne arrived at the gates of Rome on 23 November 800. Leo III understood this well and personally came out to greet him 12 miles from the city, thus doubling the distance required by the ancient ritual of the *adventus Caesaris* that regulated the imperial entrance to the city. If we consider that on Charles's previous journey to Rome in 774, Adrian I had awaited Charles at St. Peter's, rather than going out to meet him, and had gone no further than applying to the letter the ceremonial procedure for the exarch of Ravenna, we realize how much the balance of power had shifted between the king of the Franks and the Roman pontiff. On 1 December Charles, acting as the new Constantine, opened the proceedings of the council in the Vatican basilica that was to pronounce on the accusations against the pope.

By that time, everyone knew that it was a political trial and that Leo would come out of it entirely vindicated. The assembly confirmed that technically no one could stand in judgment over him and allowed him to prove his innocence by a solemn oath on the New Testament, which the pope lost no time in doing.

According to a contemporary, it was the council itself, while in session with the pope, the bishops of Italy and Gaul, and several lay magnates, that officially decided on Charles's coronation and justified it through the vacancy of the imperial throne.[20] The title adopted by Irene was not in fact recognized by the papacy, so the throne usurped by a woman appeared in all respects to be vacant. In reality, it is probable that the council limited itself to accepting formally a decision that had been taken months before through negotiations about which unfortunately we know nothing. During his stay in Paderborn, Leo III had already declared his willingness to crown Charles emperor, although the final decision was probably postponed until after the council had made its ruling. What is certain is that on Christmas morning Leo III placed the crown on Charles's head, in accordance with a ritual that we would now consider conventional but at the time was more familiar to the Graeco-Roman world than to the Germanic one. The pope anointed him with holy oil and, according to a royal chronicler, he prostrated himself before the king in the oriental ritual of *proskynesis*.[21] The Roman people, represented on this occasion by the Vatican clergy who accompanied the pontiff, hailed Charles as their emperor and Augustus. This ritual was not simply an honorific flourish but had legal force in accordance with the Roman imperial tradition and officially ratified the election of the new sovereign.

Emperor against His Wishes?

We still have to explain Einhard's surprising assertion that Charles was much vexed with the coronation and would not have gone to church if he had known what was being prepared, in spite of the solemnity of that day.[22] Of course, it may be that Einhard, modeling himself on Suetonius, merely wished to emphasize Charles's modesty, in the same way that Claudius had not considered himself worthy of the imperial title and had to be invested by force. It may be that Charles's vexation did not concern the coronation itself but its ritual trappings and their possible political consequences. With all his humiliations, in the end Leo III had succeeded in bringing about the restoration of the empire and making it appear as though everything was directed by the Church. By putting the crown on the new emperor's head, the pope de facto claimed the supremacy of papal authority over imperial authority.

For the moment it was a purely theoretical claim, given that all the power was on Charles's side. Indeed he obtained every possible recognition of his sovereignty from the pope. After subduing the duke of Benevento a few years earlier, the Frankish king had insisted that all documents produced by the Benevento chancellery should be dated by the years of his reign and that the duke's coins should carry Charles's name and monogram.[23] Immediately after the coronation the new emperor demanded the same recognition from Rome. The papal chancellery, which under Adrian I had started to date documents by the years of the papacy and under Leo III had only added the years of Charles's reign in second place, now started to date exclusively on the basis of the years of Charles's reign, as had been the practice in the past with the reign of the *basileus*. Leo III's coins now carried Charles's name and imperial title next to the papal monogram and the name of Saint Peter. Today we are somewhat indifferent to these symbolic manifestations, but things were different in the past. By mentioning Charles's reign in his documents and imprinting his name on coins minted in Rome, the pope was to all intents and purposes acknowledging the political sovereignty of the emperor over the Eternal City.

For the same reasons, public acts that remained impressed in everyone's memory also had enormous political significance. The act of Leo III placing the imperial crown on the head of the kneeling king was of this kind. The implications of this gesture could not have escaped a politician of Charlemagne's intelligence, and this is more than enough to explain his unease. Not surprisingly, when thirteen years later he wanted his son Louis the Pious crowned emperor to support him in government and prepare the succession, Charles organized the ceremony in accordance with an entirely different protocol and eliminated all the features that would have upset him in his coronation. Louis was crowned in the palatine chapel at Aachen, and he was acclaimed not by the Romans but by the Franks. Most importantly the new emperor did not kneel before the pope but was crowned by his father or, according to another chronicler, he placed the crown on his own head. The choreography was clever, but by then it was too late. The 813 ceremony was overshadowed by the one in 800, and the empire was always to suffer from its unresolved and ambiguous relationship with the papacy. A thousand years later another emperor, Napoleon, who was well aware of these implications, purposefully invited the pope to his coronation but made sure that he himself was to place the crown on his own head.

THE NEW EMPIRE IN INTERNATIONAL RELATIONS
Relations with the Empire of the East

News of the coronation was greeted in Constantinople with derision and contempt. Up until then Roman emperors had deigned to acknowledge the subordinate title of king for Germanic chiefs, but it was unthinkable that one of them could assume the title of *imperator*. The Byzantine chronicler Theophanes described the ritual of Charles's coronation in deliberately ironic terms and claimed that the pope anointed him with oil from "his head to his toes," as though it were extreme unction. He concluded coldly, "Since then Rome has been under the dominion of barbarians."[24] Charlemagne himself appears to have worried about the hostile reactions that Leo III's action might have provoked in the East, and in 802 he sent a count and a bishop to Constantinople to reassure the empress of his peaceful intentions. Rumors even circulated in the capital that the Frankish envoys had proposed a marriage between Charles and Irene, which would have made it possible to reunify the two empires. In any case, their approach encountered coldness and hostility on the part of senior Byzantine officials who shortly afterward organized a coup to remove Irene and put one of her ministers, Nicephorus I, on the throne.

Although neither Charles nor the new *basileus* had any desire to go to war, the border between the two powers in the northeast and the south of the Italian peninsula was uncertain enough to cause continuous incidents, which were exploited by the merchants of Venice and Zara to gain autonomy from Byzantium and by the duke of Benevento to rebel once again against Frankish hegemony. In 811 Nicephorus I was killed in battle by Krum the Bulgarian khan, and his successor, Michael I Rhangabe, preferred to seek peace with the West. A Byzantine delegation went to Aachen and acknowledged Charles's title of emperor, albeit through gritted teeth. The Royal Annals report, "They acclaimed him after their own manner, that is in the Greek language, and called him emperor and *basileus*,"[25] although they saved face by failing to qualify him as Roman. Charles replied with a letter in which he expressed his contentment that peace had been established "between the empires of the East and the West."[26] The division of the Roman Empire brought about centuries earlier by Diocletian provided a model or at least the legitimation for the coexistence of two empires, both Roman and both within a single Christendom.

In the West at least, the solution appeared a sensible one that remained in use for a long time, while Byzantine emperors obstinately continued to raise objections. In 824 the *basileus* Michael II addressed Louis the Pious as "our dear brother Louis, glorious king of the Franks and the Lombards, by whom he is called emperor."[27] In 871 Charles's great-grandson Louis II received a letter from the *basileus* in which he was acerbically reminded that there was only one empire. The Frankish sovereign politely replied that he, Louis, having been crowned in Rome, had every right to call himself emperor of the Romans, while his colleague was quite free to call himself emperor of the New Rome.[28] These were significant diplomatic skirmishes of an ideological nature, but we should not overestimate their urgency, particularly at the time of Charlemagne. His Europe, in which people prayed and wrote in Latin, had few relations or indeed no relations at all with the other Europe in which they wrote and prayed in Greek, and rivalry over protocol with the monarch of that distant country was not so important.

And yet Charles, who had been acclaimed emperor of the Romans at the time of his coronation, decided to modify that title and in his edicts entitled himself "the most serene Augustus, crowned by God, the great and peace-loving emperor and ruler of the Roman Empire, as well as by the grace of God king of the Franks and the Lombards."[29] It has been argued that strictly speaking being emperor *and* ruler of the Roman Empire does not necessarily mean emperor of the Romans, and that by adopting this title Charles showed his sensitivity to Byzantine concerns and was able to match them in the subtle use of protocol. But this may not have been the case, because the formula *Romanum gubernans imperium* was one of those used by Justinian, and that was undoubtedly an authoritative example of a Roman emperor to emulate. On the whole, the symbolism of power adopted by the Carolingians after 800 always referred back to that of the empire of Rome. Charles had himself portrayed on coins with the laurel crown and purple cloak and his seal carried the wording that was to remain an extraordinarily effective political slogan for centuries: *renovatio Romani imperii.*

It becomes increasingly clear that the problem was ultimately not one of defining the empire as Roman, but its connection to the Romans, who in the eyes of Franks of the time were primarily the pope and the endless ranks of clergymen who surrounded him and were often of doubtful morals. The refusal to call himself emperor of the Romans probably arose from the same reasons that, according to Einhard, made Charles unhappy with the acclamations received in St. Peter's. It was important not to diminish his title of king of the Franks, which was still the true basis of his power, and not to create the politically dangerous suggestion that the priests of Rome rather than the Frankish magnates were the political elite of the reborn empire.

The Empire and the Papacy

In spite of the ambiguity that Leo III introduced into the proceedings, the imperial coronation endorsed Charles's supremacy over the Latin Church and the pontiff himself. By adopting the title of emperor, the sovereign officially claimed a primacy that as the mere king of the Franks he could not so easily justify, even though Charles had in practice been behaving like the leader of Christendom even before 800. In his capitularies, he used to refer to himself as, "by the grace of God and by the bountifulness of His mercy, king and rector of the kingdom of the Franks and devoted defender and humble assistant of the Holy Church."[30] But we should not let his apparent humility mislead us. The assistance that the king provided the Church consisted of deciding the appointments of bishops and abbots, checking up on their behavior, convening them in council when he considered it appropriate, personally setting the agenda, and promulgating the conclusions, all duties that today we would expect the pope to carry out. When in 799 Pope Leo III came to Paderborn as a refugee accused of immorality and financial irregularities, the humble defender of the Church sent him back to Rome under escort and then followed to preside personally over a council that was to pass judgment on him.

There can be no doubt: if Christendom had a supreme leader, then that leader was the king of the Franks and certainly not the pope. In 775 the Irish priest Catwulf wrote to Charles: "because you are here to represent God, and to protect and govern the limbs of his people, and you will be accountable for this on Judgment Day, while the pope is in second place and only represents Christ."[31] In critical moments, the sovereign did not fail to point out that he was the helmsman guiding the ship through a tempest, whereas the pope's only responsibility was to pray that the waters should become calm. When he condemned the conclusions of the second Council of Nicaea against the opinion of Adrian I, Charles peremptorily asserted, "we have been entrusted with the government of the Church through the tempestuous seas of this world."[32] A few years later, faced with a more pliant pope than the aged Adrian, the king went further in his letter to the newly elected Leo III:

> With the aid of Providence, it is our duty to defend the Church externally with arms against pagan aggression and the devastation of infidels, and strengthen it internally by imposing the Catholic faith. It is your duty, most holy father, to sustain our fight by lifting your arms to God as did Moses, so that through your intercession the Christian people may be victorious over its enemies.[33]

But surely the pope was supposed to be the successor to Saint Peter? Even this was not so significant. In 800, when Charles was about to leave for Rome to pass judgment on Leo III, Theodulf of Orléans wrote that Saint Peter had personally handed over to Charles the earthly keys, that is the keys to the Vatican basilica, while preferring to keep for himself the keys to heaven, and therefore it was the duty of the king to govern the Church, the clergy, and the Christian people.[34] The low opinion in which the pope was held emerges from an obscure episode that occurred in the winter of 804. Charles was informed that Leo had set his heart on spending the Christmas festivities in his company. The emperor was rather surprised by this unusual request, which required the pope to cross the mountains in winter before traveling on to Aachen, but he deigned to go as far as Reims to meet him. After barely eight days in each other's company, the emperor dispatched him back to Rome, forcing him to retrace the interminable journey in bad weather.[35] Leaving aside the pressing needs that had caused the pope to undergo such an arduous trip, its outcome clearly showed which of the two was the superior. It also confirmed that there was not the same rapport between Charles and Leo as there had been between Charles and Adrian.

This is the sense in which we should interpret the title of assistant and defender of the Church that Charles adopted with so much humility. In the *Divisio regnorum* of 806, the document that divided up the kingdom among his heirs, the emperor personally emphasized the duty of his sons to defend the Church.[36] He defined this duty as primarily the defense of the Church of Saint Peter from its enemies and the protection of its rights. Second, it was guardianship of all the churches or bishoprics, as we would call them, that came under their authority. We would not be straining the truth if we were to conclude that for all the deference the emperor felt for the incumbent of the Roman see, he still considered that see to be only the most important of all the other archbishoprics in his empire. This was exactly the place he assigned to it in his will, in which Rome's only distinction is its first place in the list ("as is well known there are twenty-one metropolitan sees in his kingdom, and their names are as follows: Rome, Ravenna, Milan, Aquileia, Grado . . .").[37]

Between Christmas of 800 and Easter of 801 Charlemagne spent five consecutive months in the Eternal City, and this prolonged stay clearly confirmed his sovereignty. For the king to winter and celebrate the main annual festivities outside his kingdom would have been inconceivable, and a long winter residence including the festivities was the way Charles symbolically asserted his sovereignty over recently conquered countries such as Saxony and Bavaria. Besides, the author of the Royal Annals justified the imperial coronation of 800 on the basis that God had seen fit to give Charles authority over Rome, "where the Caesars had always lived," and over the other ancient metropolitan sees of western Christendom.[38] Not that long after the events of 799 and 800, several popes would start to challenge the primacy of the emperor and to claim the leadership of Christendom for themselves, but in the meanwhile no one, least of all Leo III, would question the supreme authority of Charles over the city and the Church.

Charlemagne and Hārūn al-Rashīd

The imperial stature Charlemagne assumed in the years leading up to 800 and confirmed by his coronation in St. Peter's was also reflected in his relations with his Muslim equivalent, the caliph of Baghdad. At the time, the prince of believers was Hārūn al-Rashīd, caliph from 786 to 809 and one of the protagonists of *Thousand and One Nights*. Like

Charles, he was to become a legend among his people. There were excellent relations between the Christian emperor and the Muslim one, whom the Frankish chroniclers called "Aaron rex Persarum."[39] In 801 the caliph's ambassadors landed at Pisa and also brought home the Jew Isaac whom Charles had sent to Baghdad four years earlier. They brought the gift of the famous elephant, Abul Abbas, which caused such a sensation that it was repeatedly mentioned in the Royal Annals.[40] Einhard asserted that the elephant had been expressly requested by Charles for his menagerie, and the caliph was so determined to please him that he gave away the only elephant he had, although it would be quite legitimate to doubt the latter detail.[41]

One of the intellectuals at the Aachen court, the Irishman Dicuil, used direct observation of the elephant to disprove the Roman geographer Solinus, who had claimed that these animals were incapable of lying down: "while it is certain that they lie down like an ox, as all the people of the kingdom of the Franks often saw the elephant do at the time of Emperor Charles."[42] Clearly the pachyderm was a great attraction, and possibly many of the inquisitive people who gathered outside Charles's palaces and encampments were more eager to see the elephant than the king. Yet the possession of an elephant or any other exotic animal had symbolic importance. It was the prerogative of an imperial figure to whom God had entrusted the government of a large portion of the world and whose name had been heard in infinitely distant lands. Both Charles and Hārūn were certainly well aware of all these connotations.

In 807 another legation from the caliph in Baghdad brought rich gifts that included monkeys, costly fabrics, oriental aromatic herbs and ointments, a mechanical clock with moving figures and chimes, orichalc candelabras, and even a pavilion for encampments. There was every extravagance the East could provide, as the chroniclers themselves concluded.[43] Charles could not compete with the splendor and ingenuity of such gifts, but he returned the compliment with hounds, horses, mules, and precious fabrics, which do not appear to have made a similar impression on Arab chroniclers. It is clear, though, that the two rulers had every intention to maintain cordial relations, in spite of the different religions. Their empires were far enough apart for them to have no fear of the other, and knowledge of the alliance served to rattle their common enemies, the Byzantine Empire and the Umayyads of Spain.

Charles had another reason for maintaining good relations with Baghdad, given that the benevolence of Hārūn al-Rashīd was indispensable to Christians in the Holy Land, who lived under Muslim rule and had frequent disputes with Bedouin tribes. Concerned about those communities to which he often sent financial assistance, the emperor undoubtedly suggested to the caliph that a gesture of goodwill in that direction would considerably enhance relations, and Hārūn al-Rashīd decided to grant him his wish. He actually extended it to a symbolic gift of the land on which the Holy Sepulchre stood. Hence we can appreciate why in this very period in which the Frankish king exchanged ambassadors and gifts with the caliph, the patriarch of Jerusalem acknowledged him as the protector of the holy places and sent him the keys to the Holy Sepulchre.[44] Charles's prestige as the supreme leader of Christendom did not rest on his military strength alone.

FIVE

Charlemagne and Europe

As far back as the summer of 799 when the king received the fugitive pope in Paderborn, an anonymous poet had referred to Charlemagne as the "father of Europe."[1] Just a year later he had become emperor, and the territories over which his dominion stretched were now officially identified as the re-created Roman Empire. But could the Europe we know today have been prefigured by a political construct whose attitudes were so determinedly preoccupied with the past and whose model was an empire that had flourished half a millennium beforehand? Since the nineteenth century historians have not ceased to pose this question, one that has taken on different significance according to the prevailing cultural climate. During the period of nationalism, which as we know lasted well into the twentieth century, the problem appeared to be one of identifying the Latin or Germanic roots of the resurrected empire, and therefore by extension, of the modern European civilization. No one could fail to understand the political implications of such historiographic debate.

Just after the Second World War, mainly as a result of Henri Pirenne's seminal work *Mohammed and Charlemagne*, the debate shifted to the survival of the ancient economy and institutions.[2] It appeared that neither had been swept away by the Germanic invasions as completely as had been previously believed, so it was now a question of establishing whether ancient history ended before or after the era of Charlemagne. As we shall see, there are strong arguments in favor of both propositions, and hence the response depends very much on the perspective in which the question is posed. Experience teaches us that the future of Europe in the twenty-first century is likely to influence considerably the way in which coming generations of historians view the Carolingian story. In this chapter we will examine the two perspectives just referred to, which we could define as the national one and the economic and institutional one. In so doing, we will attempt to assess in the light of current attitudes whether and to what extent Charlemagne's empire can really be considered the indirect forerunner of modern Europe.

GERMANS AND ROMANS
Karl der Grosse or Charlemagne?

The scholars who posed the question in national or, as we would now say, ethnic terms were principally French and German, the intellectual spokespeople for two ferociously adversarial nations. Was the main component of Charlemagne's empire Roman, to which France was heir, or Germanic, as proudly claimed by the new German Reich? It is easy to understand the passions unleashed by this debate in the climate of nationalistic fervor that prevailed in Europe in the nineteenth and twentieth centuries. To insist that Charlemagne was essentially German rather than French and had to be thought of as Karl der Grosse rather than Charlemagne was to assert Germany's centrality in modern Europe, in place of France. Equally, to declare that the empire built by Charles was not based on the legacy of Rome but rather the youthful energy of the Germanic peoples was to adopt a political position with extremely clear contemporary parallels.

Today, the question can no longer be posed in these terms. Charlemagne was not and could not have been either German or French, because neither of these two peoples had yet come into existence. For historians this has been obvious for some time, although Professor Karl Ferdinand Werner, who for many years was the head of the Institute of German History in Paris, had great difficulty persuading the German ambassador not to mention Karl der Grosse as one of the great Germans of the past in an official speech.[3] Not only did Germans not exist at that time, but there are even doubts about whether the various Germanic peoples, as we now define them for purely linguistic reasons, had any sense of a collective identity over and above their individual ethnicity, and whether there was any form of solidarity among them. Whatever our assessment of Charlemagne's importance in the formation of modern Europe, the national dimension as it was understood by nineteenth-century historians must resolutely be rejected. The European nations as we know them were only to be established once his empire had fallen apart.

"Stulti Sunt Romani, Sapienti Sunt Paioari"

This does not mean that Charlemagne's Europe was not riven by an ethnic division whose importance cannot be denied. Even though the empire was officially the *Romanum imperium,* Romans were almost looked on as foreigners. The name Roman referred to both the inhabitants of the Eternal City governed by the pope and the inhabitants of Aquitaine, long associated with rebelliousness against the Frankish king. They were contrasted with the western Franks of northern Gaul, the eastern Franks who still lived in Germany, the *Alamanni,* Bavarians, Saxons, and Thuringians, not to mention the Lombards of Italy, all of whom felt superior to the Roman world.

Charlemagne himself was a Frank. He was very conscious and proud of this identity. He was careful not to imitate the appearance of the Roman emperors whose title he carried. "He would wear the national, that is Frankish, dress," Einhard tells us; "he rejected and refused to wear foreign clothes, however splendid they were, except when he was in Rome. On one occasion at Pope Adrian's request and on another following the entreaties of Adrian's successor, Leo, he put on a long tunic and chlamys, as well as shoes in the Roman fashion."[4] When these popes implored their ally, the Frankish king they wished to elevate to imperial rank, to kindly dress like a Roman at least while he was in Rome, they were clearly aware of the artificial, even forced, nature of a coexistence that was unavoidable for purely political reasons.

Even before Charlemagne's conquests, the irresistible rise of the Franks meant that an ideological clash with the Roman world was inevitable. This antagonism is nowhere expressed with such clarity as in the highly official prologue to the Salic law, which was drawn up in the final years of Pepin's reign. It exalts the Franks, who represent the new Israel, for having shaken off "the heavy yoke imposed by the Romans" and replacing them as the people who led Christendom.[5] The national dimension became entwined with the religious one: the Franks deserved to govern the world because they had never sullied themselves with heresy, while for centuries the Romans had persecuted and executed Christians. Their hostility toward the Greeks of Byzantium also implied an admission that the latter were heirs to the Roman Empire, but only in its presumptuous and pagan form, over which the Franks had already triumphed and were ready to triumph again, as suggested by the *Libri Carolini*. This antagonism was destined to endure for a long time. Bishop Liutprand of Cremona visited Constantinople on behalf of Emperor Otto at the end of the tenth century and was discourteously received. The *basileus* Nicephorus Phocas declared that his master was a barbarian and not an emperor, adding "You are not Romans but Lombards!" Liutprand replied that he was not ashamed of not being Roman, indeed he would not have wanted to descend from fratricidal Romolus and his gang of thieves and fugitive slaves. "You who call yourselves *kosmocratores*, that is emperors, descend from this nobility, but we Lombards, Saxons, and Franks despise you so much that when we wish to insult an enemy of ours we simply call him a Roman."[6]

The fact that Liutprand obviously spoke in Italian and would class himself linguistically among the Latins and not the *Teutones* does not take anything away from the solidarity between Germanic peoples he was expressing in his invective. This sense of community was not in fact the product of a shared linguistic identity, which probably had not even existed in earlier times and was now entirely a thing of the past, following the adoption of the Romance language by the Lombards and large sections of the Frankish population. In 813 when the Council of Tours ordered that priests should no longer preach in cultured Latin but in "rusticam Romanam linguam aut Theotiscam," so that everyone could understand what was being said from the pulpit, it was acknowledging a linguistic reality that in no way reflected a division between nations: the Franks of Neustria, who spoke the "Roman language" were no less Franks than their compatriots in Austrasia.[7]

The collective identity of the Germanic peoples arose from their memory of the invasions. There was still a clear distinction between the Romans who had inhabited the empire in ancient times and the invaders who had triumphed over them by conquering Gaul and Italy. It should perhaps be added that this enduring distinction was based on a substantially mythical rewriting of history, due to ignorance of the process of integration between the invaders and the original inhabitants. Today we know that the Franks in Gaul were only a tiny minority within the Roman population into which they were rapidly absorbed, but at the time of Charlemagne everyone who lived north of the Loire was considered Frank, without any memory of their probable Latin origins. Chroniclers of the time considered it obvious that Clovis had annihilated the Romans or at least driven them from the country at the time of the invasions. Once again language had nothing to do with ethnic identity, and the fact that many Franks by then spoke a Romance language appeared no more than curious. A ninth-century manuscript states, "It seems that at that time the Franks learned the Roman language we still use today from the Romans who were living there. No one here knows what their mother tongue was."[8]

Equally symbolic of a division arising from history and not from language was the fact that the invaders who settled in imperial provinces always referred to the indigenous population with the untranslatable appellative Welsche, which to this day retains in German its negative connotations, and applied it without distinction to Celts and Romans, irrespective of their language. The term was in general use at the time of Charlemagne and continued to express the ancient hostility between the conquerors and the conquered. In a translation textbook of the era, the Bavarian author takes pleasure in using the following derisive expression as a grammatical example: "Tole sint Uualha, spahe sint Peigira / Stulti sunt Romani, sapienti sunt Paioari," the Bavarian and Latin versions of the sentence, "Romans are stupid; Bavarians are clever."[9] Even the geographic perception of Europe at the time of Charlemagne was dominated and radically remodeled by the settlement of Germanic peoples. Of course, intellectuals continued to use the ancient categories of classical geographers and spoke of Gaul, Germany, and Italy, as though nothing had changed since the times of Julius Caesar, but the common people who were unaware of these scholarly abstractions knew very well that the invasions had created a very different Europe. Their attitudes are demonstrated by an eighth-century manuscript containing so-called "glosses," that is, a list of Latin words with the translation into a Germanic language. This vocabulary, similar to the ones Charles would have had in front of him when he was learning to write, translated classical toponyms as follows: "Gallia uualho lant. Equitania uuasconolant. Germania franchonolant. Italia lancpartolant. Ager Noricus peigiro lant."[10]

The geographic panorama was therefore entirely different from the classical one for those who thought in a Germanic language. A man who found himself in Aachen, the preferred residence of his king, would consider himself to be in the land of the Franks, *Franchonolant*. Moving south, he would sooner or later come to *Walholant*, the land of the *Welsche* or Romans who lived beyond the Loire, in a foreign country where the Franks had very little presence. Further on in the southwest of Aquitaine, there was *Vuasconolant* or the Basque country, whose name now represents a beleaguered minority in its Pyrenean refuge but in the past covered a wider area that gave its name to Gascony. If, however, our man from Aachen went up the Rhine toward the east, he would reach the area that had once been *Ager Noricus* and had now become the land of the Bavarians, *Peigirolant*. From there, crossing the mountain he would arrive not in Italy but in the land of the Lombards, *Lancpartolant*. Here was a geography that only superficially paid homage to the ancient terminology but in reality interpreted Europe through the settlement of Germans in place of the preexisting peoples, the *Welsche*. This distinction denoted a consciously antagonistic attitude and not just a simple diversity.

The Comeback of Rome

An empire does not only define itself through the genuine or manipulated national sentiments that make it up, or even through the personal sentiments of its emperor. Charlemagne may have felt Frankish and been irritated when wearing a tunic and a chlamys, but in the most solemn moment of his life when he dictated his will, it was the empire that he had before his eyes. He decreed that two-thirds of all his treasures should be shared out between twenty-one archbishops of his subject lands, and the twenty-one metropolitan sees were listed in the following order: "Rome, Ravenna, Milan, Cividale, Grado, Cologne, Mainz, Salzburg, Trier, Sens, Besançon, Lyons, Rouen, Reims, Arles, Vienne, Tarantaise, Embrun, Bordeaux, Tours, and Bourges."[11] Their sequence reflects the administrative geography of the Roman Empire rising from the ashes and regaining contemporary relevance through an ecclesiastical geography that had been created in the first few centuries of Christianity and never amended since. It started with Rome in its rightful position, followed by the ancient capitals of the western empire, Ravenna and Milan, and then by the two sees into which the ancient patriarchate of Aquileia had been split, Cividale and Grado, which occupied crucial positions on the border with the Avars and Byzantium.

The metropolitan sees of the *regnum Francorum* appear only after the five Italic sees. We now consider these to be German cities, but they were actually all ancient Roman cities on the left bank of the Rhine: Cologne, Mainz, and Trier, with the exception of Salzburg, which

Charlemagne himself elevated to the status of archbishopric in order to organize the conversion of the Avars and the expansion of Bavarian settlers east of the Danube. Not surprisingly it is the only see whose classical name was not sufficient to identify it, so the cleric who was drawing up the will preferred to translate it into contemporary usage: "Juvavum quae et Salzburc." Then came the cities of ancient Gaul, Sens, Besançon, Lyons, Rouen, Reims, and then going down the Rhône toward the Mediterranean, Arles, Vienne, and the two Alpine sees of Tarantaise and Embrun, and then Bordeaux, the metropolis of Aquitaine, and finally returning toward central Gaul, Tours and Bourges.

It should be made clear that this was a very peculiar geography, because an ecclesiastical regional breakdown that reflected the spread of Christianity toward the end of the classical era no longer corresponded in many cases to the contemporary population distribution or the trade routes. Some metropolitan provinces were minuscule, while others were too big, as with those along the Rhine that oversaw the vast plains of northern Germany, only recently converted to Christianity at the point of a sword. Some archbishoprics were in insignificant cities like Sens or Reims, whereas Paris and Aachen, vastly more important urban centers in Charles's empire, did not have a metropolitan. What interests us here is the principle on which Charles dictated the list, which was, as already stated, a kind of summary of the empire, and the principle is very clear. We have no Romans or Germans here, nor is there a place for Franks, Bavarians, or Aquitanians. This is a Christian empire, which is Roman and cannot be anything else, because Rome had been chosen by God as the center of Christ's religion.

THE END OF THE ANCIENT WORLD
AND THE BIRTH OF EUROPE
Pirenne's Theory on Mohammed and Charlemagne

In 1937 Henri Pirenne's famous work *Mohammed and Charlemagne* was published posthumously. It brought about a turning point in the debate on Carolingian Europe as it had been waged by nineteenth-century historiography.[12] Pirenne was himself a nineteenth-century historian, and a glance at the photographs that portray him with a large beard and a pince-nez confirms his birthdate, 1862. As a Belgian who had been born and brought up on the border between the Roman and Germanic worlds, he put forward a solution that overcame the impasse between the opposing nationalisms of French and German historians. By analyzing trade patterns and the circulation of money, Pirenne came to the conclusion that Charles's empire did not resemble the Roman Empire in the slightest way, but the end of antiquity did not in his opinion date from the barbarian invasions that only had a negligible effect on the economy. It had been the Arab expansion in the Mediterranean basin that shattered the unity of the ancient world built around the *mare nostrum* of the Romans, and only then did the Europe we know today begin to take shape, with the Mediterranean representing its frontier rather than its center.

Pirenne's theory has now been completely abandoned in the essentially economic terms in which he presented it. There can in fact be little doubt that the decline of Mediterranean trade, the monetary crisis, and the decay of cities can be dated back to the last few centuries of the empire and the barbarian invasions, with a further deterioration at the time of Justinian's disastrous wars. Equally, these factors do not justify the extreme interpretation of a widespread collapse of civilization and the almost total disappearance of the market that emerges from *Mohammed and Charlemagne*. What actually occurred in the early Middle Ages was the creation of a new economic space based on continental Europe rather than the Mediterranean, with trade routes directed toward the North Sea. In spite of these limitations, Pirenne's insights proved extremely fruitful, precisely because after him the debate no longer hinged on the Roman or Germanic nature of Charlemagne's empire, but on its relationship to previous and subsequent eras. In other words, the argument shifted to whether the empire that styled itself as Roman had any similarities, at least in its structure, to the empire of

Diocletian or Constantine if not Augustus, or whether the continent over which Charles ruled was radically different and pointed the way to modern Europe.

The first interpretation that argues for continuity currently enjoys considerable support. This does not mean an unqualified victory for Pirenne's main adversary, the Austrian historian Alfons Dopsch, who saw an underlying continuity between the era of Julius Caesar and that of Charlemagne. If anything, the prevailing interpretation is a third way: historiography has been able to determine with increasing clarity the notion of an era of late antiquity that is quite distinct from the classical era and commences around the third and fourth centuries with Diocletian's reforms and the advent of Christianity. It is this antiquity, and not the era of Caesar and Augustus, that many historians feel they can stretch out to cover the times of Charlemagne or even to the end of the millennium. Perhaps without realizing it, they are echoing Max Weber's quip that Charlemagne was "Diocletian's belated executioner."[13] Even though this position implies the rejection of a radical break produced by the advance of Islam, it pays homage to Pirenne's fundamental insight that the Germanic invasions did not represent a decisive rupture in the history of the West.

We are also indebted to Pirenne for the other interpretation that perceives the continent unified by the Franks as a profoundly different reality from that of the Roman Empire. Its main proponents, archaeologists and economic historians, adopt perhaps the most persuasive image in *Mohammed and Charlemagne*, of a Carolingian Europe isolated by the Mediterranean and deprived of its relationship with Africa and the East that had been so crucial to antiquity. Even if we accept that the Roman world did not contain those features of advanced capitalism that were once attributed to it and that its economy was in reality dominated or even crushed by state intervention, it is still clear that the Rhine-based Europe of Charlemagne had very little in common with the Mediterranean-based Europe of Diocletian and Constantine. The turning point, which in many other ways, including the extremely important matter of religion, has to be placed in the third or fourth century, is shifted forward again, just as Pirenne wanted it to be. However, Muslims were not the primary cause, but rather the steady breakdown of public finances following the Germanic invasions and the new orientation of trade routes toward northern Europe that reached its high point precisely during the era of Charlemagne.

"La chute de Rome n'aura pas lieu": *The Hyper-Romanist View*

Clearly, if these are the two arguments under consideration, it is essential for supporters of continuity between late antiquity and the Carolingian age to demonstrate that the influence of the government apparatus over the Western economy was not eliminated by the invasions. This is precisely the kind of fundamental argument that is put forward in a more or less provocative manner in order to show the persistence of a late-antiquity-type social, economic, and legislative organization through to the times of Charlemagne and beyond. Scholars, whom their adversaries have maliciously called hyper-Romanists, have attempted to demonstrate that tax collection, a central and all-pervasive feature of the empire of Diocletian and Constantine, survived the barbarian invasions and continued to function in the Frankish kingdom and then in the re-created empire of the Carolingians, without substantial changes. In their opinion, the wealth that was confiscated by Frankish kings and generally redistributed among the powerful and the churches, which still in Charles's time constituted the main foundation of royal taxation policies, large noble estates, and monastic and episcopal assets, did not technically speaking consist of landownership but of taxation of the land that had remained unchanged since the times of Diocletian's reforms. Unfortunately, the demonstration of this continuity rests on such a tendentious interpretation of sources and their terminology that it discredited the hyper-Romanist scholars, or fiscalists, as they prefer to call themselves, in the eyes of the great majority of their colleagues.[14]

The French historian Guy Bois has provided us with another approach, which attempts to maintain continuity while still criticizing the hyper-Romanist dogma. He has put forward a reinterpretation of the tenth and eleventh centuries based much more on the social and productive reality than on the administrative and financial one, suggesting that Charlemagne's Europe was not so different from the ancient one.[15] His arguments center on an analysis of slaves, whom Latin sources from antiquity and the Middle Ages refer to as *servi* and historians used to call serfs. Bois came to realize that in the Carolingian era these agricultural laborers, who were subservient to rich peasants in the village as well as to great landowners, were juridically slaves in every sense of the word, exactly as they had been in the time of Cicero.

Like that of the hyper-Romanists, Bois's theory has been severely criticized and indeed largely demolished. It has been shown that this enslaved workforce was by that time very different from the squads of rural slaves employed by large landed estates, or latifundia, in late antiquity, in terms of integration into the peasant community, working conditions, and even civil rights. By the time of Charlemagne, slaves lived in their own houses, had wives and children, and worked side by side with free laborers and smallholders. However, Bois's stimulating suggestion has been much more useful than the substantially manic ideas of the hyper-Romanists in forcing us to recognize that the Carolingian age was undergoing a far-reaching transformation and was anything but settled. Many features of this transition, the ones that would have been much more evident to contemporaries, related back to antiquity, while only historians manage to perceive the shape of the future crystallizing out of the past.

The European Perspective

If we leave the debate on society and the economy and return to the one on the political space in which Charlemagne moved and which he had to a large extent helped to create, it is difficult not to recognize how through Frankish hegemony the idea of Europe first started to take shape and adopt the features that, for better or worse, we associate with it today. Whatever the inherent weaknesses of Pirenne's theory, there can be no doubt that the ancient Roman Empire was a Mediterranean reality extending its dominion over the European, African, and Asian shores of *mare nostrum*, whereas Charles's empire was a continental reality, whose center of gravity was the Rhine Valley. It was already taking on the national and regional profiles that were to shape Europe in the second millennium.

Of course, the development of this notion of the West went back to the later Roman Empire and accelerated dramatically with the barbarian invasions. But it is precisely for this reason that such importance has to be attached to the moment in which the ancient Roman provinces that suffered the disaster and for a few centuries underwent more or less independent histories were unified by a new political entity only formally linked to the ancient one. When we say that they were unified, we do not only mean that they obeyed the same emperor, which they only did for a few decades, but that the laws, governmental institutions, and economic rules developed in one of the provinces, Gaul, dominated by Franks, were extended to Europe as a whole. The basis of this slow process could be detected in the hegemony exercised by the Franks over the surrounding kingdoms during the Merovingian era, though it was not formally ratified until Christmas Day of 800.

Charlemagne's imperial coronation consecrated the birth of a new political space, which at the distance of over a thousand years still appears familiar. This is a Europe in which France and Germany are the principal partners, northern Italy is more integrated than southern Italy, Catalonia more than the rest of Spain, and from which Great Britain is in some way removed. This Nordic and continental Europe, which is Latino-Germanic in its culture, diffident toward the Mediterranean regions, and almost entirely ignores the Greeks and Slavs of the East, is a legacy of Charlemagne. It is not at all surprising that today the union's heart and head are to be found in Brussels, Strasbourg, and Maastricht, all at the core of the ancient Frankish lands.

Equally we should not be surprised that during the era of Charlemagne the name of Europe suddenly starts to appear in the writings of Western intellectuals, as in the case of that anonymous writer who during Charles's childhood celebrated the victory of Charles's grandfather at Poitiers, perceiving it as a triumph of the *Europenses* or Europeans, united under the leadership of the Frankish mayor of the palace to stem the Islamic tide, or of the priest Catwulf who wrote to Charles from Ireland in 775 proclaiming that God had elevated him to the throne "for the greater glory of the kingdom of Europe."[16] Not to forget our old friend the poet of Paderborn, who referred to Charles in the summer of 799 as *rex pater Europae*, or the king and father of Europe.

SIX

The Man and His Family

THE KING'S PHYSICAL APPEARANCE

What was Charlemagne really like? Is it possible, over a thousand years later, to rediscover the human dimension to this man who was so successful at administering his inheritance and whose power has rarely been equaled in the history of Europe? Einhard, who knew him personally, wrote about him after his death. It is true that he plundered Suetonius' *Lives of the Caesars*, because he had to demonstrate that Charles was in every sense a true Roman emperor and a genuine successor to Augustus and Tiberius, but as an eyewitness he also introduced a great number of personal observations.

> He was heavily built, sturdy, and of considerable stature, although not exceptionally so, given that he stood seven foot tall. He had a round head, large and lively eyes, a slightly larger nose than usual, white but still attractive hair, a bright and cheerful expression, a short and fat neck, and a slightly protruding stomach. His voice was clear, but a little higher than one would have expected for a man of his build. He enjoyed good health, except for the fevers that affected him in the last few years of his life. Toward the end he dragged one leg. Even then, he stubbornly did what he wanted and refused to listen to doctors, indeed he detested them, because

they wanted to persuade him to stop eating roast meat, as was his wont, and to be content with boiled meat.[1]

When a medieval chronicler outlines the portrait of a king, it is obviously wise not to take his words too literally. Intellectuals in the Middle Ages, particularly at the time of Charlemagne, were Platonists rather than Aristotelians. They were more interested in models than specific cases, and abstract perfection than imperfect realities. Thus the portrait of a monarch often conformed to the model of the ideal king rather than the individual and transient features of the subject. Einhard, however, luckily avoids these perils: in the way he describes Charles, we can see all the ravages of age and bad diet that a man of that time could suffer, particularly when he was rich enough to eat as much meat as he wanted. The fact that the words chosen by the chronicler are mainly found in Suetonius should not cause uneasiness: medieval writers considered elegance of style to be the reworking of words previously used by the ancients or the Bible, while molding them to put across exactly what they wanted to say.

The physical portrait provided by Einhard is confirmed by contemporary depictions of the emperor.[2] The image stamped on his coins is that of a corpulent man with a fat neck and drooping mustaches. His hair is cut short and his head crowned with laurels in the manner of the Roman emperors. A similar portrayal can also be found in an equestrian statuette of gilded bronze, about 8 inches high, which is kept in the Louvre. The subject is undoubtedly a Carolingian monarch, which tradition identifies with Charlemagne, although there is much evidence to suggest that the work belongs to a later period. The statuette portrays a sturdy man with a round head, a chubby face, short hair, large mustaches, and a crown on his head, very much as Einhard described Charlemagne. The most likely explanation is that it was a portrait of the emperor commissioned by one of his successors, probably Charles the Bald.

Pictorial representations are rather less satisfactory. The mosaic commissioned by Leo III for the Lateran Palace around 796–800 has been lost, but we do still have several sketches from the sixteenth and seventeenth centuries. The image of the Frankish king kneeling at the feet of Saint Peter was undoubtedly intended to be realistic, given that the king is represented in barbarian costume with strips of cloth wrapped round his legs. The problem is that in some of these sketches Charlemagne has not only a mustache but a short bushy black beard. It is true that traditional iconography of a later period depicted the emperor with a long white beard, but what we now know about Frankish fashion leads us to believe that Charles's chin was clean-shaven. When Duke Grimoald of Benevento was defeated, one of his symbolic acts of submission was to shave his chin and those of his men according to the Frankish custom.[3] It is therefore quite possible that the artist who created the Lateran mosaic depicted Charles with a beard according to the Italic custom, given that he had never personally seen the emperor. The mosaic in the apse of Santa Susanna in Rome, which was commissioned by Pope Leo III possibly in 799, has also been lost, but if we go by the same sketches, the king was portrayed with a more credible set of mustaches. The ninth century produced the first portrait of Charlemagne in a miniature. It is therefore a late work, but one produced by an artist who worked in the Frankish kingdom and not in Rome, and here again there is no trace of a beard. The emperor is still depicted as a sturdy man with a bull neck, large mustaches, and the suggestion of a double chin, thus confirming Einhard's description once again.

We might perhaps be more inclined to doubt the reliability of the biographer when he claims that the emperor was 7 feet tall, which would correspond to more than 6 feet 3 inches in modern imperial measures. This was a Herculean stature, particularly in a period in which people were a little shorter than we are today: indeed, it seems odd that Einhard did not consider it at all exceptional. Yet here again archaeology has confirmed the information provided by the biographer: in 1861, Charlemagne's tomb was opened by scientists who reconstructed his skeleton and found that it indeed measured 74.9 inches (192 centimeters).[4] The only conclusion we can make is that yes, men of antiquity and the Middle Ages were shorter, but exceptions did exist. The Germans, of whose formidable stature Roman writers spoke with awe, were even then taller than Mediterranean people, and in all probability the chiefs were considerably taller than the peasants thanks to all that roast meat.

What language did this colossus speak? By the time of his birth, the Franks who had settled in Neustria had already adopted the "Roman language" of the local population, while the Franks of Austrasia continued to speak what was beginning to be referred to as the *lingua Theotisca* or "German language." In a few capitularies, Charlemagne himself used technical terms in their original language and introduced them with the clause, "as we say in the German language."[5] Einhard does not use this term, but every reference to the emperor's *sermo patrius* or native tongue confirms that it was a Germanic tongue and therefore Frankish. As with other ancient Germanic dialects, it was rich in vowel-endings and the vowel sounds themselves would have sounded broader than in present-day German. For example, the Frankish people were called *theoda Frankono* and their language *frenkisga zunga*.[6]

Einhard adds that Charles also learned Latin and could speak it as fluently as his mother tongue.[7] This meant that he was capable of speaking to the Franks of Neustria in their Romance dialect and also express himself in a more grammatically correct Latin when he was discussing theology with his men of learning or even with the pope. He must have learned his first smattering of Latin when he was a child, given that it was only possible to learn to read in that language, but it was the Lombard Peter of Pisa who helped him perfect his scholarly Latin when he was over thirty years old. He was probably taught the softer pronunciation used in Italy, which would have been different from that used by northern European intellectuals like Alcuin.

DAILY LIFE

The King's Routine

Whereas in modern times our day is measured out by its sequence of meals, Charlemagne's depended to a much greater extent on the liturgical services that he felt himself obliged to take part in with an almost monklike zeal. After all, one of his most pressing commitments was his dialogue with God, who watched over him from the heavens and whose representative on earth he considered himself to be. He therefore had himself awakened at dawn, and before he had even gotten dressed, he went off to take part in matins wrapped in a cloak that stretched down to his feet, "a garment which today," wrote Notker a century later, "has not only fallen out of use, but whose name has even been lost."[8] Underneath he wore a linen shirt and linen underpants, items that were worn by everyone and were not royal or aristocratic finery.

Once the service had ended, the emperor would return to his room where a fire would be burning, and there he got dressed in a more or less luxurious manner according to the circumstances. Over his underwear he wore a long tunic reaching his knees and tightened it with a belt. This was the typical garment of the Franks, and only the quality of the cloth and the presence of braids distinguished the king and his nobles from the peasants, apart of course from the color: the poor dressed in undyed wool, which was therefore gray or brown, whereas the rich wore clothes of bright colors, particularly red and purple. Charles would have worn trousers under his tunic, as was the general but not universal practice, because there were those who left their legs bare. Socks were always worn, and they must have had leather soles, as often no other footwear was put on top of them. They were held up by strips of cloth bound around the feet and legs. When it was cold, the king would wrap himself in his customary cape that stretched down to his feet. Notker observed that during Charles's life fashion tended to shorten the cape, but Charles commented with characteristic coarseness that such short cloaks meant that your feet froze when you went out to answer the call of nature, and he discouraged their sale.[9] Apart from the cape, which he preferred blue, when necessary he would wear a common fur jacket made of otter, rat, or lambskins. Lastly, the sword on his belt and a knotted mace made of apple wood with a golden or silver handle were an integral part of his everyday garb.

Even if the descriptions provided by the chroniclers appear on the whole to be reliable, we should never forget their ideological dimension. It may very well be that Charles did not cherish simplicity of dress as Einhard and particularly Notker claim, because both wished to celebrate the simplicity and therefore the superiority of the old days compared with the corrupt times they lived in. This is certainly the way we should read an anecdote told by Notker. One Sunday after mass, Charles decided to go hunting with the nobles of his retinue and he ordered them to mount their horses immediately without giving them time to change their clothes. The emperor was wearing a cheap lambskin, while the others were in their holiday finery and, what is worse, being in Italy they had only just provided themselves with precious silks and purple cloth imported by Venetian merchants from the East at the market in Pavia. After dragging them through the mud and rain for a few hours and then back again to the palace, Charles commanded everyone to dry themselves at the fire without undressing and then kept them working late into the night. The following day he wanted to see what was left of their clothes and having ascertained that they had been reduced to rags, he showed them his lambskin jacket, which had not suffered at all, and he chided them for having spent their money so wastefully.[10]

Charlemagne was already busy at work when he was getting dressed and would on occasion receive ministers, give orders, and even pronounce sentences at this time. He was therefore one of those impatient men who wake up with a mass of ideas in their heads. This squares with the fact that he slept badly at night, woke several times, and might even get up to work, although it should be remembered that Einhard knew him as an old man, when insomnia becomes more frequent. So far there has been no mention of breakfast, and obviously there was no coffee, tea, or chocolate at the time. Therefore the concept of breakfast as we know it did not exist. It is most probable that he did not eat anything until late in the morning, when he had soup or bread soaked in milk or wine.

The morning ended with mass, which Charles attended every day— a little earlier in summer, and later in winter. We have to remember that the time of day was not fixed as it is with us but varied according to the seasons. An hour was one twelfth of the day, and the day was the period between sunrise and sunset. Consequently an hour by that system could last for one and one-half of our hours in the summer, while in the winter it could be shortened to three-quarters of an hour. This variability makes it difficult and ultimately also pointless to attempt to establish precise times corresponding to the habits of that age. Moreover, monks were the only people whose timetables we know with any degree of certainty, and even though we have established that the precision with which Charles followed his liturgical duties was similar to that of a monk, there can be no doubt that he would have been freer in the timing.

As with the ancients, the main meal was *coena*, which was served after mass and therefore roughly speaking in the early afternoon. The king rarely had guests, except during religious holidays, when great numbers of people would be invited. On the whole, he ate alone or in the company of his children. After the king had finished eating, it came the turn of the magnates in his retinue, who up till that moment had been respectfully observing his meal. The other officials and servants then followed them in turn. During Lent when it was obligatory to fast until the evening, Charles had vespers celebrated earlier, and he started to eat when it was still light. A bishop who dared to reproach him over this was ordered not to sit down at the table until the last of the servants had dined, and so he was obliged to fast until midnight. The emperor had little difficulty in persuading him that Christian charity required him to start as soon as possible, although Notker wishes to stress that Charles was not in any case breaking the fast, as he observed it at exactly the same time every day, just as it is commanded in the Bible.[11]

The retinue of courtiers present at the royal meal and the precise sequence of servings remind us of more recent situations, such as the Sun King's meals at Versailles, and they further increase our doubts over the patriarchal simplicity that chroniclers claimed for Charles's court. There is more than one account of a count or even a bishop attending the king's dinner standing up and even helping to wait upon him like a servant. Of course etiquette had not reached the degrees of sophistication to be found in the Byzantine Empire, something they made much fun of in the West. It was rumored, for example, that down in Constantinople it was prohibited to turn over fish or game in the presence of the emperor, so everyone only ate the upper side and transgressors were put to death.[12] Still there were rules to be observed in the presence of the Frankish king, and Charles, who appears to have been somewhat easily offended, was the first to make sure they were observed, and not without savagery. When a bishop who had been invited to his table blessed a loaf and then immediately cut a slice for himself, offering the bread to the emperor only afterward, Charles replied angrily, "You may as well eat it all yourself."[13]

He enjoyed eating, although he did not get drunk, which was remarkable for a barbarian and we might be tempted not to trust Einhard on this point. He found fasting unbearable, and on meat days he took great pleasure not only in roast meats but also game cooked on a spit, as was appropriate for such a powerful monarch, of whom no one expected a life of privations. While he ate, he liked to be read to and would listen to ancient histories, the endeavors of his ancestors, or the occasional moral work, particularly Saint Augustine's *City of God*, or that at least is Einhard's version.[14] But other sources recall the drinking songs and even lewd storytelling that was enjoyed at the emperor's table.[15] During the summer, after eating fruit and drinking the last glass, he would undress as for the night and allow himself a long afternoon sleep. On waking, he probably ate something before attending vespers that ended the day, given that even monks were allowed two meals when the days were long.

Eating, sleeping, working, and attending mass: so far the emperor's life looks like that of a pope. However, there was also room for physical pleasures in the life of a king. Without dwelling too much on the pleasures he indulged in with concubines, we can say that Charles devoted much of his time to horse riding and hunting. Apart from these pastimes so typical of his people, he had also inherited the Roman taste for baths, particularly hot baths, which had been far from forgotten in the Middle

Ages. He was a good swimmer and happily frequented spas. In his old age, he chose Aachen as his preferred residence precisely because of the quality of its waters. The palace was equipped with a spa complex where the emperor took the waters in the company of his children, his friends, and magnates of the kingdom. Occasionally, Einhard adds, even the guards were invited to come into the pool, so that more than one hundred people could be in the water at any one time.[16] Alcuin recalls in a letter having discussed theology with the emperor while they were in the hot waters of the spa.[17]

Our knowledge of the furniture that Charles used in his daily life derives from miniatures that depict the life of the king and his nobles, generally in a biblical context. We know that they did not eat lying down, as the ancient Romans did, but seated at round or rectangular tables or even low individual tables covered by small white tablecloths. They used to sit on high-backed chairs, stools, or folding chairs with colored cushions, or even chairs with backs not that dissimilar to the ones we use today. Obviously, they ate with their hands, because the fork had not yet been invented. This does not mean that there was no other cutlery and that good table manners were not observed. Meat and bread were cut with a knife, and soup was taken with a spoon.

The other important piece of furniture in daily life was the bed. It was low and wooden with four, eight, or ten legs. A soft oval mattress was placed over planks of wood, with one or two pillows. When going to bed, people wrapped themselves up in a sheet, which was white or more rarely purple. It cannot be excluded that it was made of wool, because it seemed to be in place of a blanket. When it was cold, the same cape that was used for keeping warm during the day was also used at night. This explains why Charles preferred it to be long. Although furniture was occasionally painted, mainly red, and cushions and mattresses might have had braided and fringed covers, the interiors depicted in the miniatures have a rather spartan air, even in wealthy palaces. A minimum of comfort was provided by the fireplace, the carpets that covered the floors, and the wall hangings made of expensive cloth.

The King and His Circle

A fascinating though not at all impartial account of daily life at Charles's court has come down to us through his poets. During the long winters poetry provided a pastime and an opportunity for lively competitions that the emperor liked to judge, and for those who were obliged to spend time away from the court, the composition of letters in verse form was a way of staying in contact. Analysis of these literary outpourings, often of excellent quality, reveals the esprit de corps that inspired those close to the emperor. It was characterized by a continuous and dense tangle of allusions, jokes, and witty anecdotes that only the initiated could understand. Charlemagne himself took part in this intellectual amusement, although the verses that bear his name were probably revised for him by one of his poets. When Paul the Deacon had only recently joined the court, the king sent him a poem that had been polished up by Peter of Pisa, in which he asked him if he would prefer to be put in prison or sent to convert the Danes. Paul the Deacon's response to this sample of black humor was deft (he said he would rather go to convert the Danes, but unfortunately he did not know their language).[18] Here we see the private and everyday side of the official policy of subjugating pagans and spreading the Christian faith as it would have appeared in conversations between the king and his friends rather than through the sober language of capitularies and councils.

Sometimes the poets' accounts become wickedly satirical. Theodulf of Orléans is the most caustic in his description of a court filled with third-rate poets, where the holders of the highest offices, such as the chamberlain Meginfredus or the seneschal Audulf, desperately try to squeeze out of their sluggish brains at least one clumsy hexameter in order to please the king. A fierce rivalry divided the palatine intellectuals, who were almost all foreigners, from the harsh men of war who constituted the other circle of Charles's favorites and accompanied him on his hunting expeditions and military campaigns. Theodulf caricatured one of the number, Count Wibod, who was so big and fat that when he moved the whole palace shook and was too stupid to understand the poetry in which Theodulf made fun of him, so he had to make do with mumbling resentful curses against his tormentor.[19]

As can be well imagined, no one risked being so insolent with the master. Charlemagne is only ever mentioned with extravagant praise and exalted as the supreme connoisseur of literature and an omnipotent protector, the latter being something he really was. This does not mean that the occasional vignette does not convey a certain realism, as in Theodulf's description of the monarch's return to his palace, with his sons jostling to take his gloves and sword, while his daughters bring him flowers and fruit and then sit down to chat and laugh with him.[20] More generally, the image of a Charles who enjoyed sitting among his men of letters and having them compete before him in the composition of verses, in the production of riddles, and even in debate on subtle questions of grammar undoubtedly adds another dimension to the portrait we have of the man. However, such a laborious adherence to a culture he personally found difficult to master is more suggestive of a barbarian chief than a Roman emperor.

Charles displayed his marked authoritarianism and pedantry also in the way he controlled cultural and liturgical activities. Seated in his chapel among clergymen who took turns reading from the Scriptures, the emperor was in the habit of suddenly pointing to one of them with his finger or his stick, and that person had to start reading immediately from the right place. When he felt that he had heard enough, he would, according to Nokter, grunt and everyone was so eager to please him that the reader would stop that very instant, even if the sentence was unfinished.[21] The anecdote gives a good idea of the state of terror in which the old tyrant kept his servants, but on consideration it was only the less noble side of the formidable attention to detail that Charles applied, as far as was possible, to every aspect of government. Besides, Notker's conclusion was that his treatment of his chaplains made them the best readers in the world and no one made a mistake even if they did not know what they were reading!

Charlemagne's Character

Can we now hazard a guess at Charles's character? In spite of his emulation of Suetonius, Einhard's portrait clearly has its own individualism. Here is a man both well meaning and violent. He was also a sensuous man capable of enjoying the pleasures of life, something that could not be said of Augustus. The great Austrian historian Heinrich von Fichtenau has suggested that Charles's temperament veered between depression and expansiveness, although not to a maniacal degree or showing genuinely pathological symptoms.[22] According to psychologists, such people termed cyclothymics are extremely practical and capable and have a love of physical pleasure. They also have supreme and even excessive self-confidence and a tendency to be unable to impose limits upon themselves. They tend to get depressed when on their own or in silence and occasionally erupt into violence. Although in the first half of the twentieth century when Fichtenau was writing people had more faith in these semiscientific characterizations than we have today, it is a fact that these traits are to be found in the Charlemagne described to us by chroniclers.

We know in fact that the emperor loved speaking in public so much that he even induced his adoring biographer to consider him a little too verbose.[23] We know that he never wanted to be on his own and had an unremitting need to be surrounded by his comrades in arms, his councillors, his daughters, and his bodyguard, when he was eating and even in the bath, so that visitors were first struck by the commotion in which Charles found himself perfectly at ease. We know that while he was affable with everyone, he could sometimes fall prey to terrible bouts of anger and could on occasion prove viciously brutal. This is without mentioning his unspecified cruelties to which Einhard refers with not a little embarrassment, attributing them to the bad influence of one of his wives.[24] We cannot help being struck by Nokter's story that one day, while Charles was attending church service in the company of a bishop, he proudly pointed out to him one of the clerics, who was singing the

Hallelujah in excellent voice. The bishop, who did not know that the cleric in question was a relation of the queen's, replied jokingly that he had heard peasants scream like that while they goaded their oxen. The enraged emperor reacted by knocking him to the ground with a punch. The story may well be apocryphal, but it is no less significant that it was propagated by an author whose declared aim was to celebrate Charles's greatness.[25]

The stories that spread among the people attributed to the king a propensity for boastfulness. Once, when he was reflecting on the sea that divided his dominions from those of the Byzantine Empire, he is supposed to have exclaimed, "Ah, if only there wasn't this little pond, then we would be able to share out the treasures of the East."[26] Entirely persuaded of his own brilliance, he was susceptible to flattery. Theodulf of Orléans wrote that the emperor's virtues were greater than the Nile basin, larger than the Danube and the Euphrates, and more majestic than the Ganges, and it does not appear that Charles was the least surprised.[27] At the same time, the emperor had an ability to take a joke, and his more trusted councillors would address him with the most extraordinary freedom of expression. In order to give the king an opportunity to show off, Alcuin asked him for clarifications over a complicated question concerning the liturgical calendar. Charles sent a written reply and pretended to be the author. Alcuin considered it completely mistaken and he advised the king next time to seek the assistance of less ignorant clergymen.[28] Another time Charles went so far as exclaim with his customary presumptuousness, "If only I could have just a dozen learned clerics like Saint Augustine and Saint Jerome." Alcuin promptly replied, "But surely even God has only two at that level, and you would like a whole dozen!"[29]

One last trait, which is not out of place with what has already been said, was the coarseness or even vulgarity that often appeared in Charles's behavior and language. An ambassador returning from Constantinople reported that the *basileus* had wished to be informed on the progress of the war in Saxony, and on hearing that the country had not yet been pacified, he had declared he was unhappy to hear that his son was having such difficulty in so trivial an enterprise. That manner of referring to the Frankish king was probably correct in terms of Byzantine etiquette but Charles took it badly, and when the ambassador added that the *basileus* had spoken of the Saxons as an insignificant people that would be very easy to beat, he took it even worse. The Byzantine emperor is supposed to have concluded by saying to the stunned Frank, "Listen, I bestow them on you." The anecdote, which is undoubtedly false, is an example of the delusions of grandeur that people in the West attributed to monarchs in the East. But what interests us here is Charles's purported reply, which had something unequivocally authentic in its vulgarity: "He would have done better to bestow on you a pair of underpants for the journey!"[30]

THE KING'S FAMILY
Marriage at the Time of Charlemagne

The image of vigorous sensuality and a love of physical pleasure that emerges from the portrayal of Charles is substantiated by the emperor's sexual behavior. Throughout his life he was surrounded by a multitude of wives and concubines, who came one after the other following death or rejection and ended up cohabiting. This tumultuous family life, which unfolded in full view of everyone else, was the cause of scandal among historians until it was realized that for Charlemagne's generation, the institution of marriage was something completely different from Christian marriage as it was only then beginning to be perceived by the more advanced bishops. Equally it should not be forgotten that the king's family life, in relation both to his wives and to his brother, sisters, and children, was not only part of the sphere of affections and physicality, as it is for us, but also had a clear political dimension.

Marriage, as Charles understood it at least during his youth, still corresponded to the traditional Germanic concept that did not acknowledge any sacramental value. It was purely a legal agreement. The king married to have children that would guarantee the succession, for nothing worse could happen to a people than the death of its king without an heir. Consequently, a wife who was unable to provide her husband with children could be and indeed had to be repudiated (nobody considered the possibility that the husband might be sterile). This then was the primary feature of Frankish marriage, and it contrasted drastically with ecclesiastical precepts. While the Church attempted to convince Christian men that they should only take one wife and should not remarry even if they became widowers, the reality was that repudiation was practiced with great casualness and was generally followed by a second marriage.

For a king, marriage was also a means to form alliances, and therefore a wife did not need to be personally agreeable. On consideration, this was true for everyone, because whether you were in a position of power or a peasant, you had to look after the interests of your family before assessing any personal inclinations. Germanic customs also made provisions for this by distinguishing between a real marriage established by a public contract and the practice of forming what might be called provisional or private marriages. In reality, this so-called *Friedelehe*, an ambiguous term that we would like to translate as a love match, was only possible in situations where there was a considerable difference in social position. A powerful man would take a woman from a family of more modest conditions with the consent of her family, who were quite happy to form a prestigious friendship. There would be no need for the legal and financial trappings of a real marriage. The union was still legal and honorable, but it was entered into by a simple private act, and as the woman was not removed from the authority of the father to be put under that of the husband, it could be dissolved without too many formalities, when family interests or, in the case of a monarch, the interests of the state required it.

The Church, it has to be said, was pretty uncomfortable with these customs and unforgivingly compared wives married in accordance with *Friedelehe* to vulgar concubines. In 755 a council ruled, "All laymen

should marry by public marriage, whether they are nobles or plebeians."[31] However, the bishops were paying for the long neglect of matrimonial matters by their predecessors, who had tended to consider the
whole thing repugnant as it involved carnal relations. As a result, the
Church did not really have a clear doctrine on marriage. It had not yet
been defined as a sacrament, and reflection on its nature had not even
commenced. Carolingian theologians, who pondered with great sub-
tlety on the nature of baptism and the Eucharist, had nothing to say
about marriage. The same lacuna is to be found in the liturgy, which
meant that the priest's role in the marriage ceremony was not considered
obligatory. On the rare occasions when bishops referred to marriage in
their diocesan rules, they only did so to prohibit their priests from taking part in profane and licentious festivities.

The commitment to reform of the religious life that was started by
Carloman and Pepin, and continued by Charlemagne, did end up
changing matrimonial customs. On the death of the emperor in 814, the
boundaries between what was permissible and what was not had shifted
considerably from the time of Charles's birth or even his coronation.
Friedelehe was the first casualty. While the powerful still continued to
indulge in the occasional concubine, it was no longer so easy to confuse
her with a wife. Consequently the distinction between the children of
lawful wives and those of concubines, now considered illegitimate, became much sharper. As we shall see, this development, which Charles
was obliged to uphold in light of his commitment to improving Christian morals, was to have painful consequences in his private life.

The King's Family of Origin

The evolution of manners and morals during the reign of Charlemagne
is also clear from the embarrassment with which the chroniclers speak of
his birth. Einhard declared that it was impossible to make any judgment
about the emperor's childhood, because no one had left written accounts
of it and there was no one alive who remembered it.[32] Many people have

found it strange that the biographer should depart so conspicuously from the model provided by Suetonius, who always described the birth and childhood of the Caesars. Of course, Einhard's reticence could be explained by the methodology of medieval chroniclers who were in the habit of distinguishing between what they had seen with their own eyes, what had been reported by eyewitnesses, and what had been written down. It was entirely obvious that it would be difficult to find verbal accounts that went back fifty years, and Einhard is only observing the rules of his trade when he declares that he does not want to write anything on such distant facts as the first few years of Charles's life.

But it is also possible that this reticence has some hidden cause. When Charles was born, his mother, Bertrada, was joined to King Pepin not by a public marriage but by a *Friedelehe* private contract. She only became his wife in the complete sense a few years later. According to the more advanced religious interpretation, Charlemagne was therefore born outside wedlock. In other words, he was an illegitimate child and a bastard. His very right of succession could have been challenged in favor of the second-born, Carloman, who came into this world after his parents had formalized their situation. For King Pepin and for Charlemagne, the question must have been entirely of secondary importance, and they would even have had difficulty understanding the terms in which the Church explained it. We can therefore dismiss the idea that consciousness of the irregularity of his birth constituted a psychological problem for Charles, as some people have suggested. But at the time that Einhard was writing, during the reign of Louis the Pious, the Church's influence over private lives was growing much greater, and it cannot be excluded that his father's birth was an embarrassment to the new emperor.

Whatever the reason, Einhard is responsible for leaving us with no knowledge of Charlemagne's childhood or his relationship with his father, who died when he was twenty-six. His mother, Bertrada, survived until 783, although she never again had a political role comparable with the period 768–70, in which she was a strong influence on relations between Charlemagne, his brother, Carloman, and the Lombard kingdom.[33] After her death, the king had her ceremoniously buried in the monastery of St-Denis, where Pepin had also been buried. We know nothing about the relationships between the brothers during childhood, before their father's death brought to light the deep rivalry that divided them. We know little of Charles's relationship with his only sister, Gisla, to whom he must have been fairly close, given that he made her abbess of the important convent of Chelles. The *Annals of Metz*, one of the most important historical works produced during Charles's reign to glorify the Carolingian dynasty, were probably written at Gisla's instigation and may have actually been written by her.[34] We also have some letters between her and Alcuin, and this implies a continuing close relationship between the powerful abbess and her even more powerful brother.

The Wives: Himiltrude, "Ermengarda," Hildegard, and Their Children

Charles's early marital and familial experiences mirrored those of his father, a sign that the influence of the Church had yet to be felt at the court. Charles's first union, like his father's, was not with a wife married in public with a formal commitment but with a *Friedelfrau* called Himiltrude. As is to be expected, Einhard is extremely reticent about this relationship, given the developments in official morality by the time of his writing.[35] But when Charles was young, things had been very different. Pope Stephen wrote a letter referring to this marriage (in which he had a vested interest) as "a legitimate union" and therefore indissoluble.[36] In other words, Himiltrude was Charles's wife, just as Bertrada had been Pepin's wife, and when around 770 she gave him a son, the child was baptized with his grandfather's name, Pepin, demonstrating that Charles considered him his rightful heir.

The choice of names for sons had political significance. Newborn children had to reproduce the names of ancestors, and it was precisely this identity provided by the name that gave them the right to their inheritance. During the period under discussion, the most representative name for the dynasty was not Charles but Pepin. It had been the name of the founding member of the family and of the first of his descendants to be anointed king, and thus historians prefer to refer to them in this period as Pepinids rather than Carolingians. When the son of Charles and Himiltrude was born, his brother and rival, Carloman, already had a son who naturally was also called Pepin. This must have driven Charles to speed things up and give his own son the same name, in order to ensure that he had an heir, without concerning himself too much as to whether the child was born into a private arrangement or a public marriage. After all, his own father had eventually married Bertrada publicly, and there was nothing preventing Charles from doing the same with Himiltrude, thus definitively legitimizing Pepin's situation.

But politics forced him to make another choice, one that created a wound that would be difficult to heal. During those tumultuous years in which his position did not appear at all stable, good relations with the Lombard kingdom were important and so Charles agreed to marry the daughter of the Lombard king Desiderius, on Bertrada's advice. We do not know her name, although some people call her Desiderata, which appears to be a confusion with her father's name. Manzoni, who could not have had an anonymous heroine, called her Ermengarda, but there is no historical evidence to support this suggestion.[37] In any case, the marriage did not last, because Charlemagne's policy became hostile to the Lombards, and in order to have his hands free he lost no time in repudiating her, which probably occurred in 771, hardly a year after the marriage. In the meantime, this publicly formalized marriage had swept Himiltrude into the shadows, thus stressing the provisional nature of her relationship with Charles.

The speed with which the king got rid of his Lombard wife may indicate resentment on his part over having to renounce Himiltrude, the woman who had provided him with his first child. Why exactly he did not marry her after the divorce is difficult to say. Possibly Himiltrude was no longer available, either because she was dead or because she had married someone else. Altogether it was a nasty mess, and the king could not have been pleased that he had followed his mother's advice. No one could have imagined the extent to which the consequences of this affair were to complicate and indeed poison Charles's existence. Himiltrude's son, Pepin, was still a child and fully accepted as the firstborn and the heir, in spite of being deformed, according to Einhard, and thus referred to by historians as Pepin the Hunchback in order to distinguish him from all the other Pepins.[38]

Charles wanted the company of another woman and wanted more children, so he lost little time in choosing his new queen, Hildegard. She gave him nine children, four boys and five girls, before she died in April 783 at the age of twenty-five. She had been married at the age of twelve: at that time, girls married as soon as they reached puberty in order to exploit their reproductive abilities to the full. Naturally, the four boys were baptized with the traditional names of Frankish kings. The first was called Charles, after his father and great-grandfather, while the second, born in 777, inherited the name of his uncle and his great-uncle, Carloman. The twins born in 778 were baptized with more ancient names that did not belong to the Carolingian stock. One was called Louis, which in spite of its apparent diversity is in fact the same name as Clovis, the first Christian king of the Franks. His twin, who died within a few months, was called Lothar, the contemporary form of Chlothar, who was another glorious Merovingian king. Clearly these names reveal a desire to create a link with the Merovingian dynasty by using its names taken from ancient chronicles in order to emphasize the continuity of the Frankish kingdom after the dynastic change. Charles probably became urgently aware of this political necessity in the disastrous year of 778, which saw the defeat of his campaign against the Arabs and the first dramatic insurrection of the Saxons.

The political significance of names was not so rigid for girls, as they did not inherit. Yet where possible, their names tended to continue the family tradition. Of the five girls that Hildegard produced, one was named after the mother and another Adelaide, but both died young. The daughters who survived were called Rotrude after Charles's grandmother, Bertrada after his mother, and Gisla after his sister.

The Crisis of 781

Precisely because of their political importance, names could even be changed, as occurred in 781 when the second-born by Charles and Hildegard, who had been called Carloman up until that moment, was baptized in Rome by the pope and adopted the new name of Pepin. Since his birth in 777, it had been decided that Pope Adrian would baptize him in order to renew the godparentage that had united his predecessors with King Pepin and symbolically reinforce his friendship with the Franks. Charles had promised to bring his son to Rome for Easter of 778, but a sudden change in the political situation in Spain forced him to postpone it in order to lead the abortive expedition beyond the Pyrenees. But the commitment to the pope had been made and it would have been impossible to cancel without a diplomatic incident. The baptism was therefore postponed until the king had time to travel to Rome, and this occurred at Easter of 781.

The most surprising thing was that they used the occasion to change the child's name to Pepin, although the first Pepin was still alive and well. There can be only one explanation: the priests were beginning to have a greater hold over the mature king, who was now approaching his fortieth year. They explained to him that the first Pepin, the Hunchback, having been born to a marriage that the Church by now considered illegitimate, was not qualified for the throne. Of course, Hildegard must have played her part in persuading her husband, as this meant depriving the son by "the other woman" of his inheritance and shifting her own children into the foreground. What mother would have been able to resist this temptation, especially when the Church was giving her such encouragement?

Charles gave in, just as he had given in to the removal of Himiltrude in order to marry the Lombard, and as soon as possible he created another Pepin, this time a legitimate one. By choosing this name, he made known to the world that his firstborn had been marginalized. If he agreed to give up his hereditary rights, the Hunchback may have been promised that he would become bishop of Metz, a position that had been held by Arnulf, the founder of the dynasty. While waiting for him to become an adult capable of making his own decision, people tried not to make the situation too difficult for him. So Pepin continued to live with his father and was officially the firstborn, even though it was clear that the young Charles now filled this position. When in 791 the bishop of Metz died, the pressures were renewed with the sole result that the Hunchback, by now twenty years old, organized a conspiracy against his father. Arrested and condemned to death by the assembly, Pepin was saved by the king and sent to the monastery of Prüm, where he died in 811. The see of Metz remained open until then, as though Charlemagne always hoped that his rebellious son would one day give in and accept his destiny.

Fastrada, Liudgard, and the Concubines

In 783 when Hildegard died, Charles had only just reached the age of forty. He had had three wives, of whom two had been legitimate, and he still had four surviving sons and three surviving daughters. Although the first duty of a king was to provide an heir for his people, anyone else in his place might have been contented with his lot and perhaps listened to his priests who counseled celibacy for widowers. Charles, however, did not like to be on his own. A few months after his wife's death, he returned to his homeland from the war in Saxony for the sole purpose of marrying Fastrada, an extremely young bride who gave him two daughters, Theodrada and Hiltrude, in eleven years. She died in August 794, during the Council of Frankfurt. There should be no surprise that these women died before their husband, because although they avoided the risks and hardships of war, those of giving birth were even more serious. Moreover, the wives of kings, whose duty it was to give the kingdom and the dynasty as many potential heirs as possible, were literally worn down by continuous pregnancies. "Alas," wrote Paul the Deacon in Hildegard's epitaph, "oh mother of kings, alas, the glory and the pain!"[39]

Fastrada's influence on Charles does not appear to have been a good one. It is perhaps no coincidence that the two principal plots against the king, Hardrad's in 786 and Pepin the Hunchback's in 792, both occurred when she was queen. In the second case the plotters, according to the royal chronicler, decided upon this course of action precisely because of the queen's cruelty.[40] It may also be that relations between husband and wife deteriorated over time. Einhard reluctantly admits that during his marriage to Fastrada a concubine whose name he claims not to remember gave birth to a daughter by the king, called Rothaid.[41] Even making allowances for Charles's rather exuberant vitality, this is the only reference we have to a professed concubine during a period in which the king was officially married. It is also true that the only surviving private letter of Charlemagne's is a letter to Fastrada in which, like so many soldiers over the centuries, he complains that she does not write to him enough.[42]

When Fastrada died, Charles was over fifty, and he married once again to the Alamanna called Liudgard, who did not provide him with any children, or at least none that survived the dangers of the first few months of life, as at the time one baby in two died before the age of one. In 800, a few months before the imperial coronation, Liudgard also died and was sadly mourned by the court scholars, who had detested Fastrada.[43] After her, the emperor had no more legitimate wives, only concubines, possibly because in the meantime his three legitimate sons had become adults and two of them had already had children, so the succession had been ensured for the kingdom, and there was no point in complicating matters further by putting other heirs into the world.

Einhard, who provided us with these details, also gives us the names of Charles's four female companions who followed the death of his last wife. The first, Madelgard, gave him a daughter, Ruothild. The Saxon Gersvinda gave birth to another daughter, Adeltrude. Regina had two boys, Drogo and Hugo, and Adalinda produced another son, Theodoric.[44] These three sons, who were conceived when Charles was sixty years or more, were clearly considered illegitimate, and no one thought that they could share the inheritance of the kingdom with their half brothers. It is true that they were given the names of ancestors, but these were all ancestors who did not become kings. On their father's death, all three of them were tonsured and dispatched to an ecclesiastical career by their half brother Louis the Pious, who did however treat them generously. Drogo became the bishop of Metz and the imperial arch-chaplain. Hugo was the abbot of several important monasteries, including St-Bertin, St-Quentin, and probably Novalesa, before being killed in battle in 844 during the civil wars between Louis's sons. Only Theodoric died as a child in 818. At least two other abbots, Ricbodus, abbot of St-Riquier, and Bernard, abbot of Moutier-St-Jean, are believed to have been sons of the emperor by unknown mothers, but we are now in the realm of affections and sexual relationships that were entirely private and about which many things have been lost to us forever.

Paternal Feelings

The final balance sheet for Charles's sexual appetites is impressive, and that is only taking into account the women and offspring of whose existence we can be certain. It appears that by five wives and six concubines the king had ten sons and ten daughters. In his own way Charles was inordinately fond of this numerous progeny, although in purely emotional terms the relationship with the girls was more important than the one with the boys. Leaving aside the tragedy of Pepin the Hunchback, both the other Pepin and Louis were established from early childhood in their respective kingdoms of Italy and Aquitaine, where their presence was purely symbolic but no less indispensable for that. Their familiarity with their father could not therefore have been particularly great, but this was certainly not the case with the girls and the illegitimate sons.

The last years of the emperor's life were marred by a series of premature deaths. Pepin, the king of Italy, died in 810 at the age of thirty-three. The same year saw the death of Charles's eldest daughter, Rotrude, whom he had promised as a wife to Constantine VI but then refused. The following year, Pepin the Hunchback died in the monastery of Prüm in which he had been shut up for many years, and what was worse, so did Charles, the oldest of his legitimate sons, the one destined to succeed him in the Frankish kingdom and perhaps to take the imperial crown. Of all his male offspring only Louis, the king of Aquitaine since 781, survived to become co-emperor a year before his father's death. He was perhaps the most distant in character from his energetic, sensuous, and unscrupulous father. Einhard, who would have liked to show that his hero had the stoical nature of the ancient philosophers, was almost embarrassed to admit that Charles could not accept the death of his children with Christian resignation but openly displayed his grief and cried.[45] Only Pepin left a son, Bernard, and five daughters, and the grandfather wanted his grandson to succeed to the throne of Italy, but this did not save him from his sad fate under the reign of his uncle, Louis the Pious.

The company of his daughters rendered Charles's old age less unhappy. The emperor would not allow any of them to marry, but the looseness of morals at the Frankish court meant that more than one had semiofficial and long-term relationships. Thus Rotrude had a son called Louis by Count Rorgon of Maine, and that son went on to become the abbot of St-Denis. Bertrada had several sons by the poet Angilbert, the abbot of St-Riquier, one of whom was the historian Nithard. During the very last years of Charles's life, his adult daughters were joined by the five orphaned daughters of King Pepin of Italy, whom he wanted with him in Aachen. It was this multitude of women and girls who on 28 January 814 organized the old emperor's funeral, and if their brother and uncle, Louis the Pious, hastened as soon as he arrived at the palace "to drive away that crowd of women who were far too numerous" (as one of his biographers praises him for doing),[46] we can only conclude once again that father and son had very different characters.

SEVEN

Government of the Empire

The Institutions

THE KING AND HIS SUBJECTS
King and Priest

"The fundamental institution in the Frankish kingdom is kingship itself."[1] With these words, the Belgian historian François-Louis Ganshof describes perfectly the situation at the time of Charlemagne. The king exercised sovereign power over his kingdom. All its inhabitants were completely subject to his authority, without distinction of rank or nation. Franks did not enjoy any privileges in relation to the Romans, Burgundians, *Alamanni*, or Bavarians, at least not in legal matters (in politics they did). Nobles and prelates had to obey their king just as readily as any other free man, and the king had the power of life and death over all of them. King of the Lombards as well as the Franks, Charles could have repeated the words of his distant predecessor Rotharis: "If someone together with the king shall decide on the death of another person, or shall kill a man by his order, he shall not be guilty of anything; since we believe that the hearts of kings are in the hands of God (Proverbs 21.1), it is not possible to defend any man whom the king has ordered to kill."[2]

Yet this absolute power had nothing to do with tyranny. It was a salutary kingship modeled on the example of the kings of Israel, of which

Charles, the new David, was considered the successor. Christians were in the habit of interpreting the world around them as a new edition of the biblical world that had come before them. In their eyes, everything that happened had been prefigured in the Bible, and there the kings of the chosen people maintained a constant relationship with God, who conferred on their kingship an almost priestly quality. In 794 the bishops who gathered at the Council of Frankfurt expressed their wish that the king "should assist the oppressed, console widows, bring solace the unhappy, and be both master and father, king and priest, and a wise sovereign for all Christians."[3] Of course, this concept of *rex et sacerdos* was strictly speaking only rhetoric: Charles would never have dreamed of going up to the altar and saying mass and therefore was not a priest. However, as he had been anointed by the Lord and consecrated by bishops with holy oil, he was unlike any other member of the laity.

The coronation of 800 added the imperial dimension to his kingship, but even before this Frankish kings knew they had to subordinate their actions to the demands of Christianity. Bishops reminded them of their duty to rule their subjects with paternal affection rather than cruel dominance. Although political expediency occasionally drove him to cynical intrigue and calculated cruelties, on the whole Charlemagne did his best to follow this established tradition, which can be seen in his treatment of defeated enemies. For anyone who has lived through a savage era like the twentieth century, it is rather surprising that for the most part Charles was happy to have his worst enemies tonsured and sent to a monastery to do penitence for the rest of their lives, as in the case of the Lombard king Desiderius or the Bavarian duke Tassilo. He did not indulge in those mutilations for both symbolic and preventive reasons that were customary in similar circumstances in Byzantium.

As a direct interlocutor with God, the king of the Franks acted as a mediator between heaven and earth. This role was fulfilled by a series of events that were repeated every year with unchangeable and reassuring regularity. The spring assembly gathered all the free men around the king in order to approve his decisions and listen to his admonitions. The military campaign in the summer demonstrated his ability to lead the Franks to victory and plunder, thanks to God's favor that accompanied him always. The religious festivals of Christmas and Easter marked out the long winter rest, celebrating the concord between God and the king during the transition from one year to the next. In other words, time for the Franks was cyclical. Its rhythm structured the collective existence around the king, with a symbolic significance that went beyond practical requirements. It should not surprise us then that in the summer of 790, when quite exceptionally he found himself without enemies to fight, Charles, "in order not to give the impression of sluggishly lolling about and wasting time, sailed along the Main to his palace at Seltz, built on the Saale, and from there going back down the river he came to Worms."[4] Until old age slowed him down, the king would never stop, because the entire Frankish people lived through him.

Unlike the absolute monarchs of later ages, the king of the Franks was not only responsible for his actions before God, but also before his people. Originally, this had been the meaning of the spring assembly. The two ways in which royal power was legitimized, divine will and the consent of the Franks, coexisted not without ambiguity. Charles himself appears to have tried to find a remedy, albeit in a rather confused manner. First, the king's direct contact with God made it increasingly unacceptable that he should be subject to the judgment of men. Hence the gradual dissipation of the functions of the assembly, whose task was by Charles's time simply one of applauding, and the tendency to turn it into a religious occasion by taking the opportunity of this annual gathering to bring together a council of bishops as well. Second, the king's responsibility to the whole of Christendom meant that the consent of just the Franks was no longer sufficient to legitimize his actions. Hence the need to find another way to enter into a relationship with the totality of his subjects, irrespective of their ethnicity, which led to the extremely wide use of collective oaths of loyalty.

The Assembly and Consensus

The Marchfield or annual assembly had since time immemorial been the place where the harmony between the Frankish people and its king found expression. The ordinances about which the monarch had reflected during the long winter months were published on this occasion, which meant that they gained validity from collective approval. Back in 596 King Childebert felt the need to conserve a written memory of the assembly's decisions and ordered the transcription of this body's resolutions over the previous three years.[5] Here is proof that even in those distant times this gathering, which has always been considered by historians to have mainly a military function, had become a forum of political discussion. Indeed, that may have been its principal role.

At the time of Charlemagne, the nature of the assembly had changed in more than one way. Until the reign of his father, Pepin, it had been the tradition to convene the meeting for the calends of March, but it had now been put back to a later date. The Frankish army was made up of an increasingly large proportion of warriors on horseback and the wide range of the operations required the logistical support of an immense baggage train pulled by oxen. The grass therefore had to be already high in the meadows before a campaign could start. Moreover, the increasing presence of bishops at a meeting that was no longer exclusively for warriors meant that it was inconvenient to hold the assembly in a period approaching Holy Week.

An even more important change was that not all the Franks could take part in the meetings. Now that the name no longer signified the actual ethnic descendants of the invaders, but more generally all the free men living in the kingdom, the presence of every Frank would be unthinkable. The assembly now gathered together the ecclesiastical and lay magnates—bishops, abbots, and counts—and even this meant several hundred persons, each accompanied by his own followers. Some chroniclers continued to refer to the assembly as the "meeting of the Franks" or the "gathering of all Franks,"[6] in order to stress that this gathering expressed the consent of the entire people to the king's decisions, albeit through the mediation of the most powerful men in the kingdom.

Another innovation introduced by Charlemagne was the frequent duplication of the assembly. Apart from the spring gathering, now officially called the Field of May (even though it often occurred in June or even July), it was not uncommon to hold a second meeting some time in the autumn. In this case, the king did not convene all his warriors or even all the lay and ecclesiastical magnates, but only those to whom he wished to give precise instructions, such as royal envoys or *missi dominici* charged with implementing some new provision or bishops called upon to discuss some theological or liturgical problem. In the latter case, the assembly was difficult to distinguish from a council, and no one found it surprising that a king convened and presided over a meeting of prelates.

There is also the question of the extent to which the assembly was able to oppose or even just influence the sovereign's will. In such situations the balance of power is decisive. Under an energetic king like Charlemagne it is doubtful that the assembly ever enjoyed some form of autonomy. Of course, the chroniclers often write that the king took his decisions with the "advice of the Franks,"[7] and the prologue to a capitulary sometimes contains the words "everyone agreed."[8] Yet that consent, even if we do not want to consider it mere propaganda, meant the acceptance of the royal will and the commitment to obey it. It certainly was not a conditional approval that in some way could have been withheld, thus invalidating the sovereign's decisions.

Even this popular consent, which was little more than symbolic, was superfluous when the king had to make a practical decision such as a declaration of war. He was king and that was why he was there. What he could not do was introduce new laws without submitting them to collective approval through the assembly or, if necessary, on an even wider basis. When in 803 he issued a series of additions to the national laws of his peoples, which represented the first step toward the juridical unification of his empire, Charlemagne decided that the assembly's approval would not be sufficient. At least on paper it was still the assembly of the

Franks, and he had to legitimize changes that would also affect the laws of the Bavarians and the Lombards. He therefore organized a general consultation of the entire population of the empire and told his envoys, "the people should be questioned on the articles recently added to the law, and after they have all agreed, they should place their signatures or crosses on the aforementioned articles."[9] The possibility that someone might refuse to agree was not even taken into consideration, but the fact that when amending traditional laws the emperor planned to have the changes signed by all his subjects in spite of the immense organizational difficulties demonstrates that his power was based on a consensual principle.

Charlemagne displayed a similar respect for the will of the people in his *Divisio regnorum* in 806.[10] In this extremely important act over which he reflected deeply, the emperor who was by then over sixty established the division of his legacy among his three legitimate sons, who were all still alive. Having given each his portion, Charles played safe and made provisions for the inheritance in the event of one of them dying. The dead brother's part would be divided between the other two, and he established the exact terms of this division. But, he immediately added, "if any one of these three brothers has had a son whom the people wish to choose as a successor to his father in the kingdom, we desire that the uncles shall agree and shall allow the son of their brother to reign over the portion that previously belonged to the father." Of course, here again it would have been the magnates who interpreted the popular will. Yet it is worthy of note that even when issuing provisions of such importance Charles is willing to subordinate them to the consent of the *populus*.

The Oath of Loyalty

The enlargement of the consensus from the Frankish people alone to the multiethnic empire as a whole was implemented in part by the frequent use of oaths of loyalty. In principle, obedience to the king was obligatory solely on the basis of having being born in a country subject to him. Contrary to theories sustained in the past by German historians, the foundation of royal power was not at all a personal relationship. It was a territorial power, exactly as in a modern state. Yet, according to the mentality of the time, one undertaking could prevail over obedience due to a king, if entered into voluntarily. This undertaking was the oath, which took on an enormous political importance in a society convinced of its sacred, and perhaps even magical, value. An oath could be binding on a group of men intent on organizing a conspiracy. In such a case, each of the conspirators became convinced that the undertaking he had made to his accomplices had greater moral weight than the loyalty due to the king. This explains Charlemagne's distrust of all forms of collective oath on a private basis, so much so that he forbade his subjects to take oaths even when they formed religious confraternities or associations for mutual assistance.[11]

His suspicions proved more than justified in the spring of 786, when Charles discovered a conspiracy planned by nobles in Franconia and Thuringia, led by a Count Hardrad, with the intention of arresting the king by surprise and perhaps even killing him. Before the plotters had time to act, they were arrested and shut up in monasteries far apart from each other. Some were even sent to Rome. After having being forced to swear loyalty to Charles and his heirs on holy relics, the conspirators were tried and condemned to exile and the confiscation of their property. In a few cases, they were also blinded. It is not clear whether the leaders were put to death: Einhard wrote that only three of the plotters died while resisting arrest.[12] Even if we believe that he was embellishing the truth, it is significant that he felt he had to do so. Even in such extreme circumstances, the duty of a Christian king was still to show leniency.

The question of loyalty became acutely relevant in the spring of 788, when Duke Tassilo of Bavaria was tried for treachery by the assembly in Ingelheim. It was the dramatic conclusion to a conflict that had been simmering for decades between a prince who had originally been independent and the Frankish kings who wanted to force him to acknowledge his subordinate position to them. It was a murky affair, in which it is now difficult to understand who was responsible and if there was any bad faith on the part of one of the contenders. What is certain is that Tassilo was accused of having breached his duty of loyalty to Charles and having attempted to persuade his subjects to do the same: "he commanded his men to make mental reservations and falsify their oath when they swore allegiance to Charles."[13] The duke was condemned to death and then pardoned by the king, who shut him up for the rest of his days in a monastery. The point is that for days and days the assembly listened to an unending succession of witnesses and accusations, in which the same matter arose again and again: loyalty and the ways to ensure it.

These experiences undoubtedly encouraged Charlemagne to impose an oath of loyalty on all free men in the kingdom. It was something not entirely new, as the ancient Frankish kings had made use of similar collective oaths, but for some time they had fallen into disuse. There were other ways in which subjects were called upon to manifest publicly their loyalty. In times of danger, public prayers for the king were ordered throughout the kingdom, and it was specifically demanded that everyone should take part enthusiastically. After Hardrad's conspiracy and Tassilo's trial, the king felt that something more than a prayer was required. In 789 royal envoys were sent out to the various provinces of the kingdom with the task of gathering together all free men and making them recite the following formula. Even in the Latin of the time it sounded a bit ungrammatical, but its effectiveness cannot be doubted, particularly if uttered in church with one hand on the Bible or relics, "I, [the oath-taker], promise that in relation to my lord King Charles and his sons I am faithful and I shall be so for all of my life without treachery or evil intentions."[14]

The oath's implementation must have been very uneven, as is perhaps obvious given the inherent difficulties in carrying out such an enterprise in a kingdom inhabited by many tens of millions of inhabitants with no form of registration for births or deaths. It did not in fact prevent another conspiracy, which was discovered a few years later in 792 and was led by Charles's illegitimate son, Pepin the Hunchback. He had decided to risk everything when he realized that his father intended to disinherit him in favor of his brothers. Once the conspirators had been uncovered and arrested, they denied that they were guilty of betraying their oath by arguing that they had never made the often-mentioned declaration. This was a cause of considerable concern for Charlemagne, who, after having Pepin enclosed in a monastery and the majority of his followers either hanged or decapitated, immediately ordered further measures for collective oath-taking, so that on this occasion everyone really would be forced to do it.

The instructions to the *missi dominici* that organized the oath of loyalty in 793 were one of the most impressive measures carried out by the Carolingian administration, and they demonstrate how much importance the king attached to the whole question. The envoys had first of all to explain that the recent discovery of a conspiracy had made this oath urgently necessary, and they had also to reassure people that it was nothing new, but rather an ancient practice. This throws some light on the failure of the previous oath of allegiance: "The envoys must explain with reference to ancient custom the reasons why these oaths are necessary, and that now these disloyal men wished to cause great disorder in the kingdom of our lord King Charles and plotted against his life and, when interrogated, said that they had not taken any oath."[15]

The envoys, each of whom was responsible for a large area, had to arrange personally for oaths to be taken by bishops, abbots, counts, royal vassals, archdeacons, canons, and other ecclesiastical dignitaries. Every count was required to organize under the supervision of the royal envoys the swearing of allegiance by all the inhabitants of his county over the age of twelve, starting with holders of public office and priests and then continuing with other free men. It did not stop there: freed slaves and slaves who worked on lands belonging either to the crown or to the church were also included, as were even slaves belonging to private individuals, if they had been entrusted with duties of some importance or were part of their owner's armed retinue. It is difficult to imagine a more deliberate assertion of royal authority, one that went far beyond anything in the past: only the most humble of rural slaves who toiled on the vast estates of private landowners escaped the watchful eye of the king.

All other men who lived in that immense kingdom, even when not free in legal terms, had to undertake to obey his authority.

The general oath was repeated in 802, after the imperial coronation. Charles felt that the oath of loyalty to a king had to be confirmed and enlarged now that his responsibilities had been increased, and moreover many young who had reached the age of twelve since 793 had not yet taken any oath. This time the envoys were charged with enforcing the following declaration:

> I hereby swear that from this day forward I shall be loyal to my lord
> Charles, the most pious emperor and son of King Pepin and Queen
> Bertrada, with a pure mind, without deceit or evil intentions on
> my behalf in relation to him, and for the honor of his kingdom,
> as a man should be to his lord in accordance with the law, and may
> I have God's assistance and the assistance of these holy relics that
> are to be found in this place.[16]

The instructions added that everyone should be made aware of the magnitude and the significance of the undertaking resulting from the oath and should be made to understand that any disobedience would amount to perjury, even in the case of tax evasion. At least on paper, this was the highest point that the idea of royal power had reached in Romano-Germanic Europe: obedience to a sovereign was no longer simply a question of belonging to his people or living in his kingdom; it had been reinforced by a personal religious commitment that brought into play the state of one's soul in the next life. Even though no one actually ever thought of cutting off the hands of disloyal taxpayers, which would have been the appropriate punishment for perjury, on a symbolic level the emperor's authority over his subjects could hardly have gone any further.

By the end of Charlemagne's life, the collective oath had become a permanent fixture in the imperial constitution. In March 806 the emperor ordered that all those who had not yet taken the oath, mainly those young men who had become adults in the meantime, should take it. A few days earlier he had issued his regulations on the division of his empire among his sons, known as the *Divisio regnorum,* so he ordered that everyone should also publicly declare their agreement with this document too.[17] The last renewal of the oath took place in 811, three years before the emperor's death. On that occasion the envoys were given the order "to make our people promise loyalty again in accordance with the custom established for some time, and they should explain to the people and illustrate the manner in which the said oath and loyalty toward us should be observed."[18]

While Charles felt reassured by the idea that all his subjects had sworn an oath of loyalty, he felt equally disturbed by the habit of swearing on the life of the king and his sons, which had spread among the people. Undoubtedly those who used this formula meant it as a solemn undertaking that was even stronger than swearing on their own lives or those of their own sons, but how could he be sure that their number did not include the occasional perjurer willing to get off lightly in the various situations, particularly juridical ones, in which persons were called upon to take an oath? Moreover, how was he to overcome the superstitious fear that such oaths, if false, might bring down some terrible misfortune on the heads of the emperor and the young kings? To avoid such problems, Charlemagne ordered his envoys in 803 to make sure that no one, from that time on, should use such a formula when taking an oath.[19]

CENTRAL GOVERNMENT
Residence or Capital?

Unlike the Byzantium or the Lombard kingdom, the kingdom of the Franks did not have a real capital. The king was constantly moving about, convening the spring gathering in the theater of military operations expected for that year and leading the army in its campaign throughout the summer. After the great hunting expeditions of the autumn, Charlemagne would winter in one of his country residences and generally spend the entire period from Christmas to Easter there, although there might be an occasional visit to some city or other for political or liturgical reasons. Analysis of his itineraries shows that while his father had preferred the palaces in Neustria, such as Verberie, Attigny, Quierzy, and Compiègne, Charles preferred localities in Austrasia, between the Meuse and the Rhine: above all Herstal, the ancient property of his ancestors, then Thionville, Worms, where the palace burned down in 790 and had to be abandoned, Ingelheim, and Nijmegen. From 794 the king started to show a preference for residing in Aachen, where a few years earlier he had embarked upon the construction of the most imposing of all his palaces.

The new center was only a day's journey from Herstal and was not chosen for geopolitical reasons. Its attraction consisted solely of its spa waters, which were excellent for an aging man who had to treat his arthritis. Some historians, dazzled by the buildings that Charles had built in the style of Rome, Ravenna, and Constantinople, have come to the conclusion that the emperor had finally decided to provide his empire with a capital. In reality, Aachen was no more than a favored residence and not the fixed center of his administration. This explains why Charles never turned it into an episcopal see, which he could have done very easily and would have needed to do if he really wished to make it the new Rome. The longer durations of his residence in Aachen were mainly due to the king's increasing years. He had less and less desire to be on the move, although political and particularly military reasons still forced him to do so from time to time. Although after 807 he was not in the habit of leaving Aachen in either winter or summer (except of course for the obligatory hunting expeditions in the nearby Ardennes forest), incidents on the Danish frontier in 810 and Norse incursions on the western coast in 811 did mean that he had to hasten personally to oversee the situation, in spite of his nearly seventy years of age.

The Palatium

In the absence of a capital, the main instrument of government available to the king was the *palatium*. This term did not mean a residence, but rather the whole collection of personal assistants to the sovereign, who followed him on all his travels and whom chivalric literature rendered immortal with the name of paladins. For reasons that are not difficult to understand, the office of mayor of the palace had been abolished since the time of Pepin. The most important minister was now possibly the count palatine, who was responsible for examining the judicial appeals that arrived at the palace in great number.[20] Then there was the chamberlain, who was responsible for the finances or, to put it in less anachronistic terms, was the keeper of the royal purse. The seneschal, originally just the name for the head steward in charge of royal meals, developed into a supervisor for the crown properties, who ensured provisions for the palace. There were also a butler responsible for the cellars and therefore the production of wine in the vineyards of the large crown estates, and a *comes stabuli* or constable, who looked after the royal stables and therefore also the supply of horses for the army.

We should not overestimate the specialization of these ministers, each of whom would almost certainly have had a large team of assistants to whom they would delegate the day-to-day management of their duties, while keeping their political responsibility. Being all in the king's confidence and meeting him on a daily basis, they could be charged with missions that had nothing to do with the office they held, such as embassies or, more often, the command of military expeditions. Several leading figures, whom we might have expected to find at the palace directing their various departments, were killed in battle while acting as military commanders. Thus the seneschal Eggihard and the count palatine Anselm fell at Roncesvalles in 778, and the chamberlain Adalgisile and the constable Geilo at the battle of Süntel in 782.[21]

Chapel and Chancellery

The chaplains or clergymen responsible for the chapel were part of the palace staff. The term "chapel," which today has a very general meaning, was only used by the Franks at the time, and it referred specifically to the palace oratory, which contained a very precious relic, the cape of Saint Martin, the patron saint of Gaul, that the saint cut in two with his sword in order to clothe a poor man. Every day the chaplains offered mass in the presence of the king. When they entered into service at the palace, they put themselves in his hands and took an oath of loyalty similar to the one for his vassals. Understandably, when Charlemagne had to appoint a bishop, the choice not infrequently fell on one of these men who knew him personally and were dedicated to serving him. The chapel was therefore the training ground for a large part of the upper ranks of the imperial clergy.

The head of the chaplains was the arch-chaplain. Fulradus, the abbot of St-Denis, held this extremely important ecclesiastical post until 784, then Angilramnus, bishop of Metz, who died during the campaign against the Avars in 791, and finally Hildebald, bishop of Cologne, who was to be the first signatory to Charles's will. The arch-chaplain was responsible for the liturgy and was also the highest religious authority in the kingdom; the king asked his advice on affairs of ecclesiastical hierarchy and discipline. Charles expressly obtained the title of archbishop for both Angilramnus and Hildebald (but not, it should be noted, for their sees, which remained simple bishoprics, while they were archbishops "of the holy palace") and dispensation from the requirement of residence in order to keep them at his side. When one of the chaplains was to be put forward for promotion to a bishopric, it was the arch-chaplain who dealt with the process, and this suggests that he had a powerful role in making and breaking the careers of the senior clergy.

The excessive power of the chaplains was not without its critics. Wala, Charlemagne's cousin, and the abbot of Corbie condemned "the clergymen who serve at the palace and are vulgarly called chaplains (because this is not at all an ecclesiastical order). They are only there to further their careers and get rich. They are not answerable to a bishop like other members of the clergy, nor to an abbot like monks, and so they live without any rules and without being responsible to anyone."[22] Clearly the political and economic advantages enjoyed by the staff of the palatine chapel riled many people, but it is significant that these mutterings only came out into the open after Charlemagne's death. Before making his accusation Abbot Wala waited for the reign of Louis the Pious, who was more willing than his father had been to listen deferentially to the critical pronouncements of prelates.

Some of the clerics in the service of the royal chapel were charged with drawing up edicts and possibly correspondence and capitularies. This group was directed by an ecclesiastic official who went under the title of protonotary or chancellor and solely because of his dominant role over the keeping of records must have had considerable political importance, even though he was subordinate to the arch-chaplain. We should not exaggerate the importance of this chancellery, which was not yet the real driving force of government that it was to become in the principalities of the late Middle Ages. The reign of Charlemagne has left a very limited number of edicts—an average of three or four every year. Of course, only a tiny part of acts actually drawn up has come down to us, but there is a striking difference in relation to the acts issued by Louis the Pious, which average twenty-five per year, and this figure tends to rise slightly with the following emperors.[23] We have enough evidence to conclude that Charlemagne's chancellery had a very modest output when compared with those of his successors, and this activity even declined during his reign, falling from six or seven acts in the early years to one or two in the final ones. Everything suggests that the empire was not governed through the chancellery.

The chancellery gained the addition of an archive, as mentioned under the year 813 by the royal chronicler, who also referred to the councils convened at the emperor's orders in Mainz, Reims, Tours, Châlons, and Arles: "those wishing to see these acts will find them in the aforementioned five cities, but there is also a copy in the palace archive."[24] It is generally thought that this archive was not of great importance. Thirteen years after the death of Charlemagne, for instance, Abbot Ansegisus of St-Wandrille was charged by Louis the Pious with the task of collecting together the available capitularies but only found twenty-six, while today we know of around a hundred.[25] This would mean that the palace archive conserved roughly a quarter of the capitularies published by Charlemagne. However, it is possible that the abbot made a selection of the available material, and the archive had more importance than has generally been believed. This would be more in keeping with the wide use of written records by the imperial administration, which will be shortly examined.

LOCAL GOVERNMENT

The Subdivision of the Empire into Counties

As has been shown, the governmental team at the emperor's immediate disposal was rather limited. The question now arises of how Charles could govern such an immense country in an era of slow and unreliable communications along the ancient Roman roads that had largely deteriorated or on the slow-moving barges along the great rivers. The solution was to establish a highly homogeneous legislative and administrative system across the empire by extending the methods of local government in force in the Frankish kingdom to the newly annexed territories. It is precisely because of this drive for unification that the Carolingian empire left such a deep and easily recognizable mark on all the countries conquered by Charles, in spite of its relatively short duration.

At the height of its expansion, the empire was divided into several hundred provinces, each of which came under the king's delegate, called a count. In itself the system was not new, because Frankish kings had already made use of a network of local representatives who went under this title, whose origins went right back to the administration of late Roman Gaul. It should therefore be made clear that Charlemagne did not divide his empire in counties, as school textbooks still occasionally claim, but rather he bolstered a system of deputies that was already well established in the local government of the Frankish kingdom. At the same time, there can be no doubt about the clear-sightedness with which Charles strengthened the system by extending the subdivision of newly conquered countries into counties and thus accelerating their integration in the kingdom. From 774, but particularly after the Lombard rebellion of 776, Frankish counts were installed in Italy. Between 778 and 781 the administrative system based on counts was introduced in Aquitaine at the same time as it was raised from the status of province to that of kingdom for Charles's son Louis. In 780 the organization into counties was extended to Thuringia and in 782 to Saxony, which the king mistakenly thought he had pacified. After Tassilo had been deposed in 788, it was Bavaria's turn.

In the administrative terminology, the province entrusted to a count was called a *pagus* (which led to the words *pays* in French and *paese* in Italian) and was generally equivalent to the territory of a Roman city or, in a non-Romanized area, the area settled by a German tribe, although there were plenty of examples of several *pagi* being put under the authority of a single count. In Charlemagne's time another term, *comitatus*, started to gain currency, which today we translate as county. In Gaul and particularly in Italy, the county corresponded to the diocese, while in areas that had been Christianized later, the dioceses were much larger and covered several counties. Every count was therefore obliged to work alongside a bishop, sometimes on a one-to-one ratio, while in other situations several counts corresponded to a single bishop. In his instructions to his officials, Charles never tired of stressing the need for constant cooperation with and deference to the church authorities.

Some historians have argued that the organization into counties did not cover the entire territory. In other words, each count was supposed to represent a center of power that coordinated areas of varying sizes, which were possibly not even adjacent to each other. They purportedly had power mainly over areas where the land and the people belonged to the crown. The reality appears to have been different. The empire was entirely divided into specific administrative areas, each of which came under a count. The only limitation on his power was the presence of church properties on which the count usually could not act to arrest wrongdoers, collect taxes, or execute sentences because of concessions from the king that were called immunities. This did not of course mean that the powers of the state were suspended in these areas, because all the duties were entrusted to someone who enjoyed the bishop's or the abbot's confidence, but whose appointment was vetted by the king. Such a person was in any case required by the law to cooperate with the count.

The Count's Powers

The territory governed by a count was about the same size as an English county, and it could therefore be controlled with relative ease. Within it, the count was to all effects and purposes the representative of the king: he collected taxes, maintained public order, administered justice, published and enforced royal decrees, and, when it was necessary, called up the men capable of bearing arms and led them to where the army was gathering. It goes without saying that the count was in no way the lord of this area but simply the delegate of the emperor, who could dismiss him whenever he pleased. In other words, he was a public official, although no qualification or particular professional skills were required for the job. There was, however, a requirement for ability to take command, considerable means, and influential relations. As long as he did not make any serious mistakes or commit any openly disloyal acts, a count could expect to keep the position for his whole life.

There were in fact several examples of the same family handing down the position of count from father to son or from uncle to nephew through several generations. The office of count of Oberrheingau or Upper Rhine was held by a certain Rupert who died before 764, then his son Cancor who died in 771, followed by his son Eimeric who died in 785, and then in 795 the county was again in the hands of a relation, a cousin, another Rupert. When he died in 807, he was succeeded by his son, who was also called Rupert. Such cases have made a great impression on historians, and there can be no doubt that in some areas a family of wealthy landowners whose support was important to the king managed to establish and consolidate its hereditary authority by controlling the post of count. It is also true that a family monopoly such as the one just referred to can only be documented in a very few cases. For the most part, counts were undeniably very rich men who owned large family estates and were members of a kinship network at the highest level, but the office itself was certainly not the exclusive and hereditary prerogative of the aristocracy.[26]

Charlemagne made provisions for counts to have resources other than their own personal revenues and allowed them to keep one-third of all fines. The economy of Carolingian Europe was based on the land and its harvests, particularly corn and wine, and not so much on money. In order to guarantee that his representatives had sufficient means, the king therefore had to assign to them part of the crown lands in the territories under their control. Unfortunately we have almost no knowledge of these land allocations, which did not involve the drawing up of any legal document, as they were not actual changes in ownership but simply temporary changes in the beneficiaries of their use. In legal terms, the allocation of crown properties could be considered an integral part of the office of count or, to use the expression of the time, of the *honor*. By this time there was already a clear trend toward the assimilation of these allocations into all the other lifelong benefices by which the powerful compensated loyal followers, and they had become so widespread as to enjoy a special legal status. Indeed, in current usage governmental posts were referred to as benefices, and in the future this association was to have disastrous consequences for the administration of the empire, but at the time of Charlemagne no one could have predicted this.

Frontier Commands and Multiple Offices

All school textbooks tell us that as well as counties, the empire was divided into marches, which were entrusted to marquises. In reality the situation was somewhat different. The fundamental territorial unit was the county in all parts of the empire, and the march was simply a term used in common parlance for frontier regions of the Frankish kingdom, where the Christian world came up against the pagan one. There was the danger in these border areas that counts, who had only a rather limited field of action, would have had difficulty in coordinating defense against any military incursions. Military commands were established along the borders, and more erudite writers were keen to give these the ancient Roman name of *limes*. Thus there was a *limes Avaricus* toward Pannonia, which became the nucleus of the future *Ostmark* (i.e., Austria), a *limes Hispanicus* beyond the Pyrenees to protect the march snatched from the Muslims, a *limes Britannicus* on the border with the barbarians of Brittany, and so on.

These regions, which were much larger than the counties, did not replace them but rather incorporated a certain number to coordinate military action. The Spanish *limes*, for instance, contained ten counties. Their military commanders were not yet called marquises, as the name only came into use under Louis the Pious. They were either called counts or took on the title of prefect. Thus Count Roland, who died in the battle of Roncesvalles, was referred to by Einhard as the "prefect of the march (*limes*) of Brittany."[27] Count Gerold, Charles's brother-in-law, was called the prefect of Bavaria after Tassilo had been deposed, and he was sent to rule over the Bavarians until he died in the campaign against the Avars in 799.[28] In some cases, these administrative and military responsibilities in frontier regions were attributed with the ancient title of duke. Back in 748 Grifo, the half brother of Pepin the Short, had been created duke and installed in Le Mans to oversee the march of Brittany, with as many as twelve counties under his authority, and in 790 the same title and position were temporarily given to the oldest of Charlemagne's legitimate sons, who was also called Charles.[29]

Notker refers to these military commands when praising the emperor who, unlike so many monarchs of his time, "did not assign more than one county to a single count, except when they were stationed on the borders or were in contact with barbarians."[30] It appears that the accolade was not altogether merited, because Charlemagne did give a single count the control of more than one county, at least in the final years of his reign. In 808 the instructions for assembling the army ordered every count to lead all his vassals to the gathering place, except two who will remain behind to guard his wife "and another two who will be commanded to remain at home to attend to his duties and carry out our administration." Charles then added that "the count shall be able leave at home as many pairs of men as he holds offices, as well as the two who shall remain with his wife," and this clearly means that a count could be responsible for several counties at one time.[31]

The Royal Vassals

When capitularies refer to royal vassals, the *vassi dominici*, they seem to imply that such men were to all intents and purposes the king's provincial representatives, who came immediately under the counts and held a much higher position than that of local agents such as vicars and centeniers. Generally speaking, they were simply those landowners or their sons who entered into the king's service by "commending" themselves and swearing loyalty to him. They undertook to serve him in war with arms, horses, and undoubtedly a squad of armed followers at their own expense, and as long as they remained at the palace, they were at his disposal to serve on any mission. This association with domestic service, which was the original sense of vassalage, was never entirely forgotten. In his old age Charles was reproached by a bishop for having too often chosen his envoys from "the poorest vassals living in his palace," who in his opinion were too easily corrupted.[32] After Charles's death, Walafrid Strabo drew a parallel between the royal vassals and royal chaplains, the former being laity and the latter being clergy, but both equally commended to the king and dedicated to serving him at the palace.[33]

It was the custom for most king's vassals to receive allocations from the crown properties, either through merit or simply thanks to influential connections. In this way vassals were installed throughout the provinces and formed a transmission belt capable of integrating local government through their cooperation with counts in running the justice system and recruiting armed men. When a new province was annexed, counts were appointed and royal vassals were sent to the territory. Following the final submission of Aquitaine and the installment of the child Louis as king, a chronicler wrote that Charles sent to the province not only counts and bishops in his trust, but also "many others who are called vassals, of Frankish nationality."[34] The systematic introduction of Frankish vassals to live among the Romans of Aquitaine and other conquered countries was a decisive feature in the integration of the empire.

The Royal Envoys

The real weakness in the system, as Charlemagne's successors were to discover, was the lack of control over the way counts behaved. It is true that they had to attend the general assembly every year, and it gave the emperor an opportunity not so much to listen to their advice as force them to give an account of their administration. But the only way to restrict their abuse of power was to find out what they were up to in their remote provinces. Given that each county came under a city of some importance, the emperor relied heavily on the local bishop. In 813, after endlessly repeating that counts and bishops had to get on with each other, he clarified that in the event of unresolved conflict, particularly involving the courts, counts had to obey their bishops. At the same time bishops had to verify that judgments had been made correctly and counts did not take bribes or give false witness.[35]

But the institution that was specifically charged with reporting on the conduct of counts was that of the *missi dominici*. A *missus* was simply a royal envoy who was delegated full powers and was charged to visit the area in question. In some cases, he was sent to carry out a specific mission, for example, passing sentence in an important court case or bringing news of a royal decision. In other cases he would monitor the conduct of the local authorities, especially when there had been reports of abuses. In the latter case, Charles established a simple and extremely effective procedure: the envoy installed himself in the house of the count guilty of not having administered justice correctly and remained there at the count's expense until all the wrongs had been righted. In a sense, the envoy was perceived in what we might consider rather archaic terms, as an extension of the king's physical person. Indeed, armed resistance to an envoy was tantamount to lèse-majesté and was punishable by death. In another sense, the systematic use of these envoys represented Charlemagne's considerable commitment to centralization of the administration, an effort to rationalize governmental procedures. It is extremely revealing that the envoys had to keep a written record of their actions and present a report of their missions on return to the palace.

For the greater part of Charles's reign, the royal envoys were appointed to meet each particular contingency in groups of two or even three or four. Occasionally they were appointed on their own, especially for missions of a very specific nature. On several occasions and particularly when organizing the swearing of loyalty by all subjects in 789 and then later in 793, the entire territory of the kingdom was divided into different operational areas to which a few envoys were assigned. It would appear that these envoys were not always able to resist bribery when carrying out their missions in provinces that were often very far from their king's watchful eye. In 798 the bishops Theodulf of Orléans and Leidrad of Lyons were sent on a mission to southern Gaul. They reported that nobles of the region had offered them rich gifts and were very surprised when they were not accepted, as the previous envoys had not had any such qualms.[36]

Bishop Ricbodus of Trier, who was also the abbot of Lorsch and wrote the annals named after that monastery, felt he knew exactly why the envoys were so easy to corrupt. Too often the king chose them from the vassals who lived at the palace and had not yet been allocated a benefice, which made them more susceptible to the bribes they were offered. In 802 the emperor, who had become aware of the problem, is supposed to have expressly refused to send such people on his missions ("because of the bribes," is the chronicler's comment), and he preferred to send cler-

n and counts, "who had no need to obtain gifts from poor people." Yet even before that date, envoys had often been bishops, counts,
or prefects, so we should not give more credence to this development
than it deserves. Besides, there is a great deal of evidence that even powerful figures could be corrupted, in spite of Ricbodus's prejudices. If anything, we might speculate that in 802 Charles took measures to restrict
the qualification for becoming a royal envoy and obtaining the related
privileges to those high-ranking officials that he sent to oversee entire
provinces, while excluding those innumerable palace envoys widely used
for more minor matters, such as tax collection.

More important in terms of rationalizing the system was another
innovation introduced in 802, which established the concept of the legation or *missaticum*, a specific territory assigned to two envoys or *missi*.[38]
The borders of such territories were fixed by using essentially geographic
criteria, and following the borders of counties and dioceses only to a limited extent. The envoys were bishops, abbots, and counts whose positions
meant they were already active in those areas or in immediately adjacent
ones. For example, Archbishop Maginard of Rouen, together with Count
Madelgaud, was assigned a very large area consisting of eight counties to
the west of the Seine and reaching the Breton border. As his archdiocese
was cut in two by that river, the emperor considered it more practical to
make only the western bank part of the *missaticum*. Other envoys, like
Archbishop Magnus of Sens and Count Godefridus, were not given a list
of counties but an itinerary, which in their case started from Orléans and
led over an extremely wide area as far as Besançon, before returning up
the Loire back to their point of departure.

In practice, in 802 Charles charged his most trusted archbishops,
abbots, and counts with the task of overseeing the operations of the
entire administrative and ecclesiastical apparatus over a wide area that
was convenient for them and in which they were already carrying out
their everyday business. This is usually seen as a policy reversal, because
from then on, the envoys were no longer genuinely sent out from the

palace or extraneous to the area they had to control. Indeed under the new setup, the whole point was that they had interests in that particular area. But in fact, in the past Charlemagne was already in the habit of choosing envoys who were local figures with strong links through their office, kinship, and economic interests with the area in which they had to operate. The guarantee of their correct behavior did not depend on an ignorance of local situations, which might have proved counterproductive, but on the trust the emperor placed in each one, and on the fact that they had to answer to him personally for their actions.

We should not exaggerate the consistency of the system, in terms of either the composition of the missions or the areas in which they had to operate. It is true that in 802 each *missaticum* was allocated two envoys, one of whom was either an archbishop or an abbot, and the other a count, but there are records for the following years showing that missions were sent out with three or four members to areas demarcated for a particular contingency. For instance, in 804 the emperor sent a priest and two counts to Istria to investigate abuses by the local governor.[39] Two years later, a mission was made up of two counts and an abbot, who was also head of the imperial chancellery, but when he became ill and had to abandon the idea of leaving, two abbots took his place.[40] In other words, the system had not yet been formally structured in bureaucratic terms as would occur under Louis the Pious, who was to make every archbishop take on the duties of envoy for his own archdiocese. Charles had a free hand in the choice of his envoys, and that choice fell on those who had proven their loyalty. Hence the royal envoys should be considered one of his most flexible instruments of government.

The type of action Charlemagne required of his envoys transpires from the circular that one of these missions sent to the counts who were about to be investigated:

We and all our lord's other envoys have been ordered to inform him by the middle of April of what has been done in his kingdom, of what in recent years he has ordered to be done, and what has been neglected, in order to be able to reward sufficiently those who have done their duty and to rebuke as befits those who have not. What else can we tell you? He desires no more than that we verify what has been done in accordance with his orders, what has been neglected, and who was responsible for such negligence. We therefore instruct you to reread your capitularies and remind you of all that has been asked of you verbally. Make every effort to merit God's grace and the just reward from our great lord.[41]

Charlemagne knew very well that he could only trust his men so far, but he was determined to make sure that his orders were followed through.

The Use of Written Records

As the above quote demonstrates, writing had an important role in the administration of the empire. Although the majority of the population was illiterate, Frankish society in no way resembled primitive societies based on oral communication. Its religion was a religion of the book, which demanded that all its clergy be competent in using the written language. Although its legal proceedings were for the most part conducted orally, its legal system was based on juridical traditions conserved in written form, and written evidence was given considerable weight. Equally, governmental practice encouraged the wide use of written documentation, although the fact that it was necessary to urge this activity repeatedly does imply a certain resistance or laziness on the part of administrative staff.

The use of the written word is documented at all levels. Before the annual assembly, a draft of the items for discussion was drawn up and may have been sent out to the participants in advance. Some of these agendas have survived.[42] The decisions made were sent out in the form of circulars to the local authorities required to implement them. The royal envoys received lengthy written directives as well as the oral instructions obtained directly from the king. Written orders for military mobilization were sent to bishops, abbots, and counts, with detailed instructions on the date and the place in which they were to gather with their men and on the equipment they were to bring. Envoys and ambassadors departed with letters of requisition, which entitled them to obtain transport, accommodation, and provisions during their mission exactly in the manner stipulated in the document.

The written reports that Charlemagne demanded of his officials were no less important. Every bishop, abbot, or count had to have access to the services of a notary, and there was no shortage of occasions on which these would be required. Such occasions were not limited to judicial proceedings, which obviously required the written records of court sentences. The envoys had to submit lists of the échevins, lawyers, and notaries they appointed during their mission, the names of all those who failed to report for military duty and did not have the means to pay the fine, the names of the immigrants who moved into each region, and the list of all crown properties whose revenues had been reallocated with a report on their condition. Even priests had to keep written records of the tithes they collected and the use they put them to, and the horses gifted to the king on an annual basis had to be listed along with the names of the donors.

Land agents who administered the royal estates were required to keep accounts. The *Capitulare de villis* ordered that they should keep records of everything they consumed or spent and notify the palace in writing of their stores. Every year they had to send a complete and fully itemized report of all their harvests and revenues "that by Christmas informs us of everything, subdivided and categorized, so that we can know what we have and how much of each item," the emperor concluded.[43] Clearly, it is quite possible and perhaps even probable that not all the local administrators were capable of fulfilling what was required of them. However, careful examination shows that Charlemagne's government relied more heavily on written documentation than prevailing historical conditions would lead us to expect.

THE ROLE OF THE CLERGY IN GOVERNMENT
The Ambiguity of the Institutions

Up until now we have described the manner in which Charles governed his peoples as though it were through a modern state apparatus with a central administration and local officials stationed around its territory. Such an approach is legitimate, because at that time there was also a clear concept of public power controlling a specific territory and governing everyone who lived there, in the collective interest and in accordance with the laws. The increasing importance of benefices should not confuse us or make us forget that counts were public officials in every sense of the word, however weak governmental control may have been over their conduct and however frequent their abuses of power and acts of violence.

Nevertheless this description of how the empire was governed is only partial. Charles controlled his kingdom, organized his peoples, and maintained public order almost as much through the Church, in an entirely matter-of-fact manner without anyone finding that the least bit strange. Bishops and abbots were the pillars of public order and answered to the emperor as though they too were in every sense officials appointed by him, which after all they usually were. The intrinsic ambiguity of its institutions, which was a feature of the Europe created by the Franks, resulted from the clergy's wide-ranging involvement in governmental activity, including the judiciary and even military affairs. This may be difficult for our mentality to understand, given that our outlook has been molded over the last few centuries by an increasingly clear distinction between the state and the Church.

The king was in the habit of using bishops and abbots as experienced political personnel who were more cultured than his lay ministers. Their organization had roots in the entire territory of his kingdoms, they were accustomed to working in a hierarchical manner, and they were therefore extremely well placed for relaying and implementing his orders. We can examine one eloquent example of the normal practice established in

Charles's time, although it actually occurred in the early years of the reign of Louis the Pious. In 817 Archbishop Hetti of Trier wrote to his suffragan, Bishop Frotarius of Toul:

> We have received a fearsome order from our lord the Emperor, according to which we must notify all the inhabitants of the entire region in which we represent him to prepare themselves to take part in the war in Italy. We therefore order you on behalf of our lord the Emperor to notify immediately and zealously all the abbots, abbesses, counts, royal vassals, and all the people of your diocese, that is all those who are required to do military service for the king, to prepare themselves.[44]

In this case, the archbishop is handing on the king's orders in his capacity as a royal envoy with responsibility for a large area, which was more or less the same as his archdiocese. The same person was therefore holding two offices, one ecclesiastical and the other governmental. As he was the metropolitan, Hetti considered it natural to use his suffragan bishops to implement the orders locally, and so in the area of Toul not only abbots and abbesses but also counts and royal vassals were to receive the king's orders from their bishop and were to answer to him concerning their implementation. It should be noted that Frotarius, unlike Hetti, did not hold any governmental office. He was simply a bishop, but that was sufficient for his involvement in the regular administration of the empire, even with onerous responsibilities.

A further example concerns the final years of Charlemagne's life. In 813 Abbot Adalard, another royal envoy and member of the clergy who resided in Italy, received an appeal from a priest who had been excommunicated and deprived of his church by the bishop of Lucca. The abbot ordered the count of Lucca to reopen the case, and after he had examined the situation, the count decided that the procedure followed by the bishop had not been legal. He therefore ordered another trial, but this time in the company of at least one other bishop and a certain number of priests, as required by canon law. For greater safety, he also had his own échevin take part in the trial, an échevin being one of the legal experts that every count had working for him. Thus we have a case that intrinsically concerned ecclesiastical law and in which the norms of such law were discussed, and yet the case was overseen by a count at the request of a royal envoy, who happened also to be a member of the clergy.[45]

It would be difficult to imagine a more tangible expression of the systematic overlapping of the governmental and ecclesiastical hierarchies, both in the service of the emperor. Indeed, there is a certain awkwardness in distinguishing between the two hierarchies and putting the counts and royal vassals on the one side and the archbishops, bishops, abbots, and abbesses on the other. The reality was that they clearly considered themselves members of a single organism at whose apex stood their sovereign, even though their fields of action were partially differentiated ("each to the part that has been assigned to him," Louis the Pious was to say).[46] Members of both hierarchies were holders of a governmental office or *ministerium* that had been entrusted to them by the king. That was enough to bind them to unquestioning obedience.

Being in the king's service often meant that bishops and abbots had to deal with matters that would appear completely unrelated to their pastoral or monastic vocation. Gerold, the abbot of Fontenelle, was appointed superintendent of the Channel ports and most importantly of the great international emporium at Quentovic, with the task of collecting customs duties.[47] Because most of the trade with England passed through Quentovic, Charles unfailingly turned to Gerold whenever he wanted to send an ambassador to King Offa. It seems unlikely that the abbot ever had any time for praying, but it was another generation before this systematic distraction of churchmen from religious duties started to appall some people. In Charlemagne's time, the custom of treating bishops and abbots primarily as the king's men prevailed over every other consideration.

It should be added that the political commitment required of bishops was in any case less than it had been. At the time of the Merovingians, the bishops of Gaul had been given wide-ranging fiscal, judicial, and military powers in their cities, and with the decline of royal authority they had occasionally begun to exercise them independently, giving rise to veritable episcopal republics. However, in the kingdom Charlemagne inherited from his father, Pepin, the power of bishops had been drastically reduced. The episcopal republics had all been removed, and counts had been made responsible for all duties of a fiscal, judicial, and military nature. Bishops kept only some privileges of varying significance, such as the jurisdiction over the clergy and church employees and the third or half of tax revenues, commercial duties, or fines that many counts continued to pay their local bishops.

Some of these prerogatives, particularly those concerning jurisdiction, which may occasionally have covered tens of thousands of peasants working on church lands, were of considerable importance and helped to consolidate the position of bishops as agents of public authority. Yet it was not so much the exercise of specific administrative responsibilities as the complete availability of their persons and their possessions to any order from the sovereign that turned the clergy in Charlemagne's empire into public officials. In particular, it was their willingness on all occasions to pass on the king's orders, their involvement in the chain of command down to local populations, their supervision at the king's request of the way counts conducted themselves, and lastly the frequency with which they were appointed royal envoys.

The Control of Episcopal Appointments

In the great majority of cases, bishops were genuinely the king's men in the sense that he was the one who chose them. The West had not yet been shattered by the investiture conflict, and nobody was the least shocked if the election of bishops, formally the responsibility of the local clergy, was manipulated by the monarch. There would have been cause for scandal if incompetent or corrupt bishops were appointed in this manner, but the fact that the supreme leader of Christendom monitored the nominations would if anything have been considered a safeguard.

We should therefore forget the modern organization of the Catholic Church, in which the appointment of bishops is the sole prerogative of the pope, and try to imagine a world in which the king chose the most suitable candidates, precisely because of his concern for the smooth running of the Church and the spiritual well-being of his subjects. This often simply meant that he chose those he most trusted and whose abilities he had had the opportunity to test out. This explains the high number of bishops who had served in the royal chapel, a regular breeding ground for brilliant careers in the clergy. It also meant that the king who created bishops could remove them as well. He deprived those who most incurred his displeasure of their sees, although he did have to provide good reasons for such a serious move. Playing on the etymology of the term bishop, which comes from the Greek for "overseer," Notker refers to Charles as the "bishop of bishops," and it is difficult to think of a more appropriate title.[48]

Clearly, many people were very happy when news of the death of a bishop arrived at the palace. The machinations over who would fill the vacant post would start immediately. The more powerful ministers and the queen herself would have their own candidates from their retinues, and they were not afraid to put pressure on the king to influence his decision.[49] Numerous anecdotes about the criteria Charlemagne adopted for vetting his candidates for a bishop's see were circulating in the Church long after his death. It was told that on the eve of St. Martin's, one of the most important festivals in the liturgical calendar, a cleric was informed of his promotion to a vacant diocese, and "full of happiness, he invited many palace officials and also many guests from that diocese, and he provided them all with a magnificent banquet. But having eaten too much and having drunk even more, to the point of drowning himself in wine, he did not attend the nocturnal oration for that most holy night." The liturgy of the palatine chapel was organized so that everyone had to sing a specific response. When it came to the absent cleric's turn, no one knew who was supposed to sing and, to everyone's embarrassment, the liturgy was interrupted. "Well, let someone do the singing," the king ordered with irritation. At that point a poor cleric nobody took much notice of had the boldness to sing the response, and although everyone tried to silence him, he kept going until the end. Predictably, the bishopric was taken away from the drunk and handed over to the poor man.[50]

The only occasions requiring papal approval were the appointments of those bishops in Italy who were suffragans of the Roman see, and of archbishops, as the pope was the only authority in the West able to ordain a metropolitan by bestowing on him the pallium, the symbol of his office. Whether the pope was willing to stand up to the royal will in these cases depended very much on the pope's personality, which means that Charles had a much easier time of it with Leo III than he did with Adrian I. Around 790 the king appointed Abbot Waldo of Reichenau as regent for his son Pepin, who had been made king of Italy while still a child, and as a matter of course he asked Adrian to appoint the abbot bishop of Pavia, the capital of the Italic kingdom. But Adrian did not agree with the appointment, and Waldo never officially became bishop, although this did not stop him from administering the diocese of Pavia for a time.[51]

The election of Leo III ushered in a period of greater adherence to the political line handed down by the Frankish king. This was demonstrated in 798 when Charlemagne decided to change the bishopric of Salzburg into an archbishopric to make it the center of missionary work among the Avars. Formally, the application came from the bishops of Bavaria, and Leo replied somewhat haughtily that he was happy to agree to their entreaty by appointing their brother bishop Arno of Salzburg to the rank of archbishop. But he wrote to Charles in a very different tone: "your royal majesty, whom God protects, has ordered us to grant the pallium to Bishop Arno and to install him as archbishop in the province of the Bavarians." He went on humbly to assure the king that he had already implemented his orders.[52] During Charles's reign, the king of the Franks really was the head of the Catholic hierarchy in every practical sense, and the pope was little more than his subordinate.

The abbots of the imperial monasteries also owed their position to their sovereign. Primarily, this category included those abbeys that had been founded by Charlemagne and bequeathed with substantial amounts of crown lands. Since it was common knowledge that they owed their existence to him and lived, as it were, at the expense of the state, these monastic communities were totally compliant to his will, to the point of accepting his appointment of their abbots without the slightest argument. There were also monasteries, including some very important ones like Lorsch and St-Gall, whose abbots at some stage had considered it opportune to commend themselves to the sovereign by placing their monks under the king's protection. In exchange, the monks not only undertook to pray for the king, his family, and his army but also allowed the monastery and all its possessions to pass under his complete control.

It is self-evident that the emperor could not always be aware of the local situation and would on occasion accept the candidate suggested by the diocesan bishop or by an abbot who wished to arrange his own succession. Nevertheless, the regulation issued by Charlemagne on this question demonstrates just how little he trusted such submissions:

> Neither the bishop nor the abbot should prefer the worthless to
> their betters, and they should not give them position because one
> is a relation or because they have come under some pressure, by
> presenting them to us for ordination after having hidden and elimi-
> nated better candidates. We absolutely demand that this shall not
> occur, because we would feel cheated and made fun of. In every
> monastery, a candidate should be raised such as to be useful to us
> and bring merit and advantage to those who proposed him.[53]

Charles concluded by reminding everyone that the final decision was in any case his.

The Assimilation of Posts to Benefices

The assimilation of church appointments to public ones is also demon-strated by the fact that these too tended to be seen as benefices in the contemporary usage. (The term referred to any asset, be it land, income, or position, that was not held as property but as a concession in the gift of the emperor, and as such retractable.) In a capitulary issued in the final years of Charlemagne's life, envoys were ordered to draw up an inventory of public properties, and "that they should not only detail the benefices of bishops, abbots, abbesses, counts, and our vassals, but also our own crown properties."[54] In an ordinance of 819, Louis the Pious established "that envoys who are bishops, abbots, or counts shall not have themselves maintained by others, when they are close to their benefice, while when they are away, they shall have the right to requisition provisions."[55] Of course, it could quite reasonably be argued in all these cases that the benefice was not the position but rather the possessions associated with it. In practice, the distinction was not so clear. Bishoprics and abbeys ended up being considered benefices that the king could assign at his pleasure exactly like the administration of a county or even just the benefit of a crown property for life.

Some considerable time after Charlemagne's death, a few more critical spirits were to challenge the established practice of treating senior clergymen as the king's vassals. In 858 Archbishop Hincmar of Reims wrote angrily that "the churches entrusted to us by God are not a kind of benefice or in any way the king's property, which he can give and take away at his pleasure, because all that belongs to the Church is devoted to God. We bishops, who are devoted to God, are not men who can commend themselves in vassalage to another, as lay people do, although we can commit ourselves and our churches to the defense and assistance of the government to promote the good management of ecclesiastical institutions."[56] But these were isolated arguments and the general consensus continued to perceive bishops and abbots as the emperor's men. Charlemagne's great-grandson Charles the Fat dreamed one night of being transported alive into the next world where he witnessed the sufferings of hell. The first of the damned that he encountered were prelates. "We were your father's and your uncles' bishops," they told him and explained that they had been cast among such torments for having spread discord rather than fostering peace. "Here shall come your bishops, too," they concluded, "if their present behavior is anything to go by."[57] "Your bishops": there could be no simpler expression of how the clergy ultimately answered to the emperor just like all other holders of governmental office, even though the Church was a separate organization and clearly distinguishable from lay society.

EIGHT

Government of the Empire

The Resources

PUBLIC ASSETS
Crown Properties

The crown properties were an essential part of monarchical rule. Frankish kings had established crown properties at the time of the barbarian invasions and had been augmenting them with every new conquest through aptly named seizures at the expense of ejected leaders and their followers. They had come to constitute an immense fortune: perhaps a thousand estates, which were called *villae* in the terminology of the time. They varied greatly in size but on average must have organized a workforce of a few hundred peasants. This meant that half a million men worked all over the immense empire on crown lands, and they had no lord other than the king. The entire surplus produced by their work was at the king's disposal and, as we shall see, he knew very well how to use it.

The king's possessions were particularly dense at the heart of his kingdom. In Neustria, for example, there is documentary evidence of the presence of crown properties in over four hundred localities, and there is hardly a diocese in which the king didn't own something. The picture is not one of a uniform division of land but rather an overall scattering of properties with a few areas of high concentration. No more than a quarter of the dioceses are densely populated with crown employees. Such places would have been regularly visited by the king, as he would stay in his *villae* when he was traveling in a region. Crown properties were less common and more set apart from each other in more recently subjugated areas, such as Provence, Aquitaine, Italy, and Saxony, which he visited only very occasionally. This was perhaps the reason why the original identity of the *regnum Francorum* was kept alive even after it had been enlarged and transformed into an empire.

"Quasi Alteram Rem Publicam": *Church Properties*

The crown properties, which included the vast private assets of the Pepinid family, were supplemented by the no less extensive properties of the Church. It has been calculated that Charlemagne's empire grew to include nearly two hundred bishoprics and over six hundred monasteries, whose possessions were sometimes enormous. The abbey of Fulda, Christianity's outpost in Germany, employed something like fifteen thousand peasant families, and the abbey of Tegernsee in Bavaria, another outpost close to the Avar frontier, employed twelve thousand. Church properties were continuously supported by donations from the king, but it would be wrong to perceive these transfers of ownership as progressively eroding crown properties, as Charlemagne, like his father and grandfather before him, considered the lands of the Church to be just another category of public assets, whose revenues were entirely at his disposal. Indeed when the emperor ordered his royal envoys to draw up an inventory of "whatever we own in the area assigned to each one of them," the order concerned not only crown properties in the strict sense of the term, but also church properties.[1] The chancellery devised a form for the description of both ecclesiastical and crown properties, which were clearly considered to be of the same kind.

It was not that church properties could be confiscated by the king at will and handed over to others. Such behavior would have been considered tyrannical and would have provoked violent reactions, even though in isolated cases churchmen preferred to keep quiet rather than clash with the king. It was simply that Charles, accustomed to treating bishops and abbots who owed their positions to him as his own men, found it entirely natural that they should make the revenues from their Church available to him and that he could use them as he saw most fit. This was like a second public domain: "quasi alteram rem publicam," to quote the expression used a few years after Charles's death by his cousin Wala.[2] The transfer of large estates and a large number of peasants from the crown to a bishop or abbot only meant that the latter was given responsibility for making those possessions produce revenues and organizing the labor of those men, but always ultimately on behalf of the king.

THE ECONOMIC EXPLOITATION
OF CROWN PROPERTIES
The Maintenance of the King

Many crown estates, probably between 150 and 200, were genuine royal residences, complete with a *palatium* in which the sovereign and his retinue could reside for several months, if necessary, in the certainty of being properly provided for. This was achieved by stores held in the warehouse and also by convoys of supplies that the factors of other crown estates in the surrounding area hastened to send off as soon as they were notified of the king's arrival. These residences, of which there were a great many in the ancient Frankish dominions in the valleys of the Seine, the Oise, the Meuse, the Moselle, and the Rhine, were spread out at regular intervals along the roads that led to the frontiers, so that they have been referred to as a planned system of stopping-off points. If Charlemagne traveled from Aachen to Saxony or Italy, he would always be able to spend the night in his own house, while perhaps occasionally staying with a bishop or in a monastery. This aspect also confirms the substantial equivalence of crown and church properties, given that, while the former were sufficient, at least on paper, to guarantee the maintenance of the king and his retinue, bishops and abbots also had an obligation to provide him with hospitality at their own expense, every time the need arose.

We should not give credence to the myth that Charles was obliged to move constantly from one of his properties to another and to consume grain, wine, and hams where they were produced, because there were not enough roads and means of transport to bring them to him. It is true that the palaces in which the king preferred to stay organized several estates in the vicinity in order to ensure the maintenance of the court for long periods of time, and that he generally stayed in parts of the empire where there were more crown properties. But there were so many *villae* and they were so dispersed that most of their factors never needed to host their master, undoubtedly to everyone's great relief. This does not mean that grain was left in warehouses to be eaten by mice or that wine was left to go bad in the casks in which it was stored. Every year each factor received precise instructions on what was to be done with the surplus. If the estate was not too distant from the palace where the emperor expected to winter, it would be transported there; if the planning of the summer campaign required it, it was sent to become part of the immense baggage train that accompanied the army. Otherwise, as was more generally the case, the factor had to sell it and send the proceeds to the palace, together with a detailed written account.

Management techniques may have been even more sophisticated. The king, like many of his abbots, realized the usefulness of allocating a different use to each *villa* and stipulated which were to supply the royal household and which to supply the army. Clearly, such a system implied a certain initiative on the part of the administrators: not perhaps the *maior*, the peasant foreman who organized the laborers in each *villa*, but the *actor* or factor who kept the accounts and was responsible to the king for an individual estate or, more often, for a group of estates, which in the administrative terminology was called a *fiscus* or even a *ministerium*. If we then consider that these factors were sometimes promoted from foremen and had therefore once been serfs, it becomes clear how the presence of crown lands could stimulate not only the economy but also rural society as a whole.

The Exploitation of Church Lands

The Church's wealth was also used for the benefit of the crown. Monasteries in the areas most visited by the king cooperated with local land agents in providing for the royal household by sending contributions that soon came to be considered custom and could not be changed. The abbey of St-Denis, which owned immense vineyards, was required to provide the adjacent *villa* every year with something like 3,200 gallons of wine.

More generally, bishops and abbots were required to send supplies every year to the emperor's residence or the place of annual assembly. These supplies were euphemistically called *dona*, or gifts, but were in every sense mandatory and extremely onerous levies, as can be seen from the letter Charlemagne sent in 806 to the abbot of St-Quentin. At the end of very detailed instructions on the contingent of armed horsemen that the abbot had to lead to the annual assembly, the emperor added,

> Regarding the gifts that you must bring to us at the assembly, send them by the middle of May to the place where we shall be staying at that time, and we would prefer it if by any chance you could organize your itinerary so as to be able to present them to us personally during your journey. Make sure that you are not negligent, if you wish to remain in our favor.[3]

Equally revealing is the story that Charlemagne unexpectedly turned up in a city and made himself a guest of the bishop. As it was Friday, he could not be served meat, and the bishop, who could not find any fish, was obliged to offer him cheese. The emperor took a knife, cut away the rind, and started to eat the soft part of the cheese. The bishop, who attended the king's meal together with the other servants, could not contain himself and said, "Why are you doing that? That's the best part you're throwing away." Charles, who did not like to be contradicted, tasted the rind, found that it really was good, and acerbically replied, "You're right. Arrange to have two carts of these cheeses sent me in Aachen every year." The bishop, distressed and fearful for his bishopric, said, "My lord, I can get the cheeses, but I cannot be sure that they will be exactly the same. I fear that I might be reprimanded." But Charles was implacable and ended the conversation: "Then you must cut them in two, and if you find that they are like this one, then put the two halves back together with a sharp spike and send them to me. You are welcome to keep the others for yourself, your clergy, and your servants."[4]

It is clear from the emperor's tone that there was nothing spontaneous about these gifts, and we might even be tempted to consider them a kind of tax. We would be wrong, however, because at that time the presentation of gifts was a way of expressing acknowledgment of the king's supremacy, and yet it also triggered a chain of reciprocal actions that the king too was obliged to observe, thus giving a concrete demonstration of the favor in which he held the donor. Notker, who provided us with the anecdote about the cheese, ended it by observing that once the bishop had fulfilled the emperor's order for three years at considerable expense, Charles compensated him with a generous donation of crown lands. In 817 Louis the Pious established that after his death, his two younger sons were to be subordinate to the oldest one and to bring him appropriate gifts every year. But he immediately added that the firstborn on receiving the presents had to give them presents of even greater value, reflecting the fact that he had been given greater power.[5] Clearly our understanding of these exchanges would be impoverished if we were to consider them a form of taxation solely because they were mandatory. Such gifts were brought by lay magnates as well as bishops and abbots. A court poet described with satisfaction the powerful figures who honored the king with gifts of great piles of gold and silver, chests of precious stones, purple garments, and horses.[6]

But there were other ways in which the church properties could be exploited to the king's advantage. On the lands of some abbeys such as

Fulda that were created almost entirely out of huge royal donations, the peasants had to pay a *census* to the king as well as rent to the monks, just as though they had been working on crown lands. In general, the medieval Latin term *census* was more akin to a form of rent than a tax, although when the king donated land and the people working on it to the Church but still insisted on collecting the *census* from its tenants, it more closely resembled a tax. In other cases, the obligations imposed on monasteries involved their workers' making an annual payment to the royal treasury. The monastery of St-Germain-des-Prés required its tenants to make a payment called a *hostilitium* in order to fit out a baggage train to supply the army. It is not surprising that some historians have looked on this levy as a kind of public tax, since in fact the monastery acted as an agent for the king, collecting a levy for the treasury among its employees.

Of course, not all the monasteries had the same obligations. In principle, only the so-called royal monasteries were affected. These were the houses founded by the king or at least beholden to him. The other abbeys, which answered to local bishops or even to the family of some private benefactor, were not legally required to pay any levy. In 812 the abbot of the monastery of San Bartolomeo in Pistoia submitted a legal petition to the court of the royal envoy currently on duty in Italy, asserting that his monastery was a private foundation, which was not therefore required to make a contribution, but when ownership of the abbey had been illegally acquired by some lay people, the custom of paying the levy had been established, "and from that day, they have been forcing me to go to the army, contribute toward accommodation for envoys, and pay levies to the palace, all things that are not required by the law, because the late Gaidoaldo, who built the monastery, left heirs who do military service." The judge ruled that as the family of the founder had already fulfilled its public duties, it was not right to force them on their monastery as well, thus finding in favor of the abbot.[7]

Not all the royal monasteries, moreover, had to pay the same amounts. When Louis the Pious succeeded to the throne, he found himself surrounded by complaints from monks who claimed they had been reduced to penury by excessive levies, and shortly afterward he had a list drawn up of the monasteries under his protection, only part of which survives.[8] Of those listed, fourteen were required to provide both gifts and contributions to the armies, sixteen were only required to provide gifts, and eighteen, with more modest resources, "do not have to provide either gifts or military service but only prayers for the salvation of the emperor and his sons, and for the stability of the empire." Diversity was the rule, but the underlying principle was that the Church, if required, had to provide for the sovereign's needs.

The Allocation of Abbeys as a Form of Recompense

As a further resource, the king could hand over entire abbeys for life. For example, a monastery could be granted as a benefice to a local count, on the agreement that he would use the revenues to carry out his duties. Concessions of this kind risked provoking discontent among the monks affected, and although Charles was not one to be discouraged by occasional mutterings, even he could not have been unaware that counts had the unfortunate habit of exploiting such an unexpected godsend to the point of bleeding an abbey dry. A much more practical use of monasteries was to appoint as abbots those whose services the king wanted to reward or whose maintenance he wished to guarantee while they continued to serve him.

The first category included many men of learning who worked for the palace. The best example is Alcuin, who was installed as abbot at the extremely wealthy abbey of St-Martin at Tours in 796. In the second category, appointment to the position of abbot did not involve the requirement of residence, given that the officeholder had to continue to serve his king at the palace. The chancellor responsible for the royal chancellery was regularly remunerated through an abbey. Iterius, chancellor until 777, was the abbot of St-Martin at Tours, and his successor, Rado, was appointed abbot of St-Vaast d'Arras. Another politician who obtained an appointment as abbot while continuing to serve the king in various roles was the Lombard Fardulf, who in 792 reported Pepin the Hunchback's plot to Charles and was rewarded with the wealthy abbey of St-Denis.

It should be made clear that it was not essential to be a monk in order to become an abbot, since such a constraint would have undermined its worth as a form of reward. Hence abbots by royal appointment were called "lay abbots," although they were usually members of the clergy rather than of the real laity (for example, Alcuin was a deacon). Very often the king enhanced the resources and strengthened the loyalty of a bishop by appointing him abbot of one or more monasteries. One of the most famous bishops of the time, Angilramnus, the bishop of Metz and royal arch-chaplain, was also the abbot of both Chiemsee and Senones; Hildebald, the bishop of Cologne and successor to Angilramnus as arch-chaplain, was abbot of Mondsee; Ricbodus, the bishop of Trier, was abbot of Lorsch; Arno, the archbishop of Salzburg, was abbot of both St-Amand and San Candido; Theodulf, the bishop of Orléans, was abbot of both St-Aignan and Lobbes; and so we could go on, although some of these cases include abbots who had been promoted to bishoprics.

For monks, it was not always very pleasant to be allocated an abbot from above, particularly because of the rapidity with which these out-siders used up their community's resources. The monks of Tours were dismayed at the large number of guests their new abbot, Alcuin, enter-tained at the monastery's expense: "Yet another Briton or Irishman who comes to visit his fellow countryman. My God, free our monastery from these Britons!"[9] It was not unusual for monks of an abbey placed under royal protection to petition the king to reconsider such a move and grant them the right to elect their own abbot. A collection of standard texts to be used in drawing up legal documents contains precisely the model for a petition of this kind: "from the day in which you granted us to him as a benefice and we lost your guardianship, from that day forth we have had neither clothes nor good food, neither soap nor food, as had previ-ously been the practice."[10] But while Charlemagne was alive, these heartrending complaints were unlikely to meet with a great deal of success: the allocation of abbeys as supplementary resources for bishops, counts, and men of learning and officials attached to the palace was too important a feature of his system of government for the emperor to relinquish.

CROWN PROPERTIES
AND THE ORGANIZATION OF LABOR
Factors as Iudices *or Judges*

The crown properties had a central role in the exercise of power, not simply because they were the main source of income, but also because they allowed the king to control territories and men directly without intermediaries. This was the result of the actual possession of large tracts of inhabited land where everyone was either a slave or at least an employee of the king. There can be no surprise that in the *Capitulare de villis,* in which Charlemagne regulated the administration of crown properties in an incredibly detailed manner, local factors are called *iudices.*[11] In the tradition of the Frankish kingdom, this term was generally used for public officials, but given that the etymology alludes more specifically to the disciplining of men, it implied a political rather than an economic role. It appears certain that the residents of crown lands were judged and punished directly by the factor and not the count when they committed some infraction or went to litigation. Of course, a distinction was made between free men, who had the right to be judged in accordance with their own law, and slaves, who were subject to brutal corporal punishment.

Church Lands: Advocates and Immunities

Here again the parallels with church properties are very clear. The right-hand men who administered church lands for a bishop or abbot were called *advocati* and were referred to in capitularies as though they were public officials on a par with counts and their subordinates. In effect, that is exactly what they were, given that they had to discipline and punish the multitude of laborers who lived with their families on church lands. The emperor stressed that advocates were required to know the law and judge justly, and to be sure of this, he stipulated that they should be appointed by royal envoys or at least in the presence of a count.[12] Although they served ecclesiastical masters, they were effectively part of the public administration. Louis the Pious was to give an explicit formulation to an idea that had already been implicit at the time of Charlemagne, when he spoke of "our advocates" alongside "our bishops, abbots, counts, and vassals."[13]

The judicial role of the advocates arose from the fact that bishops and monasteries normally enjoyed immunity. This royal concession barred counts or other judges from entering church lands to try wrongdoers, impose fines, collect taxes, demand hospitality from church employees, or requisition carts and horses, as they were allowed to do elsewhere. The diplomas of immunity were a development from the right of sanctuary that the earliest Christian emperors had accorded the Church and Frankish kings had later recognized. However, we should not infer from their widespread application that entire territorial areas and categories of people thus escaped the control of public authority, because the simple fact was that bishops, abbots, and their advocates held public offices on a par with counts and their subordinates. In the lands covered by immunity, public justice continued to be guaranteed and levies for the treasury and the army continued to be collected, but the agents of the Church were responsible, rather than those of a count. In other words, the granting of immunity did not mean the abandonment of powers and jurisdiction by the king, but rather their transfer from one service to another, both of a public nature.

Immunity also had specific limitations. If a thief or murderer sought refuge under the protection of the Church, the count would enjoin the bishop or abbot to hand him over. In the event of refusal, a fine could be imposed and the request would be repeated. On a second refusal, the fine would be doubled and the order to hand over the guilty party repeated. A third refusal entitled the count to use force in entering the area under immunity to detain the wanted man (although, in order to reduce the risk of abuse of power, Charlemagne did stipulate that any use of force required his prior knowledge and consent). The procedure may appear rather involved, but in practice it left ample room for negotiation, allowing each side to assert its rights and save face without definitively obstructing the maintenance of public order.

Obviously immunity did occasionally cause conflicts, as in the famous case in which Alcuin, then abbot at Tours, granted the cover of immunity at his church to a cleric who had committed a crime in Orléans. The man had been pursued by the local bishop's men, and that bishop turns out to be Theodulf, perhaps Alcuin's most famous rival among the men of learning at Charlemagne's court. Even though Theodulf's men produced a royal warrant that authorized them to arrest the fugitive, the abbot refused to hand him over and the people of Tours, fearing that their basilica might be attacked, armed themselves with sticks and threatened to beat the outsiders to death. A furious Theodulf complained to the emperor, and Charlemagne curtly informed Alcuin that he was in the wrong. The envoy sent by the emperor to carry out an investigation had some of the monks accused of provoking the riot arrested, whipped, and imprisoned. This conflict cannot be interpreted as an attempt to remove an area of private life from the jurisdiction of public authority: if the fugitive was protected by an abbot's men, his pursuers were the men of a bishop, while the king found in favor of the latter simply because in his judgment Alcuin and not Theodulf had abused his authority, which was public in both cases.[14]

BENEFICES USING CROWN AND CHURCH LANDS

A particular use of crown properties was their allocation as a benefice. A revocable right that lasted for life at the very most, a benefice granted considerable resources to a count charged with a *ministerium* or to a royal vassal who undertook to serve his king with arms and horses. It also drew on church assets. Since the times of Charles Martel, allocations using church lands were significantly called *precariae verbo regis*, where *precariae* meant the requests or entreaties presented by the interested party, and *verbo regis* stood for the royal decree that forced the bishop or abbot to give his consent. The Church was not happy with these allocations, which came dangerously close to permanent transfer of its assets, and Charlemagne, as a face-saving gesture, took care to ensure that beneficiaries at least paid the rent required by the law, but he would certainly not have entertained any idea of abolishing the system, as the clergy would have wanted.

Here again, the discontent emerged only after Charlemagne's death. In 828 Abbot Wala, while acknowledging the fundamentally public nature of church assets, proposed that their use should at least be distinguished from that of the crown properties: "so that the king should have public properties for the maintenance of his army, and Christ should have church properties, almost like a second public domain, for the benefit of the poor and of his servants."[15] The lay magnates retorted that no one should meddle with the system and that, if anything, it would be better to leave the bishops and abbots with just enough to live on and distribute the rest among combatants, given that the genuine crown properties were no longer capable of meeting military requirements. The abbot then quickly went into reverse and declared that, as long as due reverence was paid to the Church, the clergy would continue to pay as they had in the past, if there was a need to make contributions to the maintenance of the army.

The temporary granting of church and crown lands as a benefice to counts who represented royal authority in the provinces or to people of high standing who swore allegiance to the king and undertook to serve him in war with arms and horses, was a feature of what was later to become feudalism and was starting to appear at the time of Charlemagne. Historians used to perceive these practices as risking the breakup of the public domain, leading to a weakening of royal authority. There can be no doubt that abuses were the order of the day, although the emperor did everything he could to stamp them out. In Aquitaine, a foreign region in which Charles hardly ever set foot, crown possessions were already much less significant than elsewhere and were practically privatized by Frankish counts and abbots installed in the country following its conquest. This was so much the case that when Louis was appointed the new king of Aquitaine by his father in 781, he encountered real difficulties in organizing sufficient resources for his own maintenance. But more often the risk was exactly the opposite: the beneficiaries exploited the crown lands assigned to them without any scruples, and because they did not consider them their own, they reinvested the profits in their own privately owned properties. Charlemagne repeatedly ordered his envoys to make sure that this did not occur.[16]

TAXES

Obligations

The fact that the main royal revenue in Charlemagne's time came from crown property does not mean that there was no system of obligations imposed on his subjects that could in some ways be compared to taxation, albeit at the risk of a slight anachronism. In the first year of his reign, Louis the Pious granted uninhabited land requiring repopulation to refugees from Spain wishing to settle north of the Pyrenees, and he gave them a guarantee that they could live there in complete liberty:

> in such a manner, that is, that like other free men they shall serve in the army with their count and, as they shall live in a frontier region, they shall not neglect to carry out reconnaissance and surveillance, which in current parlance are called guard duties, when they are so commanded and advised by their count, and within reasonable limits. Moreover, they shall offer due hospitality and make available horses to our envoys and our sons, when for our requirements we shall send them to those parts, and to ambassadors who shall be sent

to us from Spain. But no count nor any of his subordinates or officials shall demand any other *census* of them.[17]

Here we have a description, albeit an incomplete one, of the obligations that were traditionally imposed on inhabitants of the empire. The king's envoys and ambassadors, foreign ambassadors on their way to the king, and more generally all officials when carrying out their duties had the right to be given shelter by the inhabitants and to requisition their horses. Columns of armed men traveling to join the army were authorized to graze their horses and, if necessary, to requisition fodder. The organization of supplies also required the preparation of carts and the provision of oxen, horses, and victuals, in lieu of which cash payments could be accepted. In principle, these obligations represented the participation of citizens in the running of the state and mainly fell upon the private landowners and free tenants, although there is the impression that, because they found it easier, the king's agents tended to direct these requisitions mainly at those who worked on the crown properties, including slaves who lived in their own households, while ecclesiastical bodies attempted with varying degrees of success to exempt their employees from such obligations.

Censi

None of the obligations referred to so far constitutes a tax on property. The obligations required of the empire's inhabitants were aimed directly at assisting the administration to operate and never involved the payment of sums directly into the imperial treasury for unspecified uses. Does this mean that there was no longer any taxation as either ancient Roman or modern society would understand it? Recently historians of the "fiscalist" school, which their adversaries prefer to call "hyper-Romanist," have argued that the ancient property tax, from which the later Roman emperors drew most of their revenues, had not disappeared, and they claim to have found evidence of it in Carolingian documents, but only after systematically distorting the wording. It is true that Charlemagne's legislation is very concerned about the payments called *censi*, which a great number of subjects were required to pay the king, and there are provisions that "no one should dare to forget the *census* that must be paid," "that the royal *census* should be paid wherever it is due, both the personal *census* and the one for land," and "that whoever pays the royal *census*, shall pay it in the same place as his father and his grandfather were in the custom of paying it." In reality, the *censi* were simply annual rents that had to be paid by "free men who own our properties *per precariam* and must therefore pay a *census*," as well as simple tenants on crown properties and even freed slaves, in which case the payment due for renting land would be doubled by a payment in recognition of personal dependency.[18]

Of course, there are aspects of the *census* that are similar to a kind of tax. In some cases it was collected on lands that did not belong to the king but to the Church. This apparent inconsistency is explained by the fact that when Charles donated land to the Church, he often added a clause stipulating that the peasants should continue to pay the *census* to the king, even though he was no longer formally their master. In such cases where peasant villages belonged in their entirety to abbeys such as Fulda or St-Germain-des-Prés and all the inhabitants answered to the abbey and paid it a rent as well as the royal *census*, the latter could ultimately be interpreted as a public tax, but it did not represent the uninterrupted existence of the Roman property tax.

Tolls

One form of genuine taxation was the *teloneum* or toll collected on the circulation and sale of goods. These were not arbitrary taxes but contributions required of merchants when the government provided a real service in exchange, such as the maintenance of a bridge or port, or the superintendence of a market. On several occasions Charlemagne, like Pepin before him, ordered that only goods actually destined for commerce should be taxed, and not convoys that a large landowner was moving from his lands to his place of residence. He also stipulated that new tolls should not be introduced arbitrarily, that tolls should be demanded only of merchants and not of pilgrims, and "that no one should be forced to go to a bridge and pay a toll, when they could cross without loss of time somewhere else, and that tolls should not be demanded in the middle of the countryside where there is neither bridge nor ford."[19] All these measures demonstrate the tendency of local authorities to increase the number of these levies, which clearly represented a tempting and difficult-to-control source of revenue. It was not without significance that the breakup of the empire, long after Charlemagne's death, was accompanied by a remorseless proliferation of tolls.

WAS TAXATION EXCESSIVE?

It is difficult to quantify the burden that the maintenance of imperial government imposed on its subjects. In other eras, for instance the later Roman Empire following Diocletian's reforms, historians have been able to argue that imperial taxation was so onerous that it obstructed economic development and created widespread social malaise. The impression is that the burden of taxation at the time of Charlemagne was and was perceived to be rather heavy. This caused real difficulties for independent small farmers and forced them to grant allegiance to local church authorities or powerful men, or even to become their slaves, in order to escape some of the obligations to which all free men were subjected. The conflict that arose in Istria in 804 provides an eloquent demonstration of the sudden increase in the tax burden in that province when it passed from Byzantine dominion to that of the Franks.[20]

In that year three royal envoys, a priest and two counts, were dispatched to Istria following local complaints against Duke John, who governed the region on behalf of King Pepin of Italy and his father, the emperor. Istria had been occupied seventeen years earlier during the war with the Byzantine Empire, and the inhabitants were in a position to make an immediate comparison between the conditions existing at the "time of the Greeks" and those introduced by Frankish government. They claimed that when Duke John took power, he confiscated the forest and meadows where the people grazed their livestock. When questioned by the envoys, the duke confessed, "These forests and meadows of which you speak, I thought they belonged to the crown, property of the emperor. But if you now swear that this is not the case, then I shall not challenge it."

Their complaints did not stop there.

> At the time of the Greeks, we were never forced to provide fodder, we never worked free for public estates, we never fed dogs, and we never had to raise money as we do now. We never paid for flocks, as we do now, having to hand over sheep and lambs every year. We have to provide transport services as far as Venice, Ravenna, and Dalmatia, and along the rivers, which we did not have to do before. When the duke has to leave for the emperor's war, he takes our horses and forcibly leads our sons away with him. He makes them bring carts and then takes everything and sends them home on foot. He leaves our horses behind down there in France or he shares them out among his men. At the time of the Greeks, they took one sheep for every hundred from those who had that many, for the needs of the imperial envoys. Now anyone who has more than three must hand over one every year. We are compelled by force to fulfill all these requirements and payments, because our fathers never did so, and we are laughed at by our relations and neighbors in Venice and Dalmatia, and even by the Greeks who previously governed us.

It may very well be that many of these levies of which the inhabitants of Istria complained were collected unlawfully by Duke John, who they accused of having been interested in enriching himself and his family rather than sending to the emperor his due. Yet the majority of the taxes complained of by the people of Istria are not difficult to identify as the levies habitually imposed in the Frankish kingdom. Everywhere else free men were accustomed to them, but to those who had lived under the Byzantine government they must have seemed oppressive. Although the duke was found guilty of overbearing behavior and abuse of office and was forced to renounce nearly all of the challenged taxes, this does not mean that the regime he introduced was significantly different from the one enforced elsewhere in the empire. For political reasons Charlemagne preferred to release his new subjects from such levies, which were simply accepted without protest by everyone else.

Equally significant were the protests against the patriarch of Grado and his suffragans, who displayed an entirely new attitude from the moment they came under the government of Charlemagne. They started to behave as though they were joint holders of public authority, which in effect they were in the western empire. "Once the Church paid half of all the taxes collected by the empire, but now it no longer does. In the public sea, where all the people previously fished together, we no longer dare to fish because the men of the Church attack us with sticks and cut our nets." The interminable list of complaints went on in a similar vein against the sudden arrogance of the bishops and their employees, which paralleled the complaints raised against the abuses perpetrated by Duke John and his men.

It may also be that on the periphery of the empire and in conquered lands, the Carolingian government appeared in its worst light. We should not forget that we know about this affair because, in spite of everything, one fine day the emperor's envoys left Aachen for distant Istria in order to investigate what was going on. This is a sign that the government machine was working, albeit in a laborious manner. All the same, we still have the distinct picture of a government in which public and ecclesiastical agents worked closely together to manage a command structure and a tax system that had sweeping, almost arbitrary, powers. It was not easy for free men to safeguard their rights, even when the justice system intervened on their behalf.

NINE

Government of the Empire

The Justice System

JUDGES
Local Tribunals

The main administrative activity carried out by Carolingian officials was the maintenance of the legal system, apart of course from the organization of the population for military purposes. Indeed the very concept of such things as officials, for whom there was no appropriate word in contemporary vocabulary, was often translated as *iudices*, or judges. The litanies chanted in Frankish churches implored God to concede long life to the king, his sons, all the judges of the kingdom, and the Frankish people as a whole.[1] The clear meaning of *iudices* in this context was generally all those to whom the king had delegated part of his authority. This use of the word was made possible by the fact that justice was not entrusted to specialists and therefore did not constitute what today we would call a separate power. It was administered directly at the local level by officials who represented the king, primarily by counts.

Every count was required to preside periodically over a public assembly, called a *mallus*, and on that occasion he would hear and rule upon the cases presented to him, with the assistance of a jury made up of people from the area. These *boni homines* were chosen from those notables who had practical knowledge of the law. Regretfully they also probably had interests to defend and influential friends. Each session was called a *placitum*. As convening a *placitum* involved not inconsiderable expense, which a region's inhabitants were obliged to cover, Charlemagne laid down that counts were not to hold more than three a year, and no one was to be forced to take part unless their case was heard.[2] At a more local level, the same organization was replicated using officials of lower rank, often referred to as *iuniores* of the count. They were called vicars or centeniers in the Frankish kingdom and *gastaldiones, sculdahis,* and *locopositi* in the Lombard kingdom. They held *placita* more often and dealt with cases of lesser importance. The emperor ordered that every case threatening a person's property or liberty had to be heard before a count, irrespective of the accused's social rank.[3]

This general description obviously leaves room for a certain diversity between local situations. In the Italic kingdom, for instance, the county system was introduced only gradually and with some difficulty. Counts were therefore often flanked and not uncommonly substituted by a local bishop or even a *gastaldio* or *sculdahis* when presiding over a *placitum*. In many areas, even quite extensive ones, inhabitants even though still subject to public jurisdiction were judged by separate officials. For instance, on large crown estates everyone, free laborers and slaves, answered to the factor: it was no accident that the latter were referred to as *iudices* in capitularies.[4] Equally, justice was dispensed among those who worked on the properties of a bishopric or a monastery by an advocate acting in the name of his bishop or abbot.[5] Then there were the episcopal tribunals, to which all the clergy were subject, as were lay people when they committed misdeeds of a religious nature, as in the context of matrimonial law. In spite of this multiplicity of courts, public justice was accessible for all free men within Charlemagne's empire and constituted a unifying element whose importance should not be underestimated.

The Tribunal of the Palatium

Apart from local justice, there was also the personal justice dispensed by the sovereign in his palace. Charlemagne specified on several occasions the types of trial that he wished to examine personally, and which therefore had to be referred to the palace. One sometimes has the impression that the emperor attempted to keep too many things under his own control. Among others, he demanded the referral of monks accused of homosexuality, priests who kept concubines rather than enter into proper marriages, and men who branded their dogs with the imperial mark in order to hunt unlawfully in game preserves. The reality was that legal proceedings heard at the palace fulfilled a twin requirement: religious on the one hand, by taking on jurisdiction for crimes that posed particular moral problems, and political on the other, by attempting to maintain the emperor's control over the more important cases concerning bishops, abbots, counts, and "persons of good family" in general, as one of the capitularies stipulated.[6]

The royal palace also acted as a supreme court of appeal for the entire kingdom, and later for the empire, although the devolved kingdoms of Italy and Aquitaine had their own *palatia* with similar functions. In truth, Germanic laws did not recognize appeal in the proper sense of the word, as defined by Roman law and still familiar to us today. Those who lived under the *lex Salica* or the *lex Langobardorum* could present a petition to the king when they felt that a judge had ruled unjustly and, if the petition was upheld, it led not only to acquittal but also to punishment of the judge. A capitulary states, "If someone wishes to say that they have not been judged justly, then let them come before us. But they should not dare to do so solely in order to delay justice for someone else."[7] We will leave it to the sensitivity of the reader to decide whether this form of appeal was so barbaric or, in any case, backward, as legal experts tend to think. The important thing here is to clarify that the majority of the cases heard at the palace were of this nature.

Justice at the palace was administered in accordance with a specific procedure. Lawsuits were examined by the count palatine, who would rule in the simpler cases himself and then prepare the other cases for submission to the king. Einhard wrote that Charlemagne used to receive the count in the morning while he was dressing, and if there was a particularly urgent case to be heard, he was quite capable of having the parties brought in, listening to their arguments, and pronouncing sentence on the spot.[8] In more important cases, the king did not pass judgment on his own but with the help of councillors, who were convened in numbers adequate to the importance of the case. In 783 a sentence was signed by three bishops, eleven counts, and as many as forty-four councillors, as well as the count palatine.[9] In order to speed up the trials of poorer people who had difficulty meeting the expenses, and to save on his own time, Charlemagne laid down that lesser cases should be expedited by the count palatine without the king's personal involvement.[10]

Knowing the ways of the world, we find it very difficult to believe that poor people really had access to personal justice dispensed by the emperor. Yet to our surprise, we have many examples of groups of peasants appealing to the *palatium* and protesting against the way those in authority treated them. Their cases were heard in the supreme court: so, for instance, when Charlemagne returned from Maine in 800 after having held courts of law, he found himself inundated with petitions from peasants in that province who were working on church and crown lands and had not been called to the *placitum*. Perhaps the local authorities felt that the sovereign should not be vexed with endless lawsuits about the extent of the laboring work that had to be provided by peasants on a landowner's land, but the king was of a different opinion. When he returned to the palace, he issued a general decree that was valid for the entire province, to forestall all disputes between landowners and their workforce.[11]

LEGAL PROCEDURE
Written Evidence

There is a preconception today that medieval justice was based on profoundly irrational procedures. Films and novels set in the Middle Ages repeatedly portray judicial procedures as involving some form of trial by ordeal with varying degrees of brutality. In reality written evidence was always decisive in Charlemagne's courts. Any dispute over property in which one of the parties was able to produce a valid document proving his rights was immediately resolved. Not surprisingly, anyone facing a trial in which they knew they were in the wrong would attempt to conceal any incriminating documents. A capitulary expressly makes provision for the case of a master fraudulently claiming back a slave who has in fact been freed, by first of all destroying the man's charter of liberty.[12]

This kind of fraud was often recorded in the minutes of trials. Bishop Theuto of Rieti took legal action against his brother Pando, who claimed the monastery of Sant'Angelo in Rieti as private property and won the case by demonstrating that the monastery was under royal protection. However, what modern sociologists call amoral familism prevailed when the bishop was dying, and he handed over the ruling that established the public ownership of the monastery to his brother and nephews. "And we," confessed Pando, "immediately burned it in the fire." When the judge asked him what was written in the document, Pando replied, "If it had not been unfavorable to us, we would not have burned it."[13]

This does not mean that such acts were carried out lightly, because the sacred nature of a written document was in some ways intimidating. Moreover, it was best to avoid personally dirtying one's hands, because sooner or later one might be called upon to take an oath. In a trial that took place in 786 before the duke of Lucca, the incumbent priest at the church of Sant'Angelo, called Deusdona, was accused by another priest of having first granted him the right to take over that church and then having stolen the related document because he wanted to give the church to someone else. Deusdona forcefully denied that he had done it but stated that as the cleric Alpertus was in service at the same church and wished to take it over himself, he, Deusdona, had advised him to get his hands on the document and destroy it.

And thus this cleric Alpertus stole the document and brought it
to me and said, "Here is the document that you told me to take,
now give me the church." But I told him, "If you don't destroy this
document, I cannot give it to you." When I had said this, the cleric
Alpertus in my presence gave the document to a British pilgrim who
was passing by, and in our presence the said Briton threw it in the
fire and there it burned.[14]

It is no surprise then that documents were often missing when it
came to the trial. Equally, when they were there, their validity could not
be above suspicion in an age when forging documents was far from
difficult. Not for nothing did one of Charlemagne's capitularies order
that a freed slave who had no other proof than his charter of freedom
would have to prove that he had really been freed by his owner by
demonstrating the authenticity of this document. This had to be done
by comparing it with another two documents signed by the same notary,
"and the notary must be a person known to and accepted by the inhabitants of the area."[15]

Witnesses

The relative scarcity of written documents meant that the most frequent procedure involved the summoning of witnesses. Summons is
not perhaps the correct term, given that it was not the judge who summoned them and there was no law forcing witnesses to appear. The
general idea was that one of the parties in the dispute, usually the
defendant and less often the plaintiff, was invited to demonstrate the
justness of his case, and consequently the judge granted him an ad-
journment in exchange for bail in order to produce his sworn statements. The outcome of the trial ultimately hinged upon the ability to
produce witnesses and have them testify, and it can only be expected
that this involved various hidden machinations. Trials were not without
sensational coups de théâtre, because it was not unheard of for witnesses who had been painstakingly persuaded by one of the parties to

declare suddenly, when it came to the moment, that they knew nothing about the matter.[16]

A genuine summons of witnesses by the court only occurred with one specific procedure called the *inquisitio per testes*, which had long existed in Lombard judicial practice and was deliberately introduced by Charles into Frankish practice as well. In this case the judge, who was often a royal envoy sent to investigate an unresolved crime or to examine a petition to the palace, summoned witnesses and interrogated them in relation to the case. Unlike the normal procedure, the witnesses were not called by the accused to prove his innocence or by the plaintiff to uphold his accusations but were chosen by the judge from the best-known and most respected inhabitants of the area. Their evidence was the basis for the judgment, which could not be influenced in any way by the parties and was pronounced by the king immediately after the envoys had provided him with the evidence of the witnesses, or even by the envoy himself. The procedure certainly had the merit of producing a swift decision, but precisely because of the impossibility of influencing the outcome, it risked the appearance of a heavy-handed and possibly detestable legal imposition.

Oath-Taking and Trial by Ordeal

In the absence of either written evidence or witnesses, the defendant could prove his innocence by taking a special oath. It was a last resort, which the judge was to make use of only when he could not solve the case in any other manner. The law of the Bavarians (*lex Baiwariorum*) states, "the case that has been examined and resolved with certainty must be ruled upon by the judge. No one shall be permitted to take an oath, and the ruling must be accepted. On the other hand, oaths shall be taken in those cases in which the judge's examination has not found any evidence."[17] It was an extremely formalized procedure that was a lot less irrational than we are led to believe. The defendant's oath was not enough: other people were required to take the oath with him. They were not technically witnesses in that they were not cross-examined over the facts, and in effect they swore that they did not believe that the defendant could be guilty. The law established the number of oaths required for each type of charge. According to the law of the Ripuarian Franks (*lex Ribuaria*), a man accused of stealing a flock of sheep could demonstrate his innocence by having seventy-two people take an oath. Charlemagne reduced this number to twelve.[18] Given that taking an oath meant calling on God as your witness and putting your own soul at risk, it is not so absurd that the presence of men willing to take an oath was considered convincing when there was no other evidence. In any case, this was preferable to an arbitrary sentence or an acquittal for lack of evidence.

Only when faced with very serious accusations and contradictory evidence was the defendant invited to prove his innocence by ordeal, or the "judgment of God." The most common form required the defendant to place his hand in boiling water or to walk barefoot over red-hot plowshares. The defendant would be found not guilty if the burns healed within a set period. The "judgment of God" could also be exercised in the form of a contest between the defendant and the plaintiff, particularly when the latter refused to accept a not-guilty verdict based on an oath, as the law provided for in specific cases. This meant a legal duel, but not one that led to the death of one of the parties, as it was usually fought with a cudgel and shield. Another system, which Charlemagne encouraged because it was less brutal, was the judgment of the cross. It involved the two adversaries standing before a cross with their arms raised: the first to yield to the strain lost the case. Louis the Pious first advocated its use in all cases in which the litigants were not physically capable of fighting or simply did not have the courage but then decided to prohibit this form of ordeal on the grounds that it was disrespectful to the sufferings of Christ.[19]

The "judgment of God" was also used in disputes over property, when there was a lack of clear evidence. It was in fact considered preferable to a human sentence, which could only be arbitrary in the circumstances. When in 775 the bishop of Paris and the abbot of St-Denis were disputing the ownership of a monastery, they both submitted apparently authentic written documents to back up their claims. The king decided that each party should nominate a representative to take part in the judgment of the cross.[20] But not everyone liked the system. Indeed, some time later there was even a bishop, Agobard of Lyons, who found the idea of resolving a lawsuit lacking in evidence through the "judgment of God" to be absurd and argued that in difficult cases it was up to the judge to demonstrate that he was worthy of his position by finding out the truth through skillful examination, as Solomon had done.[21]

Agobard is well known to historians for his skepticism, but even before Charles's birth the Lombard king Liutprand introduced drastic restrictions on the use of trial by ordeal and let it be known that if it had solely been up to him, he would have abolished it altogether, "because we cannot be sure of the 'judgment of God,' and we have heard that many lost their cases through judicial duels, but we cannot abolish this law because of the customs of our Lombard people."[22] In comparison, Charlemagne appears to have adopted a substantially conservative position, although he did try to limit the more brutal aspects of trial by ordeal. He published instructions to his subjects stating that, in the rare cases in which the "judgment of God" was to be used, it was incumbent on all good Christians to believe in its efficacy.[23]

Public Justice and the Settlement of Disputes

Public justice was not the only way, or even the most common way, to resolve conflicts peacefully. A negotiated solution was far more typical, and it involved the participation of friends and possibly the appointment of arbiters whose decision the parties swore to observe. Only when the interventions of such peacemakers did not succeed in finding an acceptable compromise, or one of the parties was sure of its rights and determined to meet the other head-on, did a court ruling replace the search for agreement.

The king's justice too was primarily a means of resolving disputes. It even applied to situations that we would consider to be subject to criminal law. This explains one of the most surprising inconsistencies of their judicial practice: the fact that theft was punished much more cruelly than murder. In 779 Charlemagne ruled that for the first offense thieves should have an eye removed and on the second their nose cut off, while on the third offense they were to be put to death.[24] On the other hand, murderers could and effectively did get away with the payment of compensation. This may have outraged the occasional bishop with particularly advanced ideas, but it seems to have been perfectly acceptable to everyone else.

At first sight, we might conclude that this harsh and primitive society attributed more importance to property than to human life. Theft was in fact a deliberate and mostly premeditated crime, while in a world in which everyone went around armed, got drunk easily, and was ready to pull out a knife whenever offense was perceived, murders must have been too frequent to cause real concern. To people of the time, theft was fully a crime and as such had to be punished by the law in its most severe and repressive capacity, particularly when the guilty party repeated the offense and placed himself outside society. On the other hand, murder was an extreme form of litigation. It was often the result, probably an unforeseen one, of an act of violence by which a man or an entire family wished to resolve a dispute that otherwise appeared irresolvable. The state therefore had to intervene, not to punish a crime, but to settle a dispute and to put an end to a spiral of vendettas, generally considered legitimate, but which a Christian king was required to discourage. The best solution was for him to force the guilty party to pay compensation and the injured party to accept it. This would publicly seal the end of the dispute, without anyone feeling that the offense remained and thus wishing to pursue the vendetta, something that would occur unfailingly if the murderer was put to death.

CHARLEMAGNE AND REFORM OF THE JUDICIAL SYSTEM
The Struggle against Corruption

The judicial system's real problems at the time of Charlemagne were entirely different. Particularly worrying was the unreliability of judges. The finger is pointed primarily at counts, who too often lacked any legal skills and were committed to the unscrupulous sport of family aggrandizement. This meant they were particularly susceptible to favoritism and corruption. The excessive number of complaints against counts testifies to the fact that in the administration of justice they were overbearing with the weak and acquiescent to the strong. Once the more important cases had been heard and it was time to provide justice to common folk, they were quite capable of terminating the *placitum* early and going hunting.[25]

The poor state of the justice system is betrayed by stories worthy of a crime thriller, like the case of a judge who was appointed guardian of a rich widow and administrator of her possessions. The judge falsified the deeds and took over the lands as though they were his own. He drove the widow from her property, and a petition to the emperor led to the dispatch of a royal envoy. However, the judge somehow produced witnesses that proved his rights and the case was put aside. The widow then set off in person for Aachen, and as the affair took place in Italy, she had to cross the Alps in the middle of winter. The emperor appointed a new commissioner to examine the case, this time his cousin Wala. Before Wala could set off, the judge had the widow murdered and then her assassins dispatched. On his arrival, Wala found that the usual witnesses were willing to swear that nothing had happened. It took a long and laborious investigation to uncover the crime and particularly to prove the judge's guilt, as he was protected by a great number of influential friends who held important posts at the palace of the king of Italy.[26]

It is understandable then that members of the clergy with considerable influence over Charlemagne, primarily Alcuin, insisted on the importance of reforming the justice system and argued that this was one of the most crucial aspects of the imperial project. First of all, corruption had to be stamped out. Starting with the *Admonitio generalis* of 789, many capitularies restated the prohibition on accepting gifts.[27] This ban was all the more difficult to impose in a society that was in many ways still similar to the primitive societies studied by anthropologists, in which gifts represented the normal way of establishing a reciprocal relationship. When Theodulf of Orléans on a mission in the south of Gaul tells of how people were stunned by his refusal to accept gifts, we should not simply infer that everyone was used to corruption, but that there was a deep-rooted tradition whereby the powerful, including judges, were supposed to be honored in that manner.[28] There was even a dispute between the abbots of St-Denis and St-Benoît-sur-Loire, in which the latter accused the judge of having accepted his adversary's gifts but not his own, so we might conclude that in the eyes of litigants it was a duty as well as a right for judges to receive gifts.[29]

Yet historians take anthropological teachings too far when they believe that any widespread custom in an archaic society was necessarily acceptable to everyone. Theodulf of Orléans, who after all lived in that period and surely knew more than we do about his world, observed that the use of gifts inevitably resulted in the purchase of sentences and that when judges did not receive them, they extorted them, sometimes causing the ruin of litigants. The reform of royal envoys or *missi dominici* in 802 also arose from the conviction that officials who accept gifts cannot carry out their duties properly.[30] The fact that a gift generally triggered the exchange of publicly acknowledged favors in a way accepted by contemporary morality does not mean that there was no perception of corruption as we would understand it. As far back as 755 King Pepin had ordered "that no bishop, abbot, or layman should accept unlawful bribes when acting as a judge, because when gifts start to be exchanged, the justice is invalidated."[31]

The main instrument for reducing abuse and corruption available to the emperor was the supervision carried out by his envoys. Local judges were perfectly aware of this and took countermeasures, as can be seen from a circular sent out by a commission of envoys to counts in an area they were about to visit: "Make sure that you do not say to those who wish to submit petitions, 'Be quiet until the envoys have gone, and then we will sort out the administration of justice among ourselves,' because in this manner court cases are shelved. It would be better for you to make every effort to conclude before we arrive."[32] If nothing else, it cannot be said that court officials had any illusions about what went on in the provinces.

Reform of the Jury System

Another priority Charlemagne identified was the need to increase the skills and the number of legal staff without further burdens on free men, who were already overly susceptible to the oppressive behavior of counts. It was undoubtedly in order to respond to this requirement and to make the fight against corruption more effective that after 802 royal envoys were charged not only with supervising county courts but also with taking over their functions. Envoys personally held *placita* as many as four times a year. The composition of courts was reformed for the same reason. Previously jury members were appointed in each county when the assembly of its inhabitants met for the *placitum*. After the reform, professional juries of échevins were established. They were appointed for life and were directly supervised by the envoys. Échevins were recruited from minor officials in the county and where possible they were notaries, although there was the occasional local dignitary who might have been illiterate but nevertheless expert in legal procedures. They worked in permanent groups, with a minimum of seven per county, and on occasion they could even pass judgments in the absence of the count to whom they were responsible. Indeed the frequent imperial directives to *iudices* in general are perhaps to be interpreted as referring to échevins, as well as to counts, vicars, and centeniers.

On paper, the advantages of the reform were clear, both because of the greater professionalism of the échevins in relation to popular juries and because as genuine officeholders they would be less vulnerable to pressures from their counts. However there is reason to believe that in many cases échevins had no professional training and their selection largely reflected the count's patronage. The most significant advantage was probably the abolition of the obligation to serve on juries, which lightened the load on the local population when it came to the maintenance of the judicial system. In 809 the emperor expressly ordered "that no free man shall be obliged to attend the *placitum* or *mallus*, except échevins and vassals of the count, unless it is their case that is being heard."[33] But even here, the measure led to unexpected consequences: although free commoners were personally released from the expenses and loss of time involved in attending *placita*, counts had increasing leeway to use their own vassals in the management of legal proceedings. This foreshadowed the privatization of the justice system, which was later to play a not inconsiderable part in the decline of collective liberties.

The Multiplicity of the Laws

On several occasions Charlemagne instructed his counts to base their judgments on written law and not on their whims.[34] It was above all a demand that procedure should be respected, even in cases on which a count would be loath to waste time. For instance, there was a summary procedure for criminals caught in the act, which was considerably more rapid than the ordinary procedure, but it was still essential that it was fully observed. A count who hung an offender without following procedure risked being accused of murder and having to pay compensation.[35]

In order to observe procedure, judges had to know the law. Hence they had to have books and many at that, because there was not just one legal code for the whole empire and every man was entitled to be tried in accordance with the law of his own people. Pepin had clearly established this principle shortly before his death, when he ordered that in Aquitaine "all men shall have their own law, and this is as true of the Romans as it is of the Salian Franks. Anyone who comes from another province, lives under the law of his homeland."[36] A case could therefore be conducted in accordance with the laws of the Salian Franks (*lex Salica*), Ripuarian Franks (*lex Ribuaria*), Bavarians (*lex Baiwariorum*), or Lombards (*lex Langobardorum*). The principle of personality in law contrasts with the principle of territoriality that prevails in the modern world.

By the time of Charlemagne, the indigenous population of each province considered itself to be a single people and identified with a single juridical tradition. For example the inhabitants of Neustria all saw themselves as Franks, all those of Aquitaine as Romans, and all those of the kingdom of Italy as Lombards. Accordingly some scholars choose to speak of territorial rather than personal law at this stage, but the distinction risks descending into little more than a play on words. The fact is that everyone had the right to be tried in accordance with the law of their own land, even when they moved to another country. The outward migration of Franks into every region of newly conquered countries meant that everywhere there were at least two legal systems in force. Indeed there were three, because Roman law in the simplified form of the Theodosian code was usually preferred for matters concerning the Church.

A judge therefore had to establish with the agreement of the litigants which law was to apply before he could go on to hear the case. Charlemagne told an envoy who had asked him to clarify the payment of legal expenses, "read the Roman law and do what you find written there. If, on the other hand, the case concerns Salic law, and you cannot find reference to what you should do, put your query to our general assembly."[37] Yet national laws, too rigid to deal with new situations and often written in an inadequate form, were beset with too many lacunae and contradictions for the administration of justice to rely solely on their provisions. They were therefore supplemented with the provisions of imperial capitularies, which could be of a purely administrative nature but not infrequently took on a prescriptive nature and in any case applied to the empire as a whole.

This was not absolutely new, as in the past any Germanic king could issue directives of a general nature that were valid for the entire territory under his rule, irrespective of ethnicity, and which supplemented national laws. But it was only under Charlemagne that this legislation, first royal and then imperial, became so complex and systematic as to replace entire sections of preexisting laws. Charlemagne was perfectly aware of the crucial importance of the interventions that aimed to give increasing cohesion to the peoples of his empire. In 803, after having issued a series of supplementary directives to national laws, he ordered his envoys to gather populations together, explain the innovations, and have everyone sign them with a signature or a cross.[38]

Shortly afterward, some particularly astute scholars started to question whether it was really necessary for everyone to remain attached to the legal traditions of their own people, given that they were all Christians and subjects of the same empire. In 817 Agobard of Lyons wrote to Louis the Pious pointing out this absurdity. "Of five men, who pass their time together and perhaps sit together, and who are bound by the same law as far as their eternal destiny is concerned, none of them observes the same law when it comes to earthly matters."[39] But these were problems that concerned the next generation, grown up in the empire and accustomed to its unifying force. Charlemagne's generation was happy just to harmonize national laws so that there weren't too many obvious contradictions among them. At the same time, they valued the sense of national identity that everyone gained from adherence to the traditional customs of their own people.

The multiplicity of the laws in force obviously complicated efforts to force judges to acquire real legal competence. As not all the national laws were written down, Charlemagne encouraged this to be done. The most important example and the one of greatest political significance was the drawing up of the law of the Saxons (*lex Saxonum*) in 785, when submission of Saxony appeared complete and plans to integrate its people into the empire were under way.[40] Up until that date, their law had been handed down orally. Legal systems that already existed in written form were also updated and attempts were made to spread information on the revised texts. A standardized production of legal handbooks for everyday use by judges would not begin until the reign of Louis the Pious, in part under the direct supervision of the imperial chancellery.

The efficacy of Charlemagne's attempts at reform is a matter for discussion. Too often the norms announced in capitularies had the flavor of moral exhortations rather than concrete measures, and they did nothing to change the social context in which the arrogance and corruption of judges flourished. When an emperor is forced repeatedly to order his counts not to hold *placita* after they have eaten, in order to stop them turning up drunk, we clearly should not expect very high standards of behavior from the justice system.[41] Yet in spite of all its limitations, public justice was not simply a facade, since all free men were able to turn to it in case of need and even appeal directly to the king if the local judge did them any wrong. The gradual deterioration in the conditions of the peasantry and the mass enslavement of men whose ancestors had been free, which all occurred after Charlemagne's death, were not unrelated to the deterioration and the eventual disappearance of the public justice system.

TEN

An Intellectual Project

THE EDUCATION OF A KING

One of the reasons why Charlemagne amazed his contemporaries and quickly became a legendary figure after his death was his unbounded intellectual curiosity, which involved him in all fields of knowledge. Einhard wrote that he spoke well and with ease not only in his native Frankish, a Germanic tongue, but also in Latin. This report is credible, because Latin in its popular form was the language of the Franks of Neustria, while in its classical form it was the only language in which it was possible to hold an intellectual discussion, as the vernacular languages of the time lacked adequate vocabulary. Equally credible is the report that he tried to learn a little Greek, which was indispensable for diplomatic relations with Byzantium, but without great success, as he rarely attempted to speak it.[1]

In all probability Charles did not have a genuine formal education, beyond learning to read, which, we should not forget, meant learning to read Latin. We know nothing of his childhood. Even his biographer, who met him when he was advanced in years, knew nothing. It may be that some kind of formal education was considered necessary for the son of a mayor of the palace, but even this is not certain. His father had been brought up in the abbey of St-Denis, but it is not certain that the monks provided Pepin with a formal education. There is therefore no need to speculate about Charles's education being intentionally neglected, perhaps because of his illegitimate birth, an unfounded concern that we have already disposed of.[2] The fact is that for a Frankish magnate of his generation, the ability to read was probably more than enough.

Charles, however, had an insatiable curiosity, and once he reached adulthood he searched everywhere for men of learning capable of giving him instruction. After conquering the Lombard kingdom, he had Peter of Pisa come to the court to teach him Latin grammar, which then corresponded to elementary education. He then turned to Alcuin, a scholar from England, in order to receive what we might call a secondary education, based on what were termed the liberal arts. Of the humanistic arts of the *trivium*, the royal pupil particularly applied himself to the study of rhetoric and logic, which were closest to his oratorical bent and also indispensable in politics. Of the scientific subjects of the *quadrivium*, he was mainly interested in astronomy, once he had learned arithmetic, and he studied the paths of heavenly bodies with lively interest.[3] This was a very suitable subject for a king, as the sky was an immense palimpsest on which God wrote his messages to humanity, and the ability to interpret them was of great assistance in affairs of the world.

He had a particular passion for linguistic questions, and it may be that this personal inclination was stimulated by the difficult task of governing a multiethnic empire. Once he had mastered Latin grammar, Charles started to compose a grammar for the Frankish language, which had none at that time. He clearly understood that his mother tongue risked falling into disuse, dragging the ancient traditions of his people with it into oblivion. He did all he could to prevent this. He had ancestral songs that celebrated the great deeds of ancient kings transcribed, and he wished to coin specific words in the Frankish tongue to designate the twelve months of the year and the twelve winds, so that it would no longer be necessary to resort to Latin to mention them.[4]

The modern reader will perhaps be amused to know that, in spite of these varied intellectual activities, Charles did not know how to write. Einhard assures us that he tried to learn and indeed made great efforts, including the use of wax tablets and parchment that he kept under his pillow for writing exercises when suffering from insomnia, but the task proved too onerous for a man already of advanced years and he had little success.[5] Before we feel too superior, it should be remembered that in that period reading and writing were not immediately associated activities to be learned at the same time. Although Charlemagne had readers who would read out loud to him, a standard practice since antiquity, there can be no doubt that, if necessary, he knew how to read to himself, but writing was a different matter. Learning was not based on writing, as it is today, but on reciting out loud and exercising the memory. It was therefore possible to learn Latin, for example, without ever writing a single word. Writing was a uniquely technical activity that required the mastery of complicated equipment and had no practical purpose in daily life. It was therefore the reserve of specialized craftsmen. The only occasion on which a king was required to hold a quill was to sign letters and decrees, but writing one's own signature was a demonstration of skill that any king could learn by heart. Clearly this was also the case with Charles, whose signature or monogram is conspicuous in its authority at the bottom of so many decrees.

PALATINE SCHOLARS

In the cultural field, Charlemagne could count on the assistance of a wide circle of men of learning, the best available at the time. The most important of them, Alcuin, spoke of that circle as an academy,[6] and the name has been taken up very readily by historians, even though it might imply a degree of organization and permanence that in reality did not exist. The majority of these men of letters were not Franks, which demonstrates the sorry state of Frankish culture at the time. Many came from Italy, like the grammarian Peter of Pisa who had already had an important role at the court of Desiderius, the historian Paul the Deacon who among other things left us a famous *History of the Lombards*, and the poet Paulinus, later patriarch of Aquileia. Others were Goths, refugees from Muslim Spain, and these included several figures we have already come across, such as Theodulf, the theologian and poet whom Charles appointed bishop of Orléans, and Agobard, another theologian and man of letters who was made archbishop of Lyons. Finally, there were enough Irishmen to provoke the resentment of other palatines, although their names mean little to us now.

The most important was Alcuin, who in his own country had been in charge of the cathedral school of York. He specialized in teaching, as the titles of his works show, devoted as they are mainly to grammar, logic, rhetoric, and orthography. Practically all the scholars of the following generation had been his pupils at some time or other. In one of his letters, he spoke of a palatine school when referring to the teaching provided at the court. He thus coined an expression that historians have enthusiastically taken up.[7] But Alcuin's influence went far beyond the field of education. On several occasions Charles requested his advice on matters of great political significance, such as the approach to take in converting the Saxons and later the Avars, or the legitimacy of his imperial coronation.[8] He probably had a decisive role in drawing up some of the most important planning documents during Charles's reign, such as the *Admonitio generalis* and the *Epistola de litteris colendis*, two general policy statements on the education and morality of the clergy and the people.[9]

Alcuin's services were lavishly rewarded. No fewer than five abbeys were allocated to him, without troubling him with the taking of monastic vows. These abbeys included the most ancient and richest one in the Frankish kingdom, St-Martin at Tours, where he resided from 796. Its possessions were so immense that it was said that Alcuin could travel throughout the empire and always be able to take a rest in one of his properties. Archbishop Elipandus of Toledo, who was a theological adversary, harshly criticized him for this, arguing that twenty thousand slaves had to work to keep him in such luxury.[10] Alcuin really was awash with riches, even though his works extolled the virtue of poverty, the true friend of learned men.[11] In his old age, he began to be disturbed by this contradiction, and he regretted his greed, fearing that it might endanger his soul.[12] To put this right, according to the custom of the time, he invested some of his gold in prayers, mainly through large donations to churches in his native England.

It was common practice at the court to reward palatine scholars generously. The granting of bishoprics to those who had taken holy orders and of abbeys to the others seemed to the king to be the easiest and most practical way to ensure the maintenance of his advisers. This easy distribution of prebends, which was consistent with Charles's conviction that his court scholars were one of the pillars of imperial power, established a tradition that was later to degenerate, but under his rule the system worked. There can be no doubt that it suited Charles to invest the wealth of the Church in this manner, not so much for the pleasure of having his men of letters call him a doctor of grammar, a master of rhetoric, and a most excellent logician, superior to Cato, Cicero, and Homer,[13] as for their responsibility in developing imperial ideology. Their pens, sharpened like swords, were always ready to intervene in any ideological conflict.

Bitter rivalries emerged within this group of scholars, such as the one between Theodulf and Alcuin. In 796 both were asked to compose an epitaph for Pope Adrian to be inscribed on a marble slab that was to be sent as a gift to his successor, Leo III. In the end the king chose Alcuin's text. Both men were deeply involved in the revision of the Bible, one of the priorities in Charlemagne's program of reforms, but here too the version submitted by Alcuin met with greater success than Theodulf's, which today appears unarguably the more advanced. It is hardly surprising then that the bishop of Orléans bore a grudge and in his satires afforded himself the pleasure of taunting Alcuin over the pedantry of his riddles and his excessive love of porridge, particularly when sprinkled with generous amounts of wine or beer.[14] Alcuin responded in kind after he had been installed in Tours, by refusing to hand over a condemned man who had escaped from Orléans and taken refuge in the basilica of St-Martin. He also attempted to put all the blame for the scandal that ensued on Theodulf and wrote to the emperor that he and not the guilty man should have been clapped in irons.[15]

A fact often overlooked but worth stressing is that this generation of scholars was not present at the court throughout the entire reign of Charlemagne. Peter of Pisa and Paulinus arrived there only after 776, while Alcuin, Paul the Deacon, and Theodulf entered the service of the king around 782, and then Paul the Deacon returned to Montecassino around 787. When Paulinus was appointed patriarch of Aquileia, he had already returned to his see of Cividale for some time. Peter of Pisa appears to have returned to Italy by 790. After long stays in his native England between 790 and 793, Alcuin left the palace to take possession of his monastery in Tours in 796. Theodulf was bishop of Orléans by 797. Of course, this did not stop them from working for the king, with whom they maintained a copious correspondence, and besides they were probably called upon to visit him regularly at the annual assembly, along with the other bishops and abbots. But there was no longer the daily intimacy of the eighties and early nineties. That was in fact the period of grand interventions in the field of culture and the beginning of a profound change. Language was freed from the widespread grammatical and orthographic solecisms of the Merovingian era and consciously returned to classical usage. It would appear that this reform was directly related to the arrival of Alcuin and others from countries where the knowledge of Latin had survived much better than it had in Gaul.

When they died or went into what we might call retirement, the men of learning of Alcuin's generation were replaced by natives whom they had trained and who displayed all the self-assurance of young men growing up at the center of culture and power. These included the poet Angilbert, who felt no embarrassment at being called Homer by his friends and had a long and notorious relationship with one of Charles's daughters; another poet, Modoinus, who was nicknamed Naso as in Publius Ovidius Naso, or Ovid, and later became bishop of Autun; and above all Einhard, who was to become Charlemagne's biographer. At the palace Einhard was mainly known as one of the leading experts on Latin literature, but toward the end of his reign Charles used him for important diplomatic missions. In 806, for instance, he sent Einhard to Rome to notify the pope of his plan to divide the empire among his three sons. The date of Einhard's *Life of Charlemagne* is not known, but it certainly followed Charles's death, perhaps by many years, when memories of the emperor began to fade. Those were the years when the empire started to suffer the consequences of Louis the Pious's weakness and the rivalry among his sons. Einhard, who by then had retired from the court and was peacefully enjoying his old age at his abbey of Seligenstadt, must have felt the need to sort out his memories by writing the panegyric of the great emperor under whom he had passed his youth.

REFORM OF THE CHURCH
Renaissance or Limited Reform?

Notwithstanding Charles's genuine interest in cultural fields, there must be no confusion: the program of reforms he undertook, which we usually refer to as the Carolingian renaissance, was essentially of a religious nature. The fundamental ideals, which were to improve the education of the clergy and rectify their behavior, were not new. Christian emperors since the times of Constantine and later the kings of the Romano-barbarian realms had repeatedly set themselves these aims. "He who does not rectify does not govern," wrote Isidore of Seville, one of the most influential authors of late antiquity, and went on to warn rulers that God would judge them on the basis of the way the faith was taught in their kingdoms. Governing Christendom by the grace of God, Charles felt very strongly throughout his life that one of his most important responsibilities was to guarantee the moral and educational standards of the clergy who preached the word of the Lord to his subjects. It was perhaps the heaviest responsibility of all.

It was therefore for primarily religious reasons that the reforms promoted by the emperor took on such cultural significance. Christianity is a religion of the book and Charles considered it indispensable that books were corrected or amended, as they said at the time. This was not just a question of orthodoxy, but also of language, given that a grammatical error could lead people to pray in a mistaken manner that would displease God. "Whoever attempts to please God by living righteously must not neglect to please Him also by speaking righteously," wrote Charles in a circular to all the bishops and abbots of his kingdom. "Indeed it is written, 'For by thy words thou shalt be justified, and by thy words thou shalt be condemned' (Matthew 12.37)."[16] For the same reason, priests had to have a good command of the language in which the sacred texts were written and in which they prayed, in order to avoid gross errors when they addressed the Lord. The *Admonitio generalis*, the great capitulary of 789, called on the Church to observe the ancient canons that for so long had been forgotten and trampled upon. It stressed that to achieve this aim, a proper knowledge of Latin, the liturgical language, was indispensable. Hence priests had to attend good schools, and bishops had to be concerned with priests' intellectual training even in the most remote dioceses of the immense empire.[17]

The elegant Latin that was written at Charlemagne's court, so unlike the barbaric forms of previous centuries, and the rather inflated style in classical hexameters in which writers in his service turned out one book after another, are simply the most superficial result of efforts whose motives were radically different. The Carolingian renaissance can be defined as a period in which culture and particularly education were revived for the express purpose of reforming or rather rectifying the way the Church worked and the way the Christian people lived. The intention was not to invent something new, but to recover an ideal purity that had supposedly been corrupted through the disruptive effect of the passing years and human weakness. Carolingian intellectuals did not value originality and, as we might expect, this was particularly true of theology and liturgy. Florus of Lyons wrote of the astonishment felt by an assembly of bishops when one of their number, Amalarius of Metz, being asked about where he had read certain doctrines that he was preaching, "replied that he had not taken them from the Scriptures nor from the teachings handed down by the church fathers, nor even from the heretics, but had read them in his heart." The bishops replied in unison, "Here is the very spirit of error!"[18] Historians are not unjustified when they want to replace the term renaissance, which has now become entrenched through use, with the less misleading one of a "rectification" in education and standards of behavior.[19]

The Reforms under Carloman and Pepin

Charlemagne's character was undoubtedly of crucial importance in the success of the reforms. The emperor undertook the task with a great deal more energy and larger resources than any of his predecessors. But his father, Pepin, and his uncle, Carloman, had been fully aware of the need to do something. In 741 Carloman had inherited a catastrophic situation from Charles Martel, who had been more preoccupied with the field of battle than the fields of scholarship and religion. Education had nearly disappeared in Gaul, and its intellectual life had been reduced to a state of enervation. With the exception of a tiny handful of monasteries that remained reasonably active, there was hardly a trace of theological or literary production, even in terms of copying manuscripts. The Latin of royal decrees and even capitularies would make even the most lax schoolteacher shudder.

As for the Frankish Church, this is how the Anglo-Saxon missionary Boniface described the situation to Pope Zacharias in 742:

> According to the oldest bishops, they have not met in council for over eighty years. They have no archbishops. Most of the episcopal sees are occupied by avaricious laymen or adulterous, licentious, and worldly clerics. Bishops make no claim not to be fornicators and adulterers, and they drink, neglect their duties, and spend their time hunting. The deacons, or at least those who go by this title, are people who live in sin; they take four or five concubines to their bed

but feel no shame when reading the Gospel or over attaining the priesthood or indeed a bishopric.[20]

Monasteries and properties belonging to bishoprics were widely plundered during the struggles between the mayors of the palace and their opponents, leaving them poor and impotent. Consequently reform of the Frankish Church was an absolute priority if the Carolingian mayors of the palace were to create a stable power base and to become credible defenders of the faith in the eyes of the Christian people.

Reforms started in earnest immediately after Charles Martel's death, at the initiative of both Pepin and Carloman, with possibly the greater involvement of the latter. Initially they were directed by Boniface, who had been granted wide-ranging powers by the pope, and then later by Franks such as Bishop Chrodegang of Metz and Abbot Fulradus of St-Denis. The latter was to be at Charlemagne's side in the early years of his reign. The capitularies produced by the two brothers incessantly reiterated the same measures: every city needed to have a bishop, and all the clergy in his diocese must obey him. Every year bishops had to meet at a synod to give a report to their sovereign on the progress they had made. The riches illegally taken away from the Church had to be returned. Monks and nuns were not to leave their monasteries without permission. Adulterous and licentious priests and deacons should be demoted and forced to do penitence. Unafraid of using severe measures to punish the guilty with beatings and imprisonment on bread and water, the mayors of the palace made every effort "to revive the law of God and the ecclesiastic religion, which in the times of past sovereigns had fallen into dissipation, in order that the Christian people can achieve salvation of the soul and do not perish through the deceits of false priests."[21]

Carloman and Pepin did not hesitate to involve their officials in the battle for reform and informed them that they should consider themselves defenders of the Church in their provinces. As well as undertaking to uproot every remaining vestige of paganism, counts were also expected to ensure by force that priests obeyed their bishops when they were convened for the annual synod. Of course, they made clear that this did not mean that counts could interfere with church justice, as the trial of those who committed such disobedience was still under the jurisdiction of the bishop. However, the extremely heavy fine of 60 *solidi* imposed upon any priest who did not attend the synod was collected by the count and paid into the royal treasury.[22] During Charlemagne's childhood, an ambiguity appeared that was to continue throughout his reign: with the declared aim of protecting the Church, the king and his officials actually exercised an authority over it that was both brutal and summary. Yet its results proved on the whole to be positive, as the Church needed first and foremost to be protected from itself.

Metropolitan sees were fundamental in guaranteeing discipline among bishops but, as Boniface had complained, the custom of grouping dioceses together under the direction of an archbishop to whom suffragan bishops owed obedience had completely disappeared in Gaul. The trend was reversed through Boniface himself, when he was appointed archbishop by the pope with Carloman's consent. So as not to be outdone by his brother, Pepin also hastened to reestablish two metropolitans in the traditional sees of Sens and Reims. In the meantime Boniface returned to his original vocation and established his archbishopric at Mainz as a center for coordinating missionary work beyond the Rhine and ordaining new bishops to Christianize Germany.

Charlemagne's Reforms up to the Admonitio Generalis

Charlemagne therefore inherited from his father a Church that was already engaged in the struggle to reform, even if it was finding it an arduous task. Unsurprisingly, the first measures taken by the young king largely followed in the footsteps of his father and his uncle and mainly concerned the morality and discipline of the clergy, as well as occasionally regulating previously secular matters like marriage from a religious standpoint. Lastly there were measures to ensure that the Church had the necessary resources to carry out its duties in a dignified manner, by forcing everyone to pay tithes to maintain the clergy, "whether they like it or not," as Pepin had flatly commanded.[23]

Charlemagne also completed the work of his predecessors in the restoration of ecclesiastical provinces. In Pepin's time, it often happened that a bishopric that had become vacant or had perhaps been usurped by a lay magnate was assigned temporarily to the abbot of a local monastery. Charles managed to do away with the old anomalies and ensure that every diocese had a genuine bishop. Even the restoration of archbishops proceeded in a systematic manner once he came to the throne, and within a few years all the ancient metropolitan sees recovered their rights. Naturally this was not only advantageous for pastoral activities but also for governmental ones, given that archbishops were part of the command structure connecting the king to their suffragans, to whom they handed on orders and summons from the palace. Not surprisingly, they were regularly appointed as royal envoys.

From 789, when the *Admonitio generalis* was promulgated, the scope of Charles's actions in relation to the Church suddenly became considerably more wide-ranging than that of his predecessors. He no longer spoke as king of the Franks but as sovereign of the entire Christian people, and the call to observe ancient canons took on a political significance as well as a moral one. It was no longer simply a question of fighting the corruption and ignorance of the Frankish clergy: now everyone, both lay people and the clergy, was involved in a great striving for universal betterment, organized in conjunction with the pope. The collection of canon law known as the *Dionysio-Hadriana*, which Pope Adrian I had produced for Charles fifteen years before, was to constitute the main part of the text issued in 789. These regulations established over the centuries by a wide variety of popes and councils were gathered together under the direction of the papal court at the king's request. They became the basis of Christian life throughout the West that had been united under his scepter.

In the prologue to the *Admonitio*, Charlemagne, who had been proclaimed a new David and a new Solomon, looked to another biblical model, that of Joshua. "Indeed we read in the Book of Kings that saintly Joshua tried to revive the worship of the true God in the kingdom that God had given him, by traveling throughout it and correcting and warning the people. I do not claim to compare myself with his saintliness, but we must always follow the example of the saints."[24] The commitment to reform that he had inherited from his predecessors was now transformed into Charles's much more ambitious and even utopian project to persuade Christians to live truly as a community of brothers. Although this plan could not have been realized in practice, there is an unquestionable greatness in this sovereign who addresses his people and invites them all, laymen and clerics, rich and poor, to live in peace and justice, and to love their neighbors with evangelical goodwill.

The reforms promoted by the king were immediately taken up by his more competent bishops. During the final years of the eighth century and the early years of the next one, many bishops followed Alcuin's example and wrote short tracts explaining the main liturgical questions to their clergy, with a particular emphasis on baptism and penitence. These tracts were usually dedicated to the king and he fully approved of their declared aim to ensure that the officiation of the sacraments was not reduced to a mechanical ritual but entailed a genuine understanding of the mysteries symbolized by the liturgy. Pierre Toubert has argued that the episcopacy was mobilized "to instruct its priests and through them the faithful, to explain the meaning of words and sacramental rites, and to guide them through this difficult universe of signs and symbols, in which their didactic vocation was to be tested."[25] Didactic vocation was exactly what Charles felt, and he untiringly passed this on to his clergy, making every effort to have the effects reach out to the whole of the Christian people.

Besides, the emperor was not working in a vacuum. The involvement of his bishops was a constant feature, as is shown by the frequency with which he convened councils. The fact that bishops were normally summoned for the annual assembly simply as high officials of the king makes it difficult to establish the exact number of synods convened during

Charles's reign. We would not, however, be straying very far from the truth if we were to assert that in at least eighteen years out of a total of forty-six an important ecclesiastical council was summoned in the presence of the king and occasionally under his chairmanship, as in Frankfurt in 794. Thus the Frankish Church, which when Charles was born had not held a council for eighty years, was now in the habit of convening in an almost permanent assembly to collaborate in the reforms promoted by the king. Over the same period, only three councils were held in Rome, including the one that tried Pope Leo in 800, and the contrast confirms that in terms of quantity, it was the king of the Franks and not the pope who led the western Church. Moreover, the conclusions reached by councils, even when they involved the enactment of canons, were usually published in the form of capitularies and therefore had the full force of law.

Measures Introduced in Later Years

The education and morality of the clergy remained one of Charlemagne's principal concerns. In 802, following the imperial coronation, the sovereign issued wide-ranging measures that as a whole recalled the moral commitment of the *Admonitio generalis* and to some extent went beyond it. Aware of his new responsibilities, the emperor called on his subjects to cooperate with him and personally undertake to do everything within their power to establish peace and justice between Christians, "because he, the lord Emperor, cannot dedicate the appropriate attention and corrective measures individually to everyone."[26] It was up to bishops, abbots, priests, and monks to set a good example, and the emperor produced a stream of rules just for them. The first ones were of a general nature, but the following ones gradually became more specific and detailed, suggesting that the reports he received from the provinces had denounced widespread immoral behavior.

On this occasion, there was no repetition of endless and unchanging exhortations against indiscipline, immorality, concubinage, simony,

drunkenness, violence, embezzlement, and disobedience. The emperor
sent his envoys to the provinces with a specially prepared questionnaire
and authorized them to subject the entire clergy to a thorough investigation, irrespective of rank. They had to examine them all on their doctrinal education, have them recite the liturgy to verify its correctness,
and have them sing psalms to check that they were following the Roman
tradition. Given that all this effort was not an end in itself but aimed at
raising the educational level of the people as a whole, they also had to
interrogate the laity to make sure that everyone knew the Creed and the
Lord's Prayer by heart. It had once happened that during the festivities
for Epiphany the emperor attended the joint baptism of a large number
of children, and he decided to verify how well prepared the godfathers
actually were. He tested them one by one on the Creed and the Lord's
Prayer, "and there were very many of them who did not know them at
all," concluded the horrified Charles.[27]

But the main concern remained the behavior of the clergy. A few
years later, in 811, the emperor wished to proceed with another investigation, and this time he wanted to do it personally. All the bishops and
abbots of the empire were called to Aachen for the annual assembly.
There he subjected them to an interrogation about which we have a little information, and which occasionally turned into a genuine tirade full
of sarcasm.

> Tell us what it means to renounce the worldly life, and how you
> can recognize those who have renounced from those who still live
> in the world. Is it perhaps just that they cannot bear arms and are
> not legally married? Explain to us whether someone has really aban-
> doned worldly things, when every day he attempts to increase his
> riches by every means and strips the ignorant of their possessions
> to the ruin of their heirs, by enticing them with heavenly bliss and
> threatening them with eternal suffering in hell.[28]

The image of the Frankish Church that emerges from these inquiries
is certainly not a flattering one. Bishops and canons continued to go

hunting and kept dogs and hawks. Shady dealings still occurred in some monasteries, and more or less everywhere priests and monks looked after their own affairs, lived with women, carried knives, engaged in usury, and drank in the taverns. The aging emperor's efforts to put right all these bad practices might seem utopian, and the very fact that after so many years it was still necessary to repeat the same prohibitions might appear to demonstrate their futility. Some scholars have even inferred from the inquest of 811 that there was increasing indiscipline in the Church and therefore a considerable breakdown in imperial authority. They conclude that the final years of Charlemagne's reign have to be considered a period of decline and failure, and the old man's invectives against this were only a sign of impotence.[29]

Reality was somewhat different. The problems that the emperor identified in the behavior of too many of the clergy are to be found in any era, and there is no reason to believe that things deteriorated markedly in the years running up to his death in 814. The measures introduced in 802 and 811 were therefore a product of the king's particular intentions and not external circumstances. These intentions were based on a consistent set of beliefs about which he had thought deeply. He had pursued them for many years and it is easy to identify the way they developed by reading the texts of imperial decrees. One example will suffice: after having ordered, like his predecessors, that all monks in the empire should observe the Benedictine rule, Charlemagne clearly started to have some doubts and attempted to find out whether there had been any monks in Gaul before the introduction of the rule, whose Italic origins were well known. When it was proved that there had been, he wanted to find out from the clergy what rule they had followed, "because we have read that Saint Martin was a monk, had many monks under him, and lived long before Saint Benedict."[30]

The same serenely rational approach is to be found in his rebuke aimed at bishops and abbots who were more concerned about the number of clerics and monks rather than their quality, and who preferred ones who sang well to ones who lived an honest life.

Let it be clear that skill in singing and reading is not at all despised in the Church, indeed it should be encouraged at all times. However, all things being equal, we are of the opinion that imperfections in singing are more acceptable than imperfections in living. Although it is a good thing that church buildings are beautiful, the ornament of good behavior is preferable to buildings, because it is our belief that the construction of churches relates in a certain way to the Old Testament, while the improvement in behavior belongs, strictly speaking, to the New Testament and the teachings of Christ.[31]

For an age in which most people experienced religion in strictly formal terms, the ability to distinguish between form and substance, which is revealed by these arguments, is proof enough of how Charlemagne thought deeply about what it meant to be a Christian.

Later measures taken by the emperor certainly reflect a prophetic tone that could raise some concerns, but before we jump to the conclusion that by that stage the old man was out of touch with a world he could no longer control, we should consider whether he intentionally ran the risk of some utopian excess. There can be no doubt about the utopian nature of the plan to have all Christians truly live by divine law and in harmony as required by the Gospels, but if there was ever a moment in history in which it was worth running that risk, then it had come. Western Christendom was once again led by an emperor anointed by God, and all around him pagans bowed their heads before Christ's victorious banners. When, if not then?

LITURGICAL AND EDUCATIONAL REFORM
Standardizing the Liturgy

In the context of reforms, one of Charlemagne's main concerns was the correction of liturgical books, the foundation of the complex liturgy celebrated every day by priests in the empire's countless churches. Its correct performance was essential to satisfy the Lord so that He should show His goodwill toward His people. So concerned was the king about the philological correctness of texts and the exact pronunciation of chants that he got personally involved and became a real expert, although Einhard tells us that he avoided reading during services and accompanied chants in a half-voice, like the rest of the faithful.[32] The *Admonitio generalis* states, "Some people who wish to pray to God properly, pray incorrectly because of incorrect books," and adds that for the same reason novices need to be stopped from introducing errors into sacred texts when reading or writing, "and if a gospel, psalm book, or missal has to be written, it should by men of adult age."[33]

These measures also had a political side, although at the time people did not find it useful to distinguish between religion and politics in their thinking, as they were to do after Machiavelli. Given that the empire was one, as was Christendom, the liturgy had to be officiated in a uniform manner everywhere and, given that religious legitimacy was founded on the alliance with the pope in Rome, it was appropriate that Roman liturgical customs were imposed. This decision also implied the desire to resist any Byzantine influence, which obviously would also be loaded with political significance. King Pepin had understood this in the past, and it was following his example that priests in all the churches of the empire were officially invited to sing psalms in accordance with Roman ritual, and they were provided with a copy at the expense of the government. This meant renouncing local customs that had developed in Gaul over the centuries.

The reforms proved to be far from simple. In 785 Charlemagne asked the pope to send him a copy of the Gregorian sacramentals setting out the liturgy practiced in Rome.[34] When the precious manuscript arrived, however, it was realized that a profound revision would be required before getting on with the business of producing copies. The text sent from Rome was in fact fifty years old and no longer reflected the liturgy actually used in the Eternal City. Perhaps the pope mistook Charles's reasons, believing that he wanted a gift rather than a tool, and thus sent him an expensive but outdated codex. Revision took many years of work, which was mainly organized by Alcuin. The Gregorian sacramentals had to be collated against the liturgical texts already in use. Missing passages had to be filled in and grammatical errors had to be corrected. All this effort was necessary in order to create an instrument for effectively standardizing liturgical practice throughout the entire empire.

The results of the reforms should not be overestimated. A century later Notker referred to these efforts with amazement, even incredulity. "It is something," he wrote, "that our contemporaries will find hard to believe. Indeed, I myself, who am writing about it, tend not to believe it, given the enormous difference between our chanting and that of the Romans."[35] The German monk continued with the tale of when the pope, at Charles's request, sent twelve clerics who were expert in psalm singing to introduce the Frankish kingdom to Rome's liturgical customs. "As the Greeks and Romans had always been envious of Frankish glory," the clerics agreed to teach a different and corrupted usage in each place. Once the deception was discovered, Frankish clerics had to be sent incognito to Rome in order to study those customs and bring them back to their homeland; otherwise the bad intentions of the Romans would never allow them to resolve the problem. The anecdote is obviously apocryphal, but it does at least testify to the difficulties that the king encountered in his attempt to uproot ancient customs and impose a unitary model on his multiethnic clergy.

Correcting the Bible

The most important of all the texts used for holy worship was clearly the Bible, and Charles was always interested in producing an amended and corrected version to replace the partial texts, ridden with errors, that priests had used up until that time. The challenge attracted many scholars, particularly those who had conspicuous financial and organizational resources as well as intellectual abilities. Among those proposing their own versions of the Bible were lesser-known figures, like Abbot Mordramnus of Corbie and Bishop Angilramnus of Metz, as well as leading men of learning, such as Theodulf of Orléans and Alcuin himself, who devoted the last years of his life to that work, while he was abbot of St-Martin at Tours.

Today, we value Theodulf's text above the others. Its modernity is such that it provides notes in the margin on the manuscript tradition from which each reading originates. Modern scholars tend to turn up their noses at Alcuin's version, but his was the one that obtained the greatest success. The reason for this was not so much the philological qualities of his work as the support he enjoyed at the court and above all the immense means he had at his disposal. The market was swamped with Alcuin's Bibles, which were sumptuously produced by the Tours scriptorium in large format, copiously illustrated, and very suitable for prestigious gifts, so that we have a much higher number of them than we have of those produced in Orléans under Theodulf's supervision. The latter came in a smaller format with a tighter script and an apparatus criticus that clearly went beyond the requirements of the time.

Increasing School Attendance

Textbooks for learning Latin were just as important as the Bible and liturgical texts, because they were indispensable for training an educated and informed clergy to officiate in the churches. In the circular addressed to all the bishops and abbots of the kingdom, which is known as the *Epistola de litteris colendis*, Charlemagne talked of often having received letters from monasteries in which he was assured of the zeal with which the monks prayed for him. The intention, he said, was good, but the language was full of mistakes, and the knowledge of the writers was not equal to their piety. "We therefore started to fear that as they were not that accomplished in writing, they were perhaps even less accomplished in understanding the Sacred Scriptures, and we know very well that the incorrect use of words is dangerous, errors of meaning being the most dangerous of all."[36] Charles went on to argue that the Bible is not written in simple language and is full of rhetorical figures. Whoever wants to understand its spiritual meaning must, above all, have a literary training. The king then expressly ordered that, from that time on, priests and monks were to devote themselves, over and above their religious commitments, to the study of Latin.

In this context, it became imperative to revitalize church schools. In 789, the *Admonitio generalis* ordered that priests were to bring together boys for instruction, and it did not matter whether the boys were born into freedom or slavery. The resulting schools taught "psalms, notes, singing, the ecclesiastical calendar, and grammar."[37] Although it was some time before these perfunctory instructions could be seen as a genuine educational reform, there was a clear strategic aim. Diocesan statutes published some time later by Theodulf of Orléans demonstrate their practical application.[38] All priests were requested to teach elementary education, which meant essentially reading in Latin. Boys who wanted to continue their studies were sent to the church or monastic schools of the episcopal city. During the years that followed, Frankish synods regularly discussed the opening and maintenance of rural schools. The depth of their concerns suggests that it was by no means an easy task.[39]

The only school that did not depend on an ecclesiastic institution was the one that was run at the imperial palace for the sons of officials and possibly also servants. One of the most famous anecdotes told by Notker portrays Charlemagne busy correcting the exercises carried out by these children. Those who came from more humble origins had worked hard and much better than expected. Those from noble families had been slacking. The emperor, imitating the Christ of the Last Judgment, called the best students to his right side and encouraged them to continue: "I will give you the wealthiest bishoprics and monasteries, and I shall always honor you." He brusquely told the others that their nobility made no impression on him, and they were very mistaken if they thought that it was enough to be the sons of important people in order to have a successful career.[40] The anecdote illustrates very well the true significance of the palace school in Charlemagne's system. It was the breeding ground for the highest church officials, who had to be able to serve the emperor zealously, while the cathedral schools had to replicate the training system at the local level.

BOOKS AND LIBRARIES
Book Production

Charlemagne directed his energies at libraries as well as educational reform. At the time, a book constituted a considerable investment, given the cost of parchment and the specialized workforce required. The king's policy was precisely one of encouraging such investments by favoring and if necessary financing those abbots who intended to expand their libraries. First of all, a library had to be built at the palace, where, as far as we know, Charlemagne would have been almost unable to find a book when he came to the throne. It was only at the beginning of the eighties, at the time when the court was becoming a center of intellectual debate and literary production, that the king sent out a circular requesting that everyone who possessed works by classical authors or the church fathers should make him a gift of them or have them copied for him.[41] Once the palatine library had been constituted, it was possible to organize the reliable copying of those texts that the king wanted used throughout his kingdom. These ranged from Paul the Deacon's specially commissioned homilies to the Benedictine rule that Charles personally had ordered at Montecassino from a copy that was believed to have been written by Saint Benedict himself.[42]

Although it retained its craft nature, book production underwent a considerable expansion during the Carolingian age. The first eight hundred years of Christianity have provided us with altogether 1,800 Latin manuscripts, whereas more than 7,000 have survived from the ninth century. The Bible and liturgical works, indispensable tools for the work of the clergy, were the main beneficiaries of all this activity. For example, the scriptorium of St-Martin at Tours produced at least two complete Bibles every year, and these were distributed through the imperial court even to the most far-flung episcopal and monastic sees. The enormity of this task can be better understood if we consider that the parchment for just one Bible required the butchering of several hundred sheep. The binding was no less expensive. Charlemagne donated a forest with all the deer within it to the abbey of St-Denis, so that the skins could be used for binding the books in the monastic library.[43]

Every manuscript turned out in Tours required the hard work of a team of monks, and this collective work of both monks and nuns is documented in other workshops. A codex of Saint Augustine's *De trinitate* was produced by a team of fourteen nuns, who worked at the same time on thirty-three separate quires before the book was bound.[44] A single scribe could be responsible for an entire manuscript, as was Agambert who, after having copied Saint Jerome's *Commentarii*, entered a note that he finished the work in thirty-four days, from 1 July to 4 August 806, an average of eleven pages a day.[45] The majority of copyists were monks, but there is reason to believe that even clerics working for a cathedral and sometimes even professional lay people were used in the production of manuscripts.

The increase in book production did not apply only to the distribution of Bibles and works by the church fathers. Chroniclers and hagiographers of the time also found that their works were valued and distributed, as were works by Latin authors of the classical period, which have nearly always survived to the present day because of Carolingian copies. Apart from sacred texts, Charlemagne's library contained Lucan, Terence, Juvenal, Tibullus, Horace, Martial, Cicero, Livy, and Sallust, and many of these texts were copied at the palace for the more important monastic libraries. This interest in the secular literature of antiquity is characteristic of the age of Charlemagne and is one of those features that justify, at least superficially, the name of renaissance usually attributed to the cultural revival in the Carolingian era.

Contrary to legend, classical texts were not buried in monastic libraries but were in circulation. Leading scholars, who were often abbots of one or more abbeys and all knew each other, seem to have been busy borrowing and lending books to have them copied. Lupus, abbot of Ferrières, wrote to Einhard, who was then abbot of Seligenstadt, apologizing for not yet being able to return his codex of *Noctes Atticae* by Aulus Gellius, because a third abbot, Rabanus Maurus of Fulda, was having a copy made for his library.[46] The catalogs of the principal monastic libraries were public, so librarians would consult them and then commence the laborious procedure of borrowing the codices they were interested in and having them copied. Literature from late antiquity was read with pleasure, and moreover the court poets could be considered direct followers of that tradition, which was perceived as still alive and not merely a matter of imitation, as was to be the case with humanists. The encomium of Charlemagne dictated by Theodulf of Orléans would not have seemed out of place if it had been written in Theodoric the Great's court in Ravenna.[47]

This culture was not the exclusive preserve of churchmen. While the majority of learned men close to Charlemagne were members of the clergy, and almost all of them ended up as bishops or abbots of one or more monasteries, a few were technically lay people. One example was Angilbert, who had a protracted relationship with one of Charlemagne's daughters (one of their sons became the historian Nithard). He donated two hundred books, a very considerable number, to the monastery of St-Riquier of which he had been appointed abbot.[48] Books were not absent from the homes of the nobility, although most of them were religious books and, possibly, mainly for use by wives and daughters. Less developed than in the monasteries was the instinct to establish permanent libraries, destined to survive generations. In his will, Charlemagne himself ordered that whoever wished to buy his books could do so at a fair price, and the money was to be distributed among the poor.[49] The enormous prices that manuscripts could fetch clearly affected the way they were perceived and meant that they were not valued solely for their intellectual content. But even today, a scholar's library is often dispersed after his death.

The Carolingian Minuscule

One of the lasting legacies of the Carolingian renaissance was the script we still use today in printing. When Charlemagne became king, the script most commonly used by copyists was intentionally complicated, full of squiggles, curlicues, and enormous pen strokes, but in a few monastic scriptoria in Gaul they were already experimenting with a much more practical script. Its letters were uniform and properly aligned, and the overall effect was that they were much more legible. This script, which experts call the Carolingian minuscule, had an unprecedented success under Charlemagne and gradually replaced all previously used scripts across the immense territory of the empire. As Bartoli Langeli has put it, this brought about the creation of "a single European script that left its mark on all writing practices for many centuries to follow, right up to the present day and who knows for how much time to come."[50] It was to the Carolingian script, which had been intentionally modeled on ancient lettering, that early printers of the Renaissance turned for the type from which modern types derive.

Specialists tend to deny that the success of the Carolingian minuscule can be attributed to Charlemagne's specific demands, and we have no direct evidence that there were any. Undoubtedly the emperor was deeply concerned about the errors that were being introduced into sacred texts by incompetent scribes. The creation of a script that was as clear and legible as possible was therefore very much in line with his own aims. Even in the absence of a deliberate campaign, the fact that Carolingian scholars were so often transferred to distant episcopal sees and abbeys after having served in the palace, bringing their books with them, and that there was such an effort to increase book production by copying works in the palatine library, is more than sufficient to explain the gradual affirmation of a uniform style of writing, even though significant local variants still survived at the time of Charlemagne. The spread of the new script can rightly be seen as part of the drive for unification of the religious and intellectual life of the empire, a distinctive feature in the policies of successive Carolingian emperors.

Even the punctuation that we use today is essentially a legacy of the scholars who gravitated toward Charlemagne's court. Alcuin, Abbot Mordramnus of Corbie, and others were committed to getting the scribes working in their scriptoria to adopt a uniform system in place of the arbitrary and, above all, disparate criteria that had previously been in use. The question mark first made its appearance in manuscripts of this era, with a curved shape that unequivocally heralded its current form.

GUARDIANSHIP OF THE FAITH
The Defense of Orthodoxy

The religious dimension to Charles's program of government is demonstrated by the frequency of his interventions in the field of theology, in competition with the pope and occasionally in disagreement with him. The first question in which he felt he had to intervene was that of adoptionism, a theory developed by the Spanish bishops Elipandus of Toledo and Felix of Urgel, according to which Christ was only God's adoptive son. The second of these two prelates resided in the Pyrenean march recently incorporated into the Frankish kingdom, but the first was a bishop *in partibus infidelium*, working in an extremely difficult situation in the heart of Arab-dominated Spain. It was not the pope but the king of the Franks who organized the debate on their theories, and this confirms that even before his imperial coronation Charles already considered himself the supreme Christian authority in the West.

It is worthy of note that the Christian Church continued to operate in Spain under Muslim domination, not clandestinely but with the tolerance of the Arab authorities. Inevitably, the bishops of that Church had little contact with their brethren beyond the Pyrenees, which explains why their theology was able to take on forms that elsewhere were considered rather unorthodox. Elipandus of Toledo could not be reached, but Felix of Urgel was invited in 792 to present himself at the royal palace in Ratisbon. There a council of Frankish bishops con-demned his doctrine as heretical and then sent him to Rome to recant his errors before Pope Adrian. When he returned to his homeland, Felix resumed his old beliefs, which then started spreading in Septimania, now the Languedoc, where there were many refugees from Spain. Charlemagne, who precisely during that period was beginning to pre-sent himself openly as the defender of orthodoxy against the deviations of Byzantium, must have been rattled by the alarming accusations that came to his ears.

In 794 the Council of Frankfurt, which met to discuss the theologi-cal positions of the Greeks in relation to the worship of images, added the question of adoptionism to the agenda and duly condemned it. Afterward Alcuin and others wrote persistently to Elipandus and Felix urging them to abandon their theory. The two bishops were immovable, even when Pope Leo III decided to get involved in the affair in 798, by publishing an anathema against the new heretics. In the following year the king summoned Felix to come and justify his actions in Aachen. The men of learning at the court had no doubts that such measures came under the authority of the king. Alcuin wrote that Felix had to come and "account for his doctrinal beliefs to the king."[51] As Claudio Leonardi has commented, it was the king who examined and repressed doctrinal devi-ations: "the Holy Office was in the palace."[52] It was a Holy Office, it should be said, that completely lacked the cruelty of later eras, as Felix, after being defeated by Alcuin in a public debate, returned home peace-fully to Spain and many years later continued to preach his theory to anyone who wanted to listen. The important point here is that Charlemagne considered himself personally responsible for orthodoxy, while the pope only backed him up with an auxiliary role.

The Council of Frankfurt very much symbolized the role the king of the Franks had now assumed at the head of the western Church. This synod, which had been called at the king's behest to debate his agenda, was expressly intended as an ecumenical council. Italian, Anglo-Saxon, and Spanish bishops sat alongside Frankish ones, although the unprecedented choice of venue demonstrated a concept of Christendom heavily skewed in favor of the Frankish kingdom. The matters under discussion were genuinely of common interest, including both adoptionism and the condemnation of the worship of images decreed by the eastern bishops in 787 when they gathered in Nicaea.[53] If we then consider how this ecumenical council convened by the king decided to condemn the Nicene conclusions, openly rejecting the line advised by the pope, we can judge just how far Charles had ventured, managing to get himself accepted by the church hierarchy as the true leader of the Church, even when it came to matters that were quintessentially theological.

The emperor's involvement in the so-called *filioque* question was no less audacious. Today, few Catholics realize that when they recite the Creed, they are repeating a formula that was personally imposed by Charlemagne. There was disagreement among Christians over how to interpret the traditional text drawn up for the first time in Greek at the first Council of Nicaea in 325. According to the Orthodox clergy, the Holy Spirit descends from the Father through the Son. In the Latin West, the tendency was to believe that the Holy Spirit descends equally from the Father and the Son. The Latin term *filioque*, meaning "and from the Son," had been introduced in the formulation of the Creed, although it did not exist in the Greek text. A few years after Charles's imperial coronation, Frankish monks installed on the Mount of Olives near Jerusalem quarreled with the Greek monks of St. Sabas and called on the pope to intervene, stressing that in the imperial chapel the liturgy was based on the *filioque* formula.

In Rome, the more ancient formula was still in use, as it was among Orthodox Christians, and the pope therefore considered the Frankish monks to be in the wrong. Yet he wanted to hear Charles's view on the matter, and this was in itself highly significant. Rather than consider the matter resolved by the pope's pronouncement, the emperor convened a council of the Frankish Church at Aachen in 809, which had no problem in finding Leo to be mistaken and establishing the orthodoxy of the *filioque* formula, after which Charles took the trouble to write to the pope to inform him of his error. To Leo III's credit, he refused to acknowledge this decision and continued to use the traditional formula in Rome, but in the rest of the western Church, the decisions of the Council of Aachen were automatically accepted. For the following two centuries, the liturgical usage of the Roman church remained different from that of the other Latin churches. This difference was compounded by the spread throughout Charles's empire of the custom of reciting the Creed during Mass, while the ancient use of reciting it only during baptismal services still prevailed in Rome. Finally, around the close of the millennium, Rome gave way and introduced the Creed into Mass in the form used everywhere else in the West, namely, the one with *filioque*. To this day Catholics say, "I believe in the Holy Spirit, that proceedeth from the Father and from the Son," according to the formula imposed by Charlemagne.

The Conversion of Pagans

Since the times of Charlemagne's grandfather, the idea of reforming the Frankish Church was linked to that of evangelizing the Saxon and Frisian pagans of the north. The energy and cultural training required to restore discipline and propriety among the bishops and monks of Gaul were the same qualities required to undertake missionary work beyond the borders of Christendom. It is no surprise then that the most important churchman and the architect of the first reforms under Charles Martel and later under Carloman and Pepin was a missionary. Boniface enjoyed the friendship of the Frankish mayors of the palace, and they provided him with the indispensable political and military backing for his apostolate in Germany. This was the reason why Boniface agreed in his old age to undertake the reform of the Frankish Church, before returning in his eighties to his true calling and getting himself killed in 754 by Frisian pagans.

Under Charlemagne, as we know, the question of converting pagans was dealt with in a much more drastic manner. Yet for the Frankish king and his ecclesiastic advisers the conversion of the Saxons to Christianity was never simply a matter of forced baptism at sword point. In reality, the task required a massive effort in terms of missionary work and ecclesiastical organization, and these proceeded in tandem with the military submission of the country. Mistakes were made, giving rise to polemics and requiring continuous policy adjustments. Initially, the conquered country was organized into missionary areas, mainly entrusted to priests and monks from Frankish monasteries. The abbey of Fulda alone sent no fewer than seventy or eighty missionaries to Saxony between 775 and 777.

The outposts of the faith in a conquered land were to remain exposed to insurrections for long time. Only later, when there was firmer control of the territory, was it possible to transform the more important missionary sees into bishoprics, at the same time as changing the preexisting tribal territories into counties. By 787 the missionary Willihad was ordained as bishop of Bremen and Verden, and around 796 a Frankish bishop was installed in Minden. By 799 there was also a bishop at Paderborn, the new royal residence in the heart of the conquered country, and, what is more significant, for the first time the bishop was a Saxon, Hathumar. Saxony was thus on its way to becoming in every sense a province of the Frankish kingdom, in both its political and ecclesiastical administration, although a final definition of diocesan boundaries was not possible until long after Charlemagne's death.

The missionaries' principal objective was to baptize pagans, and chronicles record that on several occasions there were mass baptisms. They were not always imposed by force, even when they followed military defeat, as was often the case. The Germans had always shown themselves willing to abandon their gods when these had been unable to protect them in battle, and from this point of view the god of the Franks was clearly proving to be much stronger. Also, we should not underestimate the fact that some missionaries, like Boniface himself, were Anglo-Saxons: the collective memory conserved a record of the ancestral relationship between the Saxons who emigrated beyond the sea and those who remained on the continent. Their languages were fairly similar, so preaching by these missionaries, who were perceived as close cousins, must have been particularly effective.

Yet it was no less common for Saxons, having accepted enforced baptism, to take advantage of the first opportunity to rebel. It is significant that every insurrection always started with the burning of churches and the massacre of priests. Following the great insurrection of 782, exasperation with these atrocities and the desire to find a definitive solution persuaded Charles to produce the terrifying *Capitulare de partibus Saxonie*, whose declared aim was to ensure "that Christ's churches, that are currently being built in Saxony and are consecrated to God, are no less honored than those vain temples of idols, indeed they should be honored more and better." In reality, he pursued this aim by imposing a reign of terror in which the death penalty was inflicted not only on murderers and arsonists but also on anyone who refused baptism, continued to practice pagan rites in secret, or breached the obligatory fasting during Lent.[54]

Not everyone approved of this policy of terror, even in Charles's closest circle. Alcuin wrote that "faith arises from the will, not from compulsion. You can persuade a man to believe, but you cannot force him. You may even be able to force him to be baptized, but this will not help to instill the faith within him."[55] Alcuin's criticism was particularly harsh when it came to the imposition of Christianity along with military defeat and therefore the plunder of the Saxons by victors. Saxony needed "preachers, not predators." In Alcuin's opinion, the system of tithes that existed throughout the kingdom had been extended too quickly to the newly conquered land, with the result that Saxons associated the imposition of Christianity with violent extortion: "the tithes, they say, destroyed the faith of the Saxons." He speculated on what would have happened if the apostles had endeavored to exact tithes from their listeners, after Christ had sent them abroad to preach his word.[56]

These reflections had their weight when it came to organizing the conversion of another defeated people, the Avars. In 796 an episcopal conference was summoned for this purpose, and its proceedings produced the condemnation of the methods applied in Saxony. The Franks now had to avoid repeating the same mistakes. Hurried mass baptisms were no longer an aim, and it was understood that a more sophisticated approach was needed. Paulinus, patriarch of Aquileia, who presided over the conference together with Bishop Arno of Salzburg and was charged with coordinating the missionary work among the Avars, wrote that although they were a "brutish and irrational people, and anyway ignorant and illiterate, so that only reluctantly and with difficulty could they come to understand the sacred mysteries," nevertheless they were not to be baptized without first being instructed and persuaded, while the teaching was to be based more on love than on terror. The suffering of hell had to be mentioned, but so had the joys of paradise, and in any case the sacrament was not to be imposed by the sword, and only those who requested it were to be baptized. As for tithes, Alcuin forcefully suggested to the king to defer their imposition on the new converts, stressing that even he, who had been born a Christian and educated as such, did not find it easy to pay his full share.[57]

The influence of this conference was enormous, and not just in Pannonia, where past mistakes appear to have been avoided, but also in Saxony, where it led to an immediate change of policy. By the following year, the king promulgated the new capitulary for the Saxons, which repealed the previous one and drastically reduced the regime of terror. Thus, for example, the murder of a priest, which previously was punished by death, was once again an ordinary crime that could be atoned for by the payment of *wergeld*, as normally occurred in all Germanic judicial systems.[58] Although the correspondence and poetic compositions that men of learning such as Alcuin and Paulinus addressed to their patron too often strike us as a monotonous succession of shameless adulation, we would do well to remember that on this occasion, those scholars knew how to express extremely critical views on one of the most delicate questions, and the king, in turn, was ready to accept those criticisms.

The Fight against Superstition

It was not only to the Saxons and Avars that the true faith had to be preached. The reason why Charlemagne devoted such energy to educating the clergy was that they were responsible for the religious instruction of his entire people. It was not enough simply to be born Christian in order to experience the faith in a conscious manner. In the *Admonitio generalis*, the king reminded bishops of their personal duty to preach to the people and organize the preaching of their priests. He even went so far as to establish exactly what it was necessary to preach to the faithful. They had to teach everyone that the Father, the Son, and the Holy Ghost were a single omnipotent God, according to the Creed that Charles himself imposed, and which made it possible to avoid the perils of heresy. They then had to explain that God who became flesh incarnate and was made man shall return in all His majesty to judge all men according to their merits and to ascertain whether they truly believed in the resurrection of the dead, so that reward or punishment can be experienced through the body.[59]

Evangelization was all the more urgent because, as Charles knew from the warnings of Matthew and Paul, *pseudodoctores* or false prophets would appear before the end of the world and attempt to lead the Christian people away from the path of righteousness. Although the end of the world could have been far off for all they knew, some of those false prophets had already manifested themselves in order to confuse the faithful. Before Charles was born, a certain Adalbert suddenly achieved great popularity. He erected wooden crosses in fields and at springs and gathered people together for extempore prayer meetings. We do not know what he preached, but he must have had a big success and caused great concern to the authorities, because in 744 Pepin ordered that all the crosses he erected should be burned.[60]

Each generation must have been destined to have its own false prophets, for nearly a half century later the word spread of letters filled with divine revelations falling from heaven, and some priests started to claim that they had seen them. The king prohibited the reading and distribution of such writings and ordered them to be burned. To avoid anyone else getting similar ideas, perhaps as the result of a slightly too frenzied religious ecstasy, Charles ordered that controls should be kept on all those homeless and lawless individuals who wandered around claiming to be inspired by God or those who tramped around naked carrying chains and claiming to be doing penance for their sins. The king had no sympathy for such people, and local authorities had to stop such vagabonds, particularly those who wanted to preach to the people. If they wanted to do penance, they should have done it by working rather wasting their time wandering the countryside.[61]

In Charles's eyes, the practices introduced by popular preachers, such as praying in the open air near trees and springs, came dangerously close to the pagan customs he had worked so hard to eradicate in Saxony by force of arms, yet their remnants survived even among the Franks. The problem had been even more pressing at the time of his father and his uncle. Carloman had ordered his bishops and counts to work together "in order that the people of God do not indulge in pagan practices, and repel and reject all the obscenities of paganism," and added a long list of pagan rites and superstitions.[62] Charlemagne, on the whole, did not appear so concerned, but throughout his reign he did publish ordinances that updated the list of prohibited practices. For example it was forbidden to open a psalm book or the New Testament at any page in search of an omen, to read the future in the excrement of oxen and horses, to baptize bells, or to hang up written spells on poles to ward off hailstorms.[63]

Rather than survivals from paganism, these customs reveal the popular religion as it was experienced by common people who were blithely unaware of the distinction between religion and superstition or magic, which appeared so clear-cut to the educated. There was a fundamental rationalism in Charlemagne's circle that leads us to attribute some of these repressive measures to exasperation with the superstition of the ignorant rather than fear of an increasingly improbable return to paganism. People shouted "Come on, Moon!" when there was a new moon and the sky was dark, because they believed that the heavenly body was engaged in some terrible battle and needed assistance.[64] But when the splendor of the sun had been dimmed by a black spot in 807, the author of the Royal Annals at Charlemagne's palace sat down to his calculations and established that it was the planet Mercury. He then noted with a tone of unmistakable scientific detachment that he had observed the conjunction for the duration of eight days, "but we have not been able to record when they went into conjunction and when they came out, because of the clouds."[65] It was hardly surprising that poor people who shouted themselves hoarse to express their support for the moon were looked on condescendingly, and that eventually this custom was added to the list of prohibited superstitions.

Perhaps the greatest protagonist in the battle against superstition was Archbishop Agobard of Lyons, one of Charlemagne's youngest protégés. Shocked by people's ignorance and stupidity, he wrote a tract denouncing commonly found false beliefs. In 810 an epizootic disease spread throughout the empire causing an extremely serious plague among oxen. Agobard informs us that it immediately began to be rumored among the people that Duke Grimoald of Benevento had sent out plague-spreaders equipped with poisonous powders to contaminate meadows and water supplies in order to kill the oxen. As was to be expected, many people were lynched after having been accused of spreading the pestiferous powders, and what was even more incredible, as the bishop observed, was that some people even managed to convince themselves that they really had spread the poison.

> This belief was so universal that hardly anyone was conscious of its absurdity. They never thought, as reason would require, how such a powder could be made, one that caused oxen to die but no other animal, and how they managed to spread it over such a vast territory, as this would not have been possible even if every man, woman, old

person, and child living in Benevento had left their country driving carts loaded with the powder. But this wretched world is now so oppressed by idiocy that Christians are willing to believe absurdities that even pagans would not have given credence to.[66]

In spite of Charlemagne's hard work and all the efforts of his circle of scholars, there was still a great deal to be done before his Christian people would be safe from error.

ELEVEN

The Frankish Military Machine

We have already established that in spite of the occasional setback, the Franks were generally victorious over their enemies. The prayers for the success of Charles's military endeavors that rose up out of the incense-laden air of all the churches of France and Germany could not have been responsible alone for this almost uninterrupted series of triumphs. The principal reason must have been the numerical and organizational superiority of the emperor's armies. It is time to explore the recruiting and fighting methods of these warriors who marched over the Alps to fight the Lombards and the Pyrenees to face the Arabs, pushed their way into the plains of Pannonia to destroy the Avars, and for so many years pursued the Saxons through the forests and marshes of northern Germany, gradually extending the authority of their king and their religion as far as the shores of the Baltic.

HOW THE FRANKS FOUGHT
The Age of Invasions

Given that the great majority of the Franks were subsistence farmers and not nomadic herders, like the peoples of the steppes, it is clear that originally most Franks were only able to fight on foot. Their military equipment must have been fairly rudimentary, since from a technological point of view theirs was a rather backward society and one in which there was even a shortage of metal tools for working the fields, so that peasants had to make do with wooden hoes. This was generally the case, although warfare had such prestige in Frankish society that the wealthy were willing to spend a great deal in order to obtain high-quality arms.

At the time of the barbarian invasions, the spear was the principal weapon carried by Frankish warriors. Next came the axe, which was so popular with them that the Romans called it the *francisca*, and one or more throwing-spears, often of a reinforced type called an *ango*. They were equally acquainted with the sword, but only the rich could afford the heavier type, the Roman *spatha*, while the one in wider use resembled a dagger sharpened only on one side, which the Romans called a *semispathium* and the Franks a *scramasax*. The defensive weapon was simply a round shield made of wood, which at the very most was reinforced by a metal boss. Only those in command could afford a steel helmet and perhaps a *lorica*, a Roman word that signified both a mail coat or a leather armor covered with metal plates, which was probably copied from the nomads of the steppes.

Thus the Frankish army at the time of Clovis could be summed up as a multitude of foot soldiers bristling with spears and defended by wooden shields, capable of striking the adversary even before they were at close quarters by hurling axes and throwing-spears. They were backed up by a small number of fighters on horseback, who were armed in more or less the same manner but whose greater wealth meant they could afford a mount, a long sword, and perhaps a helmet and a *lorica*. This portrayal is supported by the *lex Ribuaria*, whose more ancient compilation established that the value of a stallion was 12 *solidi*, a horse 3 *solidi*, a helmet 6 *solidi*, a *brunia* as much as 12 *solidi*, and a sword with scabbard 7 *solidi*, whereas 2 *solidi* would have been enough for a spear and a shield.[1] Clearly in the case of a mass mobilization, the number of horsemen must have been minimal compared with those fighting on foot. Even a spear and a shield, which were used to arm most of the combatants, represented a not inconsiderable sum: two-thirds of the price of a cow or horse. It becomes clear why only free men of some substance could afford to fit themselves out for war.

Arming the Cavalry under Charlemagne

By Charlemagne's time, the way Franks went to war had changed profoundly. It was not only a matter of some weapons disappearing and others becoming more widely used. Above all, there was a widening gap between the equipment of infantry and that of horsemen, who in this period began to be referred to as *caballarii*. In a capitulary of 793, it was casually observed that the armed vassals surrounding powerful figures occasionally included some slaves whose equipment was provided by their master. It consisted of "horses, lance, shield, long sword, and short sword."[2] These were the traditional weapons, but what is of interest is their mention as a set, as though it were obvious that every horseman, however lowly his status, normally possessed them all.

A few years later in 806, a summons sent by Charlemagne to Abbot Fulradus of St-Quentin established the equipment that a horseman was required to take to war. The list was identical to the one produced thirteen years earlier, and this demonstrates that it was the standard kit. However, there was one curious addition, that of a bow and arrows: "so that every *cabalarius* shall have shield, lance, sword, short sword, bow, and quiver with arrows."[3] Under the influence of the Byzantine chronicler Agathias, who claimed that the original Franks were not familiar with the bow and arrow, historians have inferred that the experience of fighting against the Avars persuaded Charlemagne of the usefulness of arming his cavalry with bows and arrows, or even that the idea was suggested to him by reading the Roman military theoretician Vegetius, whose treatise had only just been rediscovered.[4]

In reality, there is no reason to believe that bows were really an innovation, because the arrowheads found in tombs suggest that the weapon was far from unknown to the Franks. The laws of both the Salian and the Ripuarian Franks contain frequent references to the use of the bow, more so than any other weapon.[5] There might be an argument that bows were an innovation for horsemen, but even in this case there was a precedent. Fifty years before Charlemagne's birth, the armed servants who accompanied his great-grandfather Pepin of Herstal were equipped with "*loricae*, helmets, shields, lances, swords, and quivers filled with arrows."[6] Evidently the Frankish cavalry of the time was already similar to Charlemagne's, including the bow, and the clashes with the horsemen of the steppes did not teach them anything they did not already know.

The most important piece of the horseman's equipment was the *brunia*. Iconographic representations often show Carolingian warriors wearing this garment, a kind of leather jacket covered with metal scales. Not all Charlemagne's mounted soldiers could afford to buy one, as the *brunia* was so very expensive, but the emperor decided to make it obligatory for those who had the means. A law of 805 established that anyone who had at least twelve peasant families working for him was required to wear it when he was summoned to the army.[7] Procuring a *brunia* must have entailed a not inconsiderable sacrifice for those who did not already own one: a Bavarian noble called Hroadachar bought one from the bishop of Freising in exchange for part of his lands.[8]

We can therefore conclude that Charlemagne's army had a nucleus of armored cavalry, which probably counted a few thousand horsemen wearing *bruniae*, and then a more abundant supply of horsemen without *bruniae* who nevertheless could not be considered light cavalry, given their weapons. Besides, we should not make too sharp a distinction between the two groups, because the government was able to provide *bruniae* to a great number of horsemen who could not afford one. Bishops and abbots supplied their men with *bruniae* and swords. Charlemagne ordered them to distribute these to trusted followers or to outsiders only with his permission, and if they had equipment to spare after arming all their vassals, then they were to notify him of this directly.[9] If we consider that repeated bans on selling military equipment abroad, particularly *bruniae*, often accompanied these regulations, it becomes clear that at the time of Charlemagne equipping the army was no longer left to private initiative and was now an administrative concern.[10]

Arming the Infantry

Those who were not required to provide a horse had to have a spear, a shield, and a bow with a spare string and twelve arrows. The king added that no one was to report to the army armed only with a club, as evidently must have happened. Those who could afford nothing more had to come equipped with at least a bow.[11] These regulations inform us that, unlike the cavalry, the infantry's weaponry had become more rudimentary than in the past. Archaeology has confirmed that it had been reduced to the absolute essentials. No traces have been found of axes, once so popular among the Franks, or the short throwing-spears called *angones* that date from after the beginning of the seventh century. Even the sword, whether the long or the short version, appears to have become the reserve of horsemen, who would obtain one from their masters if they didn't have one of their own. It seems to have been taken for granted that if a warrior was rich enough to own a sword, he could also afford a horse.

Most significant is the insistence on a bow, which Charlemagne apparently considered the standard weapon of foot soldiers and indeed the only one for the poorest of them. This view is confirmed by the *Capitulare de villis*, which instructed administrators on how they should prepare carts for supplying the army: each cart should contain along with its load of flour or wine, "a shield, a spear, a quiver, and a bow," presumably to arm the guard.[12] Charlemagne's measures can be usefully compared with the laws of the Lombard king Aistulf, which were published in 750. These stated that all warriors who could not afford a horse "should have a bow and quiver with arrows if they can have a shield."[13] We find here the same intention to equip foot soldiers with bows and arrows as a single standard piece of equipment that we find half a century later in the emperor's ordinances, at a time when the Lombard military organization was fully integrated into the Carolingian war machine.

The adoption of the bow as the principal weapon of the infantry confirms that the cavalry was becoming the most important part of the army. Before the invention of gunpowder, an army whose main tactical strength lay in its foot soldiers had to arm these men with spears or swords in order to be effective. Only with such weapons could the infantry occupy and defend a position with little or no support from the cavalry. Conversely, infantry armed with bows and arrows could operate only in support of a mounted force that necessarily represented the army's tactical nucleus. The fact that foot soldiers were increasingly armed with bows and arrows in Charlemagne's armies demonstrates that the cavalry was gaining increasing importance during the emperor's long life. This trend had possibly occurred earlier among the Lombards but was clearly discernible among the Franks before Charles died.

Heavy Cavalry: A Revolution?

There are other indications that the cavalry, armed with lance and sword and protected by *brunia* and helmet, had acquired a considerable predominance in relation to the multitude that fought on foot. Even under Pepin, as far back as 755, the gathering of Frankish magnates and warriors that preceded the annual military campaigns was shifted from March to May: the army was mobilizing increasing numbers of horses, and it was therefore necessary to wait for the grass to be long enough to feed them. Royal chroniclers repeatedly noted the constraints imposed on military operations by the availability of fodder. In 798 the Saxons took advantage of an unusually bad year to rebel at the beginning of the spring, "when the army could not commence its campaign because of the lack of fodder."[14]

The uncertainty of the climate and the slowness of movement explain why the gathering was often held in June or even July, which in turn explains why the Franks had to suspend some campaigns, such as the one in 791 against the Avars, because the season was so far advanced that the horses could no longer find anything to eat.[15] Moreover, fodder was also indispensable for the thousands of oxen that pulled the carts in the baggage trains, the cumbersome convoys that Frankish military columns could not do without if they wanted to penetrate deep into enemy territory and maintain their presence there for several months. The manner in which the sources insist upon this aspect of strategic planning confirms that these were armies in which the horse had decisive importance.

There is no need to explain this change through the introduction of stirrups, as the American historian Lynn White Jr. has done.[16] It does not appear that they were widely used by Franks in Charlemagne's time. It is rare to find stirrups that can be dated back to the eighth century with any certainty. Even in the period of Louis the Pious illustrations in manuscripts depict warriors fighting on horseback without stirrups. Some considerable time after the emperor's death, the monk Notker told an anecdote that must have been conserved orally until then: Charlemagne had promised a bishopric to a young cleric, who in his delight left the palace and leaped on his horse in single bound, disdaining the stool that the servants offered him. The emperor, who had seen everything through the gate and did not find such behavior sufficiently dignified for a bishop, called him back and told him that anyone so athletic was needed more on the battlefield than in church. He therefore suspended the promised bishopric and appointed him instead to be one of the chaplains who followed him on military campaigns. This anecdote precludes the use of stirrups, irrespective of whether it actually happened.[17]

The fact is that the greater tactical importance assumed by the Frankish cavalry did not depend on a single revolutionary technological development. Rather, it reflected the greater wealth available in a society that had always made use of horses in warfare but in the past had encountered objective constraints on their widespread use. The increasing economic prosperity of the Carolingian age was reflected both in the slow but gradual spread of various technical innovations (including, there is no denying it, the stirrup, but also the *brunia*) and in the greater availability of horses. There should be no surprise that a new version of the law of the Ripuarian Franks drawn up in the early eighth century left the price of all weapons unchanged but heavily reduced the price of a horse from 12 to 7 *solidi*. It also reduced the price of an ox from 3 to 2 *solidi*, and a cow from 3 to 1.[18] It was therefore not a sudden and dramatic development but the growing ability to equip *caballarii* with heavy weaponry and armor that made it possible for Charlemagne to deploy an increasingly large and well-equipped cavalry.

Even more important than the causes of this development in weaponry and tactics were its consequences for the social composition of the Carolingian army. The greater availability of horses and *bruniae* meant that the relative contribution of the poorer smallholders unable to afford this equipment became less important. Rather than have them appear with a club, the emperor preferred to stipulate the use of the bow, a weapon that was distinctly cheaper than any other. There was, however, another possibility, and that was to exonerate them from military service altogether, while forcing them to contribute to the war effort in some other way. The changes that occurred under the Carolingians did not only concern the way in which the Franks armed themselves and fought but also the principle on which armies were recruited.

RECRUITMENT
Narrowing the Social Base

Strictly speaking, it was the duty of all free men to fight for their king when called upon to do so. This principle was so entrenched for some peoples, such as the Lombards, that a free man was referred to as an *arimannus*, a word whose Germanic roots correspond to the modern German *Heer*, "army," and *Mann*, "man." This term was readily translated in Latin documents as *exercitalis* and had a political and juridical significance as well as a military one. Indeed, the same sources also referred to the Lombard people as *felix exercitus*. Similarly, the litanies chanted in the Gaulish churches called on Christ to protect King Charles, his sons, his *iudices*, "and the whole army of the Franks," where that term *exercitus*, meaning "army," was again synonymous with the people.[19]

Obviously this does not mean that at each gathering every single free man had to go off to war, but simply that in principle everyone could be called up, if the king and his local representatives thought it necessary. A genuine mass conscription, which a later capitulary called a *lantweri*, a similar term to the Prussian *Landwehr* in the nineteenth century, probably occurred only when a region was directly threatened with invasion.[20] In spite of appearances, this could happen in Charlemagne's time: for instance Saxon raids along the Rhine in 778, Arab incursions into Septimania in 793, Norse forays along the western coast, and Arab attacks on Mediterranean islands, which became much more frequent after 800. On the other hand, when the Franks were planning the invasion of an enemy country, which happened almost every year, the army was generally recruited from the adjacent regions. Only in the case of more ambitious campaigns, such as the one beyond the Pyrenees in 778 or against the Avars in 791, do we hear of recruitment occurring simultaneously in all the provinces.

Local officials who received orders to gather the army were required to recruit all available men, and they were threatened with extremely harsh punishments if they granted exemptions too easily. The spirit that governed recruitment is expressed in a famous letter that Archbishop Hetti of Trier wrote to his suffragan Frotarius, bishop of Toul:

> We have received a fearsome order from our lord the Emperor, according to which we must notify all the inhabitants of the entire region in which we represent him to prepare themselves to take part in the war in Italy. We therefore order you on behalf of our lord the Emperor to notify immediately and zealously all the abbots, abbesses, counts, royal vassals, and all the people of your diocese, that is all those who are required to do military service for the king, to prepare themselves.[21]

There is a contradiction between the prevailing concept that the order refers to all the people and the specification that in reality it is only directed at those who are required to do military service. What does this contradiction mean?

The fact is that toward the end of his reign, Charlemagne's instructions started to restrict the obligation to bear arms and go to war to those who had sufficient means. The criterion used by the emperor was the number of peasant families that worked for each proprietor. Only those who had three or four families of slaves or tenant farmers working for them and therefore enjoyed a respectable degree of economic security were required to provide military service at their own expense. The others were exonerated but had to organize themselves, pooling their resources in order to equip a soldier. Thus, according to the instructions for the campaign of 808, four peasants who owned their own land but had no slaves and tilled the land by their own labor had to come to an agreement whereby one of them answered the call to arms and the others helped him with the equipment.[22]

The economic basis considered necessary to equip a combatant varied according to the impending campaign, and particularly in relation to the campaign's duration. This demonstrates that the main expense lay in the food supplies. In Saxony in 806, it was decided that six men would help equip the seventh for a military expedition into faraway Spain, whereas two men were enough to equip a third for an expedition against the neighboring Slavs.[23] Some scholars have argued that the man who was thus assisted left on horse, and that the light cavalry recruited in this manner constituted the majority of the Frankish army. The figures, however, do not support this interpretation. On one occasion, the specified collective cost incurred for equipping a combatant was 5 *solidi* or possibly 6, if we count a contribution from the man leaving for the war.[24] Given that a large part of the expenses went on victuals, it is clear that this was not sufficient to arm a horseman in accordance with the previously mentioned tariff in the law of the Ripuarian Franks, even if he were to take the absolute minimum in terms of equipment. It is therefore obvious that the less well off soldiers went to war on foot.

On the matter of how neighbors pooled resources to purchase arms, provisions, and means of transport, a Bavarian document might offer an early example of the system. Three men, Ratpald, Odalman, and

Kerperht, sold a few pieces of land to Abbot Opportunus of Mondsee in exchange for a stallion, two mares, a cow, six oxen, some shields, and a lance.[25] Clearly they were of a higher social rank than the people to whom Charles's regulations were later to apply: the oxen were too many for the transport of a single combatant, although we will see that the army used an almost infinite number of them, and altogether the expense corresponds to that required for arming a horseman and not a poor foot soldier. Yet we can infer that every time an order to take up arms reached a province, many transactions of this kind were undertaken by those who had to obtain the necessary weapons and provisions.

Integrating Vassals into the Royal Army

This change in recruitment methods, which clearly reduced the number of foot soldiers or at least those with little equipment, was accompanied by another, which was to prove no less consequential. It reflected the importance that vassalage had assumed in Frankish society. Every powerful man was surrounded by a group of vassals, whose service was primarily of a military nature and involved the possession of weapons and horses, possibly gifted by the lord, and the knowledge of how to use them. In the case of such people, Charlemagne considered it pointless wasting time calculating the size of their possessions and adjusting their armaments accordingly. In his eyes, it was obvious that anyone who belonged to a group of vassals was going to be a trained fighter, particularly when he had received a benefice from his lord. It went without saying that he would be called to arms. In 807 the emperor decreed, "first of all, those who are in possession of benefices shall all come to the army."[26]

But there was more. Each of these teams of vassals constituted a group of trained fighters accustomed to fighting together, so it would not have been sensible to split them up. The emperor therefore established that every man wealthy enough to be obliged to come to the gathering could join the army as part of the retinue of his own lord, if he had one. Only those who had no patron or who answered to a lord who on that occasion was not taking part in the campaign could arrive at the gathering place in the retinue of the local count, in accordance with traditional custom. Naturally, the order referred to free men, but there is reason to believe that the spread of armed followers actually modified the traditional rule that identified free men with those who could bear arms. The previously mentioned capitulary of 793 took for granted the existence of a great number of "slaves who have been honored in vassalage by their lords and can have horses and weapons, shield and spear, sword and short sword."[27] They were required to swear allegiance to the sovereign just as free men did, and it would have been very odd if they had been integrated into the army outside the units brought by their lords. In effect, Charlemagne made no distinction between followers who were free and those who were slaves and established that generally they should all follow the count, abbot, or bishop to whom they owed allegiance.

At the same time that he proclaimed the call to arms for all free men throughout the empire, the emperor sent individual ecclesiastical and secular magnates instructions that made them personally responsible for their vassals. One example was the celebrated letter to Abbot Fulradus of St-Quentin in 806, which gives us a good idea of the way the army was assembled in practice.

> You should know that this year we have convened our general
> assembly in eastern Saxony, on the river Bote and in the place
> called Stassfurt. We therefore order you to be there on 17 June
> complete with your men well armed and fitted out with arms,
> equipment, and all that is needed for the war in terms of food
> and clothing. Thus should every horseman have shield, lance,
> sword, short sword, bow, and quiver with arrows, and your carts
> should contain tools of all kinds, namely axes, planes, drills, hatchets,
> spades, iron shovels, and other tools required by the army. As for the
> stores, there should be rations for three months commencing from
> that date, and arms and clothing for six months.[28]

Engaging the Clergy in Military Service

There should be no surprise that the call to arms was sent to an abbot in such a peremptory tone. The military commitment asked of the Church was an integral part of the Frankish war effort, perhaps even an essential part. Since the time of Charles Martel, the immense estates owned by the clergy had been used by the mayors of the palace, and later the kings, to install their own armed followers, who thus had the means for equipping themselves with weapons, *bruniae*, and horses. The peasants who worked on those lands were still formally employees of the bishop or abbot, to whom they paid annual rent in return, but their work was required above all to maintain and equip the men-at-arms who had received the concession. As time went by, these outsiders pledged themselves to the bishops and abbots whose lands provided them with income. Thus the clergy provided patronage to armed men who gravitated around them in a manner no different from that of the vassals who surrounded the king and powerful secular figures. Clearly the king then considered such prelates responsible for these armed men, and for greater certainty, they had to lead their men to the army in person.

In the king's eyes, this involvement of the senior clergy in his military affairs was justified by the religious nature of his power and his certainty that God's blessing protected Frankish swords, engaged as they were in a just war against pagans. Yet some people were not happy about these powerful clerics who, at the express orders of their sovereign, carried a sword and a knife on their belts and wore boots and spurs, as one chronicler described them with pained disapproval.[29] One of Charles's most loyal followers, Patriarch Paulinus of Aquileia, wrote to him in respectful but uncompromising terms to explain that it was the king's duty to fight the Lord's visible enemies, and he should leave priests alone to fight against the invisible ones. The only weapons the clergy could wield were spiritual and not made of steel, and the only encampment they were allowed was the metaphoric one of the Lord, and not that of a king bearing arms, even when he was favored by God.[30] The same disquiet was expressed by his old ally Pope Adrian, who begged him not to force his bishops to take up arms: if they really had to accompany him on campaigns, then he should have let them deal solely with praying, preaching, and taking confession.[31]

Clearly the king expected much more of them, although, it has to be said, there is no proof that bishops and abbots were forced into physical combat and actually spilled blood. Taking part in military expeditions was an arduous affair that involved an absence of several months with long and grueling journeys and heavy expenses for the maintenance of men and horses. Actual involvement in fighting is highly unlikely. Nevertheless it was a dangerous and strenuous exertion for men who were often advanced in years. Alcuin wrote to his friend Archbishop Riculf of Mainz that he was "very worried about the journey you are about to undertake to join the expedition, because in these situations one encounters many dangers."[32] Two bishops died during one of the campaigns in which the army suffered its greatest privations, the one against the Avars in 791, but they died of exhaustion or illness, and not in battle. It is significant that when we hear of detachments preparing for combat, their commanders are counts or ministers of the palace but never bishops. There are endless accounts of the former dying in battle, as with seneschal Eggihard, count palatine Anselm, and Roland, prefect of the march of Brittany, who all fell at the battle of Roncesvalles, or chamberlain Adalgisile, constable Geilo, and as many as four counts at the battle of Süntel;[33] but during Charlemagne's long reign there is no record of bishops or abbots dying in battle, as was to occur with disturbing frequency during the civil wars among his grandsons.

Dealing with Shirkers

Military obligations were so burdensome that everywhere people were attempting to avoid them. Charlemagne's capitularies are very explicit in their exhortations to his counts, demanding that "no one be so bold as

to ignore their lord the Emperor's call to arms, and no count be so presumptuous as to exonerate any of those required to leave for the war,
perhaps as a result of some influential relation or in return for a bribe."[34]
The regulations were so detailed as to lay down that each count could
exempt from military service no more than two of his vassals to be left
at home to protect his wife and another two to take over his official
duties. If a count governed more than one county, he could leave two
men in each one. Bishops and abbots, who at least officially were not
supposed to have wives, were authorized to leave just two vassals.[35]

In reality, unjustified exemptions were extremely frequent; indeed
they were one of the most powerful tools magnates possessed in order to
impose their Mafia-style authority, by favoring their own men and dam-
aging those who did not play the game. A capitulary rails against those
powerful men who abused their authority by calling up for military service those they wanted to ruin in order to take over their lands:

> they say that should anyone refuse to hand over their land to a
> bishop, abbot, count, or judge, they will find a way to have him
> condemned and they always send him to war, until he is reduced
> to poverty and obliged to give up his property whether he likes it
> or not. The others who have already given up their lands stay at
> home and nobody disturbs them.[36]

But also, "others say that they force the poorest to join the army and
those who can pay, stay at home." In fact, some smallholders were willing to do anything to avoid this obligation, which was renewed inex-
orably every year and forced them to keep expensive equipment, spend
large sums on provisions, needlessly overwork and possibly lose horses,
and leave home for many months, not to mention the danger to life and
limb. The emperor even went to so far as to prohibit free men from
donating themselves and their property to the Church, in accordance
with widespread practice, "because we have heard that some of them do
not do it out of devotion, but in order to avoid the army and other services due to the king."[37] Similarly there were people who allied them-

selves to a magnate or even submitted to him as slaves, solely in ex-change for the promise of being helped to remain at home. This phe-nomenon became increasingly common in the latter years, so in 811 the emperor added to the assembly's agenda "the reasons why men do not fulfill their military obligations."[38] The preparatory material for the debate included the explicit assertion "that the inhabitants as a whole are more disobedient to counts and envoys than they have been in the past." The truth is that after many years of war, the Franks were tired of cam-paigns that were now leading to more hardships than glory and, what was even worse, more expenses than booty.

On paper, anyone who did not fulfill his military obligations was required to pay an enormous fine, the *heriban* or army fine. Royal envoys were encouraged to collect it without showing any pity or rather with-out allowing themselves to be bribed. They were supposed to enter the guilty man's house and confiscate not only his money but also his live-stock and movable goods, including clothing ("but this should not mean that wives and children are deprived of their clothes," Charles prudently advised), up to a value that for a fairly affluent man would represent half of his assets, while the proportion gradually decreased to a quarter for the less well-off. The names of anyone who could not pay were to be recorded and the procedure suspended until the emperor had been informed. In the worst cases, they could be forced to serve the crown as slaves until they had paid back the entire sum owed. The intention was to punish the guilty so harshly that they would never attempt to do it again, but without ruining them completely, "so that on the next occa-sion they would be able to equip themselves for war in the service of God and our interests."[39]

To avoid the collection of the *heriban*'s becoming another opportu-nity for the abuse of power, it could never involve the confiscation of land, buildings, or slaves. Moreover, the collection of the fine was never entrusted to local counts but to either royal envoys or specialized officials called *haribannitores*. This had the unforeseen result of making it even more difficult for counts to call up the army, given that the men in their area would object in more or less bad faith that the matter was no longer under their jurisdiction.[40] Those who arrived late at the encampment were punished with the same number of days on bread and water as the days they were late, while abandoning the army without permission, in effect desertion, "which in the German language we call *herisliz*," was punished with death and confiscation of all property.[41] The fact remains that in a society heavily imbued with patronage like that of Charlemagne's empire, abuses must have abounded in spite of all the exhortations. Collective tiredness and his own personal weariness might explain why in his later years, as we shall see, the emperor proved to be considerably less bellicose than he had been in his youth.[42]

THE STRATEGY
The Logistics

Another feature of recruitment under Charlemagne emerges from the letter to Abbot Fulradus, and that is the long time it took to gather the army together. The call to arms necessarily had to be sent out several months before the date on which operations were expected to begin, given that the abbot of St-Quentin needed about two months to travel to the Bote River after he had assembled men and provisions. Clearly the objective of the summer campaign had to be decided upon long beforehand, possibly as far back as the assembly in the preceding autumn. Equally the methods of recruitment had to be suited to gathering large forces without hurry with a view to an offensive campaign in enemy territory, in which the Franks would be able to decide the time and the place of their operations. As long as Charles was alive, the system paid off because it allowed sufficient strategic preparation to gather forces with massive numerical superiority to anything any single adversary could put into the field.

Many scholars have attempted to calculate the size of the total available military force in the empire, but attempts have produced absurdly divergent results, ranging from five thousand to fifty thousand horsemen. It would be more useful to reflect on the fact that the larger a state is, the smaller the armed forces that it puts in the field in any given moment in proportion to its population and its economic resources. In the case of an immense empire such as the one Charlemagne created, the practical difficulties in gathering men together, marching them to the enemy country, and adequately supplying them for the duration of the campaign were undoubtedly the principal constraint on the numerical expansion of the operational force. This effectively made it impossible to exploit fully the human potential, which must have appeared almost unlimited in comparison.

Rather than calculating the number of potential mounted combatants that could be recruited in the empire, it would be more sensible to consider the difficulties in marching a force of upward of ten or twelve thousand men, some of whom would have been on foot, along a single route and supplying them in a narrow sparsely populated corridor, where the enemy could have used a scorched-earth policy. The aforementioned figure must have been the optimal size of an army, even though on large-scale campaigns, two or even three armies were often mobilized at the same time to converge on the enemy country from different directions. The total availability of men and horses in the empire allowed Charles to plan these combined operations with the maximum room for maneuver, and also to organize operations on different fronts and against different enemies at the same time, while ensuring that every local commander had more than sufficient forces to defeat the enemies he faced. Ultimately, this was the secret behind the Frankish victories. It was already the case, as Napoleon was well aware much later, that God was on the side of the large battalions.

One of the factors restricting the size of an army was the staggering amount of carts and draft animals it required. Charlemagne's army, as we have seen, carried sufficient supplies with it for a campaign lasting several months, and it could not have been otherwise. Warriors undoubtedly requisitioned what they could from local inhabitants, while animals could graze on the roadside. However, requisitions were restricted to grass, wood, and water while they were still on imperial territory, and while they could seize provisions more freely once they were in enemy territory, it was always possible that crops had been destroyed on the invader's approach. There was therefore no choice but to bring rations of flour and, in order to keep the horses in good condition, they needed cereals to supplement the grass and hay found along the way.

The military columns stretched out for many miles along the Roman roads that crossed the empire, before entering enemy territory on roads that were often considerably worse or even nonexistent. The enormous size of these columns was mainly due to the baggage trains. The common two-wheeled cart pulled by a yoke of oxen was capable of carrying half a ton of flour, barely a day's ration for 500 men. The ration for 1,000 men over a 3-months' campaign was therefore 180 carts and 360 oxen. Then there was the wine, which at the time was routinely drunk by all sections of society and constituted an important supplement of calories. Given that a cart could carry 130 or 160 gallons, the same 1,000 men would need another 180 carts on the campaign. Every day a horse would require about 22 pounds of fodder, of which half could be grass or hay but the other half would have to be barley or oats. Over three months 100 horses would therefore consume the loads of another 90 carts. This is not counting the carts that transported arms and equipment, or the provisions required for the long journey from the men's own country to the assembly point where operations would begin.

The calculation is quite straightforward: a force of about 12,000 men, of which perhaps 3,000 would be on horse, would be accompanied at the moment it entered enemy territory by more than 6,000 carts pulled by 12,000 oxen! This explains some aspects of Charlemagne's strategy, like the division of his forces into two or three armies each with a separate itinerary. While in some cases, such as the invasion of Italy in 773, it was a conscious pincer movement in order to get round the enemy defenses, more generally this splitting up of the army was the only practical way to exploit the numerical superiority of Frankish armies without exhausting too quickly the limited resources of grass, hay, and water in the territories through which they passed. Clearly, when possible Charlemagne used waterways to transport supplies to the army on barges at the cost of restricting strategic movements, as in the campaign of 791 against the Avars, which was conducted along the banks of the Danube.

Obviously, baggage trains restricted mobility. Armies marched not at the pace of the infantry, but at the even slower pace of the oxen that pulled the carts: no more than 9 or 10 miles a day in the best possible conditions. The wide radius of devastation inflicted on the enemy country was carried out by squads of horsemen who spread out from the main body of the army, taking their supplies on pack horses and not carts. Given that each horse could carry 220 pounds and consumed 11 per day, while the rider consumed perhaps 2.2 pounds, in theory a squad of horsemen could be independent for about 10 days at an average speed of about 19 to 25 miles a day. The total area subject to incursions therefore proved quite extensive.

The majority of the army depended on oxen, and it has to be asked whether the postponement of the annual encampment from March to May was not in response to the need to find grass for the oxen rather than for the horses. This theory appears plausible when we consider that not only were the oxen more numerous than the horses, but the latter fed at least partly and if necessary entirely on barley or oats, whereas the oxen fed only by grazing meadows. In the final analysis, the humble ox must have influenced Charlemagne's plans a great deal more than the superb horse, although clearly when it came to the moment of crossing swords, heavily armed horsemen were the principal force in Frankish armies.

Fortresses and Sieges

When discussing Charles's wars, we should avoid the frequent mistake of equating combat with pitched battle. The importance of the pitched battle in antiquity and its renewed importance in modern Europe mean that we often do not realize that for long periods it was not central to war. The age of Charlemagne was one such period. Charles reigned for nearly half a century and organized one or more military expeditions almost every year, and yet during that period we can count battles in the modern sense of the term on the fingers of one hand: Roncesvalles in 778, Süntel in 782, Detmold and the battle on the Hase River in 783. The reason was that Charles's campaigns were nearly always invasions with superior forces and the enemy preferred to defend itself by withdrawing into a fortified area. However different their traditions and their methods of warfare, this was the strategy adopted by the Lombards, the Avars, the Saxons, and the Arabs of Spain.

The purpose of a campaign was not therefore to meet on the field of battle, which the enemy would in any case refuse to do when faced with Charles's armored cavalry and multitude of archers who supported it. It was to occupy the territory by laying siege to enemy fortresses and taking them. By the time of the wars of Charles Martel and Pepin in Aquitaine, references to successful sieges were so common that we have to conclude that the inability to lay siege to a fortified position, which once so afflicted barbarian armies, had now been overcome. At the same time, conquest was accompanied by the erection of permanent fortifications, particularly in areas with few population centers like Saxony and Aquitaine. The intention was to ensure the defense of the conquered land once the majority of the army had returned home. They also acted as advanced positions and supply depots for future campaigns.

The question arises as to whether the possession of advanced siege technologies, copied from the Byzantines and Arabs, was not perhaps the emperor's secret weapon. To be honest, the direct references to the use of siege machinery, and in particular catapults, are exceptionally rare. The first explicit mentions of the use of this equipment by the Franks date back to the reign of Louis the Pious.[43] The capitularies on gathering the army, normally so meticulous in specifying the arms and provisions that each person must bring, are completely silent on siege equipment. Yet the royal chronicler testifies to the use of catapults by Saxons during the siege of fortresses built by Charlemagne beyond the Rhine, and we can confidently exclude the possibility of those pagans possessing superior technologies to the emperor's.[44] We have to conclude then that Frankish armies used similar equipment. The omission from the capitularies can therefore be explained by the possibility that catapults and other machines were constructed at the place of combat once the decision to lay siege to a fortress had been taken. This gives a precise meaning to the orders requiring carts to be loaded with carpentry tools specifically declared necessary for the army.

We must take into account the technological limitations of siege equipment, whose effectiveness varied according to the type of fortification to be attacked. During Charlemagne's campaigns, Frankish armies frequently took enemy fortresses with apparent ease. For instance, *castella* and fortresses built in forests and marshlands were conquered during the two invasions of the Avars' country in 791 and 796 and the operations against the Bretons in 786. In 810 King Pepin of Italy occupied the islands of the Venetian lagoon in a combined action by land and sea. But all such fortifications were mainly built of wood and earth, like those erected by the Franks themselves: when it came to laying siege to ancient Roman cities defended by stone walls, it was a very different question.

During the war against the Lombards, Pavia and Verona were both taken by starving the enemy out after extremely long sieges. The first one lasted almost a year. During the campaigns beyond the Pyrenees, Saragossa and then Barcelona also fell after debilitating sieges. In his account of this last siege, which was directed by the emperor's son Louis the Pious, the chronicler Ermoldus Nigellus described the only war machines as battering rams, which ineffectually struck the solid wall of the city. As Aldo Settia has acutely pointed out, his description of Prince Louis riding his horse up beneath the walls and hurling his spear so that it pierced the marble, was both a gesture of defiance and a confession of impotence.[45] It was perhaps his experience as the king of Aquitaine,

fighting in a region full of Roman cities as was the case in Spain immediately south of the Pyrenees, that induced Louis to invest so much in
the acquisition of war machines. It was during his reign that a chronicler
described for the first time the use of the mangonel during the siege of
another Spanish city, Tortosa; this time, and from that time on, man-
gonels were to be employed regularly in medieval wars.[46]

TWELVE

A New Economy

THE MYTH OF A CLOSED ECONOMY

In twentieth-century historiography the Carolingian economy suffered from a long period of unfavorable preconceptions. According to the theory of Henri Pirenne, once the West had been deprived of its Mediterranean outlets by Arab invasions, its economy regressed to a purely agrarian level dominated by private consumption and the almost total absence of long-distance trade. That weakness in trade or even its disappearance necessarily meant a closed economy was widely accepted by textbooks that perpetuated the image of a narrow and stifling agrarian life. It then became difficult to attribute the Carolingian age with the prosperity, even if only modest, or the economic dynamism that historians before Pirenne had tended to take for granted as the obvious corollary of Charlemagne's political and military triumphs. "A complete lack of technique, land out of control, settlement barely established, rare and extremely mediocre surpluses that a few privileged people exchanged, a productive structure that was almost dysfunctional and at the very least inefficient": as late as 1981 this was how a great historian like Robert Fossier felt obliged to summarize the economic reality of the Carolingian empire.[1]

But at the time, the orthodoxy that had lasted half a century was beginning to be challenged, as Fossier himself must have been aware, as he added, "but alongside this, it is also true, a possible increase in the number of people, a few displacements, a little more money, and a desire to do better." Today these signs, which in his opinion were not sufficient to justify talk of growth, are better known and tend to form a decidedly more optimistic historical interpretation. What is more important is that this interpretation succeeds in giving an overall sense of the different forces at play: from the organization of production to the ownership of large estates and from the imperial government's economic and monetary interventions to the dynamic role of the great monasteries. It therefore allows us to perceive the Carolingian economy as a vital part of Charlemagne's administration, and not just its passive backdrop.

This, then, is how we imagine it. Agriculture dominated the economy and peasants made up the great majority of the population. Many of them were smallholders who lived in their own houses and worked their own land. We know very little about them, and it is probable that these peasants really did live a reality based on private consumption, eating their own bread and pork and drinking their own wine. The large estates had an entirely different role. They employed a great number of peasants, possibly the majority. They were different from the ancient latifundia and tended to organize themselves according to a new method that historians have called the manorial system. Above all, large estates had to provide food for their owners, often monasteries or possibly the king. But they also produced surpluses on a much more systematic basis than was previously believed, and these surpluses were traded.

As far as this trading activity was concerned, geography favored the large crown, aristocratic, episcopal, and monastic estates situated at the heart of the empire between the Loire and the Rhine. Having lost its Mediterranean outlets (Pirenne was right on that point), Europe ruled by the Franks did not stagnate in private consumption but directed its trade routes toward the north and the west. In 817 Benedictine monks were granted authorization to use lard and butter in place of olive oil, which was required by the rule but almost unobtainable in much of the empire, and this strikingly symbolizes the way trade had been redirected. The sacrifice of the Mediterranean basin in favor of the North Sea did not involve an overall reduction in the volume of trade. At the same time the monasteries kept demanding exemptions from tolls for their agents who transported agricultural produce, the king legislated on prices and money, the ancient Roman lighthouse was restored in the port of Boulogne to increase the safety of navigation, and emporia protected by royal charter were springing up all over the river basins of Neustria and Austrasia and along the Flemish and Frisian coasts. They attracted *nego-tiatores* in the service of large landowners, who were searching for those products that their masters' lands could not produce. Anglo-Saxon, Frisian, and Scandinavian merchants offered fish, cheese, textiles, furs, and slaves in exchange for grain, wine, weapons, and pottery. While the old Mediterranean ports like Marseilles were languishing and traffic along the Rhône had dried up, new trading centers like Rouen at the mouth of the Seine, Quentovic on the English Channel, and Dorestad in the Rhine estuary were becoming famous throughout Christendom.

Thus in a spectacular reversal of the traditional interpretation, the predominance of the great manorial farm no longer means that Europe was thrust into the misery of private consumption. Ultimately it gave rise to a dense network of new urban settlements, government interest in maintaining the road and river links, and the introduction of mone-tary reform to guarantee the circulation of a manageable and uniform currency throughout the West. As Giuseppe Petralia has correctly pointed out, "the place Pirenne perceived as an enclosed economy with no trading outlets has been transformed into the place where the un-stoppable dynamism of the West was nurtured."[2] From this point of view, Charlemagne's legislative activity and his policy of unification rightly appear as the starting point for the flourishing of late medieval and modern Europe.

THE MANORIAL ESTATE
The Manor or Villa

At the very heart of the economy was the large agrarian estate organized in accordance with the manorial model. This has to be our starting point, before we deal more closely with merchants and trade. It should be made clear that historical research over recent decades has persuaded us that everywhere the empire was teeming with independent peasants, who did not operate within the same economy as the large estates. They worked for themselves, and it is even possible that in many areas villages and cultivation organized on the manorial system were the exception rather than the rule. Yet it is this organizational model that attracts our curiosity, because it is thought that the large estate, not independent peasantry, was the driving force behind the entire economy. This does not mean that we should not be interested in how the peasants lived, what they ate, and how they worked. What we have not been told about this in written sources is now beginning to emerge from archaeological research, as we shall see later. However, to understand how the Carolingian economy worked, we must first describe the manorial estate.

The emperor, large monasteries, bishops, and noble families owned enormous tracts of land, with thousands of slaves, freed slaves, and tenant farmers. The properties were spread over a vast area, which in the case of the emperor coincided with the territory of the empire itself— about 400,000 square miles. For an abbot or a count, it was quite normal to own land and control laborers hundreds of miles from the main residence. For management reasons, these lands were, wherever possible, grouped together in agricultural complexes known in the Latin of the time as *curtes* or *villae*, each of which was responsible to a factor and was administered as an organic whole. It follows from this that large landowners owned not one but many *villae*, perhaps several dozen or, in the case of the emperor, hundreds. The Parisian abbey of St-Germain-des-Prés, for example, owned as many as twenty-five *villae* mainly located between the Loire and the Seine, with a total land area of over 124,000 acres.

The *villa* differed from the latifundium of antiquity in at least two ways. First, it was not a geographically compact estate with fields of grain or olive groves stretching out of sight and all belonging to the same master. Instead it came from the grouping together, for administrative reasons, of fields, vineyards, meadows, and woods that were not necessarily adjacent. Of course, as happens in any society, large estates tended to enlarge further and absorb small adjacent properties, so that in one or more peasant settlements, the majority of the land or indeed all of it belonged to the same owner and was organized within the same *villa*. The large crown estates or *fisci*, as they were called in documents of the time, were particularly likely to take on this form. In France, the territory of a modern commune or even two or three neighboring communes sometimes corresponds to the boundaries of an ancient crown property. *Villae* nearly always included scattered properties and isolated workers, while peasant smallholdings would survive among the master's fields, as might some properties belonging to other large landowners.

The Workforce

The second difference between the manorial estate and the ancient latifundium, at least in its most typical form, was that the owner no longer had enough slaves to work all of the land on an extensive basis and meet the demands of the market. Inventories of properties owned by a few large monasteries drawn up at the time of Charlemagne and his successors show that less than half the workers were slaves. We are not interested here in the reasons for this relative decline in the slave population, which was already occurring during the late Roman Empire, but only in the countermeasures taken by landowners. In the main, these involved the decision to maintain direct management of only part of the estate, which would continue to be exploited through slave labor, while the rest was divided up into farms. According to a custom that had started to spread under the last Roman emperors, each farm was entrusted to a peasant family, which took on a series of obligations toward the landowner, of which the payment of rent was not always the most important.

This gave rise to the split organization that typifies the manorial estate. Each *villa* had part of its lands cultivated directly by a team of slaves for the master's benefit, and part subdivided among peasants who organized their work more or less independently. The former part was called a *dominicum* or *pars dominica*, that is the "master's part," and the latter part was called the *massaricium* or *pars massaricia*, from the term *massarius* used to signify a tenant farmer who resided on the land. It goes without saying that this was not a more or less equal division of the land. The ratio between the land rented out and the land held under direct management was extremely variable, although at the time of Charlemagne the part divided into smaller farms probably already tended to be larger than the one reserved for the master, and this trend continued.

This development was the product of a specific policy that tended to transform slaves into independent farmers working land on their own. Their work was probably more productive as a result of that incentive. For religious reasons, the law forced the landowner to allow his slaves to marry and to respect their marriage. This was a further reason for assigning a house to each one. Religion also encouraged the freeing of slaves, which was not an unimportant contributory factor toward their constant diminution. Slave owners nearly always chose a procedure involving conditional manumission that kept freed slaves bound to the owner and forced them to work on the estate as smallholders.

The Mansus

The very nature of the *villa*, as an aggregate of properties often not adjacent to each other and with land of varying quality not always suited to the same type of cultivation, favored the conversion of the majority of land into tenant farms, which documents of the time called *mansi*. The term *mansus* meant the dwelling house and the lands farmed by one or very often more than one peasant family. The etymology of the word goes back to the idea of residence and nothing more. It tells us nothing, for example, about the type of ownership. The documents that refer to *mansi* are mainly inventories for large estates, in which each *mansus* comes under a *villa*. On the other hand, a small or medium-size land-owner, such as the ones often referred to in Charles's capitularies, would only own one to three *mansi*, which would be rented to the same number of peasants but without organizing them in a manorial estate. The dwelling and farm of a free peasant who worked his own land were probably also called a *mansus*. Indeed, with the addition of the adjective *indominicatum* ("of the landowner"), it could equally indicate the land on a *villa* reserved for extensive farming by the landowner or what could be termed the manorial farm.

It may be that the *mansus* that came under an estate ended up as a mainly administrative concept, without any geographic significance, since a peasant could be assigned, say, a house in the village, a portion of the large field plowed collectively by all the inhabitants, a portion of the uncultivated land for grazing livestock, and the right to keep pigs, take firewood from the forest, and perhaps even fish in the river. All these possessions and privileges constituted the *mansus* in the eyes of the landowner. In other cases, the *mansus* represented what we would call a farm, namely, a series of adjacent plots farmed by peasant families living in a detached house. It would not have made any difference whether they were independent smallholders or tenants of a large landowner.

Today, the question of the size of *mansi* no longer arises, although it did tax historians for a long time. Equally, it is difficult to understand their amazement at the enormous difference in the size of *mansi* within the same *villa*. Just as today in any country area, it is possible to find old men who laboriously till small plots next to prosperous farms ten or twenty times larger that are worked by two or three brothers as partners, so the division of land into *mansi*, which was not an artificial obligation but reflected the natural dynamics of a society, could produce widely different variations. Moreover, there were considerable differences in the fertility of land and between areas suited to growing cereal crops, vineyards, or livestock. All these differences contributed significantly to the size and nature of a *mansus*. Yet the techniques of measurement and accountancy were so rudimentary that, in spite of its variability, the *mansus* was considered by the rulers of the empire to be the most useful unit of measurement of landed property and therefore of wealth. Both the abbot who drew up an inventory of his monastery's properties on the emperor's orders and the local officials who had to divide up the burden of military expeditions among proprietors in the region essentially based their calculations on the number of *mansi* that made up each *villa* or belonged to each landowner. The *mansus*, as well as being used as a unit for measuring farmland and for collecting rents, also became the unit for calculating impositions levied by the government. As can be easily imagined, this must have caused many injustices and inequalities. But then what tax system does not?

The Corvée

There is another decisive reason why the split manorial system became universal and why large landowners, when obliged to convert part of their lands into smallholdings, did not split up some of their *villae* in their entirety and then keep others wholly under direct management. The reason why each individual *villa* had both directly farmed land and tenant farms was that in a society with limited technological resources, the work of the peasantry was largely subject to the rhythm of the seasons. A landowner who wished to farm a large area of field on an extensive scale, as in the case of the *dominicum* or manorial farm of a large *villa*, would have needed a great number of laborers at the time of harvesting and haymaking, but there would also have been long months when a minimal workforce would have been sufficient. It therefore made sense to employ the absolute minimum of *prebendarii*, as they called the slaves the master had to feed all year round, whether or not they were working. In the times of greater labor requirements, during the harvest for instance, landowners would then call on the assistance of their tenant farmers. At the same time, they could save the money required for keeping plows, carts, and oxen on the *dominicum*, by forcing the tenant farmers to make theirs available during the periods of greatest need for plowing and transporting the harvest to market or the master's residence.

Peasants who settled on a *mansus* therefore undertook to provide their labor to the landowner for a certain number of days, if necessary with a plow or cart. These commitments to provide labor, called corvées, generally replaced the use of a salaried workforce, which other eras considered the solution to the problem but the age of Charlemagne made little use of. The reasons were the lack of money in circulation and the country's low population, which generally meant a shortage of labor. It was therefore difficult to build up a large stratum of landless laborers willing to sell their labor for wages. It would be no exaggeration to say that the labor provided free of charge by corvées was indispensable everywhere to guarantee the cultivation of land reserved for the owner and the transport of harvests. This then was the central core of the manorial economy.

These services did not only have an economic purpose, or rather their effects went far beyond the purely economic sphere. Because tenant farmers were bound by contracts that were generally oral and handed down in inheritance from father to son, and because they worked the master's land shoulder to shoulder with his slaves, albeit for a limited period but often involving hard toil, they found their dependence on their master reinforced in both a symbolic and a concrete manner. Although they were born free, they were also the landowner's men—in a different way from the slaves, it is true, but not so different that certain parallels could not be drawn or even a kind of assimilation produced in the collective understanding. Then there is the question of the descendants of freed slaves. These *liberti* or manumitted slaves were bound by inheritance to their master and required to work for him and do him obeisance. They thus became increasingly indistinguishable from those who remained in slavery, once they were both being settled on farms that they cultivated on their own behalf. The tendency to consider all those who toiled under a master on a large estate to be a single mass of subject laborers or, let us use the word, serfs was to have a decisive importance in determining the end of ancient slavery and the birth of a new status, that of serfdom, from which the great mass of the peasantry was not to be freed until many centuries later.

The Management of the Estate

Villae could vary tremendously in size from 500 or so acres to over 50,000, although more frequently they were around 2,500 to 5,000 acres. The number of directly employed laborers was therefore equally varied. There could be a few dozen or there could be hundreds of families. One of the largest crown estates in Italy, at Bene Vagienna, organized the work of about 3,300 laborers, who with wives and children represented in the region of 15,000 people. Naturally, these sizes were not static: the *villa*, like every type of estate, was a living organism and therefore in movement. A famine year, the afflictions of an epidemic, or the devastation of war in a border region could wipe out peasant families that were difficult to replace. Monastic inventories frequently mention *mansi absi* or uninhabited dwellings with land, although it has to be said that somehow or other the fields of these *mansi* were often still being farmed.

The presence of uninhabited *mansi* might also reflect an ongoing reorganization or even the plowing up of new land on which it had not yet been possible to settle tenant farmers permanently. Although the empire was sparsely populated overall, the population was tending to grow, and when the workforce increased, the master could order new land to be put under the plow: scrubland was cleared, woods cut down, and marshes drained in order to produce new fields. There was no shortage of land, provided there was a workforce to farm it. Everything implies that in the

Carolingian era such initiatives were widespread, although they were not to have the epoch-making impact of the great increase in land use that occurred in the early part of the next millennium.

For a long time, historians believed that all *villae* were organized in accordance with the same system, irrespective of the local conditions, in order to produce everything the master needed. In that case the land reserved for his consumption had to cover an immense variety of production, ranging from wine to hemp and from meadows for livestock to woodland for firewood and raising pigs. The factor would be in permanent residence in the manor, and he represented the administrative center of the estate. Next to the manor there would be barns, granaries, stables, warehouses, premises for producing cheese, salting meat, and making beer, vegetable gardens, chicken runs, and fisheries. Sometimes there were also workshops, called *gynaecea* according to ancient usage, where workers' wives wove and made clothes for the entire *familia* of laborers held in some form of servitude.

Today we have a much more complex image. It appears increasingly evident that the majority of *villae* belonged to proprietors who owned a great many others, and they were able to specialize production with a certain amount of forethought. Clearly the factor organized the work of his men differently according to whether he was preparing to host his master in the coming winter, prepare a baggage train for the army, or sell the harvest to send the profit to his master. Although the *villa* was managed independently, it was still an integral part of a large productive cycle. In the case of large crown estates, several neighboring *villae* could be placed under the authority of a single factor, to whom *maiores* or foremen were answerable.

Local conditions also influenced the type of crops an estate grew. In particularly suitable areas, the main manorial farm specialized in the production of wine and olive oil, and this involved significant investments in the related equipment. Where the climate and soil favored it, the manorial farm could be assigned entirely to livestock farming. In border regions or less accessible areas where farmers had to struggle with thick undergrowth or marshland, such as the lower Po Valley almost all of which required colonizing, the landowner often decided to minimize the role of the manorial farm and let the settlers take on the heavy toil of putting new land under the plow. Conversely, in wide plains with rich soil, a large landowner would usually prefer to establish extensive cereal crops on a larger scale. To do so, he needed to set up a large manorial farm and exploit the free labor of his tenant farmers mercilessly.

The cultivation of cereals on large estates was carried out over large areas with fields of 250 or 500 acres, and the purpose was the creation of stockpiles rather than immediate consumption. A clear indication of this feature is provided by the preferred types of cereal grown on manorial farms. While the most valued crops in all regions were wheat and rye, the manorial farms of the great estates in northern Gaul mainly grew barley and spelt, another cereal crop that today has almost disappeared. The preference for these cereals can be explained by the ease with which they could be preserved. This favored their cultivation on large estates as a low-risk crop suitable for storage. Back in the times of the Roman Empire, frontier garrisons had their warehouses mainly filled with spelt. The idea that monks and nobles ate bread made of barley or spelt is unlikely, so the abundance of these cereals in manorial warehouses can only be explained by the deliberate decision to build up lasting stocks to feed slaves, provide supplies to the army that every year went on campaigns, and if necessary sell on the open market. It is significant that after the time of Charlemagne, when the number of slaves was further reduced, the great military campaigns were only a distant memory, and trade was becoming increasingly dangerous and difficult, the production of barley and spelt on manorial farms was abandoned in favor of rye and wheat.

THE EXCHANGE ECONOMY
The Role of Trade in the Management of Large Estates

In order to understand the dynamism of the Carolingian economy, we must abandon our preconceptions, which more or less automatically associate trade with an urban reality. The ancient Roman cities counted for very little at the time of Charlemagne. There were still many of them, perhaps as many as a hundred, but only in Italy did some, like Pavia and Rome, retain a significant role and have more than a few thousand inhabitants. The only relevance of the other cities was that a bishop and occasionally a count resided there. Jean Favier has remarked, "What was a city at that time? A church, the cathedral, on the horizon; around it a few houses on one or two floors, rarely three, and occasionally a city wall or what was left of it. . . . A dozen hectares [30 acres] and two or three thousand inhabitants constituted a city."[3] Significant sea and river ports were developing as new commercial centers on the northern coasts at crossroads for traffic, and they had an increasingly urban feel to them, but their thriving bustle was the by-product of an essentially rural economic growth. It was in the countryside that mouths and arms were slowly increasing in number, where forests were being cut down and marshes drained to make way for the plow, and where money was circulating, albeit still in small amounts. It was in the countryside that markets were springing up, and the most successful of these were later to be transformed into cities.

In this countryside where people worked, produced, consumed, saved, and reinvested on a larger scale that we had previously believed, a decisive impetus came from large monastic estates. They are the only well-documented ones, for which we have inventories of the lands, equipment, peasantry, and, in a few lucky cases, even the correspondence between owners and their factors. Whenever we can hear their voices, we realize that abbots had very clear ideas about how their properties were to be run, and they were certainly not happy just to consume passively the surplus that local agents sent them, while withdrawing into their world of prayer and reflection. Of course, they were not like the businessmen of the late Middle Ages and even less like modern capitalists. These abbots were certainly not motivated by the drive for profit, still less profit in monetary terms, but there can be no doubt that the more enterprising of them were very determined to make the monastic properties yield as much as possible.

Abbots were not businessmen, it is worth repeating, but the rule obliged them to feed and clothe their monks, charity required them to assist the poor, and the king ordered them to give shelter to pilgrims and occasionally himself and his envoys, as well as sending a squad of well-equipped horsemen off to war. All this demanded warehouses full of grain, cellars full of barrels of wine, beer, and oil, larders full of lard and salt, woodsheds full of logs, and large herds of horses and cattle. Then all this produce had to be transported to the monastery, sometimes over great distance and in staggering quantities. The monastery of Corbie consumed a ton of grain every day!

Abbots could not just sit back and live off their income: they had to accumulate and distribute and therefore plan and invest. The most widely used policy consisted of budgeting the consumption required for the monastic community, and assessing in advance the provisions that would be required of each farm owned by the monastery. After having calculated the daily requirement of grain for making bread, the abbot of Corbie established how much had to come from the harvests of manorial farms and how much from the revenues of mills owned by the monastery. The abbot of St-Denis valued all the produce required annually for the monks' meals, shared out the task of providing it among a certain number of *villae*, and ordered the remaining *villae* to provide the monks' clothes. The abbot of St-Wandrille listed everything that could be produced by the abbey's properties, categorized them by province, assigned to one or more *villae* the task of maintaining the community for each month of the year, and calculated separately the requirement that needed to be brought in to supplement the produce from monastic lands. The abbot of St-Germain-des-Prés, after having evaluated the monastery's possessions "down to the last chicken and egg," divided them up, assigning one part to the maintenance of the monks, another part to the military service required by the king, and a final part for the abbot's private consumption.[4]

However rudimentary the techniques of calculation may have been, it is clear that the rational management of large estates and, to some extent, the budgeting of requirements represented a real concern for monks. To make the system operate, abbots required an ability to organize the transport of provisions over great distances by land or water. Thus they established itineraries along which convoys could move, stopping on estates belonging to the monastery; they fitted out barges, equipped the suitably located farms with port facilities, employed a workforce for post horses and baggage wagons, and incessantly petitioned the king in the hope that he would guarantee the safety of the routes and exempt the abbey's agents from tolls and market duties. This dense transport network would itself be enough to prevent talk of a closed economy, even if self-sufficiency was widely perceived as an ideal worth pursuing.

Purchasing and Barter

Nevertheless, that ideal would have been difficult to put into practice. This is where the transport of goods became trade. Nothing is more eloquent than the list of monasteries that were attempting to buy a warehouse in the great port of Quentovic or even in the surrounding area, in order to have a base for their trading operations: St-Vaast, St-Riquier, St-Bertin, St-Germain-des-Prés, St-Wandrille, Ferrières. Of course, this was not only for buying and selling, because barter also played a part, as the case of Ferrières demonstrates. Charlemagne had given Alcuin, who was also the abbot of this monastery close to the Loire, a property located in the peat bogs of the Flemish coast, at St-Josse-sur-Mer, a short distance from Quentovic. Since then the monastery had been able to obtain supplies of wax, clothing, vegetables, cheese, and dried or salted fish and was able to fulfill its public obligations of hospitality as required by the emperor. After Charlemagne's death, one of his successors took the gift back, and the new abbot, Lupus, suddenly found himself unable to feed and clothe his seventy-two monks in a dignified manner: "we wear clothes that are worn and patched all over, the servants are almost naked and suffer the cold, and we have to keep hunger at bay with herbs from the garden."[5]

Obviously, the monks could have bought what they needed for their keep locally, and indeed in the end that is what they decided to do: Abbot Lupus's correspondence contains numerous nauseated references to the need to buy vegetables, grain, and beer to feed his community at the Orléans market. So there was a market, there were provisions on sale, and there was money to buy them, although at some stage it ran out and the abbot was obliged to sell the church's precious crockery. To Lupus, this was not the way to run a well-functioning economy: the systematic purchase of products with money seemed almost scandalous to him and destined in the long term to impoverish the monastery. Even supplies that in the past had come from St-Josse-sur-Mer would obviously have been mainly purchased at the Quentovic market, but in that there was a different logic: monastic property in the area made it possible to create surpluses and to trade these surpluses at the market, generally without the use of money.

Equally natural was the use of the primitive system of gifts and countergifts in order to make up the deficiencies in the market and the scarcity of ready cash, and without these it would have been extremely difficult to buy some goods and services. The correspondence of Lupus of Ferrières is full of requests. On one occasion, he asked a friend to give him twenty long tree trunks and provide him with some carpenters who, together with his own, would build a boat, a better one, he pointed out, than he would ever have found on sale. Then he asked the abbot of Prüm to send some expensive clothes that he wanted to give to the pope, and then he wrote to the king of England begging him to forward the lead needed to roof a church to Quentovic, where his agents were to collect it. In all these cases, no mention is ever made of payment: it is implicit that the abbot of Ferrières would pay back his correspondents, when they had need of his services. However primitive this system might appear, it worked. It was both trade and a dense web of social obligations, and anyone who tried to replace it with a more modern system of payments would have risked offending the person with whom they were dealing. This was exactly what happened to Lupus of Ferrières. When he asked the abbot of Corbie to pay for the hire of the all-important boat he had finally managed to build, he received an indignant refusal.[6]

Money had only an auxiliary role in the Carolingian economy, while today it is the key mechanism for the exchange of goods and services. Private consumption, and not profit, was the ideal even for the wealthy, let alone the rest of society. Wherever possible, gifts and barter were used in place of money transactions. Yet, however marginal and often rare money might have been, it was still required for buying at the market things that could not be procured by other means, or for the payment of tax. The more provident abbots tried to put aside money for more difficult times by selling their surpluses of grain and wine. Factors were authorized to sell livestock or flour collected from millers or vegetables from the gardens. It is true that selling sometimes meant bartering with grain or even flour, and debts were paid in barrels of wine or carts of salt, but nevertheless some money was circulating. Louis the Pious ordered that tithes owed to the Church should always be paid in kind by removing part of the harvest or livestock at their source, but he added that if bishops preferred to, they could collect them in money.[7] In so doing, he demonstrated a perfect understanding of the role of money in the economy of the time: what might be called an alternative resource, which strictly speaking was not absolutely necessary but was in practice valued and sought after by many people.

Partly, it was just convenient, as money traveled more easily than foodstuffs. In all parts of the empire, monasteries tended to demand payments in money from peasants who lived further away and in kind from those who worked nearby. Thus the abbot of Corbie expected his tenants to pay the tithes on their lands in kind and deliver them to the monastery warehouses, but he allowed those who lived further away to sell produce and fulfill their obligations through a payment in money.[8] The method of payment would have made little difference, and bishops and abbots were happy to collect money as well as bags of grain and barrels of wine. This put pressure on tenant farmers, who were forced to put together the dozen or so silver coins they needed to pay their superior every year.

Even country folk were therefore part of the market, and we must clearly distinguish between the ideal of private consumption that everyone from the king to the most lowly laborer undoubtedly shared, and its limited feasibility in practice. Of course peasants did not need to buy wax for candles, as the churches did, or good quality wine, as nobles did. The effective ability of peasants to feed themselves from the land varied from one family to another and from one village to another, as can be seen from the interminable lists of tenant farmers on the inventory ordered by Abbot Irmino of St-Germain-des-Prés. The exchange of goods must therefore have been intense within each village and among neighboring villages. It cannot be excluded that the occasional rich peasant, assisted by the proximity of a navigable waterway, may have traded his surpluses over longer distances, as occurred with wine. Rural merchants, of whom records survive more or less everywhere, were not only dealing with the agents of abbeys and powerful men. Charlemagne had to ban workers on his estates from losing time going round markets, which means that these were places where peasants gathered together, and not just to stare with gaping mouths.[9]

Merchants and Fairs

While local trade was in part organized directly by peasants, trade over longer distances was managed by merchants, people who lived off trade alone. In some areas of the empire, they constituted a rich and influential group. One example was Italy, where the Po River offered a natural line of communication for salt from the Adriatic and oriental cloth imported by merchants in Venice. When Charlemagne was still a child, the Lombard King Aistulf set down in law the armament that every subject was required to own in relation to his wealth, and he included "those men who are merchants and do not own any real estate."[10] Clearly, he took for granted that the richer merchants would be able to buy horses and armor, just as the large landowners did.

The area with the highest concentration of merchants was the North Sea coast inhabited by Frisians. Although only recently subjugated and Christianized, this country was already being integrated into the *regnum Francorum*. Indeed, incorporation into the Carolingian state was probably responsible for the high point in Frisian commercial dynamism, as it established the success of its emporium in Dorestad, a genuine gateway to the Anglo-Saxon and Scandinavian worlds. In order to be exported profitably toward northern markets, goods originating in the Frankish hinterland had to be loaded on ships, and the only people who had the necessary expertise were the men from the coast, the Frisians. This explains their virtual monopoly over international trade.

The few luxury items still imported into Gaul from eastern markets were in the hands of Jewish merchants, who mainly lived in cities along the Rhône and imported not by sea but through Muslim Spain. There are signs that the government was concerned about their presence for moral rather than political reasons. In 806 the emperor ordered bishops and abbots to keep watch over the treasures of their churches "because we have been told that Jewish merchants and others boast that they can buy anything they want,"[11] and later Bishop Agobard of Lyons complained that in order to please the Jews, it had been necessary to change market day, which previously had been held on Saturday.[12] But Agobard was alone in his malice, because Jewish merchants prospered under Charlemagne and even more under Louis the Pious, by supplying the court with wine, spices, and textiles, and they enjoyed wide-ranging privileges. These included the right to be tried only in accordance with their own law, to have Christian employees, and to practice their religion even within the imperial palace.

Less is known about the exports overland into the immense plains of Eastern Europe inhabited by Slavs and Avars. These became increasingly important following the emperor's victorious campaigns, which gradually forced those peoples into subjugation. In 805, while preparing for a campaign against the Slavs who lived along the Elbe, Charlemagne published precise restrictions on merchants operating in that sector, prohibiting them from exporting arms or armor under pain of having all their property confiscated, and designated about ten outposts along the border beyond which they were banned from going. In each of those localities, an imperial official was expressly appointed to protect the merchants but also to supervise their trade.[13]

The protection of subjects involved in international trade was one of the sovereign's specific duties. In negotiations with King Offa of Mercia, Charlemagne requested favorable conditions for "our merchants" when operating in England.[14] Later Louis the Pious granted the merchants who supplied the palace exemption from all taxes collected within the empire, with the exception of customs duties in Quentovic and other parts of the border.[15] It showed that the king had a benevolent attitude toward those subjects who were willing to take risks, go to sea, and undertake imports and exports on a large scale, and he intended to encourage their activities. Besides, he was not the only one. In 808 the Danish king, Godefrid, attacked the Slavs who lived at the mouth of the Elbe and destroyed the emporium where all the trade between Carolingian Europe and the Baltic took place. He then forced the merchants to move to a new site on the border of his kingdom at Haithabu, where he had an emporium built.[16] Although his methods were rather unorthodox, they signaled the birth of the concept of commercial warfare amid the flourishing trade of northern Europe.

Merchants operating locally are lesser known figures compared with important international traders, but it would appear that there was no shortage of them, although they did not have the same opportunities to make riches. A hagiography of the eighth century talks of a poor man whose wealth consisted solely of a donkey and who traveled with the animal from one city to another, buying provisions in one place and trying to sell them at a higher price in another. This *mercator*, as the hagiographer unhesitatingly calls him, took a load of salt from Orléans to Paris and was clearly working for himself. There may have been many people like him, with little chance of our coming across them in the sources, unless entirely by chance.[17]

We have a little more information on those merchants who traded on behalf of monasteries and under their protection, enjoying toll exemptions that the king generously lavished on monastic communities and their agents. In 775, when renewing the privilege granted to the abbey of St-Denis, Charlemagne specified that the exemption from taxation was valid for all foodstuffs belonging to the abbey, whether they were transported by cart or boat, by pack animals or porters. It was valid for purchasers who came from outside the monks' properties "to deal in or buy wine," and lastly for all those *negotiantes* or merchants who had submitted to the monastery and operated under its protection.[18]

It is true that St-Denis was not just any monastery. Since time immemorial, a fair had been held there on 9 October, the feast of Saint Denis. On that day, merchants arrived from all countries, but particularly Anglo-Saxons and Frisians from the north, who bought wine for export to their distant lands. The fair generated river trade that animated the entire Parisian basin. The abbey was itself a wine producer on a colossal scale and had a decisive role in organizing and supervising the fair. It enjoyed by royal concession the right to keep all the related taxes, not only in the area of the fair around the monastery but in the entire county of Paris.

The popularity of the fair of St-Denis and the sea and riverside emporia of Rouen, Orléans, Dorestad, and Quentovic was related to the fundamental weakness of trade. Merchants and buyers converged en masse on those places because very often they could not buy what they needed anywhere else. In old age, Einhard was the abbot of two large monasteries, Seligenstadt on the Main and St-Bavon in Ghent, situated a hundred or so miles apart. On one occasion while he was staying in the former, he had to write to the factor in Ghent requesting him to obtain wax, which was not available in Seligenstadt because two consecutive bad years had ruined beekeeping.[19] There should be no surprise that trade was not anyone's favorite sector of the economy, or that anyone who could, would try to go without. But it is precisely the obstinacy with which trade continued to take place and money continued to circulate in spite of everything that demonstrates the impossibility of understanding the Carolingian economy without devoting sufficient coverage to these factors.

THE KING'S POLICIES

Economic prosperity owed much to the king's energetic initiatives. In part, these only indirectly concerned the economy, but they were no less effective for that. Charlemagne needed to have the economic resources of the Church available to him, and thus court envoys demanded that church property be inventoried. This in turn persuaded bishops and abbots of the need to organize the management of their lands on a more stable basis. Ultimately, this pressure led to the universalization of the manorial system. But the king's direct interventions were equally important and testify to an increasing awareness of economic questions and the possible role of government in this sphere. Occasionally, they were general provisions aimed at controlling commercial activity in the interest of the consumer, such as the prohibition on trading by night in gold plate, silver plate, jewels, slaves, horses, and livestock—in other words, in all those goods that might tempt the vendor to defraud the purchaser. After sunset, only necessary provisions and hay were to be sold to travelers in inns.[20] Other measures introduced by Charlemagne involved considerable and complex planning and constituted a conscious attempt to intervene in the more delicate mechanisms of the economy: these reforms affected weights and measures, currency, and food prices.

Weights and Measures

One of Charlemagne's constant concerns was the standardization of the weights and measures in use in the empire. The starting point was, as always, moral. He wanted to guarantee that no one was defrauded, in accordance with the biblical admonition against anyone who uses "divers weights, and divers measures."[21] This preoccupation with order, stability, and harmony, which appears to dominate Charlemagne's legislation, thus produced its effects in the market square. It meant intervening in the economy, first in order to monitor and then to control. When Pepin was still mayor of the palace, he had ordered that each bishop should supervise the weights and measures in use in the local market.[22] His son went further and wished to impose the adoption of standard weights and measures throughout his kingdom.

He was possibly thinking about this already when, in 787, having recently returned from a journey through Italy involving a stay at the abbey of Montecassino, he wrote to its abbot requesting him to send a pound of bread and a measure of wine as they had been fixed by Saint Benedict.[23] The immediate purpose was to standardize usage for the consumption of food by monks in the hundreds of abbeys in the kingdom, but Charles lost no time in widening the scope of his project. By 794 a new measure of volume had been introduced, and it was valid for both liquids and solids or, in more practical terms, for both wine and cereals. It was called the public *modius* to distinguish it from the *modius* previously in use. In that same year, the Council of Frankfurt fixed market prices by ordering everyone to use the same measure, the "public *modius* that has been recently introduced."[24] The new *modius* must have been considerably larger than previous measures, and in 802 the emperor ordered that from then on anyone who paid three *modii* in rent or tax, was to only pay two.[25]

There is some uncertainty about the success of the reform. Charlemagne ordered all the factors of crown properties to keep at home a reference *modius*, which was identical to one in the palace.[26] However, complaints about the variety of measures in use and the repeated demands to use the official *modius* and no other measure demonstrate that the old measures continued to be used. Even in 822, when Louis the Pious was struggling to have his father's reform finally accepted, the abbot of

Corbie referred with ill-concealed irritation to "this new *modius* that has been forced on us by our lord the Emperor," at the same time as ordering his millers to compare the old *modii* with the new one and calculate the relative size.[27] The instinctive resistance to change and the practical difficulties in implementing it conspired against one of the Carolingian emperor's most ambitious attempts at unification, and Europe would have to wait for Napoleon and the decimal system before a start would be made on imposing uniform weights and measures on the whole of the continent.

The Currency

The standardization of weights and measures also included the so-called monetary reform, which in reality was a series of legislative measures started by Pepin and taken up by Charlemagne. In this field, the emperor was able to pursue and enlarge upon his father's policies in a well thought-out and systematic manner. The reform consisted primarily in the introduction of a monometallic system. Only silver coins were to be used in business transactions, in place of the system based on both silver and gold coins that had been inherited from the Roman Empire. Looked at in these terms, the reform might appear the result of a slowdown or even a collapse in the circulation of money and trade, as indeed it was considered by Pirenne. After all, the Merovingians had never suspended the circulation of gold coins, although those minted locally could not stand up to comparison with the gold coins of Byzantium and the Arabs. By establishing that it was no longer worthwhile minting gold coins, the Carolingian kings appear to have acknowledged a sudden and irreversible decline.

Yet the continued minting of gold coins was not in itself evidence of great economic vitality; indeed it might have been the opposite. For most of the seventh century the Frankish kings had only minted gold coins, neglecting silver. Thus the smallest unit in circulation was the gold *tremis*, which had a theoretical weight of 0.053 ounce and a value that could have kept a person alive for several months. It does not appear, then, that it was a period particularly favorable to small business transactions. When the Carolingian mayors of the palace in Gaul started to coin and put into circulation a new silver coin, the *denarius*, this clearly did not signify a crisis but rather the recovery of trade, particularly at the local level.

The legislation introduced by Pepin and later by Charlemagne was not limited to the encouragement and supervision of minting silver coins but clearly appreciated the unifying potential inherent in the new currency. The reform imposed a single currency on the whole of Western Europe, which was to last in its essential features until the French Revolution, and in England right up until 1971. Today we talk, slightly tongue-in-cheek but not overly so, of Charlemagne's "proto-Euro." The foundation of the system was the decision to mint the coin at a fixed rate that all mints had to observe. A pound of silver was to produce 240 *denarii*. The silver *denarius* was to be the only coin minted in the empire. Although transactions involved multiples of a *denarius*, the multiples were used purely for calculation and did not correspond to coins actually minted. The *solidus*, the ancient gold coin of the Roman Empire, simply designated the value of 12 *denarii*, and the *libra*, which in English is called a pound, was obviously equal to 240 *denarii* or 20 *solidi*.

The most important measure taken by Charles was the increase in the weight of the *denarius* and therefore also the *libra* in the early 790s. Since time immemorial, the *denarius* had weighed around 0.045 ounce, the equivalent weight of 20 grains of barley, in accordance with the system of weights used in Romano-Germanic Europe. Charlemagne decided to shift to a system based on wheat grains, as wheat was now the most valued type of cereal. He established that the silver *denarius* should weigh 32 wheat grains, that is 0.047 ounce. Given that a *libra* represented 240 *denarii*, this meant changing the value of the *libra* to 14.5 ounces. The not insignificant result was that the king's coins that circulated throughout the empire were larger, heavier, and more highly regarded than their predecessors, with undoubted political spin-offs.

The reform also wanted to recover the monopoly of royal mints, following centuries in which a profusion of independent mints, mainly in the service of ecclesiastical bodies, had minted coins without any form of control. The king's name replaced the minter's mark on the coin, and from that time on, it was the king and not the manufacturer who guaranteed the quality of the coin. The number of authorized mints was drastically reduced from several hundreds to a few dozen, and even those monasteries and bishoprics that maintained the right to mint had to adapt to the royal mint mark and cease to put their own names on their coins. Since a single type of *denarius* had to circulate throughout the entire empire, secular and ecclesiastical local authorities had to make sure that everyone accepted payment in this "sovereign's coin" (*dominica moneta*), under pain of losing their posts.

Charlemagne thus gave his empire a uniform monetary system, which guaranteed the quality of the currency and therefore its circulation everywhere. This intention can only be explained in the context of an economy in which trade had a specific role. Of course, the new silver coins, even if guaranteed by the name and portrait of the emperor, were not the best means for trading with the East, but this point simply confirms the reorientation of trade routes. Mediterranean trade counted for little or nothing. The important trade was in the North Sea, and there Anglo-Saxon and Scandinavian merchants were very happy to accept payment in Charles's silver. Indeed, their kings started immediately to imitate the Frankish *denarii* in their own mints, a sure sign of the currency's hegemony.

Charlemagne's decision to use only one metal did not stop gold from circulating in those parts of the empire that were still open to trade with the Mediterranean. The baggage of a merchant from southern Italy was found in the Reno riverbed close to Bologna. He had drowned crossing the river in the final years of Charlemagne's reign. His bag only contained gold coins, the majority of which were Byzantine and from the duchy of Benevento; the rest were Arab.[28] Bad gold coins imitating the gold medallions Charlemagne had made for state occasions were cheerfully palmed off on merchants from the north. The imposition of silver coins must therefore be interpreted essentially as an attempt to unify fundamental economic activities throughout the immense empire, without suffocating its innumerable regional peculiarities.

To offset any optimism that might emerge from this description, it has to be stressed that, in spite of the Carolingian reform, the West remained without any really small coins for use in everyday transactions. In 794 the silver *denarius*, the smallest coin in circulation and in large parts of the empire the only coin, was the price of 12 loaves of wheat bread and 15 of rye bread. We do not know how they managed to buy a single loaf. It is possible that everyone, including those who did not work the land, acquired flour in sacks and baked their own bread by paying the baker a percentage of the flour. More generally, people who went to market to buy or sell a chicken or a dozen eggs evidently did so on trust. The vendor would keep an account and get paid on a regular basis. Such practices would have proved easier in a rural society in which everyone knew each other.

The Food-Rationing Policy

Even though the countryside was certainly not oppressed by hopeless poverty in Charlemagne's reign, in some years bad weather caused poor, if not catastrophic, harvests in practically every part of the empire. Then hunger came and the price of bread rose frighteningly, allowing a few speculators to get rich from the suffering of the poor. Famines of this extent occurred twice during Charles's reign, first in 792–93 and then in 805–6. The first one was probably more serious, given that the chroniclers reported cases of people being reduced to cannibalism, and in several areas there were records of collective hallucinations, in which the starving thought they saw corn growing not only in the fields, but in the forests and marshes as well. They even felt that they could touch the corn, "but no one could eat it."[29] On both occasions, the government intervened energetically to lessen the effects of the famine and alleviate the suffering of the poor, although we do not know with what success.

We should not find it amusing that the first measure it took was a collective appeal to God to keep the famine away from Christian lands. People were convinced that God intervened concretely in human affairs, and if, for impenetrable reasons, He had decided to put them to the test, the evidence of their contrition might move Him to pity. In the spring of 792 the king ordered that every priest in the kingdom should celebrate mass three times, the first for the king himself, the second for the "army of the Franks" or, in other words, the Frankish people, and the third "for the current tribulation," to bring an end to the famine. The clergy were also required to fast for two days, as were counts and royal vassals and their servants. More concretely, everyone had to undertake to feed some starving person until the next harvest came.[30] As always, measures of a religious nature were undertaken in a practical and not a mystical manner, because there was confidence in their efficacy. Outside the clergy, people were given the opportunity to free themselves from the obligation to fast by a payment of money into the fund to assist the "starving poor," in accordance with their means.

In the autumn of 805 the emperor introduced an even more practical measure, explaining that in the event of famine, plague, or any other scourge, there was no point in waiting for a royal edict and everyone had to pray to God on their own behalf. Given that the immediate problem was famine, Charlemagne ordered all landowners to try to feed their own people and to sell their own grain at a low price. He also prohibited any export of foodstuffs from the empire.[31] A little later the emperor and his counselors decided that it would be still better to organize collective prayers. News of the bad harvest was arriving from all sides, the weather was not improving, and the specter of famine was impending. Charles sent a circular to his bishops, ordering all the faithful to observe three days of fasting every month for three consecutive months.[32]

The most interesting measures were those of a preventive nature.

Charles fixed the maximum price for cereals at the Council of Frankfurt in 794, when the famine was still a tragic memory. The price was not to be exceeded either in time of abundance or in time of shortage. He established that in the event of a crisis, public stockpiles (*annona publica domni regis*) were to be released into the market at deliberately low prices: half the official price for barley and oats, two-thirds for rye, and three-fourths for wheat.[33] In other words, the immense crown estates did not only have the purpose of sustaining the king and his officials and providing victuals for the army; they also amassed stocks to relieve the population in times of famine. Notker's boast that in the final years of his life Charles even sent "the riches of Europe, that is wheat, wine, and oil," to African emirs for the relief of their starving populations may have been pure propaganda, but it demonstrates that there was a government policy of amassing and distributing food.[34] In ordinary years, even bishops were encouraged to build up reserves, and they did this not only by using cereals produced on their own lands, but by purchasing harvests from the peasantry at fixed prices. This policy provoked discontent, but it certainly helped reduce the devastating effects of famine during bad years.

The regulations concerning the management of crown lands, the renowned *Capitulare de villis*, may well reflect Charlemagne's mood following the famine of 792–93 and may have been intended to head off another such catastrophe or at least to alleviate its harshest consequences. The king ordered his factors to make sure "that delinquents do not hide our seed crop underground or elsewhere, causing the harvest to be insufficient."[35] His concern may well betray the experience of a couple of consecutive bad harvests during which farm servants on crown estates may well have acted in such a manner.

In March 806, at the height of another famine, the emperor issued regulations that partly repeated those of Frankfurt and partly amended them. Anyone who owned stocks was not to keep them in his warehouse until the price had risen but to put them on sale immediately at a fixed price, after having ensured that enough stocks remained for his own people. However the fixed price in 806 was higher than the one in 794. It appears then that experience had taught Charles the difficulties of artificially imposing prices that were too low for the market. But the new measures also displayed a more pronounced punitive intention. Bishops and counts had to feed their poor and not allow them to travel around begging. Vagabonds had to be fed free of charge but were also obliged to work.[36] Perhaps the most frightening thing about famine was above all the unrest it created in society, because it flooded the thoroughfares with large crowds of destitute people that were difficult to control and created enormous problems over army recruitment that required special exemptions for stricken areas.[37] This explains the increasing amounts of preventive measures introduced in Charlemagne's final years. These invited bishops and counts to distribute grains to the poor so that they would not suffer hunger and restated that all landowners were required to feed everyone who worked for them, whether free man or slave. It was prohibited to buy a peasant's crop before it had been harvested, given that selling one's grain cheap while it was still growing during the months of desperation that preceded the new harvest, a particularly difficult moment in times of famine, was the way in which too many people ruined themselves completely and fell into the clutches of speculators.[38]

A VILLAGE AT THE TIME OF CHARLEMAGNE

So far we have examined the economy at the time of Charlemagne, the organization of the large landed interests, the development of trade, the management concerns of abbots, and the corrective measures adopted by the emperor. We still need to know how things were at the bottom of society: the life and work of the peasantry on whose toil the whole economic system in the West ultimately rested. Written sources tell us very little, but for some time a new and growing science, medieval archaeology, has been helping us learn more about this question. There is one village that in recent years has been patiently brought back to the light of day.

The Settlement at Villiers-le-Sec

At Villiers-le-Sec in the Île-de-France, archaeologists have discovered the remains of three peasant houses, each of which constituted, together with the surrounding outbuildings, the dwelling unit of a *mansus* attached to the abbey of St-Denis.[39] They were high and spacious houses, built from timber frames on a rectangular plan. The lattice walls were filled with clay, and the roofs were covered with thatch. They stood between 100 and 250 feet apart on the important road that led from Paris to Amiens. It was not a temporary settlement. The place had been continuously inhabited since the Gallo-Roman period and the settlement probably included many other *mansi* of the same kind. All of them would have been sufficiently far apart to maintain the appearance of a scattered rural settlement, not a tightly clustered village and still less a fortified one. This picture conforms to what we know in general about rural settlements at the time of Charlemagne, when the village as a cluster of houses around a church or castle was not widespread, and in many areas there was a prevalence of hamlets with just a few families or even isolated dwellings.

The three houses are all of a similar size: just under 40 feet in length and half that in width. This is large enough to suggest that part of the building was used as a cow barn leading directly into the part for human habitation, in accordance with a tradition that survived until very recent times in the peasant world. A hearth was hollowed out of the earth floor and lined with stones. It was situated directly below a hole in the thatch roof to let the smoke out. The first house had a blacksmith's forge attached to it. The second was surrounded by a barn or granary as large as the main house and several other outbuildings, including a bakery dug into the ground and protected by a wood and straw structure. The third had a sturdy rectangular granary made of particularly thick poles and a lean-to that covered a ditch about 40 inches deep, in which a loom had been constructed. Here the women wove mainly linen and some wool, to judge from numerous bits of equipment found on the site. This basement construction served to maintain the humidity necessary for linen yarn during weaving.

These buildings of wood, clay, and straw give the impression of space but also appear less solid than the stone and tile constructions typical of the Gallo-Roman period, even in the countryside. Nevertheless, they were sturdy buildings. The load-bearing beams were made of oak or at the very least beech, while the wall lattice was made of hazel, sycamore, ash, and willow. It is clear that wood was readily available, as was also demonstrated by the fact that precious oak was burned in the fireplaces. Clay, extracted in the area, was mixed with straw cut up small and then caked on the lattice internally and externally, until it covered it like a kind of plaster. Before this wattle and daub dried, it was smoothed off with a wooden trowel. The roofing was probably made of rye straw, which is longer and more resistant than wheat straw. Although thin, the walls and particularly the roof did provide some protection from the cold when the fire in the middle of the floor was lit.

The houses also had windows, which were closed with wooden shutters, and at least one door, set solidly in a wooden frame. Metal had a not insignificant role in their construction, given that not only the hinges and the latches, locks, or chains, but also the nails and cramp-irons that bound the wooden structure together were all made of iron. It hardly needs saying that there was no glass in the windows and in all probability the shutters were kept closed when it was cold. However, houses were not entirely in darkness, because apart from the fire, there were terra-cotta oil lamps, which could also be used as candlesticks for cheap tallow candles.

Outside each house, there were holes dug into the ground with narrow openings and a capacity of about 1.3 cubic yards. These were used for storing grain. Once they were filled, the silos were sealed with a layer of straw and another of clay and were then capable of conserving the grain for a considerable time in relatively good condition. The coexistence of granaries aboveground and underground silos can probably be explained by the use of the former to conserve the grain that still had to be threshed, as well as hay and straw, while once the threshing was over, it was stored more safely underground. Milling, which in antiquity had been done by querns, now regularly involved taking sacks of grain to a water mill, which would serve one or more settlements. The increasing use of water mills represented one of the main technological advances of the Middle Ages.

Women had a choice when it came to cooking. Bread was cooked in ovens hollowed out of the earth next to the house. Even though it required considerable skill and produced excellent bread, this kind of oven did not last very long, as sooner or later the earth would crumble and bury it. It has been calculated that the average life of such an oven was about twenty bakes, and therefore a maximum of a few months, assuming that bread was baked once a week. Then they had to dig out another one. Soup was cooked over the domestic fire. Cooking was done in terra-cotta receptacles, in the almost total absence of metal pots. These receptacles were shaped like rounded vases, and they were rested directly on the fire, on a stone support, or even on bricks from some ancient Gallo-Roman building. Some had handles, and it cannot be ruled out that they were hung over the fire with a chain, as was later to become common practice.

The Human Population and Work in the Fields

What was the physical appearance of the peasants who lived in these houses? Burial places have produced skeletons with an average height of 5 feet 5 inches for men and 5 feet 1 inch for women, the same heights recorded more or less everywhere up until industrialization. This gives the lie to the idea that medieval men were short in stature: they were shorter than we are, but no more or less so than conscripts of the early twentieth century. Equally normal for the time was the high mortality rate. Judging by the age of skeletons buried at Villiers-le-Sec, barely 60 percent of the population lived beyond twenty years, and more than 20 percent of children died before the age of five. These are astonishing figures for us, but it should be made clear that they were normal for a preindustrial population and have nothing to do with the supposed nature of the "Dark Ages." In France under the Sun King the figures were substantially the same. Among those who reached adulthood, bone diseases and arthritis were common, and teeth were often in a bad state. Clearly these peasants, who lacked any medical care, were on the whole very prone to illness and in a precarious state of health, even though basically well built.

In all probability, a single family consisting of a peasant, his wife, and their children lived in each of the houses the archaeologists uncovered. The widely held idea in the collective imagination that in the past peasant families were extended might be true in certain situations, for example, Italian *mezzadri* (sharecroppers) in the modern age, but research has swept them away from the Middle Ages. At the time of Charlemagne, the family was generally made up of five or six people, that is, the father, the mother, and three or four children. The sanitary and economic conditions did not allow for higher numbers, and although it is improbable that they used contraceptive methods, all the information we possess confirms that a couple rarely exceeded this rate of fertility, even though girls married very young, at around fourteen or fifteen years. Of course, there would have been cases of two or three brothers reaching adulthood and continuing to work together on the paternal *mansus*. These overpopulated *mansi* are well known to scholars and prove that in spite of the difficult conditions of their lives, the population tended to increase. But even in these cases, each brother formed an independent family or, as they said at the time, a "hearth."

Archaeological studies make it possible to reconstruct the plant life surrounding the village through analysis of the pollen. At the time of Charlemagne, cultivated land was evidently increasing at Villiers-le-Sec to the detriment of woodland. Whereas oak and beech were still common, chestnut and lime had disappeared in spite of being well represented in earlier times. Around their houses, the peasants had cherry, apple, pear, walnut, and hazel trees, as well as raspberry and blackberry bushes, which all helped vary their diet. The vegetable garden provided carrots, broad beans, and peas, in the obvious absence of potatoes, kidney beans, and tomatoes, which were to come from America. The staple for their diet was, however, provided by cereals cultivated in the surrounding fields.

The tools the peasantry used were extremely rudimentary and mainly made of wood. Metal tools were sickles for harvesting corn, scythes for hay making, and axes for cutting wood, but the hoe, which for us is clearly a metal tool in spite of the wooden handle, was made almost entirely from wood, with just an iron rim to make it cut into the ground better. The vast crown estate of Annapes covering nearly 7,500 acres raised more than a hundred cattle, almost as many horses, and more than eight hundred sheep, goats, and pigs, yet its inventory listed all its metal tools as just two scythes, two sickles, and two iron-rimmed hoes. It then added "wooden tools as necessary," as these did not have to be inventoried like those made of iron, which was a precious material.[40]

We should not exaggerate the depth of medieval backwardness: even Gallo-Roman peasants used wooden hoes. As for the lack of metal tools in the possession of crown estates, it is clear that tenant farmers had their own scythes and sickles, which were not included in the inventory. But we certainly cannot speak of progress, as can be shown by the type of plow they used. It was light, with a single handle, and was still made entirely of wood or, at the very most, was fitted with a metal plowshare. Heavier plows, which had to be pulled by a yoke of oxen and equipped with wheels, were unknown in Frankish lands, and we do not know whether they had moldboards to lift and turn the soil, which would have been a significant technological improvement. It is prudent to assume that the majority of peasants did not use such an advanced tool, and therefore most of their work was still with a hoe, the indispensable accessory to the light plow.

The Cultivation of Cereal Crops

A wide variety of cereal crops were grown in the time of Charlemagne. They include rye, which was hardier, and wheat, which was more prized, as well as smaller amounts of oats and barley, both good for feeding animals but edible for humans in the form of soups or beer. In fact, beer could be considered an alternative means of conserving cereals. With some variations in accordance with soil and climate, these same cereals were grown throughout the empire. One other important grain was spelt, which, although absent in Villiers-le-Sec, was very frequently used on manorial farms because of its easy conservation. Fields were not only used for cereals: a significant area was reserved for hemp and especially flax, from which women made cloth.

In the area of Villiers-le-Sec, as in the whole of the north of the empire, favorable climatic conditions allowed peasants to plow twice a year. The fields that were plowed in the summer were sowed in the autumn with rye, wheat, and barley, while those plowed in the winter were sowed in the spring, sometimes with flax or vegetables, but mostly with oats. This was the three-year rotation, which thanks to the alternation of winter and spring crops allowed peasants to leave one-third of cultivated land fallow each year, to avoid exhausting it. Their ancestors and even their contemporaries living on the Mediterranean side of the empire, where the climate was unsuitable for spring crops, were forced to leave half of the land fallow. The three-year rotation distributed work better over the year and diversified production, helping to avert the total failure of the harvest, while the cultivation of oats made it possible to maintain a larger number of horses. But archaeologists also believe that peasants might have been practicing another system of cultivation, the *infield-outfield* system. This involved an inner area of well-manured and permanently cultivated fields, and an outer area of less intensively cultivated fields, which were often left fallow or used for grazing.

This theory is particularly significant because it gets us round the old debate over yields: the quantity of grain produced in relation to the quantity sown. The extremely negative interpretation of Carolingian agriculture has been based on calculations that, starting with the inventories of large monastic and crown estates, established yields at one and a half or two times the seed corn. For further clarity, a yield of 2 to 1 means that half the harvest has to be put aside for the next sowing. Even assuming that yields on better land rose to 3 to 1, they would still have been very low and have left the population on the brink of famine with the first bad harvest. Clearly, if drought or high winds halved the crop, the yield would fall to 1.5 instead of 3.0. But 1.0 would anyway have to be put aside for sowing and only 0.5 would remain for consumption, a fourth of the normal amount.

Recent experiments have demonstrated that by concentrating all the available human and animal manure in small fields and working them intensively, it would have been possible to achieve much greater yields on the order of 10 to 1 or even 20 to 1. This is exactly what happened with the infield-outfield system. Hence tenant farmers on manorial estates produced large quantities of grain and barley, at the cost of very intensive labor in fields close to where they lived, and used less convenient fields less industriously for small surpluses of rye and oats in good years. Having thus ensured the survival of their tenants through a system of private consumption that did not rule out access to the market for the sale of occasional surpluses, large landowners were free to apply a different logic involving extensive agriculture on the manorial farm where, due to the economies of scale, they also returned a profit from those yields of 2 or 3 to 1, which would have been unsustainable for small independent farmers.

Domestic Animals

Analysis of animal remains at Villiers-le-Sec has produced extremely useful information on economic activity and eating habits. Hunting and fishing appear to have been almost negligible and, except for the occasional hare or pigeon, so was their part in the peasants' diet. Game and fish accounted for only 1 percent of the animal remains recovered. This percentage differs markedly from digs on urban or aristocratic sites, where bones of game animals vary between 5 and 10 percent of the total. There is therefore reason to believe that by Charlemagne's time, peasants were already increasingly obliged to leave game to the large landowners and forego eating it themselves, and in this they probably differed from their counterparts in previous centuries.

On the whole, domestic animals were smaller than the ones we see today. Dogs, which the ancient Gauls had had no scruples about eating, were now used as guard dogs and for clearing the rubbish. Their average height did not exceed 20 inches, although many were larger. An ox was on average 46.5 inches tall and weighed about 550 pounds, which was not therefore very much. Examination of ox bones reveals the disappearance of the breeding techniques that have been shown to exist in the Gallo-Roman era. Sheep and goats were also small, whereas pigs were of a reasonable size, although modern ones are fatter. At the risk of sounding repetitive, horses, donkeys, and even chickens were much smaller than they are today, but also in relation to the Gallo-Roman period. It appears that the slow and wearisome dissolution of ancient civilization had more serious consequences for breeding techniques than for farming ones. In particular, the stature of horses, not only in Villiers-le-Sec but more or less in all the Carolingian archaeological sites, has been shown to be around 55 inches and often even lower. This means that the animals were decidedly less imposing than our imaginations tend to make them, when we think of the heavily armed cavalry that formed the backbone of Charlemagne's armies.

As for diet, pork is the meat most emphasized by literature and iconography, but the digs at Villiers-le-Sec show that the most widely consumed meat was ox, with pork and mutton in second place. Peasants also ate horsemeat and donkey, while poultry had a minor role. But we can forget about the consumption of veal calves, reared exclusively for meat and killed when they are at their most tender, as we are accustomed to eating today. No more than one-third of cattle were butchered young, and in any case not before fifteen or eighteen months, while the majority were eaten only after they had been hardened by a full working life, at ten years or more. The same occurred with horses, although it is worthy of note that a similar number of them were butchered young, a sign that horsemeat was prized and not simply a standby. The only animal that was generally and traditionally butchered young was the pig, which was usually killed between a year and a year and a half, although it was not uncommon to kill pigs even earlier. To some extent this was also true of lambs and kids, of which a good half were butchered by a year and a half. Other digs in other regions have shown markedly different customs, such as butchering pigs and sheep at around two and a half years. From one end of this immense empire to the other, stretching from the Mediterranean to the Baltic, peasants clearly had very different local customs, and it would be absurd to reduce them to a single model.

In any case, this analysis of meat consumption should not lead us to have an overly positive idea of the peasants' diet in Villiers-le-Sec. Examination of their bones shows that there was a high risk of undernourishment in terms of protein, so the various meats discussed so far must be considered dishes for feast days, a fairly irregular supplement to a diet essentially made up of soup, bread, milk, eggs, butter, and cheese, with the addition of wine or beer, which were useful from a calorific point of view. Finally, as confirmation of the highly sophisticated techniques currently in use among archaeologists, findings have shown that in the great majority of cases meat was boiled and not roasted. This also appears likely because the animals were often old, and in any case, boiling is the cooking technique that is nutritionally least wasteful.

THIRTEEN

Patronage and Servitude

A SOCIETY BASED ON PATRONAGE
The Inadequacy of Legal Categories

A royal envoy once sought clarification from Charlemagne on a difficult trial involving the legal status of the children of a slave and a *colona*, a peasant woman who worked on a crown estate by hereditary obligation but distinguished on paper from genuine slaves by rules that went back to the Roman emperors. The emperor replied that the envoy should not make too fine a point of it and simply treat the mother as though she were a slave, "because there are only free men and slaves."[1] The reply was so categorical that we are tempted to take it as a key to understanding the society of the time, in which ancient slavery was still formally in force and therefore the legal distinction between free men and slaves might appear decisive in determining social conditions.

Reality was somewhat different. To start with, the sharpness of the reply reflects Charles's irritation with an envoy with whom he does not appear at all satisfied. Further on in reply to another question, he even dictates, "we have already ordered you to do this verbally, and you still haven't understood!" Moreover, the assertion that there can only be free men and slaves was not original, but a quotation from Roman law hurriedly chosen not in the search for a general theory of society but simply as a practical solution to an individual case. Finally, it is not at all clear, as the following pages will demonstrate, whether the Latin *servus* can be translated here as "slave" rather than a vaguer term like "serf." Although slavery was of great importance in Charlemagne's empire, legal categories are not the best way to understand the peasant world of this era.

The same could be said of the nobility at the other extreme of society. There can be little doubt that in the empire there was a circle of fabulously wealthy families, all related in some degree to each other and often to the emperor himself. In their provinces their word was law; they imperiously commanded the peasantry and monopolized high positions as counts and bishops. We can be equally sure that many of these families boasted ancient lineage and looked down on those who did not belong to their circle, even those who became rich and powerful through imperial favor. When Louis the Pious appointed as archbishop of Reims a new man called Ebbo, who was actually a freed slave born of peasants who toiled on crown lands, Bishop Thegan of Trier contemptuously commented, "The emperor might have made you a free man, but he has not made you noble, because that would be impossible!"[2]

This example also shows that the empire's ruling class was not made up solely of nobles. Besides, the nobility of which Thegan and his peers boasted had no legal status, as it would have later in the Middle Ages. Nobility meant being born to a family that was not only rich but also eminent and influential. It meant having friends and relations in the right places, and the longer established the contacts were the better it was, but it carried no right to privileges sanctioned by law. At least this was the situation among the Franks, even though other peoples like the Saxons had a nobility so clearly distinguished from lesser free men as to merit legal recognition in their laws. Charlemagne never introduced separate provisions or tariffs for nobles, except in the case of Saxony where conversely they were the rule.[3] Clearly these were always considered exceptions in the emperor's eyes, while the empire's legislative structure on the whole reflected the Frankish legal tradition and made no provision for nobles to be treated differently.

The Interdependence of Social Relations

A review of the different types of legal status is not therefore the best way of going about a description of society at the time of Charlemagne. When he attempted to reflect on the composition of the peoples he governed, he never made use of such criteria. He was most struck by the fact that all men, whether they were nobles or plebeians, free men or slaves, were involved in allegiances, some of them hereditary and others freely chosen, that nearly always resulted in some form of patronage. It was precisely this personal allegiance, more than anything else, that determined social status. For example, we can consider the criterion the king used to organize the collective oath of loyalty in 793.[4] Charlemagne ordered his envoys to have the oath sworn primarily by bishops, abbots, counts, royal vassals, *vicedomini* (a bishop's right-hand men), archdeacons (the highest ecclesiastical dignitaries in each diocese), and canons, in other words the upper ranks of the ecclesiastical and secular administrations.

These were followed by monks and clergy living in communities, who were exempted from the actual oath as it was not compatible with their vows, but they had to promise loyalty before their abbot, who would give a detailed report to the king. "Then advocates, vicars, centeniers, and secular priests," Charles continued, demonstrating once again how the two hierarchies overlapped. Hence not only advocates, who administered church lands and disciplined their servants, but priests as a whole constituted the lower officialdom of the Church in parallel with local officials answerable to a count. Moving on to the "people as whole," the king ordered that all able-bodied men over twelve years of age were to take the oath, and he listed them as follows, moving down the social ladder: "independent smallholders, then all bishops' or abbesses' men or counts' men or in any case other lords' men, and also servants of crown lands and *coloni,* and those slaves who are honored by their owners with commissions and benefices: let them all take the oath."

In other words, society at all levels was full of men who owed allegiance to someone else, and this allegiance defined their social status. It was not a mechanical definition: a man's rank was established by the type of allegiance, whether it was the freely chosen allegiance of vassals and more generally of those who had chosen a patron, or the hereditary allegiance of manumitted slaves and actual slaves, who were by then increasingly mixed up together. The degree of trust between liege and patron was also significant, as this could induce the king to appoint one of his *fideles* count or bishop, or induce a landowner to promote one of his slaves by entrusting him with management of an estate. But what mattered above all was the identity of the person or institution to which allegiance was due, because both for the free and armed vassal and for the slave or freed slave who worked the land, it was a very different thing to be a king's man, a monastery's man, or just a private landowner's man.

Only one category possibly escaped this interdependence of personal relations. In translation we call them "independent smallholders." They were the common free men who had originally formed the backbone of the Frankish people and had no other obligation than to fight in the army and pay taxes. As we shall see at the end of this chapter, they were not surprisingly under threat at the time of Charlemagne or possibly even fast on the way to extinction. To maintain full social, economic, and even legal independence had already become difficult for those who were not very rich, and in the future it was to become impossible.

ALL THE KING'S MEN
The Powerful

At the top, Frankish society was governed by those who managed to obtain a position of trust from the king, either in the temporal or ecclesiastic administration. They were counts, royal vassals, bishops, and abbots—men whom documents of the time quite correctly called *potentes* or the powerful. But how many of them were there? At the height of its expansion, the empire had 189 episcopal sees and therefore the same number of bishops, all personally known to Charles and probably appointed by him.[5] Monasteries were even more numerous. There were more than five hundred, but not all were under the direct protection of the king. Those that were and had an abbot appointed by him totaled about two hundred. As for the secular authorities, the emperor was represented in the provinces by some two hundred to two hundred and fifty counts, all personally appointed by him, and at least a thousand royal vassals.

Apart from the personal relationship of trust with the emperor, this elite was distinguished by its possession of vast riches, albeit with marked inequalities. In 793 when ordering special donations to alleviate the effect of the famine, Charlemagne laid down that bishops, abbots, and abbesses who could afford it should pay 20 *solidi*, those not quite so rich 10 *solidi*, and the least rich 5 *solidi*. As for counts, the richest also had to give 20 *solidi* and the others 10. The richest royal vassals, who owned at least two hundred holdings (a very substantial figure), had to donate 10 *solidi* as well. Those who had at least one hundred had to pay 5 *solidi*, and then proportionately less down to those who had only thirty or twenty holdings.[6] This means that even the poorest of the king's vassals had twenty or thirty peasant families who worked for them and the richest had a few hundred. Counts, bishops, and abbots could easily have around a thousand, indeed the wealthiest went beyond that threshold. The monastery of St-Germain-des-Prés had over 1,600 tenant farmers, most of them free men. If we count them, their families, and the slaves on the manorial farms, then the abbot was responsible for over 15,000 people.

The substantial endowments that came with the office of count or an episcopal see contributed heavily to this accumulation of wealth, but in reality most of these powerful figures were born rich. The great landowners, who possessed what in ancient times had been called latifundia and were now organized in villas, had a deeply ingrained facility for command. After all, in an almost exclusively agrarian society in which the land was worked by slaves or tenant farmers very much in the thrall of their landowners, running an estate also meant ruling over and punishing other men. It is hardly surprising then that the king chose his counts, bishops, abbots, and, more locally, his royal vassals mainly from this circle. Economic supremacy was automatically accompanied by commitment to public service, which provided the less scrupulous, that is nearly all of them, with the opportunity to inflate their riches very effectively.

Naturally, people of this rank tended to marry among themselves. At the time there were no such concepts as primogeniture and the patrilineal line, nor were there the surnames and coats of arms that were to typify nobility of the late Middle Ages and the *ancien régime*. Noble kinship involved a flexible nucleus of families allied by marriage or consanguinity, a great mass of uncles, aunts, nephews, nieces, brothers- and sisters-in-law, and cousins, always ready to pass inheritances from one to the other. Such a flexible organization of kinship had the added advantage of assisting its durability and avoiding its disappearance through the hazards of demography. Only choosing the wrong side in the event of a challenge to the regime, a catastrophe involving executions and confiscations, could brutally put an end to the fortunes of a great family. Otherwise, it obviously continued to exist, even without legal privileges guaranteed by birth.

The fact that a magnate's assets could well be the basis for political power is demonstrated by some fortuitous documents. In 739 Abbon, who governed Provence for Charles Martel, left a will leaving generous legacies to the abbey of Novalesa, on the Italian side of the Alps, which he had founded, and other churches.[7] He listed primarily his properties in the Susa Valley, inherited from his parents and often entrusted to factors, who may have been slaves or manumitted slaves, and were painstakingly listed with their families. On the other side of the Alps, the list widened out to areas that were later to become Savoy, the Dauphiné,

Lyonnais, and Burgundy and then continued along the Rhône Valley as far as the Mediterranean. Giovanni Tabacco, who first commented on this document, has observed,

> A series of the most disparate purchases and inherited *allodia* [land not subject to a superior] emerge throughout. Here and there lists of names of *ingenui nostri, liberti nostri,* and attendants appear alongside the names of vendors, the names of forbears and collateral kinsmen from whom the *allodia* came. This all demonstrates the long common history of a powerful kinship group and its dependent population, mainly of slave origin, such as the freed slave (whose wife and children were also recorded) whom Rustica, Abbon's mother, had transferred from the *pagus* of Geneva to the *pagus* of Gap.[8]

But then alongside the inherited and purchased *allodia,* there is suddenly mention of properties conferred on Abbon *per verbo dominico,* or at the behest of the mayor of the palace. As a rule, they were properties confiscated from a magnate of southern Gaul who had opposed Frankish conquest and therefore, unlike Abbon, had chosen the wrong side.

It was precisely the choice of sides that led to the establishment of what German historians have called *Reichsadel,* the imperial nobility. This was the circle of families from which Charlemagne chose his closest collaborators, as his father and grandfather had before him, and it reflects the broad international range of his activities. For the most part, these were already rich and powerful families before the advent of the Carolingians, and in southern Gaul, which was still profoundly Romanized, there were even families who boasted descent from the ancient senatorial nobility. With the increase in the size of the kingdom and eventually the empire, these kinship groups constantly saw their opportunities increase as well, and the loyalty of those who served the new dynasty was bountifully rewarded. Thus they managed to acquire and retain properties in several provinces or even kingdoms, amassing *villae* situated sometimes hundreds of miles apart and automatically putting themselves forward for positions of trust in places far from their origins. At the same time, they would enter complex networks of matrimonial alliances with families of the same rank but of different geographic origin.

Commendation and Vassalage

According to custom, counts, bishops, and abbots swore allegiance to the king from the moment they took office. They submitted themselves to his protection and promised to serve him, in the specifically patronage-based or even Mafia-like manner that had been very much alive at the time of the Roman Empire and had never gone out of fashion. But they were not the only ones to surrender themselves to the king's protection, which was certainly not a simple formality, although custom made it obligatory to all intents and purposes. In practice, anyone who entered into contact with the king and served him in any capacity had to submit publicly to his benevolence, as long as they were not in the hereditary servitude that bound slaves and manumitted slaves. In so doing, they officially became part of the most powerful of all patronage systems.

The clergy attached to the royal chapel entered into this form of allegiance, as did the warriors who undertook to serve with arms and horses and were now regularly referred to as vassals. A noble who wanted his son to enter the service of the emperor, or an abbot who hoped to draw the emperor's attention to one of his most promising young monks, would take the candidate to the palace and recommend him to the emperor, possibly also bringing a letter of presentation from some other powerful figure or man of learning who was well known to the sovereign. When a position became vacant or a benefice available, Charlemagne would then choose his new church officials and royal vassals to be sent to the provinces from this pool of young men who had come with powerful backers and lived with him at the palace.

The letters of a few eminent figures of the period that have survived, such as Einhard's, show how dense and complex was this exchange of patronage and favors, how much the career of a young man depended on the right friendships, and how much wealth the king was capable of dispensing to those who served him well or simply had enough contacts in high places.[9] He did so by forming benefices from crown and church lands. The granting of such a favor was technically called a *precarium*, because the desired effect required the submission of a public petition. The commonly used term was "benefice," because it was clear to everyone that the only reason for these concessions was the king's benevolence obtained by loyalty, powerful friends, or even gifts. In each case, it is difficult to think of a terminology that could express more explicitly the use of power and crown property based on patronage.

This network of friendships, protégés, favors, and allegiances was then repeated for every powerful figure. This did not concern the king, nor could he have done anything to undermine one of the principal pillars on which his society rested. Yet there was one aspect of this private patronage that Charlemagne was determined to change. Normally a powerful figure like a count, a bishop, or even a lesser official or large landowner would be surrounded by a squad of armed men and, if these were free men and not simply slaves armed at his expense, they would submit to his protection and swear allegiance to him. This extremely ancient tradition of the Franks was called *trustis*, from the Germanic root for trust and loyalty, and it constituted the warrior side of the patronage practices that were widespread in Romano-Germanic society.

Charlemagne did not want these armed protégés to take on a subversive role, and he ordered that the practice should be legalized in accordance with the vassalage procedure that he used to bind his royal vassals to himself. This meant that the oath of loyalty had to be made in public, and whoever entered into vassalage had to serve not only his lord but also his emperor. Vassals had to fight in the emperor's army every time their lord was called up for war. Whereas the widespread use of benefices reflected the way society was substantially based on patronage, the no less widespread use of vassalage arose from the king's desire to control and regulate the ties of patronage, or at least those that had military implications, by giving them an unmistakably public significance.

Workers on Crown and Church Lands

So far we have discussed the people who were the winners in society, those who were born well or at least had the right contacts. They therefore received concrete advantages from the patronage system, while for the majority it only meant exploitation and toil. In other words, we have looked at the protégés and not the subservient. The latter included slaves, freed slaves, and laborers tied to the land, who together represented a significant percentage and perhaps even the majority of peasants. The term *servi* still technically meant genuine slaves, as it had done in ancient times, but it was already being used on occasion to mean collectively all those men whose degree of submission to the landowner amounted to a form of serfdom. Here again, the legal status, as defined with varying degrees of precision in accordance with the circumstances, is not sufficient to describe the social status. The master to whom the peasant had to answer was no less important than the legal status itself. Someone who by obligation of birth worked on crown or church lands (circumstances that were almost the same) could hold his head high and look down on peasants who toiled on the land of a private landowner. The men who worked for the crown or for the clergy enjoyed a tiny part of the king's reflected glory.

Not for nothing did Charlemagne exclude slaves, manumitted slaves, and all laborers tied to the land on private estates from the oath of allegiance he organized in 793.[10] These were men of little importance and the king had no need of their loyalty, as that of their masters would suffice, but it was a different matter in the case of his own men and those of the Church. The oath of loyalty had to be taken by all *fiscalini* and *ecclesiastici*, as well as all *coloni*. The terms *fiscalini* and *ecclesiastici* are somewhat vague from a legal point of view, but from the social one they were very precise and basically meant all peasants, whether slaves or freed slaves, working on crown or church lands.[11] Even in the ancient laws of the Franks, they had been attributed a privileged status and in many situations were put on a par with free men, rather than slaves.

Their status was the same at the time of Charlemagne. Of course, we have to make distinctions among them: the farm laborer working alongside other poor wretches on some crown farm in a remote province was still a man of little standing, while the one who managed to obtain a supervisory position with some responsibility was transformed into a local worthy who was more powerful than many free men.

Not surprisingly some took advantage of their positions and indulged in all kinds of abuses of power to gain wealth. After all, the ability to commit abuses of power with impunity was the mark of success. Charlemagne banned royal serfs from selling slaves on royal estates, as they were clearly royal property, to local officials such as vicars and centeniers. His order reveals a web of illegality, complicity, and arrogant abuse of power that the palace had great difficulty stemming.[12] Similar opportunities tempted those who worked on church land in Istria after Charles annexed their region, previously subject to Byzantium. They had suddenly become arrogant, as the inhabitants complained in 804, "at the time of the Greeks, they would never have dared to get angry with a free man or hit him with a stick; indeed, they never even dared sit before them. But now, they beat us and threaten us with swords, and we daren't resist out of reverence for our lord the Emperor, fearing they might do worse."[13] Of course, very few were to imitate the career of Ebbo, who was born a freed slave and ended up the archbishop of Reims, but some could hope to become priests or foremen of the farm on which they worked. What little social mobility existed in Charlemagne's time was undoubtedly more pronounced on lands where the king or the Church commanded than on private estates.

THE PEASANT WORLD
The Manor and Its Local Practices

With few exceptions, only a small, wealthy elite was eligible to compete for the high offices dispensed by the king. Charles's long shadow covered a great mass of people whose economic and legal condition was much more modest. This throng of slaves and freed slaves on crown and church lands was in turn only a part—the more secure and less wretchedly exploited part—of an immensely greater sector of society, which was otherwise made up of peasants working for private landowners. In some areas these less fortunate counterparts constituted the entire rural population.

Their legal positions were somewhat different, and not only on a purely formal level. There were concrete differences between the rights and opportunities of a slave and those of a freed slave, or between those of a *colonus*, who was forced to reside on a farm, and a *libellarius*, a tenant farmer with a written contract, who at least in theory had entered freely into a contract with the landowner. Before examining these categories, it is worth emphasizing again that by Charlemagne's time and perhaps for some time before then, the difference between these situations was gradually fading into a shared subjugation in which the same obligations were imposed on everyone by the landowner and by the law. These obligations did more to shape the conditions in which the peasantry found itself than any legal distinctions between them.

The organization of large estates into villas favored this trend, as the rents and services demanded by the owner of a particular farm were unlikely to change once they had been established. The years passed, peasants died, and their sons took over the running of the smallholding, but the obligations to the landowner did not change. The peasants no longer had the contractual power to renegotiate them, and the landowner preferred the administrative convenience ensured by the observance of ancient customs. On the other hand, these obligations varied from one province to another, according to the type of agriculture that was practiced and whether the legal tradition in which the majority of the inhabitants lived was Frankish, Roman, Saxon, or Lombard. Indeed, they could change from one estate to another, in accordance with the type of investment that the landowner had made or the percentage of slaves among the peasants (on whom heavier obligations could be and were imposed).

Thus a custom that everyone observed was created in all the private estates and ended up being enshrined in law. Indeed, on some occasions the law intervened expressly to regulate it. In 800, a year in which he must have had many other things to worry about, Charlemagne had to deal with complaints presented to the palace by peasants working on crown and church lands in the province of Maine. They denounced the high-handedness with which their factors demanded corvées, "because the matter was organized in different ways, and some people were forced to work all week, others half a week, and still others two days." The emperor ruled that throughout the province, those who worked for the crown or the Church were to plow their master's fields for a day if they owned enough oxen to pull a plow, whereas laborers who did not own oxen were to provide three days of manual labor, "and we have ruled in this manner so that peasants on estates cannot avoid the aforementioned obligations, but also so that landowners cannot demand any more."[14] But even in the absence of such focused interventions, the general policy of the time established that peasants who worked for estates, including free men who had signed a contract, had to accept the justice dispensed by the landowner in the event of disputes. Thus the obligations they had to meet increasingly eluded the negotiable and transformed into perpetual customs, of which the landowner was by law the guarantor.

Slaves

Slaves were still an important part of the peasantry who worked for a master, although not as important as in antiquity. The *prebendarii* who worked manorial farms were not the only slaves in a villa; there were also those who had been assigned smallholdings and had been allowed to set up home. In some large monastic estates (the only ones we can make estimates for), little more than half the peasants working on the land were free tenants, about one-third were slaves who had set up home, and the balance were *prebendarii*. Thus the monastery of Santa Giulia in the Brescia area gave work to a thousand people on the manorial farm and over five thousand on smallholdings, of whom three thousand were free and the rest slaves.[15] Clearly these figures, which are valid for large estates, do not reflect the proportion of slaves in society as a whole, because there were far fewer slaves in places where smallholdings were widespread. Charlemagne reduced the military obligations for anyone who "finds himself so poor that he owns neither slaves nor land in his own right," which means that even a small landowner could have a few slaves to assist him in his work.[16]

Legally speaking, a slave was still the property of his owner and could be bought and sold just as in the Roman world. When in 806 he was establishing the rules to govern relations among the three sons who were to inherit his empire, Charlemagne stated that they were not to purchase in the others' lands real estate such as land, vineyards, woods, "or slaves who have already set up home," while they could purchase gold, silver, gems, arms, clothing, and "slaves who had not set up home, in other words all those goods that merchants trade in."[17] In economic terms, slaves were goods and some merchants grew rich trading in them, even though religion supported by the law placed several restrictions on the trade. The separate sale of husband and wife was discouraged and the export of Christian slaves outside Christendom was expressly prohibited.[18] To avoid these and other abuses, Charlemagne ordered as far back as 779 that every sale of slaves had to take place in the presence of a bishop or a count or at least reliable witnesses, and he prohibited the export of slaves outside the borders of the empire.[19] Many years later his son Pepin restated the law for Italy and made it illegal to buy slaves in secret and smuggle them into another region.[20]

In order to get round these restrictions, the slave trade tended to concentrate on prisoners of war from Charlemagne's victorious pagan wars against the Saxons and later the Slavs. It appears that this trade mainly consisted of exports to Muslim Spain and that the imported slaves did not significantly alter the levels of the slave population within the empire, except perhaps in the Germanic region. It is possible that there, slave labor was mainly made up of Slavs, and this gave rise to the etymological development that extended to all Western languages, whereby the ethnic name of the Slavs became synonymous with slavery. A Bavarian document divides the peasants working for the monastery of Sankt Emmeram into "Bavarians and Slavs, free men and slaves," and then at the end it reduces the two alternatives to one: "free men and Slavs."[21] But in Gaul and Italy, the majority of slaves were indigenous: they spoke the same language as their masters and like them had been baptized, although there was a distinctive usage of names for slaves, involving frequent diminutives. From an ethnic point of view, they were seen as Franks or Lombards, even though technically these terms were reserved for free men.

The availability of slaves was increased by the possibility of selling oneself into slavery, which was permitted under the law and actually occurred with starving peasants. When a fine could not be paid, the offender could become a slave of the crown, possibly on a temporary basis until the fine was paid off. Pepin had already ruled that if a free man who was married was reduced to slavery for whatever reason, then his wife was entitled to leave him and marry another, "unless he had sold himself out of poverty and was forced by hunger, and she, having agreed, avoided starvation through the price of her man."[22] In this case, it was right that a wife who had been saved by her spouse at the cost of such a sacrifice should show him her gratitude by remaining at his side in slavery. Charlemagne occasionally discouraged the practice, as when, following the conquest of Italy, he was informed that many poor people had sold themselves, their wives, and their children in order to escape destitution inflicted by the war, and so he revoked all those transactions.[23] But this was a political gesture, not the assertion of a principle, and the practice continued to occur widely.

The greatest restriction on the slave trade was of an economic nature. When a landowner arranged for a slave family to set up home by providing them with a smallholding, as occurred very frequently, he obviously lost all interest in selling them. He might do it if he sold the land, as any buyer would be interested in acquiring the workforce with the land, but otherwise the idea would never occur to him. If he donated the land to the Church for the sake of his soul, he would also transfer the peasants who worked there, possibly freeing them and turning them into manumitted slaves of the Church. In other words, slaves who had set up home had de facto security of tenure and were not going to be thrown off their land. As was made clear by Charlemagne's previously mentioned provisions of 806, they had been transformed into a kind of real estate or immovable asset. This development might not appear particularly wonderful in terms of human dignity, but in practice it represented an important conquest on their part.

With the establishment of his home, a slave also acquired the opportunity to keep any small profits he might manage to put aside through hard work. This right was first acknowledged in custom and then later by law. There were even slaves who managed to set up a small business through these savings. When Charlemagne introduced the new currency and ordered all traders to accept it without argument, he established a fine in the case of a free man, "but if he is of servile condition, and he is trading in his property, he should lose his business or be whipped publicly before the people."[24] The responsibility for a smallholding or a business placed the slave in a social situation not too unlike that of a free smallholder and allowed him to organize his work independently and even to own his own slaves. One of Pepin's laws refers to the case of a slave who has his own female slave as his concubine and acknowledges his right to leave her in order to marry "one of his peers, that is, a slave woman belonging to his master, but it would be better if he kept his slave."[25] The conclusion was a purely formal nod in the direction of the bishops, who were campaigning against divorce and polygamy.

I have already implied another improvement that was no less spectacular. Precisely because they were Christian, slaves were entitled to marry, and their owner had to respect their marriage. The Lombard king Liutprand had already ruled that if a slaveholder raped one of his married female slaves, she and her husband would obtain freedom.[26] Pepin decreed that if a married slave couple was sold separately, priests were to preach to them both on the obligation to accept the enforced chastity with Christian fortitude, but at the same time he observed that everything should be done to join them back together.[27] Charlemagne went further and ruled that if a man and woman belonging to different masters were to marry, it would no longer be possible to divide them, as long as they adhered to appropriate form and had the consent of their masters.[28] In spite of this, promiscuity persisted among slaves, particularly when there was a large female workforce involved in weaving. Among the slaves personally attending to the emperor, Notker mentions "two bastards born in the women's quarters of Colmar," suggesting a situation not dissimilar to the factory life created by the industrial revolution a thousand years later.[29]

The influence of Christianity also led to the abolition of the owners' power of life and death over their own slaves. Of course, these unfortunate wretches, who owned nothing of their own except a few animals they managed to rear and a few coins scratched together by selling their produce in the market, were still subject to corporal punishments for the slightest mistake. They would be punished with a beating and in more serious cases with hanging, for actions that would have involved a fine for a free man. But only royal judges could pass the death sentence, and slaveholders who caused death through excessive beatings were to be punished. The harshness of slavery was still evident in this submission to corporal punishment that marked the distinction between free man and slave, so much so that the evidence that a man had been "beaten like as slave" was crucial in trials that established someone's personal status.[30] However, the dehumanization of slaves that occurred in the pre-Christian era had now come to an end.

The Fate That Awaited Freed Slaves

Freed slaves were even more numerous than slaves and their social conditions were not so different. We have already examined freed slaves working on crown and church lands, but a very high percentage and possibly the majority of peasants working anywhere on large estates was made up of freed slaves. The manumitted slave, who retained a subservient relationship toward his previous owner and now his patron, had already been a familiar figure in antiquity, but with the dominance of Christianity, the liberation of slaves was expressly encouraged by the Church as a righteous act and developed apace. At the same time, the obligations toward patrons that bound freed slaves were increased so that owners would not be damaged economically. All Germanic laws acknowledged various forms of manumission, the most solemn of which was carried out in the presence of the king using written documents, and it made the freed slave a free man with full rights and no obligation to submit himself to a patron. The impression is that cases of complete manumission were extremely rare. Generally, the freed slave was obliged to live on the owner's land and work for him by paying a rent. He had no right to leave without his new patron's permission.

This was not necessarily an unfavorable solution. A freed slave left to himself without a smallholding to work and with no patron to protect him would have swelled the ranks of the poorest peasants, and whereas the rural population was still low enough for everyone to find work in the end, it was not so low that they could dictate the conditions. At the time of Louis the Pious, several dozen slaves were freed in the Rieti area all at the same time by the will of a local *gastald*, and they received smallholdings from the abbot of Farfa. They had to accept extremely harsh contractual conditions, which meant working up to one week out of two on the manorial farm at the busiest time of year, as well as paying a heavy rent in kind.[31] Freed slaves constituted a veritable rural proletariat, particularly in areas that were being put under the plow for the first time, and their work contributed in no small way to the prosperity of the manorial system. It is by no means certain that their manumission improved their living conditions.

In the great majority of cases, freed slaves remained bound to the owner who had freed them. The law turned it into a moral question. The Lombard king Aistulf wondered whether it was not a sign of ingratitude that freed slaves dared to abandon their benefactors. The king had been informed that slaveholders hesitated to free slaves if they were not sure that they could count on their labor. The king therefore ruled that even in the case of complete manumission, which turned a freed slave into a free Lombard in every sense, the former owner was still entitled for the rest of his life to claim that freed slave's service.[32] There were no such explicit measures for the Franks, but common practice was the same: the freed slave, who was called a *litus*, was not a free man but was obliged to become another of his patron's men.

The real tragedy for slaves freed in this manner was that the distinction between them and slaves was reduced to the matter of a name and nothing more. In practice freed slaves found themselves just as subservient as they had previously been, given that they were still required to remain permanently on their patron's lands and serve him how and when he wanted without being able to negotiate more favorable contractual conditions, as a free peasant was still able to do. Innumerable accounts testify that a freed slave's social condition was closer to that of a slave than of a genuinely free man. In 754 King Pepin issued a law against incest: the guilty party, if he was free, had to pay a heavy fine, and if he could not, he was imprisoned. But "if he is a slave or a manumitted slave, he should be beaten many times, and his owner should not allow him to repeat his offense."[33] In 802 Charlemagne ordered that all inhabitants of the northern coastline threatened by Norse raids were to make themselves available to the local authorities and to come immediately in the event of being called to action. Those who failed to do this had to pay a fine to the king, if they were free men, but if they were slaves or freed slaves "they shall receive a royal fine on their backs" or, in other words, more beatings.[34]

Hence, as time went by the distinction between slaves and manumitted slaves became one of little interest to those in command and to those literary figures who fixed our image of their society on parchment. *Servus*, the most widely used word to signify the ancient slave and the only one retained by the vernaculars of Gaul and Italy, had come to be used without distinction for both slaves and manumitted slaves, not to mention other categories of rural dependent laborers, such as the *coloni* who were personally free peasants but undertook that they and their descendants alike would live permanently on a smallholding. Charlemagne's time was just the beginning of this confusion, which had even crept into the capitularies, but in the long run it would lead to the disappearance of ancient slavery from the European countryside and the creation of a new form of dependence called serfdom. This was to include the great majority of peasants dependent on a landowner, all equally subject to the conditions imposed locally by the manor.

POTENTES AND PAUPERES

The emperor had little interest in the fate of freed slaves, as was made clear by his celebrated reply to the indecisive envoy: "there are only free men and slaves." Quoted at the start of this chapter in the context of treating a *colona* as a slave, this blunt remark demonstrates with absolute clarity that the subjection of the peasant multitude was not, in itself, a political problem, even though on other occasions Charlemagne did concern himself with whether their masters treated them correctly and respected their rights, as was his duty. The difficulties that afflicted free smallholders were an entirely different matter. They were crushed by the services the king demanded of them and were at the mercy of the abuses perpetrated by the powerful with impunity. Free smallholders still formed the majority of the army and paid taxes, albeit with great difficulty. The fact that too many of them were being forced to sell up and enter into the service of a master was extremely disturbing and was becoming politically significant.

Measures to protect the poor from abuses of power therefore proliferated in Charlemagne's capitularies. By "poor" we mean in this case not the real poor, slaves and freed slaves exploited by their masters, but the free men who in the traditional perception constituted the backbone of the Frankish people. Undoubtedly the most effective measure would have been exemption from military service, but the emperor was not persuaded that he could allow it and, as we have seen, he treated absconders harshly, while beseeching local officials, possibly without effect, not to take advantage of military service to ruin these men and deprive them of their lands.[35] On the other hand, Charlemagne did commit himself to easing the burden of the administration of justice. He abolished the obligation on all free men to attend *placita*, although this did risk encouraging counts and their friends to treat public justice as a purely private affair.[36] Lastly, the emperor ruled that poor people who were free and had to pay a fine could convert the sentence into a beating and thus pay their debt to the crown "with their backs," avoiding confiscation of their livestock, which would have thrown them into a state of destitution.[37]

But the majority of these measures were no more than warnings that the emperor would no longer tolerate the abuses the powerful heaped on the poor.[38] We have reason to believe that unfortunately such rebukes too often remained a dead letter. All over the empire free men were submitting themselves to the benevolence of powerful patrons, not as armed vassals but as bondsmen, and there were many more who, motivated by hunger, actually sold themselves into slavery. Not that the fate of the former was much different from that of the latter, given that, as we have seen, local custom tended increasingly to put the entire peasantry on a par in a single form of subjugation. It was no coincidence that this period witnessed an increase in the number of trials brought by groups of peasants who expected the court to reaffirm their personal freedom against a master who wished to treat them on a par with slaves. Occasionally the peasants won, but more often they lost.

After Charlemagne's death, the law itself worsened the status of free men working under a master. Louis the Pious repeatedly introduced measures that, although restating that they were to be considered free, established that they could not give evidence in court, because it was impossible to take action against them in the case of perjury, as they did not own any land.[39] A freedom that lacked any form of economic support was proving increasingly difficult to defend in practice. For a long time, both the Frankish and Lombard laws had laid down that a free man residing on another man's lands was the responsibility of the landowner, and if he committed a crime, it was up to the master to arrest him and hand him over to the authorities.[40] The contracts that peasants entered into with landowners, even the written ones still used in Italy, should in theory have given the peasant greater guarantees, but even they made provisions for the voluntary submission to justice dispensed by the landowner in the event of contractual nonfulfillment.

Squeezed between the two worlds of patronage and servitude, free smallholders led an increasingly precarious existence. The more well-to-do, those who had a few slaves and could buy weapons and horses and train to use them, could enter the local patronage network, possibly as a royal vassal, and obtain a position among the secure. Once the relative tranquillity ensured by Charlemagne had gone, the others increasingly found that they had to submit to the abuses, sell their property, and join the growing ranks of serfs working for their lord.

FOURTEEN

Old Age and Death

CHARLEMAGNE'S FAILURE?

The final years of Charlemagne's reign are often presented as a period of decline, almost as though the sovereign's gradual physical deterioration was paralleled in the empire he created. The old and sick emperor hardly moved from his palace in Aachen, where he was surrounded by a cliquish and domineering band of flatterers intent on making fortunes for themselves unbeknown to him.[1] His legitimate sons eyed each other suspiciously, while waiting for the old man to die, so that they could inherit. In their hearts, each was convinced that with luck he would be able to eliminate his brothers and reign on his own. But the tragic irony was that death took away two of the three potential heirs, the firstborn Charles and King Pepin of Italy, leaving only the weaker king of Aquitaine, Louis the Pious, and this series of bereavements soured the last years of their father's life. The wars of conquest, which for so long had created consensus and amassed riches, had ended, and the beginning of the Norse coastal raids was a frightening omen of the aggression that would speed the collapse of the empire after Charles's death and return Christendom to barbarism. The aging emperor's policies in his later capitularies have been interpreted as a desperate but unsuccessful attempt to stem the spread of corruption and the moral disintegration of the empire.

This sorry picture is not altogether false but has to be broken down into its various elements. Militarily speaking, there is no denying that in later years the emperor did not display his previous aggression. In 810 he instantly accepted simultaneous offers of peace from the *basileus* Nicephorus and the emir of Cordova, who were both tired of war. It is true that the agreement with the emir recognized the progress King Louis of Aquitaine had made beyond the Pyrenees, taking the empire's borders as far as the Ebro, but it is also true that in order to make peace with Byzantium, Charles agreed to return the Venetian lagoon, which had only just been conquered. Equally, the continual border incidents provoked by the Danes did not induce the emperor to rid himself of these irritating neighbors by invading their country, as he would have done in earlier times. Instead, he fortified the frontier along the Elbe and negotiated with their king. In 811 he went so far as to sign a bilateral treaty, as though between two equals. It remains to be seen whether this undoubted change of policy was merely a sign of the emperor's advancing years or a conscious decision by the Frankish aristocracy, whose previous victories had made them richer than they ever imagined in their wildest dreams. They now probably preferred a more prudent and less adventurous policy.

As for Charles, of course he had grown old and was not so eager to leave Aachen. Even at the time of his coronation in St. Peter's in 800, he was already nearly sixty and an old man for his time. It does not appear credible that, as some have argued, he only traveled by water because arthritis and possibly gout meant he could no longer ride. Quite the contrary, we know that, in spite of frequent fevers and pains in his legs, he continued to go hunting up until a few months before his death. Yet for some time he had preferred to let his sons lead military campaigns. As far back as 796, the destruction of the Avar khanate was carried out by King Pepin of Italy, who in the following years oversaw intermittent operations against the Byzantines along the eastern border and against the duke of Benevento in the south of Italy. Similarly, King Louis of Aquitaine directed the prolonged campaigns on the other side of the Pyrenees, leading to the siege and conquest of Barcelona. It is difficult to see anything unusual in this natural delegation of responsibilities to the men he trusted in the area, who also happened to be his sons and whom he had made kings precisely for this purpose. As for the eldest heir, Charles, who would have inherited the Frankish kingdom, it was only natural that he should be trained from a young age in taking command by being given independent control of operations against the Saxons, and that after 800 he was increasingly often given sole command of campaigns along the central front against the Slavs and Danes. The emperor was getting old, and it was certainly no indication of a crisis that he had three strapping young sons who could replace him very effectively in the direction of military operations.

Besides, the negative image of the final years of Charles's life was inspired by accounts that were far from impartial. It was the chroniclers of his son Louis, particularly the poet Ermoldus Nigellus, who claimed that subjects greeted the new emperor with delirious enthusiasm, and that he immediately set about correcting the wrongs committed under his father, opening prisons and recalling exiles.[2] According to these authors, Charles in his final years was a profoundly senile old man who was isolated from the world, and even his less corrupt counselors were obliged to insist that he place more responsibilities in the hands of his surviving son. Of course, there may well be some truth in all this but not enough to speak of those years as a period of decay. The experience of other emperors who have survived into great old age in more recent times, such as Queen Victoria and Kaiser Franz Joseph, shows that the physical and even mental decline of a monarch is not necessarily reflected in the government of the empire, even though there is always a party of impatient supporters grouped around the heir, ready to celebrate the death of the old incumbent as a liberation.

It is particularly unacceptable to interpret the legislative activity of Charles's final years as a failure. Between 805 and 813 the emperor issued a new series of capitularies, hammering away on the need to pursue efforts at reform. The year 813, in particular, saw an unprecedented mobilization of the Frankish Church, which Charles convened in five provincial councils, all of whose records have survived.[3] The capitularies of these years are legislative acts of tremendous ideological significance, which express profound reflection on the nature of imperial power. It was almost as if the old monarch, having pondered over his new name of Augustus, which initially caused him some concern, had become increasingly persuaded of the responsibilities this brought in relation to the Christian people. The bitter sarcasm he used against the corruption of judges and the inadequacies of the clergy, and the almost obsessive insistence on *concordia, consensus, unanimitas*, and above all *caritas*, which had to inspire government action and relations between subjects, may be interpreted by some as a sign of feebleness and senility, but it seems difficult to blame Charles for having wished to follow through the moral implications inherent in the concept of a Christian empire.

THE FIGHT AGAINST PIRACY

Much has been said about a new threat to Charles's kingdom in the final years of his reign. It came from pirates who increasingly afflicted the empire's coastline and made sea travel and trade unsafe. The fact that these raids continued and indeed intensified after his death almost to the point of bringing Christendom to its knees appears with hindsight to suggest that the measures taken by the aging emperor were insufficient. We must avoid interpreting events of the time in the light of things that happened fifty or hundred years later. On close examination, Charlemagne's reaction to pirate raids does not appear inappropriate for the size of the threat it could be judged at the time. Indeed it testifies to his energy and broad vision, which were extraordinary in a decrepit old man, for that is what a seventy-year-old would have been in that period.

The Norse

The most dangerous enemies were the Norse from Scandinavia, whom we more often refer to as Vikings.[4] The first Norse incursion struck the monastery of Lindisfarne, an island off the English coast, in 793. The massacre of the monks and the burning of the abbey horrified Christendom. The news reached Charles's court, and Alcuin, who came from those parts, tried to console himself with the thought that the catastrophe was God's punishment for the sins of the Anglo-Saxon people.[5] Very soon they were to discover that no one was safe from the divine wrath: the raids proliferated against England, Scotland, and Ireland and then in 799 struck the Atlantic coast of the Carolingian empire.[6] From that time, navigation was no longer safe even in the Channel, and England was one of the empire's most important trading partners. In 809 a papal legate to the king of Northumbria was captured by pirates while crossing the Channel to return to Rome.

Everything would indicate that Charles understood the nature of the problem perfectly, given that he was not content just to introduce a system of rapid mobilization of armed men in the coastal regions but also ordered the building of warships in the northern ports.[7] In 811 he insisted on personally reviewing the squadrons at the anchorage in Ghent and Boulogne. With hindsight, we might consider that he did not invest enough resources in shipbuilding, although naval power is the most difficult to improvise. Nevertheless, the emperor must have been convinced that he had dealt with the threat, when he died. In fact, pirate attacks were only one aspect of a more complex problem, his relations with the kingdom of Denmark, and after a little hesitation Charles took decisive action on this, with all the energy of his most successful years.

Since the Franks had subjugated the Saxons and shifted their borders to the North Sea, the Danes had found themselves on the border of the empire, and their king, Godefrid, had immediately demonstrated that he was not going to put up with intimidation. In 804, when Charles himself crossed the Elbe at the head of his army to eliminate the last center of

Saxon resistance, Godefrid gathered together his fleet and his cavalry at the mouth of the great river that marked the border between the two kingdoms. We do not know whether the Danish king agreed to hand over the escaped rebels to the emperor, following this show of force, but we do know that the emperor made a formal request for him to do so.

From that time on, the Franks knew that they had to be wary of the Danes, although Einhard probably exaggerated when he claimed that Godefrid "had become so puffed up with vain hopes that he intended to conquer the whole of Germany and boasted that he would soon be in Aachen."[8] It was more serious that the Slav tribes who lived around the mouth of the Elbe were under continuous attack from the Danes, because they had helped the Franks against the Saxons and Charlemagne considered them protected satellites of his empire. In 808 Godefrid sacked their coast, overcame their fortifications, hung one of their leaders, and drove another into exile. Once he had defeated these tribes and forced them to pay a tribute, he hurriedly fortified the borders of his kingdom. For a while, Charles preferred to study his adversary, investing most of his resources in his own fortifications along the border and even allowing the commencement of negotiations. His prudence may have been taken as a sign of weakness, because in 810 a Danish fleet appeared off Frisia, and, a few days' march from the palace in Aachen, these raiders forced the coastal population to pay a heavy tribute of one hundred pounds of silver to avoid pillage.

The time for delay was over, and the elderly emperor finally decided to react as he had so often done in more youthful times, by preparing a blitzkrieg against the Danes under his own command. At the beginning of the summer of 810 he was at Lippeham on the Rhine, intent upon assembling the army, when news arrived that Godefrid had been assassinated. The Danish kingdom was thrust into civil war and the need for armed intervention seemed to fade, given that the leaders who temporarily emerged were more than happy to sign a peace treaty with the emperor to ensure his goodwill. With hindsight, it could be argued that the failure to invade Denmark was to cost the empire dear, but at the time everyone was happy that such a dangerous enemy had been rendered harmless without having to go into battle. "What a pity that I was not able to see my Christians fighting those *cynocephali*," Charles joked, alluding to the legend put about by geographers that among the frozen and mysterious wastes of the north, there lived people who had the heads of dogs.[9]

This did not prevent Notker, who was writing around 887, from endowing the emperor with tragic foresight. The monk of St-Gall tells us that when Charles was visiting a Gaulish port, a Norse ship appeared off the coast, exploring the area for the first time. As soon as these Vikings knew that the emperor was there in person, they sneaked away, but Charles was not overjoyed and stood at the window for a long time with tears in his eyes. He then explained to his dismayed followers that his tears came not from fear of what the enemy could do to him, because while he was still alive they would not dare trouble that coast, but from awareness that after his death they would inflict untold horrors on his successors.[10] It appears that the Charlemagne of legends started to cry long before the *Chanson de Roland*. In the imagination of those who came afterward, the upheavals suffered by the Christian empire following his death were too dramatic not to color adversely their view of the emperor's final years.

Muslim Pirates

During the same period, the southern flank of Christendom was experiencing the first of the raids by Moorish pirates that were to create danger and uncertainty for a millennium.[11] Initially, the organizational abilities of the empire and particularly the Italic kingdom appear to have provided a degree of defense capability, even in terms of naval power, so we cannot yet talk of Arab domination of the Mediterranean. In 798 the Moors sacked the Balearic Islands, but the following year a Frankish squadron brought in to assist the islanders managed to repulse another incursion and capture the pirates' insignia, which it immediately forwarded to the emperor. In 806 the Moors attacked Corsica and this time defeated the squadron sent to intercept them by King Pepin of Italy, killing its commander, the count of Genoa. But the following year another Christian naval force succeeded in defeating them and capturing thirteen ships. Yet such successes were to become increasingly rare in the coming years, while the raids were to proliferate.

Then in 812 word spread among Christians that Saracens of Africa and Spain were preparing a great fleet to pillage Italy. The emperor seems to have realized that the resources invested in naval defense in the Mediterranean were insufficient, and he sent his cousin Wala with the task of doing something to resolve this. The measures he took had some effect, because a Muslim squadron was sunk off Sardinia, but at the same time another sacked Corsica without meeting resistance. The following year pirates were intercepted close to Majorca by a Christian squadron under the command of the count of Ampurias and they lost eight ships, leading to the freeing of more than five hundred slaves. On the whole, however, the kings of Italy and Aquitaine did not have the means to maintain domination of the sea, and the naval forces based in Mediterranean ports could not guarantee the safety of the coastal areas, although they could make life difficult for the pirates. Again in 813 the Moors appeared for the first time on land and sacked places as far apart as Nice and Centocelle, near Rome. Even before Charlemagne died, Christendom was on the defensive in the Mediterranean, but examination of these operations, with its succession of victories and defeats, demonstrates that Frankish naval capabilities and their willingness to fight to maintain control were greater than has been generally believed.

PROVISIONS FOR THE SUCCESSION
The Division of the Kingdom in 806

The most pressing of the many worries that absorbed Charles during the last years of his life was the division of the inheritance among his sons. Frankish law entitled each male to a share of the paternal estate, and no one, not even the emperor, could ignore this. In 806 at the Diet of Thionville Charles issued a decree known as the *Divisio regnorum*, which established that after his death the countries over which he ruled would be divided into three kingdoms to be given to his three remaining sons, Charles, Pepin, and Louis.[12] The real firstborn, Pepin the Hunchback, was still alive in the monastery to which the plot against his father had consigned him, but his exclusion from the will had been decided earlier, because the new rules of marriage preached by the church authorities and included in Charlemagne's own capitularies meant that he had to be considered illegitimate.[13]

Some people have interpreted this division as proof of the emperor's fundamental indifference toward the imperial title, or at least a reluctance to provide for its continuance after his death, at a time when relations with the Byzantine Empire were extremely bad and there was no sign of the East acknowledging the new title. It is as though, when faced with the urgent practical requirements of his own succession, Charles suddenly forgot the high-sounding theories on the nature of imperial power that underlay his later capitularies and started to treat the empire as his private property to be divided as he wished among his heirs. The reality was somewhat different. The carefully constructed *Divisio regnorum* testifies to Charles's strenuous efforts to safeguard the rights of his sons without destroying the immense political edifice he had so patiently built over many years.

To understand the true nature of the division planned by Charles, we need to analyze it as the product of a long sequence of decisions. As the emperor could not have known how long he would live, the problem of his succession had been concerning him for a long time. The plan's outline appeared back in 781, when his two smallest sons, Carloman who later became Pepin and Louis, ages four and three, respectively, were anointed kings of Italy and Aquitaine. The fact that the first legitimate son, Charles, was not given a kingdom did not mean he was out of favor. His name continued to take precedence over those of his brothers in the litanies read out in church services, even though they were kings and he was not. Clearly the young Charles was destined to inherit the most important of his father's kingdoms, the *regnum Francorum*, and the twin coronation of 781 was clearly a policy statement on the succession. One annalist wrote of that occasion, "the king divided his kingdoms among his sons."[14]

While Pepin and Louis were installed in their kingdoms, assisted by their tutors and counselors, and grew up there, gradually learning about local questions, their brother Charles remained at home at his father's side and acted increasingly as his lieutenant, with both military and diplomatic duties. In 800, when he was twenty-three, he accompanied his father to Rome and was crowned king and anointed by the pope alongside him.[15] He was the only king of the Franks to celebrate his own coronation in the Eternal City. Six years later the *Divisio regnorum* did little more than rubber-stamp a division of the inheritance that had been settled long before and was already operating in practice. Thus the two kingdoms of Italy and Aquitaine were partially autonomous but still subordinate to the kingdom of the Franks, although Charlemagne did his best to reduce the inequality among the brothers as far as was possible. Pepin was given the Italic kingdom, which was already his, but also Bavaria, while Louis's Aquitaine was enlarged to include Septimania, Provence, and part of Burgundy. All these annexations were entirely justifiable in geopolitical terms and in no way encroached on the traditional structure of the Frankish kingdom that was to be Charles's, and at the same they assuaged the egalitarian concerns of the Frankish tradition.

The Coronation of Louis the Pious in 813

In 806, when he issued the *Divisio regnorum*, the emperor was over sixty, and he was entitled to expect that its provisions would not have to be changed. But fate had other ideas, because Charles was to see two of his sons die, one after the other, King Pepin of Italy in 810 and Charles, who was to succeed him on the Frankish throne, in 811. Once he had recovered from this heavy blow, the aging emperor understood that the task of taking over the succession now fell entirely on Louis's shoulders and he wanted to make things as easy as he could for his surviving son. On 11 September 813, in the presence of the general assembly of Frankish magnates and bishops, Charles acknowledged his son as his heir and associated him with the empire by placing the imperial crown on his head and ordering that he should now be addressed with the title of Augustus.

The granting of the imperial inheritance to Louis did not entirely invalidate the decisions taken in Thionville in 806. While the kingdom of Aquitaine, which was already Louis's, de facto lost its autonomy, Charles safeguarded the kingdom of Italy, because the previous year he had conceded its royal title to his grandson Bernard, the son of Pepin. Bernard's coronation took place in Aachen in September 813, immediately after the coronation of Louis the Pious. The relationship between the empire and the kingdoms was based on a variable geometry, which made it possible to cut out and reabsorb kingdoms according to the needs of the imperial family, while the subordination to the emperor was beyond discussion. Hence Bernard, although taking the title of king, did not receive the anointment reserved for the king of the Franks.

The custom of crowning the emperor's son while the father was still alive, in order to facilitate the transition through a period of joint regency in which the empire was effectively ruled by two sovereigns, originated in the eastern empire and there can be no doubt that Charles was consciously imitating it, as well as copying the Byzantine ritual in his coronation of Louis. In 812 relations with the *basileus* had returned to normal, and envoys from Constantinople had acknowledged Charles's imperial title, albeit through gritted teeth. It was then possible to take the analogy between the two empires to its logical conclusion: both were Roman, and they peaceably shared the government of the Christian people, one in the West and the other in the East. Seen from this perspective, Louis's coronation in 813 loses the connotations of alarm or even emergency that historians in the past have too easily read into it. Quite the opposite, it is one more factor that confirms the idea of

Charlemagne approaching death in the certain belief that he has fulfilled
his mission and handed an ordered and secure world down to his son.

Charlemagne's Will

Apart from the empire, Charlemagne left a substantial private fortune,
which he could dispose of as he wished and was not obliged to leave to
his successor. We are not talking here about the immense crown estates.
Far too often it has been argued that in that time people had no concept
of public property as distinct from the monarch's personal property. In
reality, what was known, with good reason, as *res publica* belonged to the
crown, and Charlemagne would never have dreamed of disposing of it
privately. But he felt he could do what he liked with the treasury, the
enormous quantity of jewels and coins held at his palace in Aachen, filled
with presents from foreign ambassadors and his own counts, bishops,
and abbots, as well as booty from military campaigns, primarily the Avar
gold.

Einhard informs us that the emperor intended to dictate a proper
will, in accordance with the norms of Roman law, leaving a bequest to
each of his daughters and his sons born outside official marriage, but it
was a long and complicated affair and Charles, who left this too late, did
not manage to complete his will. In 811, however, he signed a more or
less equivalent document, although less formal, and in it gave instructions for sharing out the treasury.[16] This document, which had been
signed by eleven bishops, four abbots, and fifteen counts, announced
that all the gold, silver, and precious stones kept in the imperial vaults
should be divided in three parts. Two parts were then further divided
into twenty-one portions corresponding to the twenty-one metropolitan
sees in which the empire was divided. Following the emperor's death,
they were to be distributed to the twenty-one archbishops, who were
then to share them out with their suffragans.

The remaining third was to be kept for Charlemagne's future needs.
After his death, it was to be divided into four portions, one to be shared

equally among the twenty-one archbishops, one to be shared among his children and grandchildren, one to be distributed to the poor, and one to be given to the servants at the palace. All pots and pans of copper and iron, weapons, clothes, carpets, and household goods in general were to be added to the third portion of gold and silver, to increase the size of alms. As for the books in the library, anyone who wanted them had to pay their worth, and the proceeds would be given to the poor. The books were probably not so much to be auctioned as to be redeemed by his successor who, as far as we know, owned at least some of his father's books. Einhard, who was writing during the reign of Louis the Pious and was indebted to him for his wealth, assures us that after Charles's death, the new emperor was informed of this document and observed it scrupulously.[17]

CHARLEMAGNE'S DEATH

In the Middle Ages as in antiquity, as Suetonius testifies so fully, the death of an emperor was always preceded by sinister omens. The Middle Ages were no different and Charlemagne no exception.[18] Since 806 there had been a sudden increase in the number of eclipses of the sun and moon, and on one occasion a dark spot had obscured the brightness of the sun for an entire week. Even though these phenomena could be explained by astronomers and did not provoke irrational fears, they were cause for concern as it was firmly believed that when God maneuvered the cosmic spectacle He intended to announce something exceptional to mankind. During military campaigns Charles himself had kept an eye on the movement of heavenly bodies, and once while fighting the Saxons, he had written to Alcuin to ask him whether the conjunction of Mars with Cancer was to be considered a bad omen.[19] But now the wars were over, and given the emperor's age, it was impossible to deceive oneself over the meaning of the portent.

There was no lack of other omens that did not derive from the cosmic order. The portico that joined the royal hall to the chapel suddenly collapsed on Ascension Day. Einhard's memory was probably playing tricks on him, because the Royal Annals record the incident occurring in 817, three years after Charlemagne's death, and it was attributed simply to the bad state of the woodwork.[20] The burning of the bridge over the Rhine at Mainz was also interpreted as a bad omen. The structure, which had taken ten years to build, was destroyed by flames in three hours. Then there were the tremors that shook the palace of Aachen on several occasions, and sinister sounds coming from the ceilings of the rooms in which the emperor stayed. It is not clear whether these tremors resulted from an earthquake or simply the poor materials with which the imperial residence had been built. More serious, apart from the evil omens, was Charles's accident in 810, during his expedition against the Danes. A flaming torch appeared to him, and his frightened horse stumbled and dragged him down in the fall. Within days, his elephant Abul Abbas died. This animal had been a gift from Hārūn al-Rashīd and had followed the emperor on all his travels.

Yet Charlemagne survived all these omens by several years, dying four months after the imperial coronation of his son Louis. We are tempted to think that, having made provisions for the succession, he felt that his work was finished and he simply let himself die. But the sources contradict this romantic interpretation.[21] Once the ceremony was over, Charles immediately dispatched Louis to the kingdom of Aquitaine, which he had ruled for thirty years, and then went happily off to hunt in the forest of Ardennes, close to Aachen, as he did every year. It was autumn, the ideal season for hunting, and that had always been his principal amusement, just as game had always been his favorite dish. Faced with these attractions, old age was certainly not sufficient to hold Charlemagne back.

But during the hunt he caught a chill and had to stay in bed at his palace in Aachen. He fasted, believing this would rid him of his fever as it had done so often in the past. But instead he felt an additional pain in his side, which was undoubtedly pneumonia, and the old man's physique, already weakened by lack of nourishment, could no longer resist. He died on 28 January 814 at nine in the morning, after having received the Eucharist. His body, washed and prepared in accordance with custom, was carried to the palatine chapel. The emperor had not left instructions for his burial, but it was agreed that nowhere was more suitable than the magnificent basilica he had had built at his own expense. He was buried that same day in a sarcophagus of ancient marble he had had brought from Rome, and his tomb carried the Latin inscription stating, here lies the body of Charles, "the great and orthodox emperor."[22]

Charlemagne was dead, having reigned for forty-six years. Some, particularly those close to the new monarch, would certainly have greeted the news with joy. The times were changing, previously blocked careers could now proceed, and new opportunities would open up for those who had been straining at the leash. Others, perhaps the majority, would have felt a sense of loss, because Charlemagne had been there as long as anyone could remember. Only the very old could recall his predecessor, but the great majority of the empire's subjects were young and had known only one sovereign. But there was no reason for alarm. With the help of Providence, the crown had passed to its legitimate heir, without challenges, dissent, or the threat of civil wars as had happened so often in the past. As for the future, that was in God's hands.

NOTES

ABOUT THE NOTES

The notes are meant solely to locate quotations, sources, and bits of specific information; for the relevant literature and its discussion the reader is referred to the annotated bibliography at the end of the volume.

The following abbreviations have been used for the main sources referred to in the notes:

Alcuini	*Alcuini epistolae*, in *MGH, Epistolae Karolini aevi*, vol. 2.
ARF	*Annales Regni Francorum*, ed. F. Kurze (Hannover, 1895; vol. 6 of *MGH, Scriptores*)
CC	*Codex Carolinus*, in *MGH, Epistolae Karolini aevi*, 3:476–653
CRF	*MGH, Legum sectio II, Capitularia Regum Francorum*, vol. 1
Einhardus	Einhardus, *Vita Karoli Magni*, ed. O. Holder-Egger (Hannover-Leipzig, 1911; vol. 25 of *MGH, Scriptores*)
Fichtenau	H. von Fichtenau, *Das karolingische Imperium* (Zurich, 1949)—in English translation, *The Carolingian Empire* (Toronto, 1979)
KdG	*Karl der Grosse: Lebenswerk und Nachleben*, 4 vols. (Düsseldorf, 1965–67)
LL	*Le leggi dei Longobardi*, ed. C. Azzara and S. Gasparri (Milan, 1992)
Manaresi	C. Manaresi, *I placiti del 'Regnum Italiae,'* vol. 1, Fonti per la storia d'Italia no. 54 (Rome, 1955)

MGH	*Monumenta Germaniae Historica*
Notker	Notker Balbulus, *Gesta Karoli Magni imperatoris*, ed. H. Haefele (Berlin, 1962; vol. 12, n.s. of *MGH, Scriptores*)
PL	Migne, *Patrologia Latina*
Scriptores	*Scriptores rerum Germanicarum in usum scholarum*
Settimane	*Settimane di studio del Centro italiano di studi sull'alto medioevo*, Spoleto

The laws of Germanic people other than the Lombards are quoted from the edition in the relevant section of *MGH, Legum sectio I, Leges Nationum Germanicarum*.

References are to page numbers in the cases of *ARF*, Fichtenau, and *LL*; to item numbers in the cases of *Alcuini, CC, CRF*, and Manaresi; to book and chapter in the cases of Einhardus and Notker.

INTRODUCTION

1. See chapter 4, on the coronation in 800, and *Alcuini*, 178.
2. *MGH, Epistolae Karolini aevi*, 2:138.
3. *MGH, Poetae Latini aevi Karolini*, 1:366–81.
4. M. Bloch, "Problèmes d'Europe," *Annales ÉSC* 7 (1935): 476; L. Febvre, *L'Europe: genèse d'une civilisation* (Paris, 1999).
5. *Nascita dell'Europa ed Europa carolingia: un'equazione da verificare* (Spoleto, 1981).

CHAPTER 1

1. *Chanson de Roland*, v. 1.
2. The account by Sidonius Apollinaris is to be found in A. Ebenbauer, *Carmen historicum: Untersuchungen zur historischen Dichtung im karolingischen Europa* (Vienna, 1978), 5:237–50.
3. *CRF*, 10.
4. Einhardus, 30.
5. *ARF*, 140.
6. Einhardus, 31.
7. The question has been reopened by K. F. Werner, "Das Geburtsdatum Karls des Grossen," *Francia* 1 (1973): 115–57, by drawing attention to a passage

in the *Annales Petaviani* that claims Charlemagne was born in 747. However, the source is an isolated one and too lacking in authority to be credible, particularly when compared to the three accounts provided by Charlemagne's court. M. Becher, in "Neue Überlegungen zum Geburtsdatum Karls des Grossen," *Francia* 19 (1992): 37–60, observes that the chronicler counted years in accordance with the eastern style, and therefore, if Charles was born on 2 April, the date he provided would have been in 748 and not 747. This is useful to the arguments against the date 2 April 747, which was Easter Sunday, a coincidence that was unlikely to go unnoticed if it really was the day Charles was born. But to come down in favor of the traditional date of 742 seems more logical, rather than take it forward to 748 as Becher argues.

8. *Quellen zur Geschichte des 7. und 8. Jahrhunderts*, ed. A. Kusternig (Darmstadt, 1982), 84.

9. *Corpus Inscriptionum Latinarum*, 3:3576.

10. *CC*, 10.

11. *CC*, 12–13, 39.

12. *MGH, Leges*, IV/2:2–9.

13. *MGH, Scriptores*, 2:264.

14. *Quellen zur Geschichte des 7. und 8. Jahrhunderts*, ed. H. Haupt (Darmstadt, 1982), 272–324.

15. *ARF*, 8. It is however curious that such an important document is missing from the *Codex Carolinus*, the collection of papal letters to Frankish mayors and kings put together on Charlemagne's orders.

16. *CC*, 14.

17. *CC*, 33.

CHAPTER 2

1. *ARF*, 29.

2. *ARF*, 33.

3. *MGH, Epistulae Karolini aevi*, 2:501–5.

4. *CC*, 1–2.

5. *CC*, 10.

6. *ARF*, 31.

7. Ermengarda is one of the best-known characters in Alessandro Manzoni's highly successful Romantic tragedy, *Adelchi* (Milan, 1822). And see his *Discorso sopra alcuni punti della storia longobardica in Italia* (Milan, 1822).

8. *CC*, 45.

9. *Regesta Pontificum Romanorum*, ed. P. Jaffé (Leipzig, 1885), 2396.

10. *Cronaca di Novalesa*, ed. G. C. Alessio (Turin, 1982), 146–49.

11. Einhardus, 6.

12. *ARF*, 36; *Annales Mettenses Priores*, ed. B. von Simson (Hannover, 1905; vol. 10 of *MGH, Scriptores*), 60; *Le Liber Pontificalis*, ed. L. Duchesne (Paris, 1955), 1:495.

13. *Cronaca di Novalesa*, 148–51.

14. *Liber Pontificalis*, 1:498.

15. *Codice diplomatico Longobardo*, ed. L. Schiaparelli, Fonti per la storia d'Italia no. 38 (Rome, 1933), 291; the interpretation of the words "tempore barbarici" has been advanced by V. Fumagalli, *Il Regno italico* (Turin, 1978), 3–4.

16. *ARF*, 44.

17. *MGH, Scriptores rerum Langobardicarum*, 224.

18. Ibid.

19. *CC*, 59.

20. *CRF*, 88.

21. See chapter 6, on the crisis of 781.

22. W. Pohl, *Die Awaren: Ein Steppenvolk in Mitteleuropa, 567–822* (Munich, 1988), 323.

23. Notker, 2.17.

24. *Cronaca di Novalesa*, 168–73.

25. Manzoni, *Discorso sopra alcuni punti*.

26. The mistake was pointed out by E. Delaruelle, "Charlemagne, Carloman, Didier et la politique du mariage franco-lombard," *Revue historique* 170 (1932): 216n, who was however unaware of Manzoni and could not work out its origin.

CHAPTER 3

1. Einhardus, 7.

2. *Vita Lebuini*, in *Quellen zur Geschichte des 7. und 8. Jahrhunderts*, ed. H. Haupt (Darmstadt, 1982), 388.

3. A. Barbero, "Interpretazioni di Carlo Magno nella crisi della democrazia tedesca," *Il Mulino* 51 (2002): 23–32.

4. *ARF*, 41.

5. *CRF*, 26.

6. *Alcuini*, 107, 110, 111, 113; *MGH, Concilia aevi Karolini*, 1:172–76.

7. *ARF*, 94.

8. *CRF,* 27.

9. *MGH, Scriptores,* 2:376.

10. K. Brandi, "Karls des Grossen Sachsenkriege," in *Die Eingliederung des Sachsen in das Frankenreich,* ed. W. Lammers (Darmstadt, 1970), 5.

11. *ARF,* 44.

12. Einhardus, 8; *ARF,* 64–67.

13. There is an ample description of this battle, in fact a digression, in the annals' revised version (*ARF,* 61–65).

14. On Count Theodoric and William of Toulouse, see E. Hlawitschka, "Die Vorfahren Karls des Grossen," in *KdG,* 1:51–82.

15. The main Western source is *ARF,* 48–49.

16. *CC,* 61.

17. *ARF,* 50.

18. Einhardus, 9.

19. *ARF,* 51; Einhardus, 9.

20. See chapter 11, on the integration of vassals into the royal army.

21. Einhardus, 13.

22. Paul the Deacon, *Historia Langobardorum,* 4:1 and 37.

23. Ibid., 4:12, 20, 24.

24. The main sources for the following events, all from the Frankish side, are *ARF,* 74–85; Einhardus, 11; and *CRF,* 28.

25. *ARF,* 83.

26. *Alcuini,* 6.

27. *ARF,* 87.

28. Einhardus, 13.

29. *MGH, Epistolae Karolini aevi,* 2:528.

30. Einhardus, 13.

31. *L'oro degli Avari: popolo delle steppe in Europa,* ed. E. A. Arslan and M. Buora (Udine, 2000).

32. *MGH, Concilia aevi Karolini,* 1:172–76; and see *Alcuini,* 107, 110, 111, 113.

33. *MGH, Epistolae Karolini aevi,* 2:528–29.

34. Einhardus, 13.

35. "You miserable *khagan!* Your kingdoms are destroyed; you won't reign any more! King Pepin is approaching with a strong army; he will occupy your lands and slaughter your people" (*MGH, Poetae Latini aevi Karolini,* 1:116–17).

36. W. Pohl, *Die Awaren: Ein Steppenvolk in Mitteleuropa, 567–822* (Munich, 1988), 323.

CHAPTER 4

1. *ARF,* 112; *Alcuini,* 214.

2. *CC,* 1–2.

3. *ARF,* 8.

4. *CC,* 60.

5. P. Jaffé, *Regesta Pontificum Romanorum* (Leipzig, 1885), 1:2448.

6. Einhardus, 19.

7. *Libri Carolini,* ed. A. Freeman and P. Meyvaert (Hannover, 1998; from *MGH, Concilia,* II/1).

8. *Alcuini,* 174.

9. *ARF,* 100.

10. *ARF,* 104.

11. See particularly *Alcuini,* 159, 173, 179.

12. *Alcuini,* 136, 148, 177, 185, 200, 202.

13. *CC,* 41, 111, 118, 121–22.

14. Fichtenau, chap. 2n81.

15. Einhardus, 26.

16. *Alcuini,* 145.

17. *Alcuini,* 174 and 177.

18. *Alcuini,* 179.

19. *Alcuini,* 179, 184.

20. *Annales Laureshamenses,* in *MGH, Scriptores,* 1:38.

21. *ARF,* 112

22. Einhardus, 28.

23. Erchempert, *Historia Langobardorum Beneventanorum,* in *MGH, Scriptores rerum Langobardicarum,* 236.

24. Migne, *Patrologia Graeca,* 108:952.

25. *ARF,* 136.

26. *MGH, Epistolae Karolini aevi,* 4:556.

27. F. Dölger, *Regesten der Kaiserurkunden des oströmischen Reiches 565–1453* (Munich-Berlin, 1924), 408.

28. *MGH, Epistolae Karolini aevi,* 5:385–94.

29. *CRF,* 45.

30. *CRF,* 22.

31. *MGH, Epistolae Karolini aevi,* 2:503.

32. *Libri Carolini,* 98.

33. *MGH, Epistolae Karolini aevi*, 2:137.

34. *MGH, Poetae Latini aevi Karolini*, 1:523–24.

35. *ARF,* 119.

36. *CRF,* 45.

37. Einhardus, 33.

38. *Annales Laureshamenses*, in *MGH, Scriptores*, 1:38.

39. *ARF,* 114, 131; Einhardus, 16; Notker, 2.8–9.

40. *ARF,* 116, 117, 131.

41. Einhardus, 16.

42. Dicuil, *Liber de mensura orbis terrae*, ed. G. Parthey (Berlin, 1870), 55.

43. *ARF,* 123–24; Einhardus, 16.

44. *ARF,* 112; *Alcuini*, 214.

CHAPTER 5

1. *MGH, Poetae Latini aevi Karolini*, 1:366–81.

2. H. Pirenne, *Mahomet et Charlemagne* (Brussels, 1937)—trans. by B. Miall as *Mohammed and Charlemagne* (London, 1939).

3. K. F. Werner, *Karl der Grosse oder Charlemagne?* (Munich, 1995), 3.

4. Einhardus, 23.

5. *MGH, Leges*, IV/2:2–9.

6. Liutprand, *Relatio de legatione constantinopolitana*, 12, in *Die Werke Liudprands von Cremona*, ed. J. Becker (Hannover-Leipzig, 1915; vol. 41 of *MGH, Scriptores*), 182–83.

7. *MGH, Concilia aevi Karolini*, 1:288.

8. E. Ewig, "Volkstum und Volksbewusstsein im Frankenreich des 7. Jahrhunderts," *Settimane* 5 (1958): 648.

9. "Romans are foolish, Bavarians are clever" (R. Aman, "Medieval maledicta," *Maledicta: The International Journal of Verbal Aggression* 12 [1996]: 28).

10. *Die althochdeutschen Glossen*, ed. E. Steinmeyer and E. Sievers (Berlin, 1879–1922), 3:610. In translation, "Gallia, land of the *welsch*. Aquitania, land of the Basques. Germania, land of the Franks. Italy, land of the Lombards. Ager Noricus, land of the Bavarians."

11. Einhardus, 33.

12. Pirenne, *Mahomet et Charlemagne*.

13. Quoted by G. Petralia, "A proposito dell'immortalità di Maometto e Carlomagno (o di Costantino)," *Storica* 1 (1995): 49.

14. See the discussion in C. Wickham, "La chute de Rome n'aura pas lieu," *Le Moyen Âge* 99 (1993): 107–26.

15. G. Bois, *La Mutation de l'an mil* (Paris, 1989).

16. On the victory at Poitiers see *MGH, Auctores Antiquissimi*, 11:362, and on Catwulf's letter see *MGH, Epistolae Karolini aevi*, 2:503.

CHAPTER 6

1. Einhardus, 22.

2. See P. E. Schramm, "Karl der Grosse im Lichte seiner Siegel und Bullen sowie der Bild- und Wortzeugnisse über sein Aussehen," in *KdG*, 1:15–23.

3. Erchempert, *Historia Langobardorum Beneventanorum*, in *MGH, Scriptores rerum Langobardicarum*, 236.

4. Fichtenau, chap. 1n2.

5. *CRF*, 74, 98.

6. H. Thomas, "Frenkisk: Zur Geschichte von *theodiscus* und *teutonicus* im Frankenreich des 9. Jahrhunderts," in *Beiträge zur Geschichte des Regnum Francorum*, ed. R. Schieffer (Sigmaringen, 1990), 67–95.

7. Einhardus, 25.

8. Notker, 1.31.

9. Notker, 1.34.

10. Notker, 2.17.

11. Notker, 1.11.

12. Notker, 2.6.

13. Notker, 1.12.

14. Einhardus, 24.

15. Fichtenau, chap. 1nn92–99.

16. Einhardus, 22.

17. *Alcuini*, 262.

18. *Die Gedichte des Paulus Diaconus*, ed. K. Neff (Munich, 1908), nos. 21–22. See G. Gandino, "La dialettica tra il passato e il presente nelle opere di Paolo Diacono," in *Paolo Diacono e il Friuli altomedievale (secc. VI–X)* (Spoleto, 2001), 74–77.

19. *MGH, Poetae Latini aevi Karolini*, 1:488.

20. *MGH, Poetae Latini aevi Karolini*, 1:485–86.

21. Notker, 1.7.

22. Fichtenau, chap. 1nn5–11.

23. Einhardus, 25.

24. Einhardus, 20; compare *ARF,* 91.

25. Notker, 1.19.

26. Notker, 1.26.

27. *MGH, Poetae Latini aevi Karolini,* 1:484. I am indebted to Fichtenau (chap. 1nn22–23) for his analysis of this and the following texts.

28. *Alcuini,* 143–45.

29. Notker, 1.9.

30. Notker, 2.5.

31. *CRF,* 14.

32. Einhardus, 4.

33. Einhardus, 18; and see chapter 2, on the ancient enmity of Franks and Lombards.

34. J. L. Nelson, "Gender and Genre in Women Historians of the Early Middle Ages," in *L'Historiographie médiévale en Europe,* ed. J.-P. Genet (Paris, 1991), 156–60.

35. Einhardus, 20.

36. *CC,* 45.

37. *ARF,* 31; *Cronaca di Novalesa,* ed. G. C. Alessio (Turin, 1982), 168–73.

38. Einhardus, 20.

39. *Die Gedichte des Paulus Diaconus,* no. 26.

40. *ARF,* 91; compare Einhardus, 20.

41. Einhardus, 18.

42. *MGH, Epistolae Karolini aevi,* 2:528.

43. *Alcuini,* 197–98.

44. Einhardus, 18.

45. Einhardus, 19.

46. Astronomus, *Vita Hludowici imperatoris,* ed. E. Tremp (Hannover, 1995; vol. 64 of *MGH, Scriptores*), 23.

CHAPTER 7

1. F.-L. Ganshof, "Les traits généraux du système d'institutions de la monarchie franque," *Settimane* 9 (1962): 94.

2. *Rothari,* 2 (in *LL,* 14).

3. *MGH, Concilia aevi Karolini,* 1:142.

4. *ARF,* 87.

5. *CRF*, 7.

6. *ARF*, 14, 18, 48.

7. *ARF*, 34, 74.

8. *CRF*, 20, 27.

9. *CRF*, 40.

10. *CRF*, 45.

11. *CRF*, 16.

12. Einhardus, 20.

13. *ARF*, 80; cf. *ARF*, 74–85; Einhardus, 11; and *CRF*, 28.

14. *CRF*, 23.

15. *CRF*, 25.

16. *CRF*, 34.

17. *CRF*, 46.

18. *CRF*, 80.

19. *CRF*, 40.

20. See chapter 8, on factors as *iudices*.

21. See *ARF*, 61–65; on Count Theodoric and William of Toulouse, see E. Hlawitschka, "Die Vorfahren Karls des Grossen," in *KdG*, 1:51–82; and Einhardus, 9.

22. Paschasius Radbertus, *Vita Walae*, in *MGH*, *Scriptores*, 2:550.

23. R.-H. Bautier, "La chancellerie et les actes royaux dans les royaumes carolingiens," *Bibliothèque de l'école des chartes* 142 (1984): 5–80.

24. *ARF*, 138.

25. *Die Kapitulariensammlung des Ansegis*, ed. G. Schmitz (Hannover, 1996; from *MGH*, *CRF*, n.s., vol. 1).

26. The genealogy of the counts of Oberrheingau, who were later to call themselves Robertingians, can be found in R. Le Jan, *Famille et pouvoir dans le monde franc* (Paris, 1995), 254 and 440. Other genealogies are discussed in other parts of the work, yet very few testify to a hereditary transference of office at the time of Charlemagne. These same few examples are regularly referred to by supporters of the idea of a well-established hegemony on the part of the nobility. These families were the counts of Paris, the counts of Meaux, the Guidonides who were counts and marquises in the march of Brittany, and one or two cases of prolonged family fortunes reflecting close kinship with the reigning dynasty, as occurred with the brothers and nephews of Queen Hildegard, one of whom was the *praefectus Baioariae* Gerold. This is not really enough to justify the emphasis the author puts on the inheritance of office and favors a rejection of the hegemony of the nobility (currently the prevailing belief) and the acceptance of

the opposing and much more open-ended approach to the social origin and careers of Carolingian officials supported by D. A. Bullough, "'Leo qui apud Hlotharium magni loci habebatur' et le gouvernement du Regnum Italiae à l'époque carolingienne," *Le Moyen Âge*, 67 (1961): 221–45; and D. A. Bullough, "'Europae Pater': Charlemagne and his achievement in the light of recent scholarship," *English Historical Review* 85 (1970): 59–105.

However, it must be conceded that the lack of sources makes it an inherently difficult problem to resolve, even if we apply the most up-to-date prosopographical techniques. Take, for instance, the eighty-six counts in Neustria for which there is documentary evidence between the beginning of the eighth century and the reign of Louis the Pious, according to the list drawn up in R. Le Jan ("Prosopographica neustrica: les agents du roi en Neustrie de 639 à 840," in *La Neustrie: les pays au nord de la Loire de 650 à 850*, ed. H. Atsma [Sigmaringen, 1989], 1:231–69). Of them, as many as twelve proved to belong to collateral branches of the reigning dynasty or, in any case, closely related to it; of the remaining seventy-four only six were definitely sons of counts. If we add another three or four probables, it is still clear that at the time of Charlemagne the inheritance of the office of count does not appear to have been a regular occurrence. If however, instead of looking at all the counts we know of, we restrict ourselves to those of whom we know both father and sons, the picture changes radically, and the retention of the office of count in the same family over two generations becomes statistically more frequent. In this situation, the methodological options are capable of making the documents say more or less what we want, so it would perhaps be more correct to leave the matter unresolved.

It should also be noted, in relation to these observations, that from the same sample it would appear that counts palatine were of a more humble origin than counts employed in the provinces, given that of sixteen only one was definitely the son of a count, and none was a relation of the king.

27. Einhardus, 9.

28. Einhardus, 13.

29. J.-P. Brunterc'h, "Le duché du Maine et la marche de Bretagne," in *La Neustrie*, 1:29–128.

30. Notker, 1.13.

31. *CRF*, 50.

32. *Annales Lauresbamenses*, in *MGH, Scriptores*, 1:38. See J. Hannig, "Pauperiores vassi de infra palatio? Zur Entstehung der karolingischen Königsbotenorganisation," *Mitteilungen des Instituts für österreichische Geschichtsforschung* 91 (1983): 309–74.

33. *MGH, CRF*, 2:515.

34. Astronomus, *Vita Hludovici Imperatoris*, ed. E. Tremp (Hannover, 1995; vol. 64 of *MGH, Scriptores*), 3.

35. *CRF*, 78.

36. *MGH, Poetae Latini aevi Karolini*, 1:498.

37. See above, note 32.

38. *CRF*, 34; but see the later edition and commentary by W. A. Eckhardt, "Die Capitularia missorum specialia von 802," *Deutsches Archiv für Erforschung des Mittelalters* 12 (1956): 498–516.

39. Manaresi, 17.

40. *CRF*, 85.

41. *CRF*, 85.

42. *CRF*, 71–73.

43. *CRF*, 32.

44. *MGH, Epistolae Karolini aevi*, 3:277–78.

45. Manaresi, 16 and 26.

46. *CRF*, 150.

47. The abbot was "procurator . . . per diversos portos ac civitates exigens tributa atque vectigalia, maxime in Quentawic" (S. Lebecq, "La Neustrie et la mer," in *La Neustrie*, 1:405–40).

48. Notker, 1.25.

49. Notker, 1.4.

50. Notker, 1.5.

51. D. A. Bullough, "Bajuli in the Carolingian Regnum Langobardiae and the career of Abbot Waldo," *English Historical Review* 77 (1962): 625–37.

52. *MGH, Epistolae Karolini aevi*, 3:58–60.

53. *CRF*, 33.

54. *CRF*, 80.

55. *CRF*, 141.

56. *MGH, CRF*, 2:297.

57. Hariulf, *Chronicon Centulense*, ed. F. Lot (Paris, 1901), 144–48.

CHAPTER 8

1. *CRF*, 80.

2. Paschasius Radbertus, *Vita Walae*, in *MGH, Scriptores*, 2:548.

3. *CRF*, 75.

4. Notker, 1.15.

5. *CRF,* 136.

6. *MGH, Poetae Latini aevi Karolini,* 1:396.

7. Manaresi, 25.

8. *CRF,* 171. Only a partial list survives.

9. *Vita Alcuini,* in *PL,* 100:102.

10. *MGH, Legum sectio V, Formulae,* 262.

11. *CRF,* 32.

12. *CRF,* 102.

13. *CRF,* 152.

14. *Alcuini,* 245–49.

15. Radbertus, *Vita Walae,* 2:548.

16. *CRF,* 46, 49, 59, 80, 140.

17. *CRF,* 132.

18. *CRF,* 33, 44, 80, 140, 144. See the discussion in W. Metz, *Das Karolingische Reichsgut* (Berlin, 1960).

19. *CRF,* 20, 44, 57, 58, 61.

20. Manaresi, 17.

CHAPTER 9

1. E. H. Kantorowicz, *Laudes regiae: A Study in Liturgical Acclamations and Mediaeval Ruler Worship,* 2d ed. (Berkeley, 1958), 15, 43. *Iudices* is used in the same sense by other contemporary writers: see, e.g., *Le Liber Pontificalis,* ed. L. Duchesne (Paris, 1955), 1:495–97.

2. *CRF,* 40, 61, 102, 104.

3. *CRF,* 64–65, 80.

4. See chapter 8, on factors as *iudices.*

5. See chapter 8, on advocates and immunities for Church lands.

6. *CRF,* 79.

7. *CRF,* 69.

8. Einhardus, 24.

9. *MGH, Diplomata Karolinorum,* 1:148.

10. *CRF,* 80.

11. *CRF,* 31.

12. *CRF,* 39.

13. Manaresi, 5.

14. Manaresi, 7.

15. *CRF,* 104.

16. See for instance the Spoletine *placitum* of the year 776 in *Codice diplomatico longobardo*, IV, ed. C. Brühl, Fonti per la storia d'Italia no. 65 (Rome, 1981), 1:78–83.

17. *Lex Baiwariorum*, IX, §. 18 (in *MGH, Leges Nationum Germanicarum*, V/2:381).

18. *CRF*, 41; cf. *Lex Ribuaria*, §.19 (in *MGH, Leges Nationum Germanicarum*, III/2:81).

19. *CRF*, 134, 135, 138.

20. *MGH, Diplomata Karolinorum*, 1:102.

21. *MGH, Epistolae Karolini aevi*, 3:158–64.

22. *Liutprand*, 118 (in *LL*, 186–88).

23. *CRF*, 62.

24. *CRF*, 20.

25. *CRF*, 23, 49.

26. Paschasius Radbertus, *Vita Walae*, 1:26, in *MGH, Scriptores*, 2:543ff.

27. *CRF*, 22, 33, 35, 61, 78.

28. *MGH, Poetae Latini aevi Karolini*, 1:498.

29. *Miracula Sancti Benedicti*, 24, ed. de Certain (Paris, 1858).

30. See chapter 7, note 32.

31. "Quia, ubi ipsa dona currunt, iustitia evacuatur": *CRF*, 14. See also *Alcuini*, 254.

32. *CRF*, 85.

33. *CRF*, 61.

34. *CRF*, 33, 57, 60.

35. *CRF*, 52.

36. *CRF*, 18.

37. *CRF*, 58.

38. *CRF*, 40.

39. *MGH, Epistolae Karolini aevi*, 3:158–64.

40. Not everybody agrees on the date of 785: see F.-L. Ganshof, "Charlemagne et l'administration de la justice dans la monarchie franque," in *KdG*, 1:395.

41. *CRF*, 23, 35, 40.

CHAPTER 10

1. Einhardus, 25.

2. On this unfounded concern see chapter 6, text following note 32.

3. Einhardus, 25.

4. Einhardus, 29.

5. Einhardus, 25.

6. *Alcuini*, 170 and 308.

7. See *MGH, Epistolae Karolini aevi*, 2:177n.

8. See *Alcuini*, 107, 110, 111, 114, 173, 174, 177; and *MGH, Concilia aevi Karolini*, 1:172–76.

9. *CRF*, 22 and 29.

10. *MGH, Epistolae Karolini aevi*, 2:302.

11. *Alcuini*, 53.

12. Fichtenau, chap. 3nn77–83.

13. This is the Paderborn poet: *MGH, Poetae Latini aevi Karolini*, 1:367–68.

14. *MGH, Poetae Latini aevi Karolini*, 1:486–88.

15. *Alcuini*, 245–49.

16. *CRF*, 29.

17. *CRF*, 22.

18. *PL*, 119:82.

19. P. E. Schramm, "Karl der Grosse: Denkart und Grundauffassungen; Die von ihm bewirkte *Correctio* ('Renaissance')," *Historisches Zeitschrift* 198 (1964): 306–45.

20. *MGH, Epistolae Karolini aevi*, 1:298–302.

21. *CRF*, 10.

22. *CRF*, 13.

23. *CRF*, 17.

24. *CRF*, 22.

25. P. Toubert, "La théorie du mariage chez les moralistes carolingiens," *Settimane* 24 (1977): 270.

26. *CRF*, 33.

27. *CRF*, 122; see also 130.

28. *CRF*, 72.

29. F.-L. Ganshof, "Note sur les 'Capitula de causis cum episcopis et abbatibus tractandis' de 811," *Studia Gratiana* 13 (1967): 3–25. See also chapter 14, on assessing Charlemagne's reign.

30. *CRF*, 72.

31. *CRF*, 72

32. Einhardus, 26.

33. *CRF*, 22.

34. *CC*, 89.

35. Notker, 1.10.

36. *CRF*, 29.

37. *CRF*, 22.

38. *PL*, 105:196

39. *MGH, Concilia aevi Karolini*, 1:471, 581, 632, 675.

40. Notker, 1.3.

41. Such a circular is not extant, but it has been postulated with good reasons by B. Bischoff, "Die Hofbibliothek Karls des Grossen," in *KdG*, 2:42–62.

42. *MGH, Epistolae Karolini aevi*, 3:509–14.

43. *MGH, Diplomata Karolinorum*, 1:87.

44. R. McKitterick, "Nuns' scriptoria in England and Francia in the eighth century," *Francia* 19 (1989): 7–10.

45. R. McKitterick, *The Carolingians and the Written Word* (Cambridge, 1989), 256.

46. *MGH, Epistolae Karolini aevi*, 4:17.

47. *MGH, Poetae Latini aevi Karolini*, 1:483–89.

48. Hariulf, *Chronique de St. Riquier*, ed. F. Lot (Paris, 1894), 88.

49. Einhardus, 33.

50. A. Bartoli Langeli, "Scritture e libri da Alcuino a Gutenberg," in *Storia d'Europa*, vol. 3: *Il Medioevo*, ed. G. Ortalli (Turin, 1994), 946.

51. *Alcuini*, 193.

52. C. Leonardi, "Alcuino e la Scuola palatina: le ambizioni di una cultura unitaria," *Settimane* 28 (1981): 488.

53. See chapter 4, on the conflict between Charlemagne and Byzantium.

54. *CRF*, 25.

55. *Alcuini*, 113. See also 110.

56. *Alcuini*, 107, 110, 111.

57. *MGH, Concilia aevi Karolini*, 1:172–76; *Alcuini*, 107, 110, 111, 113.

58. *CRF*, 27.

59. *CRF*, 22.

60. *CRF*, 12.

61. *CRF*, 22, 35.

62. *CRF*, 10.

63. *CRF*, 19, 22, 23, 33, 35, 96, 108; *Alcuini*, 268, 290–91.

64. *CRF*, 108.

65. *ARF*, 123.

66. Agobard, *Contra insulsam vulgi opinionem de grandine et tonitruis* (in *PL*, 104:16).

CHAPTER 11

1. *Lex Ribuaria*, § 40; see E. H. Kantorowicz, *Laudes regiae: A Study in Liturgical Acclamations and Mediaeval Ruler Worship*, 2d ed. (Berkeley, 1958), 15 and 43.

2. *CRF*, 25.

3. *CRF*, 75.

4. B. S. Bachrach, "Procopius, Agathias and the Frankish military," *Speculum* 45 (1970): 435–41.

5. *Lex Salica*, § 13.3 and 17.2; *lex Ribuaria*, § 5.7.

6. *Vita Landiberti episcopi Traiectensis*, in MGH, *Scriptores rerum Merovingicarum*, 6:365.

7. *CRF*, 44.

8. Quoted in W. Störmer, *Früher Adel* (Stuttgart, 1973), 145.

9. *CRF*, 74.

10. *CRF*, 20, 40, 44.

11. *CRF*, 77.

12. *CRF*, 32.

13. *Ahistulf*, 2 (in *LL*, 250).

14. *ARF*, 103.

15. See chapter 3, on the 791 war against the Avars.

16. L. White Jr., *Medieval Technology and Social Change* (London, 1962).

17. Notker, 1.6.

18. *Lex Ribuaria*, § 40.

19. Kantorowicz, *Laudes regiae*, 15 and 43.

20. MGH, *CRF*, II/1:204.

21. MGH, *Epistolae Karolini aevi*, 3:277–78.

22. *CRF*, 50.

23. *CRF*, 49.

24. *CRF*, 48.

25. Störmer, *Früher Adel*, 145.

26. *CRF*, 48.

27. *CRF*, 25.

28. *CRF*, 75.

29. Astronomus, *Vita Hludowici imperatoris*, ed. E. Tremp (Hannover, 1995; vol. 64 of *MGH, Scriptores*), 378. For the analysis of this and the following texts I am much indebted to F. Prinz, *Klerus und Krieg im früheren Mittelalter* (Stuttgart, 1971).

30. MGH, *Epistolae Karolini aevi*, 2:525.

31. *CC*, 88.

32. *Alcuini*, 25.

33. See *ARF*, 61–65; and Einhardus, 9.

34. *CRF*, 33.

35. *CRF*, 50.

36. *CRF*, 73.

37. *CRF*, 44.

38. *CRF*, 73.

39. *CRF*, 44 and 74.

40. *CRF*, 57 and 73.

41. *CRF*, 74 and 98; *ARF*, 80.

42. See chapter 14, on the final years of Charlemagne's reign.

43. Astronomus, *Vita Hludowici imperatoris*, 330.

44. *ARF*, 44.

45. A. A. Settia, "La fortezza e il cavaliere: tecniche militari in Occidente," *Settimane* 45 (1998): 570.

46. Astronomus, *Vita Hludowici imperatoris*, 330.

CHAPTER 12

1. R. Fossier, "Les tendances de l'économie: stagnation ou croissance?" *Settimane* 28 (1981): 273.

2. G. Petralia, "A proposito dell'immortalità di Maometto e Carlomagno (o di Costantino)," *Storica* 1 (1995): 76.

3. J. Favier, *Charlemagne* (Paris, 1999).

4. J.-P. Devroey, "'Ad utilitatem monasterii': mobiles et préoccupations de gestion dans l'économie monastique du monde franc (VIIIe–IXe s.)," *Revue bénédictine* 103 (1993): 224–40.

5. *MGH, Epistolae Karolini aevi*, 4:nn11, 42–62, 71, 83, 88, 92. See J.-P Devroey, "Courants et réseaux d'échange dans l'économie franque entre Loire et Rhin," *Settimane* 40 (1993): 341.

6. *MGH, Epistolae Karolini aevi*, 4:nn13, 14, 66, 68, 75, 85, 111–12. See Devroey, "Courants," 353.

7. *CRF*, 150.

8. *Corpus Consuetudinum Monasticarum* (Siegburg, 1963), 1:388–403.

9. *CRF*, 32.

10. *Ahistulf*, 3 (in *LL*, 250).

11. *CRF*, 46.

12. *MGH, Epistolae Karolini aevi*, 3:182–85.

13. *CRF,* 44.

14. *MGH, Epistolae Karolini aevi,* 2:145.

15. *MGH, Leges,* V, *Formulae,* 315.

16. *ARF,* 126.

17. *Translatio S. Germani Parisiensis,* in AASS maii, 6:782.

18. MGH, *Diplomata Karolinorum,* 1:93.

19. *MGH, Epistolae Karolini aevi,* 3:137.

20. *CRF,* 55.

21. *CRF,* 22.

22. *CRF,* 12.

23. *MGH, Epistolae Karolini aevi,* 2:511.

24. *CRF,* 28.

25. *CRF,* 35.

26. *CRF,* 32.

27. *Corpus Consuetudinum Monasticarum,* 1:375, 379.

28. P. Grierson, "Carolingian Europe and the Arabs: the myth of the *mancus,*" *Revue belge de philologie et d'histoire* 32 (1954): 1064.

29. *Annales Mosellani,* in *MGH, Scriptores,* 16:498.

30. *CRF,* 21.

31. *CRF,* 44 and 46.

32. *CRF,* 124.

33. *CRF,* 28; see also 46.

34. Notker, 2.9.

35. *CRF,* 32.

36. *CRF,* 46.

37. *CRF,* 48.

38. *CRF,* 46, 48, 62, and 63.

39. The following paragraph is based on archaeological digs carried out from 1981 to 1987 by a French team: see *Un Village au temps de Charlemagne: moines et paysans de l'abbaye de St-Denis du VIIe siècle à l'an mil* (Paris, 1988).

40. *CRF,* 128.

CHAPTER 13

1. *CRF,* 58.

2. Thegan, *Gesta Hludowici imperatoris,* ed. E. Tremp (Hannover, 1995; vol. 64 of *MGH, Scriptores*), 232.

3. *CRF,* 26, 27.

4. *CRF,* 25. Cf. chapter 7, on the oath of loyalty.

5. The calculation of the size of the governmental apparatus is in K. F. Werner, "Heeresorganisation und Kriegsführung im deutschen Königreich des 10. und 11. Jahrhunderts," *Settimane* 15 (1968): 818–20, partly adjusted in K. F. Werner, *Naissance de la noblesse* (Paris, 1998), 130.

6. *CRF,* 21.

7. *Monumenta Novaliciensia vetustiora,* ed. C. Cipolla, Fonti per la storia d'Italia no. 31 (Rome, 1898), 1:20–38.

8. G. Tabacco, "La connessione fra potere e possesso nel regno franco e nel regno longobardo," *Settimane* 20 (1973): 141–42. The book by P. Geary (*Aristocracy in Provence: The Rhône Basin at the Dawn of the Carolingian Age* [Stuttgart, 1985]) also relies heavily on Abbo's testament.

9. *MGH, Epistolae Karolini aevi,* 3:109–45.

10. See note 4.

11. A. Barbero, "Liberti, raccomandati, vassalli: le clientele nell'età di Carlo Magno," *Storica* 14 (1999): 22–28.

12. *CRF,* 77.

13. Manaresi, 17.

14. *CRF,* 31.

15. *Inventari altomedievali di terre, coloni e redditi,* Fonti per la storia d'Italia no. 104 (Rome, 1979), 41–94.

16. *CRF,* 48.

17. *CRF,* 45.

18. *CRF,* 20, 90, 105.

19. *CRF,* 20.

20. *CRF,* 102.

21. Quoted by J. Schmitt, *Untersuchungen zu den Liberi Homines der Karolingerzeit* (Frankfurt am Main, 1977), 152.

22. *CRF,* 16.

23. *CRF,* 88.

24. *CRF,* 28.

25. *CRF,* 16.

26. *Liutprand,* 140 (in *LL,* 202).

27. *CRF,* 16.

28. *CRF,* 105.

29. Notker, 2.4.

30. On the meaning of expressions like "batebant eum pro servo," I do not support the interpretation of B. Andreolli and M. Montanari, *L'azienda curtense in Italia* (Bologna, 1983), 103, who see in it a public sale rather than a public

beating. See also F. Bougard, "La justice dans le royaume d'Italie aux IXe–Xe siè-cles," *Settimane* 44 (1997): 149n.

31. *Liber Largitorius vel Notarius monasterii Pharphensis*, ed. G. Zucchetti (Rome, 1913–32), nos. 7, 9, 15, 17, 21.

32. *Ahistulfi Leges*, 11 (in *LL*, 254).

33. *CRF*, 13.

34. *CRF*, 34.

35. *CRF*, 73; see chapter 11, on sanctions against shirkers.

36. See chapter 9, note 30.

37. *CRF*, 34.

38. *CRF*, 34, 35, 44.

39. *CRF*, 165; *CRF*, II/1:193.

40. *CRF*, 93–94; *Liutprand*, 92 (in *LL*, 174).

CHAPTER 14

1. So Alcuin since 802: *Alcuini*, 254.

2. Ermold le noir, *Poème sur Louis le Pieux*, ed. E. Faral (Paris, 1932), 60–64.

3. *ARF*, 138; see *MGH, Concilia aevi Karolini*, 1:245–306.

4. The main source for the following events are the yearly entries in *ARF*.

5. *Alcuini*, 16.

6. *Alcuini*, 184.

7. *CRF*, 34, 74.

8. Einhardus, 14.

9. Notker, 2.13.

10. Notker, 2.14.

11. The main source for the following events are again the yearly *ARF* entries.

12. *CRF*, 45.

13. See chapter 6, on the crisis of 781.

14. *Annales Sancti Amandi*, in *MGH, Scriptores*, 1:12.

15. *Alcuini*, 217.

16. Einhardus, 33.

17. Einhardus, 33.

18. For what follows see Einhardus, 32; and *ARF*, 122–37.

19. *Alcuini*, 155.

20. *ARF*, 146.

21. Einhardus, 30.

22. Einhardus, 31

BIBLIOGRAPHY

The bibliography is divided into two parts. The first part consists of a record of all the principal sources for Charlemagne, the editions currently in use and the most recent bibliography for them. The second part, which is made up of paragraphs that correspond to the chapters of the book, contains an annotated and updated bibliography on Charlemagne's reign.

The following abbreviations have been used:

BEC	*Bibliothèque de l'école des chartes*
BISIMeAM	*Bullettino dell'Istituto storico italiano per il medioevo e archivio muratoriano*
CRF	*MGH, Legum sectio II, Capitularia Regum Francorum*, vol. 1, ed. A. Boretius (Hannover, 1883)
DA	*Deutsches Archiv für Erforschung des Mittelalters*
EHR	*English Historical Review*
FMSt	*Frühmittelalterliche Studien*
HJ	*Historisches Jahrbuch*
HZ	*Historische Zeitschrift*
KdG	*Karl der Grosse: Lebenswerk und Nachleben*, 4 vols. (Düsseldorf, 1965–67)
MÂ	*Le Moyen Âge*
MGH	*Monumenta Germaniae Historica*

RBPH	*Revue belge de philologie et d'histoire*
RH	*Revue historique*
RSI	*Rivista storica italiana*
Savigny	*Zeitschrift der Savigny-Stiftung für Rechtsgeschichte*, in three sections, Germanistische (Germ.), Romanistische (Rom.), Kanonistische (Kan.)
Scriptores	*Scriptores rerum Germanicarum in usum scholarum*
Settimane	*Settimane di studio del Centro italiano di studi sull'alto medioevo*, Spoleto

THE SOURCES

One of the most important chronicles is the *Annales Regni Francorum*, which exists in two versions: the first is of an official nature and was written, probably by more than one person, under Charlemagne's direct control from 787 onward, while the second reworked version has strong similarities to Einhard's text, which may have been based on it or may be its source. The edition referred to is that of F. Kurze (Hannover, 1895; vol. 6 in *MGH, Scriptores*). The second important chronicle is Einhard's *Vita Karoli*, written between 817 and 831. The edition I have used is that of L. Halphen for *Les Belles Lettres* (Paris, 1938). Also very significant for the latter years of Charles's reign are Thegan's *Gesta Hludowici imperatoris* and the Astronomer's *Vita Hludowici imperatoris*, now published in a single volume by E. Tremp (Hannover, 1995; vol. 64 in *MGH, Scriptores*). Other important annals are the *Annales Mettenses Priores*, written shortly after 802, probably in Chelles at the request of Abbess Gisla, Charlemagne's sister (ed. B. von Simson [Hannover, 1905; vol. 10 in *MGH, Scriptores*]).

Later, but invaluable for its anecdotal content, we have the work of Notker Balbulus (sometimes referred to as the Monk of St-Gall), *Gesta Karoli Magni imperatoris*, ed. H. F. Haefele (Berlin, 1959; vol. 12, n.s. in *MGH, Scriptores*).

For an introduction to Carolingian historiography, see M. Innes and R. McKitterick, "The Writing of History," in *Carolingian Culture: Emulation and Innovation*, ed. R. McKitterick (Cambridge, 1994), 193–220, and its bibliography. On Einhard and the still controversial dating of his work, see H. Löwe, "Die Entstehungszeit der Vita Karoli Einhards," *DA* 39 (1983): 85–103; *Einhard: Studien zu Leben und Werk*, ed. H. Schefers (Darmstadt, 1997); and K. H. Krüger, "Neue Beobachtungen zur Datierung von Einhards Karlsvita,"

FMSt 32 (1998): 124–45. On the *Annales Mettenses*, see J. L. Nelson, "Gender and Genre in Women Historians of the Early Middle Ages," in *L'Historiographie médiévale en Europe*, ed. J.-P. Genet (Paris, 1991), 156–60.

The other official sources are the capitularies collected and edited by A. Boretius in *CRF*; the *concilia* published by A. Werminghoff (Hannover, 1906; vol. 1 in *MGH, Concilia aevi Karolini*), with the important supplement of the *Libri Carolini*, ed. A. Freeman and P. Meyvaert (Hannover, 1998); the diplomas published by E. Mühlbacher et al., *Die Urkunden Pippins, Karlmanns und Karls des Grossen* (Hannover, 1906; vol. 1 in *MGH, Diplomata Karolinorum*).

The most studied of these sources are undoubtedly the capitularies, whose editions also have many shortcomings. Apart from the obligatory work on dating carried out by F-L. Ganshof, *Recherches sur les capitulaires* (Paris, 1958), also worthy of note are the observations by A. Bühler, "Capitularia relecta: Studien zur Entstehung und Überlieferung der Kapitularien Karls des Grossen und Ludwigs des Frommen," *Archiv für Diplomatik* 32 (1986): 305–501, the supplements by H. Mordek and G. Schmitz, "Neue Kapitularien und Kapitularien-sammlungen," *DA* 43 (1987): 361–439, the volume in preparation for a new edition, by H. Mordek, *Bibliotheca capitularium regum Francorum manuscripta* (Munich, 1995; vol. 15 in *MGH, Hilfsmittel*), which has an extensive bibliography, and the collected articles of H. Mordek, *Studien zur fränkischen Herrschergesetzgebung* (Frankfurt am Main, 2000); for Italy, the edition by C. Azzara and P. Moro, *I capitolari italici* (Rome, 1998). For the *concilia*, a start can be made with W. Hartmann, *Die Synoden der Karolingerzeit im Frankenreich und Italien* (Paderborn, 1989).

For correspondence, see the first four volumes of *MGH, Epistolae Karolini aevi*, and particularly 1:469–657, containing the *Codex Carolinus* or collected correspondence between the popes and the Frankish kings, and 2:1–481, containing Alcuin's correspondence. For poetry, the four volumes of *MGH, Poetae Latini aevi Karolini*. For an introduction to Carolingian poetry, and above all its political significance, see A. Ebenbauer, *Carmen historicum: Untersuchungen zur historischen Dichtung im karolingischen Europa* (Vienna, 1978), and P. Godman, *Poets and Emperors: Frankish Politics and Carolingian Poetry* (Oxford, 1987); for a more literary approach, see F. Stella, *La poesia carolingia* (Florence, 1995).

The laws of the Germanic peoples are published in the relevant section of *MGH, Legum sectio I, Leges Nationum Germanicarum*; but for Lombard laws see the recent edition by C. Azzara and S. Gasparri, *Le leggi dei Longobardi* (Milan, 1992).

BIBLIOGRAPHIC GUIDE

Introduction: Paderborn, Summer of 799

The importance of building Paderborn for Charlemagne's policies has been demonstrated by the research of Karl Hauck, most recently in "Karl als neuer Konstantin 777: Die archäologischen Entdeckungen in Paderborn in historischer Sicht," *FMSt* 20 (1986): 513–40.

On the meeting between Charlemagne and Leo III, see the catalog and the studies on the recent exhibition in Paderborn, *799—Kunst und Kultur der Karolingerzeit: Karl der Grosse und Papst Leo III. in Paderborn*, ed.C. Stiegemann and M. Wemhoff (Mainz, 1999).

Until a few years ago, everyone dated the so-called *Paderborner Epos* at 799, but today that is fiercely challenged. Many prefer to refer to it as the *Aachener Epos*, dating its composition in Aachen some time after 801. However, there are no impelling reasons to abandon the traditional theory. For a review of recent suggestions, see E. D'Angelo, "Carlo Magno e Leone III: osservazioni sullo *Aachener Karlsepos*," *Quaderni medievali* 36 (1993): 53–72; and C. Ratkowitsch, *Karolus Magnus—alter Aeneas, alter Martinus, alter Iustinus: Zu Intention und Datierung des "Aachener Karlsepos"* (Vienna, 1997).

For the diverging opinions that emerged from the Spoleto conference in 1979 (*Settimane* 28 [1981]), compare the conclusions of Karl Ferdinand Werner's lecture ("À la question générale du Colloque, si le rôle du monde carolingien a été essentiel dans l'éclosion de l'Europe, nous répondrons donc, pour le domaine politico-institutionnel: Oui") and Robert Fossier's ("Puisqu'il me faut répondre à la question qui soutient le thème de cette 'semaine': l'Europe médiévale est-elle issue de l'Europe carolingienne, dans l'immédiat, et en ce qui concerne l'économie, je réponds fermement: 'non'!"). For a more balanced summary, see G. Tabacco's inaugural lecture, "I processi di formazione dell'Europa carolingia" (ibid., 15–43), and O. Capitani's conclusion (ibid., 973–1011).

For a survey of current opinion about Charlemagne's role in forging modern Europe, see *Carlo Magno: le radici dell'Europa*, ed. G. Andenna and M. Pegrari (Rome, 2002).

Among the many extant biographies of Charlemagne, we only mention the latest: M. Becher, *Karl der Grosse* (Munich, 1999) (a short work of synthesis); D. Hägermann, *Karl der Grosse: Herrscher des Abendlandes* (Berlin, 2000) (a substantial work); J. Favier, *Charlemagne* (Paris, 2000) (also substantial but somewhat less up-to-date).

Chapter 1. The Frankish Tradition

The historiographic perspective on the origins of the Frankish people has for some time been dominated by ethnogenesis, which perceives the origins of the main Germanic peoples as an assemblage of smaller and often heterogeneous tribal nuclei (*Stämme*). The fundamental work remains R. Wenskus, *Stammesbildung und Verfassung: Das Werden der frühmittelalterlichen Gentes* (Cologne, 1961); but see also S. Gasparri, *Prima delle nazioni: popoli, etnie e regni fra antichità e medioevo* (Rome, 1997).

The most recent general works on the original Franks are P. Perin and L.-C. Feffer, *Les Francs* (Paris, 1987), and E. James, *The Franks* (Oxford, 1988); see also T. Anderson, Jr., "Roman military colonies in Gaul, Salian ethnogenesis and the forgotten meaning of Pactus Legis Salicae 59.5," *Early Medieval Europe* 4 (1995): 129–44; and H. J. Hummer, "Franks and Alamanni: a discontinuous ethnogenesis," in *Franks and Alamanni in the Merovingian Period*, ed. I. Wood (San Marino, 1998), 9–32.

For a general analysis of the Merovingian age, a reliable account along traditional lines can be found in I. Wood, *The Merovingian Kingdoms 450–751* (London, 1994); a lighter version that covers Charlemagne's reign is S. Lebecq, *Les Origines franques: V^e-IXe siècle* (Paris, 1990); and a more complex and thought-provoking one is P. Geary, *Before France and Germany: The Creation and Transformation of the Merovingian World* (Oxford, 1988). On the question of the *reges criniti*, see A. Cameron, "How Did the Merovingian Kings Wear Their Hair?," *RBPH* 43 (1965): 1203–16.

On Charles Martel, see the collection of essays in *Karl Martell in seiner Zeit*, ed. J. Jarnut, U. Nonn, and M. Richter (Sigmaringen, 1994).

On the internal division of the kingdom of the Franks, whose terminology has changed over time, see the articles by E. Ewig collected in *Spätantikes und fränkischen Gallien* (Munich, 1976), and also in "Überlegungen zu den merowingischen und karolingischen Teilungen," *Settimane* 28 (1981): 225–53; on the two principal kingdoms, see, respectively, E Cardot, *L'Espace et le pouvoir: étude sur l'Austrasie mérovingienne* (Paris, 1987), and the 2-vol. work edited by H. Atsma, *La Neustrie: les pays au nord de la Loire de 650 à 850* (Sigmaringen, 1989).

The myth of Trojan origins had enormous ideological importance in antiquity and the Middle Ages; for a recent clarification of the arguments, see A. Giardina, "Le origini troiane dall'impero alla nazione," *Settimane* 45 (1998): 177–209. On the idea of the Franks as a chosen people, which developed from the age of Charles Martel, see E. H. Kantorowicz, *Laudes regiae: A Study in*

Liturgical Acclamations and Mediaeval Ruler Worship, 2d ed. (Berkeley, 1958); R. Schmidt-Wiegand, "'Gens Francorum inclita': Zur Gestalt und Inhalt des lingeren Prologes der Lex Salica," in *Festschrift A. Hofmeister* (Halle, 1955), 233–50; E. Ewig, "Zum christlichen Königsgedanken im Frühmittelalter," in *Das Königtum*, ed. T. Mayer (Constance, 1956), 7–73.

On the genealogy of Charlemagne, see E. Hlawitschka, "Die Vorfahren Karls des Grossen," in *KdG*, 1:51–82; E. Hlawitschka, "Merowingerblut bei den Karolingern?" in *Adel und Kirche: Festschrift G. Tellenbach* (Freiburg, 1970), 66–91.

On the family tradition and propaganda of the Carolingians, see O. G. Oexle, "Die Karolinger und die Stadt des heiligen Arnulf," *FMSt* 1 (1967): 250–364; I. Haselbach, *Aufstieg und Herrschaft der Karlinger in der Darstellung der sogenannten Annales Mettenses Priores* (Lübeck, 1970); M. Sot, "Historiographie épiscopale et modèle familial en Occident au IXe siècle," *Annales ÉSC* 33 (1978): 433–49; W. Goffart, "Paul the Deacon's *Gesta episcoporum Mettensium* and the early design of Charlemagne's succession," *Traditio* 42 (1986): 59–93; M. T. Fattori, "I santi antenati carolingi tra mito e storia: agiografie e genealogie come strumento di potere dinastico," *Studi medievali* 34 (1993): 487–561; G. Gandino, "La memoria come legittimazione nell'età di Carlo Magno," *Quaderni storici* 94 (1997): 21–41. The sacred charisma attributed to the Carolingians by official historiographers was a great deal more persuasive than the attempts by Louis the Pious to link them genealogically to the Merovingians (see Hlawitschka, "Die Vorfahren").

The bibliography on Pepin's coronation and the origins of the alliance between the Frankish monarchy and the papacy is endless. To look into it, start with T. F. X. Noble, *The Republic of St. Peter: The Birth of the Papal State, 680–825* (Philadelphia, 1984), and C. Azzara, "L'ideologia del potere regio nel papato altomedievale (secoli VI–VIII)," *Settimane* 44 (1997). On the controversial nature of the undertakings made by Pepin in 754 and later renewed by Charlemagne in 774, see P. E. Schramm, "Das Versprechen Pippins und Karls des Grossen für die römische Kirche," *Savigny* (Kan.) 27 (1938): 180–217; A. M. Drabek, *Die Vertrage der fränkischen und deutschen Herrscher mit dem Papsttum von 754 bis 1020* (Vienna, 1976); J. Jarnut, "Quierzy und Rom: Bemerkungen zu den 'Promissiones Donationis' Pippins und Karls," *HZ* 220 (1975): 265–97; A. Angenendt, "Das geistliche Bündnis der Päpste mit den Karolingern (754–796)," *HJ* 100 (1980): 1–94.

The anointment ritual, contrary to what has long been believed, did not begin as an imitation of episcopal anointment, which was introduced only later, but establishes a clear parallel between the king and the priest with clear references to the Old and New Testaments; see A. Angenendt, "Rex et sacerdos: Zur Genese der Königssalbung," in *Tradition als historische Kraft*, ed. N. Kamp and J. Wollasch (Berlin, 1982), 100–18; and J. Jarnut, "Wer hat Pippin 751 zum König gesalbt?" *FMSt* 16 (1982): 45–57.

On the bond created by the pope's becoming godparent for the king's children (*compaternitas*), see A. Angenendt, *Kaiserherrschaft und Konigstaufe* (Berlin, 1984).

For the debate on the title of patrician of the Romans, see J. Deér, "Zum Patricius-Romanorum-Titel Karls des Grossen," *Archivum Historiae Pontificiae* 3 (1965): 31–86, and H. Wolfram, *Intitulatio* (Graz, 1967), 1:225–36.

On the king of the Franks as the new David and the general use of Old Testament models that inspired Carolingian kingship, see W. Mohr, *Studien zur Charakteristik des karolingischen Königtums im 8. Jahrhundert* (Saarlouis, 1955); W. Mohr, *Die Karolingische Reichsidee* (Münster, 1962); W. Mohr, "Christlich-alttestamentliches Gedankengut in der Entwicklung des karolingischen Kaisertums," in *Judentum im Mittelalter*, ed. P. Wilpert (Berlin, 1966), 382–409; A. Graboïs, "Un mythe fondamental de l'histoire de France au moyen âge: le 'roi David' précurseur du 'roi très chrétien,'" *RH* 287 (1992): 11–31.

Chapter 2. The War against the Lombards

Relations between Charles and Carloman and their policies toward the Lombard kingdom have been subjected to detailed analysis, although it has always been hampered by the lack of sources and the partiality of the existing ones. See M. Lintzel, "Karl der Grosse und Karlmann," *HZ* 140 (1929): 1–22; E. Delaruelle, "Charlemagne, Carloman, Didier et la politique du mariage franco-lombard," *RH* 170 (1932): 213–24; M. V. Arv, "The Politics of the Frankish-Lombard Marriage Alliance," *Archivum Historiae Pontificiae* 19 (1981): 7–26; J. Jarnut, "Ein Bruderkampf und seine Folgen: Die Krise des Frankenreiches (768–771)," in *Herrschaft, Kirche, Kultur: Festschrift F Prinz* (Stuttgart, 1993), 165–76.

The overall examination of relations between Franks, Lombards, and the papacy appears to have been more fruitful: see R. Holtzmann, "Die Italienpolitik der Merowinger und des Konigs Pippin," in *Das Reich: Idee und Gestalt, Festschrift J. Haller* (Stuttgart, 1940), 95–132; and T. F. X. Noble, *The Republic of St. Peter: The Birth of the Papal State, 680–825* (Philadelphia, 1984).

On the route chosen by Charlemagne to lead his army into Italy, see G. Tangl, "Karls des Grossen Weg über die Alpen im Jahr 773," *Quellen und Forschungen aus italienischen Archiven und Bibliotheken* 37 (1957): 1–15. On the *clusae*, see E. Mollo, "Le Chiuse: realtà e rappresentazioni mentali del confine alpino nel medioevo," *Bollettino storico-bibliografico subalpino* 84 (1986): 333–90; and A. A. Settia, "Le frontiere del regno italico nei secoli VI–XI: l'organizzazione della difesa," *Studi storici* 30 (1989): 155–69. On Rothgaud and the battle of Livenza, see H. Krahwinkler, *Friaul im Frühmittelalter* (Vienna, 1992), 119–43; P. Moro, *Quam borrida pugna: elementi per uno studio della guerra nell'alto medioevo italiano (secoli VI–X)* (Venice, 1995), 32–35. For the reaction of the Lombard elites to the fall of the kingdom, see K. Schmid, "Zur Ablösung der Langobardenherrschaft durch die Franken," *Quellen und Forschungen aus italienischen Archiven und Bibliotheken* 52 (1972): 1–36.

For the history of Italy during the Lombard and Carolingian periods, see the general work by C. Wickham, *Early Medieval Italy: Central Power and Local Society, 400–1000* (Ann Arbor, Mich., 1989), and the highly original new books by P. Cammarosano, *Nobili e re: l'Italia politica dell'alto medioevo* (Rome, 1998), and *Storia dell'Italia medievale: dal VI all'XI secolo* (Rome, 2001). These are preferable to the albeit highly evocative work by V. Fumagalli, *Il Regno italico* (Turin, 1978), or the disappointing work by G. Albertoni, *L'Italia carolingia* (Rome, 1997).

On King Pepin of Italy, the fundamental analysis is by E. Manacorda, *Ricerche sugli inizii della dominazione dei Carolingi in Italia* (Rome, 1968), which also analyzes Italic legislation in detail; on this latter question, see also G. Tabacco, "L'avvento dei Carolingi nel regno dei Longobardi," in *Langobardia*, ed. S. Gasparri and P. Cammarosano (Udine, 1990), 375–403; and *I capitolari italici* (Rome, 1998), a recent edition of the Italian capitularies and their translation from Latin into Italian by C. Azzara and P. Moro.

The government of the Italic kingdom under the Carolingians has been analyzed from various angles. On the recruitment of personnel, particularly of high rank, see D. A. Bullough, "Leo qui apud Hlotharium magni loci habebatur et le gouvernement du Regnum Italiae a l'époque carolingienne," *MÂ* 67 (1961): 221–45; D. A. Bullough, "Bajuli in the Carolingian Regnum Langobardiae and the career of Abbot Waldo," *EHR* 77 (1962): 625–37. On the transfer of Frankish personnel at the highest political level, see the prosopographic analysis by E. Hlawitschka, *Franken, Alemannen, Bayern und Burgunder in Oberitalien (774–962)* (Freiburg, 1960); while for the transfer of Franks to positions of local officials and vassals in Italy, see A. Castagnetti, *Minoranze etniche dominanti e rapporti vassallatico-beneficiari: Alamanni e Franchi a Verona e nel Veneto in età carolin-*

gia e postcarolingia (Verona, 1990). For the continuing presence of Lombard nobles and free men in the administration of the kingdom, see S. Gasparri, "Strutture militari e legami di dipendenza in Italia in età longobarda e carolingia," *RSI* 98 (1986): 664–726. On the particular role of the Church in the government of Carolingian Italy, which was perhaps the most important innovation introduced following the Lombard era, see O. Bertolini, "I vescovi del regnum Langobardorum al tempo dei Carolingi," in *Vescovi e diocesi in Italia nel medioevo* (Padua, 1964), 1–26, and J. Fischer, *Königtum, Adel und Kirche im Königreich Italien (774–875)* (Bonn, 1965). For a summary, see P. Bonacini, "Dai Longobardi ai Franchi: potere e società in Italia tra i secoli VIII e IX," *Quaderni medievali* 35 (1993): 20–56.

The debate on the extension of the county system to Italy was opened by P. Delogu, "L'istituzione comitale nell'Italia carolingia," *BISIMeAM* 79 (1968): 53–114, which, perhaps under the influence of the main German historiographic trends of the time, argued that it was applied on an irregular and intermittent manner and speculated on the continuing autonomy of rural *gastaldiones*. Today, the prevailing approach emphasizes the Carolingian kings' determination to centralize, in spite of the variety of local situations, and the gradual suppression and subordination of *gastaldiones* to counts, as has been demonstrated by the careful research of V. Fumagalli, "Città e distretti minori nell'Italia carolingia: un esempio," *RSI* 81(1969): 107–17; A. Castagnetti, "Distretti fiscali autonomi o circoscrizioni della contea cittadina? La Gardesana veronese in epoca carolingia," *RSI* 82 (1970): 736–43; and V. Fumagalli, "L'amministrazione periferica dello stato nell'Emilia occidentale in età carolingia," *RSI* 83 (1971): 911–20. For a general interpretation of these conclusions, see V. Fumagalli, *Terra e società nell'Italia padana: i secoli IX e X* (Turin, 1976), and A. Castagnetti, *'Teutisci' nella 'Langobardia' carolingia* (Verona, 1995).

The operation of the justice system, which has been widely investigated in the previously mentioned works, is now the subject of a specific study by E. Bougard, *La Justice dans le royaume d'Italie: de la fin du VIIIe siècle au début du XIe siècle* (Rome, 1995); see also his article, "La justice dans le royaume d'Italie aux IXe–Xe siècles," *Settimane* 44 (1997): 133–76.

Chapter 3. Wars against the Pagans

On the Old Testament spirit with which Charlemagne conducted his wars against pagans, it is still useful to consider E. Delaruelle, "Essai sur la formation de l'idée de croisade," *Bulletin de littérature ecclésiastique* 42 (1941): 24–45—now in E. Delaruelle, *L'Idée de croisade au moyen âge* (Turin, 1980); there are also a few references to the subject in G. Fasoli, "Pace e guerra nell'alto medioevo," *Settimane* 15 (1968): 15–47; but above all see E. Cardini, *Alle radici della cavalleria medievale* (Florence, 1981), 148–69.

There is no single work dealing with Charlemagne's wars. For a brief analysis of the principal campaigns, see J. F. Verbruggen, "L'armée et la stratégie de Charlemagne," in *KdG*, 1:420–36; and above all, for its particularly acute insights, B. S. Bachrach, "Charlemagne's cavalry: myth and reality," *Military Affairs* 47 (1983): 1–20. In the wider political and cultural context, interesting comments are provided by T. Reuter, "Plunder and tribute in the Carolingian Empire," *Transactions of the Royal Historical Society* 35 (1985): 75–94, and T. F. X. Noble, "Louis the Pious and the frontiers of the Frankish realm," in *Charlemagne's Heir: New Perspectives on the Reign of Louis the Pious*, ed. P. Godman and R. Collins (Oxford, 1990), 333–47.

On the war against the Saxons, see the collection of essays edited by W. Lammers, *Die Eingliederung der Sachsen in das Frankenreich* (Darmstadt, 1970), which apart from the analysis of the military campaigns and the Christianization offers an impressive account of the ideological conditioning at work in German historiography during the thirties, particularly in the assessment of the respective roles of Widukind and Charlemagne, the *Blutbad von Verden*, and "degenerate historiography" (see 219, 238, 242). For a summary of the question in the light of the present German *Historikerstreit*, see A. Barbero, "Interpretazioni di Carlo Magno nella crisi della democrazia tedesca," *Il Mulino* 51 (2002): 23–32. Also important are the essays contained in M. Lintzel, *Ausgewählte Schriften*, vol. 1 (Berlin, 1961), where the famous theory is put forward claiming that there was a split between the people and the Saxon nobles, who favored Charlemagne. For a more recent assessment, see H.-D. Kahl, "Karl der Grosse und die Sachsen: Stufen und Motive einer historischen Eskalation," in *Politik, Gesellschaft, Geschichtsschreibung: Festgabe F. Graus* (Cologne, 1982), 49–130.

On Widukind's baptism, see G. Althoff, "Der Sachsenherzog Widukind als Mönch auf der Reichenau: Ein Beitrag zur Kritik des Widukind-Mythos," *FMSt* 17 (1983): 251–79, which argues that after his baptism the Saxon leader was forced to become a monk. For an opposing opinion, see A. Angenendt, *Kaiserherrschaft und Königstaufe* (Berlin, 1984).

On Charlemagne's *Ostpolitik* and that of his successors, see M. Hellmann, "Karl und die slawische Welt zwischen Ostsee und Böhmerwald," in *KdG*, 1:708–18; L. Dralle, "Wilzen, Sachsen und Franken um das Jahr 800," in *Aspekte der Nationenbildung im Mittelalter,* ed. H. Beumann and W. Schröder (Sigmaringen, 1978), 205–27; and more recently M. Innes, "Franks and Slavs c. 700–1000: the problem of European expansion before the millennium," *Early Medieval Europe* 6 (1997): 201–16.

For an overall analysis of the campaigns fought on the Iberian front, see B. S. Bachrach, "Military organization in Aquitaine under the early Carolingians," *Speculum* 49 (1974): 1–33; and P. Sénac, "Charlemagne et l'Espagne musulmane," in *Carlo Magno: le radici dell'Europa,* ed. G. Andenna and M. Pegrari (Rome, 2002), 55–80. More specifically on the military expedition over the Pyrenees in 778, R.-H. Bautier, "La campagne de Charlemagne en Espagne (778): la réalité historique," in *Roncevaux dans l'histoire, la légende et le mythe* (Bayonne, 1979), 1–47. See also J. Horrent, "La bataille des Pyrénées de 778," *MÂ* 78 (1972): 197–227, and particularly on the question of the *Hruodlandus* mentioned by Einhard, P. Aebischer, "Roland: mythe ou personnage historique?" *RBPH* 43 (1965): 849–901.

The obligatory reference work on the Avars is W. Pohl, *Die Awaren: Ein Steppenvolk in Mitteleuropa, 567–822* (Munich, 1988), written in the light of the most up-to-date theories on ethnogenesis. It covers the most recent debate on Charlemagne's military campaigns against the Avars, on which extremely contrasting interpretations exist. Also worthy of note is the traditional account by J. Deér, "Karl der Grosse und der Untergang des Awarenreiches," in *KdG,* 1:719–91. There are radically divergent opinions on Avar weaponry: B. S. Bachrach, "A Picture of Avar-Frankish Warfare from a Carolingian Psalter of the Early Ninth Century in the Light of the Strategicon," *Archivum Eurasiae Medii Aevi* 4 (1986): 5–27; G. Fasoli, "Unni, Avari e Ungari nelle fonti occidentali e nella storia dei paesi d'Occidente," *Settimane* 35 (1988): 13–43. For a review of archaeological digs, with an extensive bibliography, see I. Bóna, "Die Geschichte der Awaren im Lichte der Archäologischen Quellen," *Settimane* 35 (1988): 437–63. On the channel between the Rhine and the Danube, see H. H. Hofmann, "Fossa Carolina," in *KdG,* 1:437–53.

There is a considerable amount of historical research on relations between Tassilo and the Frankish kings; most recently M. Becher, *Eid und Herrschaft: Herrscherethos bei Karl dem Grossen* (Sigmaringen, 1993), and P. Depreux, "Tassilon III et le roi des Francs: examen d'une vassalité controversée," *RH* 293 (1995): 23–73.

On the wars against the Bretons, see J. C. Cassard, "La guerre des Bretons armoricains au haut moyen âge," *RH* 110 (1986): 3–27, with the warning that the wars conducted by the Franks against Brittany, consisting of pillage, sieges, and ambushes, did not differ in method from other theaters of war, as the author appears to believe.

Chapter 4. The Rebirth of Empire

There was intense historical debate over Charlemagne's imperial coronation up until the 1960s. See the following reviews: F.-L. Ganshof, *The Imperial Coronation of Charlemagne: Theories and Facts* (Glasgow, 1949)—published later in *The Carolingians and the Frankish Monarchy* (London, 1971), 41–54; and H. von Fichtenau, "Il concetto imperiale di Carlomagno," *Settimane* 1 (1954): 251–98. Following the almost simultaneous publication of the overviews by R. Folz, *Le Couronnement impérial de Charlemagne* (Paris, 1964); and P. Classen, "Karl der Grosse, das Papsttum und Byzanz: Die Begründung des karolingischen Kaisertums," in *KdG*, enlarged ed., vol. 1 (Sigmaringen, 1985), the debate has died away considerably.

On the whole, the pope's initiative can be considered decisive in the imperial coronation, although he did not act alone. On the transfer of honorary prerogatives that the pope previously reserved for the *basileus*, see P. E. Schramm, "Die Anerkennung Karls des Grossen als Kaiser," *HZ* 172 (1951): 449–515, who states that Charles was effectively almost an emperor long before the coronation in 800; of the opposite opinion was J. Deér, "Die Vorrechte des Kaisers in Rom," *Schweizer Beiträge zur allgemeine Geschichte* 15 (1957): 5–63—now available in *Zum Kaisertum Karls der Grossen*, ed. G. Wolf (Darmstadt, 1972), 30–115. On the political significance of papal coinage, see P. Grierson, "The Coronation of Charlemagne and the Coinage of Pope Leo III," *RBPH* 30 (1952): 825–33.

Of the more recent assessments of the papal initiative, a richly nuanced example is G. Arnaldi, "Il papato e l'ideologia del potere imperiale," *Settimane* 28 (1981): 341–407. The most detailed reconstruction of papal policy over the long term is that of T. F. X. Noble, *The Republic of St. Peter: The Birth of the Papal State, 680–825* (Philadelphia, 1984), subordinating Charles's elevation to the imperial throne to a well organized papal plan to achieve political hegemony over Italy. On relations between Charlemagne and the papacy, see also A. Angenendt, "Das geistliche Bundnis der Päpste mit den Karolingern (754–796)," *HJ* 100 (1980): 1–94; and G. Thoma, "Papst Hadrian I und Karl der Grosse: Beobachtungen zur Kommunikation zwischen Papst und König nach den Briefen des Codex Carolinus," in *Festschrift E. Hlawitschka* (Munich, 1993), 37–58.

For an examination of the theory on the imperial coronation as a necessary prelude to Charlemagne's judging and condemning the perpetrators of the attack on Leo III, see O. Hageneder, "Das crimen maiestatis, der Prozess gegen die Attentäter Papst Leos III. und die Kaiserkrönung Karls des Grossen," in *Aus Kirche und Reich: Festschrift F. Kempf* (Sigmaringen, 1983), 55–80.

On the mosaics commissioned by Leo III, see C. Davis-Weyer, "Das Apsismosaik Leos III. in S. Susanna," *Zeitschrift für Kunstgeschichte* 28 (1965): 177–94, and K. Belting, "Die Beiden Palasttaulen Leos III. im Lateran und die Entstehung einer päpstlichen Programmkunst," *FMSt* 12 (1978): 55–83, but all the authors mentioned deal with it. It is possible that the figure on the left is Saint Peter and not Saint Sylvester.

The debate over the Donation of Constantine is so vast that it would be impossible even to attempt to summarize it here, but for some time the prevailing interpretation has been that, whenever it was written, there is no proof of its influence on papal policy at the time of Charlemagne. For a summary of the question, see H. Fuhrmann, "Das frühmittelalterliche Papsttum und die Konstantinische Schenkung: Meditationen über ein unausgeführtes Thema," *Settimane* 20 (1973): 257–92.

The Franks' significant role in the imperial coronation can be followed in detail in Alcuin's letters and the works of the court poets, as well as in Charlemagne's building program. The theory put forward in the middle of the last century by several German scholars, that the resulting Frankish concept of the empire was decidedly at odds with the Roman one the pope proposed, has found its latest proponent in H. Beumann, "Romkaiser und fränkisches Reichsvolk," in *Festschrift E. Stengel* (Münster, 1952), 157–80; H. Beumann, "Nomen imperatoris: Studien zur Kaiseridee Karls des Grossen," *HZ* 185 (1958): 515–49; H. Beumann, "Das Paderborner Epos und die Kaiseridee Karls des Grossen," in *Karolus Magnus et Leo papa: Ein Paderborner Epos vom Jahre 799* (Paderborn, 1966), 1–54. More recently, particular importance has been attached to the following research: K. Hauck, "Die Ausbreitung des Glaubens in Sachsen und die Verteidigung der römischen Kirche als konkurrierende Herrschersaufgaben Karls des Grossen," *FMSt* 4 (1970): 138–72; K. Hauck, "Karl als neuer Konstantin 777: Die archäologischen Entdeckungen in Paderborn in historischer Sicht," *FMSt* 20 (1986): 513–40, which suggests that the idea of imitating Constantine came to Charles as early as his trip to Rome in 774, and that the idea of building, as he did, a new capital took shape in Paderborn before it did in Aachen. A recent variant of this approach is the argument that the imperial coronation served primarily to justify Charlemagne's domination of the Saxons: H. Mayr-Harting, "Charlemagne, the Saxons and the imperial coronation of 800," *EHR* 111 (1996): 1113–33. For a full discussion of recent research on the Frankish concept of empire, see H. H. Anton, "Beobach-tungen zum Fränkisch-Byzantinischen Verhältnis im Karolingischer Zeit," in *Beiträge zur Geschichte des Regnum Francorum,* ed. R. Schieffer (Sigmaringen, 1990), 77–119.

The ideological significance of the palace complex at Aachen has mainly been explored by H. von Fichtenau, "Byzanz und die Pfalz zu Aachen," *Mitteilungen des Instituts für österreichische Geschichtsforschung* 59 (1951): 1–54; and H. Löwe, "Vom Theoderich dem Grossen zu Karl dem Grossen," *DA* 9 (1952): 353–401. The conclusions of the two articles were put in perspective by L. Falkenstein, *Der 'Lateran' der karolingischen Pfalz zu Aachen* (Cologne, 1966), and H. Hoff-mann, "Die Aachener Theoderichsstatue," in *Das erste Jahrtausend* (Düsseldorf, 1962), 1:318–35; see also L. Falkenstein, "Charlemagne et Aix-la-Chapelle," *Byzantion* 61 (1991): 231–89. A different approach to the influence of imperial ideology on Charlemagne is to be found in C. Heitz, *Recherches sur les rapports entre architecture et liturgie à l'époque carolingienne* (Paris, 1963).

There has been little follow-up to Ohnsorge's theories on the continuing centrality of the Byzantine Empire in Christendom, which any ideological proj-ect developed in the West had to measure up to. This was not only true of Leo III, who was supposedly of Greek origin, but also of Charlemagne himself, for whom the imperial title was a means to raise the king of the Franks up to the same rank as the *basileus.* See W. Ohnsorge, *Das Zweikaiserproblem im früheren Mittelalter* (Hildesheim, 1947), and his collections of articles in *Abendland und Byzanz* (Darmstadt, 1958), in *Konstantinopel und der Okzident* (Darmstadt, 1966), and in *Ost-Rom und der Westen* (Darmstadt, 1983). On the origins of Leo III, see H. G. Beck, "Die Herkunft des Papstes Leo III.," *FMSt* 3 (1969): 131–37.

The debate over the identity of the author of the *Libri Carolini* has been con-tinuing in increasingly polemical tones for more than forty years, although the prevailing opinion appears to be that he was Theodulf of Orléans, as first argued by A. Freeman, rather than Alcuin, as L. Wallach believes. For the most recent view, see D. A. Bullough, "Alcuin and the kingdom of heaven: liturgy, theology and the Carolingian age," in *Carolingian Renewal: Sources and Heritage* (Manchester, 1991), 161–240, and its bibliography, n69. For an overall assess-ment of the work, see G. Arnaldi, "La questione dei *Libri Carolini*," in *Culto cris-tiano e politica imperiale carolingia* (Todi, 1979), 61–86.

The life of Empress Irene has been the subject of a recent dissertation: J. A. Arvites, "Irene: Woman Emperor of Constantinople, Her Life and Times" (Ph.D. diss., University of Michigan, Ann Arbor, 1985).

The details of the Roman plot against the pope in early 799 are not at all clear, and contemporary accounts are contradictory; see W. Mohr, "Karl der Grosse, Leo III. und der römische Aufstand von 799," *Archivum Latinitatis Medii Aevi* 30 (1960): 39–98. Even the text of Leo III's oath and its precise legal significance are highly controversial; see H. Adelson and R. Baker, "The Oath of Purgation of Pope Leo III in 800," *Traditio* 8 (1952): 5–80; L. Wallach, "The genuine and the forged oath of Pope Leo III," *Traditio* 11 (1955): 37–63; M. Kerner, "Der Reinigungseid Leos III. von Dezember 800," *Zeitschrift des Aachener Geschichtsvereins* 84–85 (1977–78): 131–60.

On the ceremony for imperial coronation, many features of which remain obscure, particularly the actual nature and meaning of the crown used by Pope Leo, see the partly divergent interpretations of E. H. Kantorowicz, *Laudes regiae: A Study in Liturgical Acclamations and Mediaeval Ruler Worship*, 2d ed. (Berkeley, 1958); P. Classen, "Karl der Grosse, das Papsttum und Byzanz," in *KdG*, vol. 1; K. J. Benz, "'Cum ab oratione surgeret': Überlegungen zur Kaiserkrönung Karls des Grossen," *DA* 31 (1975): 337–69; and most recently C. Brühl, "Kronen- und Krönungsbrauch im Frühen und Hohen Mittelalter," *HZ* 234 (1982): 1–31, which examines the concept of coronation itself.

On the coronation of Louis the Pious, see W. Wendling, "Die Erhebung Ludwigs des Frommen zum Mitkaiser im Jahre 813 und ihre Bedeutung für die Verfassungsgeschichte des Frankenreiches," *FMSt* 19 (1985): 201–38.

On the titles officially assumed by Charlemagne and their ideological significance, see P. Classen, "Romanum gubernans imperium: Zur Vorgeschichte der Kaisertitulatur Karls des Grossen," *DA* 9 (1951): 103–21; H. Wolfram, "Lateinische Herrschertitel im neunten und zehnten Jahrhundert," in *Intitulatio*, ed. H. Wolfram (Vienna, 1973), 2:19–178. For a general examination of crowns, scepters, thrones, and other physical symbols of imperial power, see the three volumes of collected essays edited by P. E. Schramm, *Herrschaftszeichen und Staatssymbolik* (Stuttgart, 1954–56), and the essays by the same author in *Kaiser, Könige und Päpste* (Stuttgart, 1968).

It should also be noted that more recent historiographic practice has distanced itself from the emphasis placed up until the sixties on the significance of iconography, architecture, and symbols of power in terms of general policy and propaganda. Note Arnaldi's amiable ridicule ("Il papato e l'ideologia," 365) of "all that great flurry of activity around scepters, *laudes regiae*, globes, thrones and crowns [that] does not appear to have contributed to changing our understanding of the history of political ideas in the early Middle Ages," or the even more skeptical views of D. A. Bullough, "*Imagines regum* and the early medieval West," in *Carolingian Renewal*, 39–96, which, among other things, challenges the idea that the chapel in Aachen was inspired by the Chrysotriclinos of Constantinople; Bullough was also responsible for comparing ownership of the statue of Theodoric with ownership of the elephant (or, for that matter, ownership of a Rolls-Royce).

On relations between the Church and empire in the Christian tradition, a fundamental work is G. Tabacco, *La relazione fra i concetti di potere temporale e di potere spirituale nella tradizione cristiana fino al secolo XIV* (Turin, 1950). On the role of the king of the Franks, and later the emperor, as head of Christendom and therefore the Church, see E. Ewig, "Zum christlichen Königsgedanken im Frühmittelalter," in *Das Königtum*, ed. T. Mayer (Constance, 1956), 7–73; H. H. Anton, *Fürstenspiegel und Herrscherethos in der Karolingerzeit* (Bonn, 1968); and H. Fuhrmann, "Das Papsttum und das kirchliche Leben im Frankenreich," *Settimane* 28 (1981): 419–56. On Catwulf, see most recently M. E. Moore, "La monarchie carolingienne et les anciens modèles irlandais," *Annales ÉSC* 51 (1996): 307–24. On relations with the caliph and the patriarch of Jerusalem, see F. W. Buckler, *Harun u'l-Rashid and Charles the Great* (Cambridge, Mass., 1931); G. Musca, *Carlo Magno e Harûn al-Rashid* (Bari, 1963); and M. Borgolte, *Die Gesandtenaustausch der Karolinger mit den Abbasiden und mit den Patriarchen von Jerusalem* (Munich, 1976).

Chapter 5. Charlemagne and Europe

Attempts to appropriate Charlemagne for nationalistic reasons have been analyzed by K. F. Werner, *Karl der Grosse oder Charlemagne?* (Munich, 1995); R. Morrissey, *L'Empereur à la barbe fleurie: Charlemagne dans la mythologie et l'histoire de France* (Paris, 1997); M. Kerner, *Karl der Grosse: Entschleiderung eines Mythos* (Cologne, 2000). The most dramatic episode was undoubtedly the conflict that occurred in the thirties in Germany between young German historians, who were hostile to Charlemagne because he was seen as the slaughterer of Saxons, and the more traditional nationalist historians, who perceived him as the exemplary Germanic figure. It was the latter current that was to prevail. See the collection of essays by various authors in *Karl der Grosse oder Charlemagne? Acht Antworten deutscher Geschichtsforscher* (Berlin, 1935); and *Die Eingliederung der Sachsen in das Frankenreich*, ed. W. Lammers (Darmstadt, 1970); for a recent assessment, A. Barbero, "Interpretazioni di Carlo Magno nella crisi della democrazia tedesca," *Il Mulino* 51 (2002): 23–32.

On the relationship between Franks and Romans in the collective imagination of the Frankish kingdom, see E. Ewig, "Volkstum und Volksbewusstsein im Frankenreich des 7. Jahrhunderts," *Settimane* 5 (1958): 587–648; on the contradictory meanings attributed to the names of countries such as Gaul and Germany, see E. Ewig, "Beobachtungen zur politisch-geographischen Terminologie des fränkischen Grossreiches und der Teilreiche des 9. Jahrhunderts," in *Spiegel der Geschichte: Festgabe M. Braubach* (Münster, 1964), 99–140. Both essays were republished in his *Spätantikes und fränkisches Gallien* (Munich, 1976).

There is an extensive bibliography on the juxtaposition of *lingua Romana* and *lingua Theotisca*, particularly on the philological side. A useful summary can be found in W. D. Heim, *Romanen und Germanen in Charlemagnes Reich* (Munich, 1984). It is now universally accepted that the linguistic identity did not coincide with the ethnic one. See R. Wenskus, "Die Deutschen Stämme im Reiche Karls des Grossen," in *KdG*, 1:178–219; and more recently H. Thomas, "Der Ursprung des Wortes Theodiscus," *HZ* 247 (1988): 295–333; H. Thomas, "Frenkisk: Zur Geschichte von *theodiscus* und *teutonicus* im Frankenreich des 9. Jahrhunderts," in *Beiträge zur Geschichte des Regnum Francorum*, ed. R. Schieffer (Sigmaringen, 1990), 67–95. A particularly good example is the Lombards, who spoke a Romance language and therefore distinguished themselves linguistically from the *Teutisci*: see A. Castagnetti, *'Teutisci' nella 'Langobardia' carolingia* (Verona, 1995). The historical consequences are examined in C. Brühl, *Deutschland-Frankreich: Die Geburt zweier Völker* (Cologne, 1990), which, however, puts insufficient emphasis on a shared sense of antagonism between Germans and Romans, founded not so much on a linguistic division as on the memory of the invasions.

Although obvious, the extreme delicacy of the matter makes it worth repeating that the ethnic distinctions of the time of the invasions had not persisted until this period. Throughout the West, the process of merging was either extremely advanced or even completed, given that by the name of Franks or Lombards, it was meant all free men living in the country, the great majority of whom were Roman in origin, according to our calculations. For all these matters, see S. Gasparri, *Prima delle nazioni: popoli, etnie e regni fra antichità e medioevo* (Rome, 1997), 161–229. But we should not forget that whereas these processes of ethnogenesis and fusion are more or less clear to us, they were completely unknown at the time. Hence, someone who claimed to be Frank or Lombard was happily convinced that he was descended from the invaders. These ethnic divisions therefore had a distinctness in the imagination of the time that we would no longer accept (this gives rise to some differences between my interpretation and that of Gasparri, for instance in relation to Liutprand of Cremona).

There is an endless bibliography on the question of Pirenne's thesis. For an understanding of it, a good starting point would be G. Petralia, "A proposito dell'immortalità di Maometto e Carlomagno (o di Costantino)," *Storica* 1 (1995): 38–87. The starting point for the whole argument is obviously H. Pirenne, *Mahomet et Charlemagne* (Brussels, 1937). A useful republication of many critical interventions on the subject can be found in *The Pirenne Thesis: Analysis, Criticism and Revision*, ed. A. F. Havighurst (Boston, 1976). The most important revision of Pirenne's thesis was probably carried out, using archaeological data, by R. Hodges and D. Whitehouse, *Mohammed, Charlemagne and the Origins of Europe: Archaeology and the Pirenne Thesis* (London, 1983), in which it was shown that the economy of the Roman Empire of the West underwent a prolonged agony from the third to the sixth century, long before the Arab invasions, and that Charlemagne's reign coincided with a recovery of trade over long distances, directed toward northern Europe.

Particularly stimulating on the transition from antiquity to the Middle Ages are the collected essays of C. Wickham, *Land & Power: Studies in Italian and European Social History, 400–1200* (London, 1994).

For the positions of the hyper-Romanist school, see in particular J. Durliat, *Les Finances publiques de Dioclétien aux carolingiens (284–889)* (Sigmaringen, 1990). In his preface, K. F. Werner praises the book precisely for demolishing the idea of an essentially Germanic Middle Ages. The main critique of the positions of Durliat and other hyper-Romanists like E. Magnou-Nortier can be found in C. Wickham, "La chute de Rome n'aura pas lieu," *MÂ* 99 (1993): 107–26.

G. Bois's position is expressed in *La Mutation de l'an mil* (Paris, 1989). An issue of *Médiévales* 21 (1991) was devoted entirely to debating this question.

On the evolution of the concept of Europe, which at the time of Charlemagne signified both the Frankish empire and western Christendom, see J. Fischer, *Oriens—Occidens—Europa: Begriff und Gedanke Europa in der späten Antike und im frühen Mittelalter* (Wiesbaden, 1957).

Chapter 6. The Man and His Family

For contemporary depictions and accounts of Charlemagne's physical appearance, see P. E. Schramm, "Karl der Grosse im Lichte seiner Siegel und Bullen sowie der Bild- und Wortzeugnisse über sein Aussehen," in *KdG*, 1:15–23; D. A. Bullough, "*Imagines regum* and the early medieval West," in *Carolingian Renewal:*

Sources and Heritage (Manchester, 1991), 39–96. On Charlemagne's character and mentality, see H. von Fichtenau, *The Carolingian Empire* (1949; Toronto, 1979), and P. E. Schramm, "Karl der Grosse: Denkart und Grundauffassungen; Die von ihm bewirkte *Correctio* ('Renaissance')," *HZ* 198 (1964): 306–45. On the pronunciation of Latin, R. McKitterick, *The Carolingians and the Written Word* (Cambridge, 1989), 7–22; R. McKitterick, "Latin and Romance: an historian's perspective," in *Latin and the Romance Languages in the Early Middle Ages*, ed. R. Wright (London, 1991), 130–45.

On clothing, furniture, and diet, see P. Riché, *La Vie quotidienne dans l'empire carolingien* (Paris, 1973), as well as the illustrations and comments in the exhibition catalog *Un Village au temps de Charlemagne: moines et paysans de l'abbaye de St-Denis du VIIᵉ siècle à l'an mil* (Paris, 1988).

On the court poets, see A. Ebenbauer, *Carmen historicum: Untersuchungen zur historischen Dichtung im karolingischen Europa* (Vienna, 1978); P. Godman, *Poets and Emperors: Frankish Politics and Carolingian Poetry* (Oxford, 1987); M. Garrison, "The emergence of Carolingian Latin literature and the court of Charlemagne," in *Carolingian Culture: Emulation and Innovation*, ed. R. McKitterick (Cambridge, 1994), 111–40; and the anthology of F. Stella, *La poesia carolingia* (Florence, 1995).

The history of marriage is one of the most historically fertile subjects of recent decades. For a general overview, see the essays collected together in *Il matrimonio nella società altomedievale* (Spoleto, 1977), particularly P. Toubert, "La théorie du mariage chez les moralistes carolingiens," 233–82; see also recent update by the same author, "L'institution du mariage chrétien de l'antiquité tardive à l'an mil," *Settimane* 45 (1998): 503–49. On Frankish marriage and its political uses, the fundamental work is R. Le Jan, *Famille et pouvoir dans le monde franc* (Paris, 1995), although its sometimes uncritical support for the systemizing theories of German *Personenforschung* is questionable. See also S. Fonay Wemple, *Women in Frankish Society: Marriage and the Cloister 500 to 900* (Philadelphia, 1981), and more recently I. Réal, *Vies de saints, vie de famille: représentation et système de la parenté dans le royaume mérovingien (481–751)* (Turnhout, 2001).

On relations between fathers and sons at the time of Charlemagne, see R. Schieffer, "Väter und Söhne im Karolingerhause," in *Beiträge zur Geschichte des Regnum Francorum*, ed. R. Schieffer (Sigmaringen, 1990), 149–64. On the role of wives and particularly daughters at the emperor's court, see J. L. Nelson, "Women at the Court of Charlemagne: A Case of Monstruous Regiment?" in *Medieval Queenship*, ed. J. C. Parsons (New York, 1993), 43–61.

Existing biographic data on Charlemagne's wives and children can be found in K. F. Werner, "Die Nachkommen Karls des Grossen bis um das Jahr 1000," in *KdG*, 4:403–82; more briefly in J. L. Nelson, "La famille de Charlemagne," *Byzantion* 61 (1991): 194–212. For an attempt at clarifying the image of Fastrada, see J. L. Nelson, "The siting of the council at Frankfort: some reflections on family and politics," in *Das Frankfurter Konzil von 794: Kristallisationspunkt karolingischer Kultur*, ed. R. Berndt (Frankfurt am Main, 1997), 149–65. On Hildegard, see K. Schreiner, "Hildegardis regina: Wirklichkeit und Legende einer karolingischen Herrscherin," *Archiv für Kulturgeschichte* 57 (1975): 1–70, mainly concerned with the queen's image in later literature, as well as contributions to the conference *Autour d'Hildegarde*, ed. P Riché et al. (Paris 1987). King Pepin of Italy has been analyzed in detail by E. Manacorda, *Ricerche sugli inizii della dominazione dei Carolingi in Italia* (Rome, 1968). On his change of name, see G. Thoma, *Namensänderungen in Herrscherfamilien der mittelalterlichen Europa* (Munich, 1985), 77–83, in which she argues that it came about because of papal pressure. On the choice of the names of Clovis and Chlothar for the twins born in 778, see J. Jarnut, "Chlodwig und Chlothar: Anmerkungen zu den Namen zweier Söhne Karls der Grossen," *Francia* 12 (1984): 645–51, which also puts forward specific and contingent political reasons for the choice of these two Merovingian names. For the theory on Pepin the Hunchback and the bishopric of Metz, see W. Goffart, "Paul the Deacon's *Gesta episcoporum Mettensium* and the early design of Charlemagne's succession," *Traditio* 42 (1986): 59–93.

On the pope as the godfather of the emperor's son, see A. Angenendt, *Kaiserherrschaft und Königstaufe* (Berlin, 1984).

Chapter 7. Government of the Empire: The Institutions

On the institutions of the Frankish kingdom and later the Carolingian empire, see first of all the essays by F.-L. Ganshof, "Les traits généraux du système d'institutions de la monarchie franque," *Settimane* 9 (1962): 91–127; and "Charlemagne et les institutions de la monarchie franque," in *KdG*, 1:349–93; for a fresher and less strictly descriptive approach, see J. L. Nelson, "Literacy in Carolingian Government," in *The Uses of Literacy in the Early Medieval Europe*, ed. R. McKitterick (Cambridge, 1990), 258–96. In preparing this book I was unable to consult the new and stimulating work by M. Innes, *State and Society in the Early Middle Ages: The Middle Rhine Valley 400–1000* (Cambridge, 2000).

There has been a wide-ranging debate on the nature of royal power; see the bibliography assembled by J. L. Nelson, "Kingship and Empire in the Carolingian World," in *Carolingian Culture: Emulation and Innovation*, ed. R. McKitterick (Cambridge, 1994), 52–87. The essential studies are those of E. Ewig, "Zum christlichen Königsgedanken im Frühmittelalter," in *Das Königtum*, ed. T. Mayer (Constance, 1956), 7–73; and H. H. Anton, *Fürstenspiegel und Herrscherethos in der Karolingerzeit* (Bonn, 1968), which mainly investigate the religious dimension; while H.W. Goetz, "Regnum: zum politischen Denken der Karolingerzeit," *Savigny* (Germ.) 104 (1987): 110–89, examines the state and territorial aspects. On anointment and its consequences, see A. Angenendt, "Rex et sacerdos: Zur Genese der Königssalbung," in *Tradition als historische Kraft*, ed. N. Kamp and J. Wollasch (Berlin, 1982),100–18.

On the oath of loyalty, the most recent analysis is that of M. Becher, *Eid und Herrschaft: Herrscherethos bei Karl dem Grossen* (Sigmaringen, 1993), which goes beyond the previous summary by F.-L. Ganshof, "Charlemagne et le serment," in *Mélanges L. Halphen* (Paris, 1951), 259–70, although I do not find convincing his proposal to shift capitulary no. 25 back to 789 (rather than Ganshof's suggested date of 793) and to relate it to Hardrad's conspiracy, rather than Pepin the Hunchback's, thus treating as one what had traditionally been considered two distinct collective oath-takings. On confinement in a monastery as a punishment for rebels, see M. De Jong, "What was public about public penance? *Paenitentia publica* and justice in the Carolingian world," *Settimane* 44 (1997): 863–902. On the sworn associations prohibited by Charlemagne, see O. G. Oexle, "'Conjuratio' et 'ghilde' dans l'antiquité et dans le haut moyen âge," *Francia* 10 (1982): 1–19.

For the debate on the origins of the assembly, and the movement of its date, the relevant bibliography may be found in B. S. Bachrach, "Was the Marchfield part of the Frankish Constitution?" *Mediaeval Studies* 36 (1974): 178–85 (I discuss his conclusions in annotating chapter 11). On its subsequent evolution, see J. T. Rosenthal, "The Public Assembly in the Time of Louis the Pious," *Traditio* 20 (1964): 25–40. A wide current of German historiographic opinion, misled by the myth that those of noble blood were entitled to participate in the exercise of power, has misunderstood the meaning of the collective approval expressed by the assembly of magnates, and the relationship between them and the king in general. Typical of this misunderstanding are the works of K. Brunner, *Oppositionelle Gruppen im Karolingerreich* (Vienna, 1979), and J. Hannig, *Consensus fidelium: Frühfeudale Interpretationen des Verhältnisses von Königtum und Adel am Beispiel des Frankenreiches* (Stuttgart, 1982).

On the question of Aachen as a capital, see E. Ewig, "Résidence et capitale pendant le haut moyen âge," *RH* 230 (1963): 25–72; C. Brühl, "Remarques sur les notions de 'capitale' et de 'résidence' pendant le haut moyen âge," *Journal des savants* (1967): 193–215; and above all the fundamental work of L. Falkenstein, "Charlemagne et Aix-la-Chapelle," *Byzantion* 61 (1991): 231–89.

More generally on Charlemagne's residences and travels, see A. Gauert, "Zum Itinerar Karls des Grossen," in *KdG*, 1:307–21; C. Brühl, *Fodrum, Gistum, Servitium Regis* (Cologne, 1968); and most recently R.-H. Bautier, "Le poids de la Neustrie ou de la France du nord-ouest dans la monarchie carolingienne d'après les diplômes de la chancellerie royale (751–840)," in *La Neustrie*, ed. H. Atsma (Sigmaringen, 1989), 535–63. On the system of palaces, see J. Barbier, "Le système palatial franc: genèse et fonctionnement dans le nord-ouest du *regnum*," *BEC* 148 (1990): 245–99.

On the count palatine, see H. E. Meyer, "Die Pfalzgrafen der Merowinger und Karolinger," *Savigny* (Germ.) 42 (1921): 380–463.

The fundamental work on the chapel is J. Fleckenstein, *Die Hofkapelle der Deutschen Könige* (Stuttgart, 1959). On the chancellery, R.-H. Bautier, "La chancellerie et les actes royaux dans les royaumes carolingiens," *BEC* 142 (1984): 5–80; and D. A. Bullough, "Aula Renovata: the court before the Aachen Palace," in *Carolingian Renewal: Sources and Heritage* (Manchester, 1991), 123–60.

On the origins of the office of count, see D. Claude, "Untersuchungen zum frühfränkischen Comitat," *Savigny* (Germ.) 81 (1964): 1–79; E. Ewig, "Die Stellung Ribuariens in der Verfassungsgeschichte des Merowingerreichs," *Vorträge der Gesellschaft für Rheinische Geschichtskunde* 18 (1969): 1–29—republished in his *Spätantikes und fränkischen Gallien* (Munich, 1976). For terminology, see J. Prinz, "Pagus und Comitatus in den Urkunden der Karolinger," *Archiv für Urkundenforschung* 17 (1941): 329–58; W. Metz, "Bemerkungen über Provinz und Gau in der karolingischen Verfassungs- und Geistesgeschichte," *Savigny* (Germ.) 73 (1956): 361–72.

For an introduction to the county system in different provinces, see S. Krüger, *Studien zur sächsischen Grafschaftsverfassung im 9. Jahrhundert* (Göttingen, 1950); O. Clavadetscher, "Die Einführung der Grafschaftsverfassung in Rätien und die Klageschriften Bischof Viktors III. von Chur," *Savigny* (Kan.) 39 (1953): 46–111; E. Ewig, "L'Aquitaine et les pays rhénans au haut moyen âge," *Cahiers de civilisation médiévale* 1 (1958): 37–54; P. Delogu, "L'istituzione comitale nell'Italia carolingia," *BISIMeAM* 79 (1968): 53–114 (cf. the observation made above in the bibliography relating to chapter 2); U. Nonn, *Pagus und comitatus in Niederlothringen: Untersuchungen zur politischen Raumgliederung im früheren Mittelalter* (Bonn, 1983); M. Borgolte, *Geschichte der Grafschaften*

Alemanniens in fränkischer Zeit (Sigmaringen, 1984); F. Cagol, '*Gaue,' pagi e comitati nella Baviera agilolfingia e carolingia* (Verona, 1997).

Following these studies, there has been a tendency among some German historians to deny that there was a systematic organization of counties and to postulate the existence of various categories of *Grafschaften*; but see also the opposing and persuasive argument of H. K. Schulze, *Die Grafschaftsverfassung der Karolinger in den Gebieten östlich des Rheins* (Berlin, 1973); H. K. Schulze, "Grundprobleme der Grafschaftsverfassung: Kritische Bemerkungen zu einer Neuerscheinung," *Zeitschrift für württembergische Landesgeschichte* 44 (1985): 265–82; H. K. Schulze, "Die Grafschaftsorganisation als Element der frühmittelalterlichen Staatlichkeit," *Jahrbuch für Geschichte des Feudalismus* 14 (1990): 29–46.

Estimates of the number of counties vary; in "Charlemagne et les institutions," Ganshof calculates there were about four hundred, excluding the kingdom of Italy; K. F. Werner, in "Heeresorganisation und Kriegsführung im deutschen Königreich des 10. und 11. Jahrhunderts," *Settimane* 15 (1968): 819, put it at five hundred at least and then raised the figure to six or seven hundred in "Missus-marchio-comes," in *Histoire comparée de l'administration* (Munich, 1980), 191, but in his more recent *Naissance de la noblesse* (Paris, 1998), 130, he reduced his estimate to about 300 *pagi* and "aux alentours de 200 à 250 comtes."

On the social origins of counts, see R. Le Jan, "Prosopographica neustrica: les agents du roi en Neustrie de 639 à 840," in *La Neustrie*, 231–69; and R. Le Jan, *Famille et pouvoir dans le monde franc* (Paris, 1995), stressing the hereditary hegemony of a small group of great families; but compare the more nuanced conclusions of D. A. Bullough, "*Leo qui apud Hlotharium magni loci habebatur* et le gouvernement du Regnum Italiae à l'époque carolingienne," *MÂ* 67 (1961): 221–45; and D. A. Bullough, "'Europae Pater': Charlemagne and his achievement in the light of recent scholarship," *EHR* 85 (1970): 59–105.

The *centena*, or "hundred," considered by the German *neue Lehre* as a group of *Königsfreien* settled on crown lands, was very probably an ordinary geographic subdivision of a county: see most recently M. Schaab, "Die Zent in Franken von der Karolingerzeit bis ins 19. Jahrhundert," in *Histoire comparée de l'administration*, 345–62. There is fuller documentary analysis in H.-J. Krüger, "Untersuchungen zum Amt des 'centenarius'—Schultheiss," *Savigny* (Germ.) 87 (1970): 1–31, and 88 (1971): 29–109.

On the empire's other internal subdivisions, see E. Ewig, "Descriptio Franciae," in *KdG*, vol. 1—republished in his *Spätantikes und fränkischen Gallien* (Munich, 1976), 274–322. K. F. Werner's analysis of the so-called dukedoms or *regna* should be treated with caution, at least as far as Charlemagne's era is concerned, as in K. F. Werner, "La genèse des duchés en France et en Allemagne," *Settimane* 28 (1981): 175–207.

On the *missi dominici* or royal envoys, see W. A. Eckhardt, "Die Capitularia missorum specialia von 802," *DA* 12 (1956): 498–516; Werner, "Missus-marchio-comes," 191–240; and for precise contextualization of the reform of 802, see J. Hannig, "Pauperiores vassi de infra palatio? Zur Entstehung der karolingischen Königsbotenorganisation," *Mitteilungen des Instituts für österreichische Geschichtsforschung* 91 (1983): 309–74; J. Hannig, "Zentrale Kontrolle und Regionale Machtbalance: Beobachtungen zum System der karolingischen Königsboten am Beispiel des Mittelrheingebietes," *Archiv für Kulturgeschichte* 66 (1984): 1–46.

On the use of written word in government, apart from the aging work by F. L. Ganshof, "Charlemagne et l'usage de l'écrit en matière administrative," *MÂ* 57 (1951): 1–25, see the fundamental study by R. McKitterick, *The Carolingians and the Written Word* (Cambridge, 1989); J. L. Nelson, "Literacy in Carolingian Government," in *The Uses of Literacy in the Early Medieval Europe*, ed. R. McKitterick (Cambridge, 1990), 258–96; and most recently, *Schriftkultur und Reichsverwaltung unter den Karolingern*, ed. R. Schieffer (Münster, 1996).

On the cooperation between the king and the episcopacy in the Carolingian empire, and more especially the contradictions it created, which were much more complex than I have been able to summarize in this book, see G. Tabacco, "L'ambiguità delle istituzioni nell'Europa costruita dai franchi," *RSI* 87 (1975)—republished in his *Sperimentazioni del potere nell'alto medioevo* (Turin, 1993), 45–94; for the particular situation in Italy, see G. Tabacco, "Il volto ecclesiastico del potere in età carolingia," in *Storia d'Italia Emaudi, Annali, 9: la Chiesa e il potere politico* (Turin, 1986)—also republished in *Sperimentazioni*, 165–208.

For a textbook providing an introduction to the ecclesiastical institutions of the Carolingian era, see J. Imbert, *Les Temps carolingiens (741–891): l'église; les institutions* (Paris, 1994) (with a rather dated bibliography).

On the elimination of the episcopal republics and the integration of their bishops into the administration of the kingdom, see R. Kaiser, *Bischofsherrschaft zwischen Königtum und Fürstenmacht* (Bonn, 1981); R. Kaiser, "Royauté et pouvoir épiscopal au nord de la Gaule (VIIe–IXe siècles)," in *La Neustrie*, 143–60. More specifically on the administrative role of the upper clergy, see Werner, "Missus-marchio-comes," 191–240; on their military duties, see F. Prinz, *Klerus und Krieg im früheren Mittelalter* (Stuttgart, 1971); J. Nelson, "The Church's military service in the ninth century: a contemporary comparative view?" in

Politics and Ritual in Early Medieval Europe (London, 1986), 117–32. On the allocation to bishops of proceeds from crown lands, R. Kaiser, "Teloneum episcopi: du tonlieu royal au tonlieu épiscopal dans les civitates de la Gaule (VIᵉ–XIIᵉ siècle)," in *Histoire comparée de l'administration* (Munich, 1980), 469–85.

On the *commendatio* of the monasteries to the king, see J. Semmler, "Traditio und Königsschutz," *Savigny* (Kan.) 45 (1959): 1–33.

Chapter 8. Government of the Empire: The Resources

On the crown estates or fisc, a fundamental work is still J. W. Thompson, *The Dissolution of the Carolingian Fisc in the Ninth Century* (Berkeley, 1935) (in spite of reservations below), as well as W. Metz, *Das Karolingische Reichsgut* (Berlin, 1960), with revisions in W. Metz, "Zum Stand der Erforschung des karolingischen Reichsgutes," *HJ* 78 (1959): 1–37, and W. Metz, *Zur Erforschung des karolingischen Reichsgutes* (Darmstadt, 1971); see also J. Barbier, "Aspects du fisc en Neustrie (VIᵉ–Xᵉ siècles)," in *La Neustrie*, ed. H. Atsma (Sigmaringen, 1989), 129–42. The theory originally put forward by Thompson that the management of the crown estates was deteriorating after Louis the Pious as a result of irresponsible selling of property has been challenged by J. Martindale, "The Kingdom of Aquitaine and the Dissolution of the Carolingian Fisc," *Francia* 11 (1983): 131–91.

The essential bibliography on the *Capitulare de villis* can be found in B. Fois Ennas, *Il Capitulare de villis* (Milan, 1981).

On the system of maintaining the king and the resulting obligations for the Church, particularly in relation to hospitality, see C. Brühl, *Fodrum, Gistum, Servitium Regis* (Cologne, 1968). On *dona* and forms of contribution to the state by monasteries, see J. Semmler, "Traditio und Königsschutz," *Savigny* (Kan.) 45 (1959): 1–33; J.-P. Devroey, "Problèmes de critique autour du polyptyque de l'abbaye de St-Germain-des-Prés," in *La Neustrie*, 441–65; J. Durliat, "Le polyptyque d'Irminon et l'impôt sur l'armée," *BEC* 141 (1983): 183–208.

On the allocation of abbeys for services to the king and the problem of secular abbots, see F. J. Felten, *Äbte und Laienäbte im Frankenreich: Studien zum Verhältnis von Staat und Kirche im früheren Mittelalter* (Stuttgart, 1980). On the use of Church assets to benefit counts, see the local study by O. Clavadetscher, "Die Einführung der Grafschaftsverfassung in Rätien und die Klageschriften Bischof Viktors III. von Chur," *Savigny* (Kan.) 39 (1953): 46–111.

On immunity, F.-L. Ganshof, "L'immunité dans la monarchie franque," in

Les liens de vassalité et les immunités, Recueils de la société Jean Bodin no. 1 (Brussels, 1958), 171–216; E. Magnou-Nortier, "Étude sur le privilège d'immunité," *Revue Mabillon* 60 (1984): 465–512; B. H. Rosenwein, *Negotiating Space: Power, Restraint and Privileges of Immunity in Early Medieval Europe* (Ithaca, N.Y., 1999). The legal subtleties of the conflict between Alcuin and Theodulf are analyzed by L. Wallach in *Alcuin and Charlemagne: Studies in Carolingian History and Literature* (Ithaca, N.Y., 1959), 97–140.

On church advocates, see J. Riedmann, "Vescovi e avvocati," in *I poteri temporali dei vescovi in Italia e Germania nel medioevo*, ed. C. G. Mor and H. Schmidinger (Bologna, 1979), 35–76.

On the obligations of holders of *precariae verbo regis* in relation to the Church whose land they occupied, see G. Constable, "Nona et decima: An aspect of Carolingian economy," *Speculum* 35 (1960): 224–50.

On obligatory services, see H. Dannenbauer, "Paraveredus-Pferd," *Savigny* (Germ.) 71 (1954): 55–73; C. Brühl, "Das fränkische Fodrum," *Savigny* (Germ.) 76 (1959): 53–81.

The theory of the survival of the property tax and the fiscal nature of the *censi* is put forward by J. Durliat and E. Magnou-Nortier in such a contrived manner that it has never appeared very convincing. See most recently E. Magnou-Nortier, "La gestion publique en Neustrie: les moyens et les hommes (VIIe–IXe siècle)," in *La Neustrie*, 271–320, and J. Durliat, *Les Finances publiques de Dioclétien aux carolingiens (284–889)* (Sigmaringen, 1990). Metz's demonstration in *Das Karolingische Reichsgut* (Berlin, 1960)—that the *censi* were nothing more than rents paid by farmers and holders of *precariae* living on crown lands under various titles—remains valid. See also E. Müller-Mertens, *Karl der Grosse, Ludwig der Fromme und die Freien: Wer waren die 'liberi homines' der karolingischen Kapitularien?* (Berlin, 1963), 74–78, and J. Schmitt, *Untersuchungen zu den Liberi Homines der Karolingerzeit* (Frankfurt am Main, 1977),110–36.

On tolls, see F.-L. Ganshof, "À propos de tonlieux à l'époque carolingienne," *Settimane* 6 (1959): 485–508; on other taxes on movement, see F.-L. Ganshof, "À propos des droits sur la circulation au sein de la monarchie franque," in *Studi storici in onore di O. Bertolini* (Pisa, 1972), 1:361–77.

Chapter 9. Government of the Empire: The Justice System

The history of law has recently undergone an extraordinary renewal since its acceptance as far too serious a matter to be left to jurists, and the adoption of an anthropological perspective helps us understand a great deal more about it. Among the more recent studies we can add the classic work by F.-L. Ganshof, "Charlemagne et l'administration de la justice dans la monarchie franque," in *KdG*, 1:394–419. For very different positions on the nature and efficacy of the Carolingian justice system, see J. L. Nelson, "Dispute settlement in Carolingian West Francia," in *The Settlement of Disputes in Early Medieval Europe*, ed. W. Davies and P. Fouracre (Cambridge, 1986), 45–64; P. Fouracre, "Carolingian justice: the rhetoric of improvement and contexts of abuse," *Settimane* 42 (1995): 771–803; R. McKitterick, "Perceptions of justice in western Europe in the ninth and tenth centuries," *Settimane* 44 (1997): 1075–1102; for a summary, see R. Le Jan, "Justice royale et pratiques sociales dans le royaume franc au IXe siècle," *Settimane* 44 (1997): 47–85.

On the office of count palatine, see H. E. Meyer, "Die Pfalzgrafen der Merowinger und Karolinger," *Savigny* (Germ.) 42 (1921): 380–463.

On the legal procedure, particularly in Italy, see C. Wickham, "Land Disputes and their Social Framework in Lombard-Carolingian Italy," in *Land & Power: Studies in Italian and European Social History, 400–1200* (London, 1994), 229–56. More generally, on the peculiarities of the administration of justice in the Italic kingdom, see P. Delogu, "L'istituzione comitale nell'Italia carolingia," *BISIMeAM* 79 (1968): 53–114 (to be compared with the works of Fumagalli and Castagnetti mentioned in the bibliographical notes on chapter 2), and above all F. Bougard, *La justice dans le royaume d'Italie: de la fin du VIIIe siècle au début du XIe siècle* (Rome, 1995); F. Bougard, "La justice dans le royaume d'Italie aux IXe–Xe siècles," *Settimane* 44 (1997): 133–76.

A classic analysis of the procedure of *inquisitio per testes* is provided by L. Wallach, *Alcuin and Charlemagne: Studies in Carolingian History and Literature* (Ithaca, N.Y., 1959), 117ff. D. A. Bullough demonstrates its Lombard origins, in polemic with Ganshof, in "'Europae Pater': Charlemagne and his achievement in the light of recent scholarship," *EHR* 85 (1970): 92–96.

The problem of personality of the law is intrinsically related to that of the fusion between Romans and Germans; for a problematical view based on the latest research, see P. Amory, "The Meaning and Purpose of Ethnic Terminology in the Burgundian Laws," *Early Medieval Europe* 2 (1993): 1–28, and S. Gasparri, *Prima delle nazioni: popoli, etnie e regni fra antichità e medioevo* (Rome, 1997).

On the privatization of the judicial system during the post-Carolingian age, see the seminal work of G. Duby, "Recherches sur l'évolution des institutions judiciaires pendant le Xe et le XIe siècle dans le sud de la Bourgogne," *MÂ* 52 (1946): 149–94, and 53 (1947): 15–38. Another insightful work is C. Wickham,

Legge, pratiche e conflitti: tribunali e risoluzione delle dispute nella Toscana del XII secolo (Rome, 2000).

Chapter 10. An Intellectual Project

There is a vast literature on the Carolingian renaissance; over the last half century we have developed an increasingly clear picture of the essentially religious nature of Charlemagne's reforms, abandoning the earlier emphasis on the renewal of literature and the rediscovery of the classical age. To appreciate the shift, we can compare the traditional overview by P. Lehmann, "Das Problem der Karolingischen Renaissance," *Settimane* 1 (1954): 309–58, with the recent works of J. J. Contreni, "The Carolingian Renaissance," in *Renaissances before the Renaissance*, ed. W. Treadgold (Stanford, 1984), 59–74, and G. Brown, "Introduction: the Carolingian Renaissance," in *Carolingian Culture: Emulation and Innovation*, ed. R. McKitterick (Cambridge, 1994), 1–51.

Equally significant is the tendency to see Carloman and Pepin as the first to commit themselves to improving the morals of the Church and reforming the liturgy, a project that Charlemagne then took up on a larger scale. See J. Hubert, "Les prémisses de la Renaissance carolingienne au temps de Pépin III," *Francia* 2 (1974): 49–58; and P. Riché, "Le renouveau culturel à la cour de Pépin III," *Francia* 2 (1974): 59–70; as well as the essays by C. Vogel referred to below under liturgical reform.

The bibliography on palatine scholars is immense, particularly in the case of Alcuin. For an introduction, see D. A. Bullough, "Aula Renovata: the court before the Aachen Palace," in *Carolingian Renewal: Sources and Heritage* (Manchester, 1991), 123–60; and J. Fleckenstein, "Alcuin im Kreis der Hofgelehrten Karls des Grossen," in *Science in Western and Eastern Civilization in Carolingian Times*, ed. P. L. Butzer and D. Lohrmann (Basel, 1993), 3–21. A recent article summarizing the subject is C. Leonardi, "Alcuino e la Scuola palatina: le ambizioni di una cultura unitaria," *Settimane* 28 (1981): 459–96. For the most interesting aspect, which concerns Alcuin's ideological support for Charlemagne and his assistance in political affairs, see L. Wallach, *Alcuin and Charlemagne: Studies in Carolingian History and Literature* (Ithaca, N.Y., 1959); I. Deug-Su, *Cultura e ideologia nella prima età carolingia* (Rome, 1984); and D. A. Bullough, "Alcuin and the kingdom of heaven: liturgy, theology and the Carolingian age," in *Carolingian Renewal*, 161–240. On Paul the Deacon, see a recent and stimulating essay by G. Gandino, "La dialettica tra il passato e il presente nelle opere di Paolo Diacono," in *Paolo Diacono e il Friuli altomedievale (secc. VI–X)* (Spoleto, 2001), 67–97.

The high literary value of the Latin poetry written at Charlemagne's court, not so much based on imitation as a direct continuation of the late classical tradition, is argued by F. Stella, *La poesia carolingia* (Florence, 1995), which contains an excellent anthology of texts. On the court's scientific and encyclopedic culture, see the previously mentioned collection of essays edited by Butzer and Lohrmann, *Science in Western and Eastern Civilization in Carolingian Times*. On schools and instruction, F. Brunhölzl, "Der Bildungsauftrag der Hofschule," in *KdG*, 2:28–41; and P. Riché, *Les Écoles et l' enseignement dans l'Occident chrétien de la fin du Ve au milieu du XIe siècle* (Paris, 1979).

On the inspirational effect of Charlemagne's reforms, see P. E. Schramm, "Karl der Grosse: Denkart und Grundauffassungen; Die von ihm bewirkte *Correctio* ('Renaissance')," *HZ* 198 (1964): 306–45.

On reform of the Church, see R. McKitterick, *The Frankish Church and the Carolingian Reforms (789–895)* (London, 1977); specifically on the measures taken in 811, see F.-L. Ganshof, "Note sur les *Capitula de causis cum episcopis et abbatibus tractandis* de 811," *Studia Gratiana* 13 (1967): 3–25. On the *Collectio Dionysio-Hadriana*, see H. Mordek, "Dionysio-Hadriana und Vetus Gallica— historisch geordnetes und systematisches Kirchenrecht am Hofe Karls des Grossen," *Savigny* (Kan.) 55 (1969): 39–63. On the synods convened by Charlemagne, see W. Hartmann, *Die Synoden der Karolingerzeit im Frankenreich und Italien* (Paderborn, 1989). On monastic reform, see J. Semmler, "Karl der Grosse und das fränkische Mönchtum," in *KdG*, 2:255–89; J. Semmler, "Mönche und Kanoniker im Frankenreichs Pippins III. und Karls des Grossen," in *Untersuchungen zu Kloster und Stift* (Göttingen, 1980), 78–111; R. Grégoire, "Benedetto di Aniane nella riforma monastica carolingia," *Studi medievali* 26 (1985): 573–610.

On liturgical reform, see C. Vogel, "La réforme liturgique sous Charlemagne," in *KdG*, 2:217–32; C. Vogel, "Les motifs de la romanisation du culte sous Pépin le Bref et Charlemagne," in *Culto cristiano e politica imperiale carolingia* (Todi, 1979), 15–41. On revising the Bible, see B. Fischer, "Bibeltext und Bibelreform unter Karl dem Grossen," in *KdG*, 2:156–216; more specifically on Theodulf's text, see E. Dahlhaus-Berg, *Nova antiquitas et antiqua novitas: Typologische Exegese und isidorianisches Geschichtsbild bei Theodulf von Orléans* (Cologne, 1975); on Alcuin's text, see D. Ganz, "Mass production of early medieval manuscripts: the Carolingian Bibles from Tours," in *The Early Medieval Bible*, ed. R. Gameson (Cambridge, 1994), 53–62, and R. McKitterick, "Carolingian Bible

Production: The Tours Anomaly," in *The Early Medieval Bible*, 63–77 (with a tendency to diminish its hegemony in relation to previous interpretations).

On book production and its costs, see R. McKitterick, *The Carolingians and the Written Word* (Cambridge, 1989); R. McKitterick, "Script and book production," in *Carolingian Culture*, 221–47; as well as other articles by the same author, collected in *Books, Scribes and Learning in the Frankish Kingdoms, 6th–9th Centuries* (London, 1994), and *The Frankish Kings and Culture in the Early Middle Ages* (London, 1995). For an exploration of the *scriptoria* active at the time of Charlemagne, see B. Bischoff, "Panorama der Handschriftenüberlieferung aus der Zeit Karls des Grossen," in *KdG*, 2:233–54. On Charlemagne's library, see B. Bischoff, "Die Hofbibliothek Karls des Grossen" in *KdG*, 2:42–62.

The question of the Carolingian minuscule is a great deal more complex than was previously thought; see A. Pratesi, "Le ambizioni di una cultura unitaria: la riforma della scrittura," *Settimane* 28 (1981): 507–23; and A. Bartoli Langeli, "Scritture e libri da Alcuino a Gutenberg," in *Storia d'Europa*, vol. 3: *Il Medioevo*, ed. G. Ortalli (Turin, 1994), 935–83.

On the reform of Latin, see J. Fontaine, "De la pluralité à l'ünité dans le latin carolingien?" *Settimane* 28 (1981): 765–805; more generally on Latin as a spoken language and a language of learning at the time of Charlemagne, see the stimulating reflections of McKitterick, *The Carolingians and the Written Word*.

On Charlemagne's theological interventions in general, see H. Nagel, *Karl der Grosse und die theologischen Herausforderungen seiner Zeit: Zur Wechselwirkung zwischen Theologie und Politik im Zeitalter des grossen Frankenherrschers* (Freiburg, 1998). On the adoptionist controversy, see W. Heil, "Der Adoptianismus, Alkuin und Spanien," in *KdG*, 2:95–155, and more recently, J. C. Cavadini, *The Last Christology of the West: Adoptionism in Spain and Gaul, 785–820* (Philadelphia, 1993). On the theological conflict with Byzantium and the Council of Frankfurt, see the collections of essays, *794—Karl der Grosse in Frankfurt am Main: Ein König bei der Arbeit*, ed. J. Fried (Sigmaringen, 1994), and *Das Frankfurter Konzil von 794: Kristallisationspunkt karolingischer Kultur*, ed. R. Berndt (Frankfurt am Main, 1997). On the question of *filioque*, see M. Borgolte, "Papst Leo III., Karl der Grosse und der Filioque-Streit von Jerusalem," *Byzantina* 10 (1980): 401–27.

In itself, Boniface's missionary work is not part of this bibliography; for reflections on its historical significance in relation to Charlemagne's reign, see G. Arnaldi, "Bonifacio e Carlomagno," *Settimane* 20 (1973): 17–39. On the conversion of the Saxons, see the collected essays in *Die Eingliederung der Sachsen in das Frankenreich*, ed. W. Lammers (Darmstadt, 1970), and H. Beumann, "Die Hagiographie 'bewältigt': Unterwerfung und Christianisierung der Sachsen durch Karl den Grossen," *Settimane* 29 (1982): 129–68. On the conversion of the Avars and the Slavs, see H. Wolfram, *Conversio Bagoariorum et Carantanorum: Das Weissbuch der Salzburger Kirche über die erfolgreiche Mission in Karantanien und Pannonien* (Vienna, 1979). For the link between the missionary work and the foundation of the archbishoprics of Salzburg and Hamburg, see B. Wavra, *Salzburg und Hamburg: Erzbistumsgründung und Missionspolitik in karolingischer Zeit* (Berlin, 1991). More generally on the organization of missionary work and the related reorganization of ecclesiastical geography, see H. Büttner, "Mission und Kirchen-Organisation des Frankenreiches bis zum Tode Karls des Grossen," in *KdG*, 1:454–87, which should be updated by the essays collected together in *Kirchengeschichte als Missionsgeschichte*, 2/1: *Die Kirche des früheren Mittelalters*, ed. K. Schäferdiek (Munich, 1978), and the bibliography produced by A. Angenendt, *Kaiserherrschaft und Königstaufe* (Berlin, 1984).

On the fight against superstition, see H. Mordek and M. Glatthaar, "Von Wahrsagerinnen und Zauberern: Ein Beitrag zur Religionspolitik Karls des Grossen," *Archiv für Kulturgeschichte* 75 (1993): 33–64.

Chapter 11. The Frankish Military Machine

The general studies on Carolingian military organization are now rather dated; see J. F. Verbruggen, "L'armée et la stratégie de Charlemagne," in *KdG*, 1:420–36; F.-L. Ganshof, "Charlemagne's Army," in *Frankish Institutions under Charlemagne* (Providence, R.I., 1968), 59–68; F.-L. Ganshof, "L'armée sous les carolingiens," *Settimane* 15 (1968): 109–30.

A revisionist approach emerged in the seventies from the studies of Bernard S. Bachrach, commencing with *Merovingian Military Organization, 481–751* (Minneapolis, 1972), which tended to bring forward to the Merovingian age innovations that had traditionally been considered Carolingian, both in the role of the cavalry and in the employment of armed vassals. This ran somewhat counter to another of his works, at least in its logic if not in spirit: "Charlemagne's cavalry: myth and reality," *Military Affairs* 47 (1983): 1–20, which tended to diminish the importance of these factors in the Carolingian age. A stimulating reflection on these and other questions is A. A. Settia, "La fortezza e il cavaliere: tecniche militari in Occidente," *Settimane* 45 (1998): 555–80. The publication of this book's original version preceded the appearance of B. S. Bachrach, *Early Carolingian Warfare: Prelude to Empire* (Philadelphia, 2001).

For the military organization of the Franks at the time of the invasions, see

H. Elton, *Warfare in Roman Europe, A.D. 350–425* (Oxford, 1996), 45–88; for the weaponry, see the work mainly based on the archaeological finds by P. Perin-L.-C. Feffer, *Les Francs* (Paris, 1987), 2:83–124; for analysis of written sources, see B. S. Bachrach, "Procopius, Agathias and the Frankish military," *Speculum* 45 (1970): 435–41.

The costs stipulated by the *Lex Ribuaria* should be interpreted as purely indicative, because other sources, perhaps reflecting excessive demands, give very different current prices; see for example J. Durliat's calculations in "Le polyptyque d'Irminon et l'impôt sur l'armée," *BEC* 141 (1983): 183–209.

S. Coupland, "Carolingian arms and armour in the ninth century," *Viator* 51 (1990): 29–50, constitutes the principal overall contribution to the question of Carolingian armament (with an unconventional theory on the *brunia*).

The idea that shifting the annual assembly was connected to the need to graze the army's horses has been challenged by many scholars, arguing that the term *Campus Martii*, which had been in use since ancient times, did not refer to the month of March, but to Mars, the god of war, and therefore the shift, which was reported much later in the Royal Annals, did not actually take place at all. See L. Levillain, "Campus Martius," *BEC* 197 (1947–48): 62–68; D. A. Bullough, "'Europae Pater': Charlemagne and his achievement in the light of recent scholarship," *EHR* 85 (1970): 85–86; and most recently B. S. Bachrach, "Was the Marchfield part of the Frankish Constitution?" *Mediaeval Studies* 36 (1974): 178–85. However, the objection does not take into account the fact that as far back as 596 King Childebert II referred to the annual gathering as *Kalendas Martias* and not *Campus Martii* (*CRF*, n7). Moreover the assembly was convened at the calends of March under Carloman (*CRF*, n11) and Pepin (*CRF*, n12), the Lombard kings held the gathering on 1 March, as can be seen in the laws of Liutprand, Aistulf, and Rachis, which were regularly promulgated on that day (*Le leggi dei Longobardi*, ed. C. Azzara and S. Gasparri [Milan, 1992]), and the same happened with the Alamans (*Leges Alamannorum*, ed. K. A. Eckhardt [Hannover, 1966]; vol. 7 in *MGH, Leges Nationum Germanicarum*, 80 and n). The idea of replacing March with Mars therefore appears to fly in the face of the evidence.

On stirrups, see L. White, Jr., *Medieval Technology and Social Change* (London, 1962). For a critique of White's theories, see P. H. Sawyer and R. Hilton, "Technical Determinism: the Stirrup and the Plough," *Past & Present* 24 (1963): 90–100; B. S. Bachrach, "Charles Martel, mounted shock-combat, the stirrup, and feudalism," *Studies in Medieval and Renaissance History* 7 (1970): 45–75.

Carolingian iconographic sources that systematically depict the use of stirrups, as in the psalter of St-Gall, are from the late ninth century, but the Gellone sacramentary and the Apocalypse of Trier, both illustrated during the life of Charlemagne, as well as the Stuttgart psalter, which dates from 820–30, and the Utrecht psalter of about 830, depict horsemen without stirrups, even when wearing heavy armor. The oldest manuscript in which horsemen appear with stirrups, among others who continue not to use them, is the Apocalypse of Valenciennes, whose date is the subject of some argument (the beginning or middle of the ninth century?), and which is possibly of Spanish origin, so it would represent the Arab stirrup of leather and wood, rather than the metal one that eventually came into use in Europe. Reproductions and details of these miniatures can be found in much of the bibliography referred to in this section, and particularly in D. Nicolle, *The Age of Charlemagne* (London, 1984).

It should be noted on this point that the reliability of iconographic depictions of the Carolingian age as sources for the study of armaments is more widely accepted today than it was in the past; see B. S. Bachrach, "A Picture of Avar-Frankish Warfare From a Carolingian Psalter of the Early Ninth Century in the Light of the Strategicon," *Archivum Eurasiae Medii Aevi* 4 (1986): 5–27, and the previously mentioned S. Coupland, "Carolingian arms and armour in the ninth century," who, however, challenges the reliability of the iconography in the particular case of the *brunia*.

For a fuller debate on the arguments that could explain the increasing importance of the cavalry in the Carolingian age, see F. Cardini, *Alle radici della cavalleria medievale* (Florence, 1981), 256–91. For the importance of cavalry in the Frankish army and society immediately after Charlemagne's death, see J. L. Nelson, "Ninth-Century Knighthood: The Evidence of Nithard," in *The Frankish World* (London, 1996), 75–87.

On free men and their military obligations in Italy and elsewhere, see G. Tabacco, "I liberi del re nell'Italia carolingia e postcarolingia," *Settimane* 13 (1966); S. Gasparri, "Strutture militari e legami di dipendenza in Italia in età longobarda e carolingia," *RSI* 98 (1986): 664–726. On the crucial, but not easily resolvable, problem of the extent of military obligations and the selection criteria actually applied at the time of recruitment, see the stimulating though inconclusive reflections of T. Reuter, "The End of Carolingian Military Expansion," in *Charlemagne's Heir: New Perspectives on the Reign of Louis the Pious*, ed. P Godman and R. Collins (Oxford, 1990), 391–405.

On the integration of vassals into the army, see J. Fleckenstein, "Adel und Kriegertum und ihre Wandlungen im Karolingerreich," *Settimane* 28 (1981): 67–94 (but he exaggerates the extent to which the Carolingian army identified itself with patronage structures). On the military duties of the clergy, see F. Prinz, *Klerus und Krieg im früheren Mittelalter* (Stuttgart, 1971); J. L. Nelson, "The church's military service in the ninth century: a contemporary comparative view?" in *Politics and Ritual in Early Medieval Europe* (London, 1986), 117–32.

For calculations on the size of the army, see K. F. Werner, "Heeresorganisation und Kriegsführung im deutschen Königreich des 10. und 11. Jahrhunderts," *Settimane* 15 (1968): 816–22.

On logistics, see B. S. Bachrach, "Animals and welfare in early medieval Europe," *Settimane* 33 (1985): 707–51.

The attempt to analyze Charlemagne's military capitularies in the light of the contingent military situation, particularly on the Pyrenean front, has produced very interesting but occasionally arguable results; see B. S. Bachrach, "Military organization in Aquitaine under the early Carolingians," *Speculum* 49 (1974): 1–33. The campaigns in Aquitaine offer typical examples of Carolingian siege warfare: G. Fournier, "Les campagnes de Pépin le Bref en Auvergne et la question des fortifications rurales au VIIIe siècle," *Francia* 2 (1974): 123–35.

Chapter 12. A New Economy

Pirenne's theory on the Carolingian economy was first expounded in *L'Histoire économique et sociale du moyen âge* (Paris, 1933)—trans. by I. E. Clegg as *Economic and Social History of Medieval Europe* (London, 1936); and then more fully in the posthumous publication of *Mahomet et Charlemagne* (Brussels, 1937)—trans. by B. Miall as *Mohammed and Charlemagne* (London, 1939). The most recent attempt to resurrect this pessimistic interpretation was in R. Fossier, "Les tendances de l'économie: stagnation ou croissance?" *Settimane* 28 (1981): 261–74 (but see also the heated debate that followed, 275–90).

For the first signs of reversing the trend, in relation to agriculture, see R. Delatouche, "Regards sur l'agriculture aux temps carolingiens," *Journal des savants* 12 (1977): 73–100. For a summary of current interpretations, in which a new approach to trade is equally fundamental, see J.-P. Devroey, "Reflexions sur l'économie des premiers temps carolingiens (768–877): grands domaines et action politique entre Seine et Rhin," *Francia* 13 (1985): 475–88; A. Verhulst, "Marchés, marchands et commerce au haut moyen âge dans l'historiographie récente," *Settimane* 40 (1993): 23–43; G. Petralia, "A proposito dell'immortalità di Maometto e Carlomagno (o di Costantino)," *Storica* 1 (1995): 38–87.

The reevaluation of trade between the Carolingians, England, and Scandinavia follows the model developed by R. Hodges, *Dark Age Economics: The Origins of Towns and Trade*, A.D. *600–1000* (London, 1982); see also R. Hodges and D. Whitehouse, *Mohammed, Charlemagne and the Origins of Europe: Archaeology and the Pirenne Thesis* (London, 1983), and J.-P. Devroey, "Courants et réseaux d'échange dans l'économie franque entre Loire et Rhin," *Settimane* 40 (1993): 327–89. Since I completed the original version of this book in 1999, I was not able to refer to some important new works: *The Long Eighth Century: Production, Distribution and Demand*, ed. I. L. Hansen and C. Wickham (Leiden, 2000), and M. McCormick, *Origins of the European Economy: Communications and Commerce*, A.D. *300–900* (Cambridge, 2002), which however fit well into the general trend toward a substantial reevaluation of Carolingian economic dynamism.

On the Frisian markets, see S. Lebecq, *Marchands et navigateurs frisons du haut moyen âge* (Lille, 1983); S. Lebecq, "Dans l'Europe du nord aux VIIe–IXe siècles: commerce frison ou commerce franco-frison?" *Annales ÉSC* 41(1986): 361–77; S. Lebecq, "La Neustrie et la mer," in *La Neustrie*, ed. H. Atsma (Sigmaringen, 1989), 405–40. The idea of complete integration of Frisian trade into the imperial economy, which is argued in these studies, might appear to be contradicted by S. Lebecq, "Francs contre frisons (VIe–VIIIe siècle)," in *La Guerre et la paix au moyen âge* (Paris, 1978), 53–71.

More generally on markets and merchants, see M. Rouche, "Marchés et marchands en Gaule du Ve au Xe siècle," *Settimane* 40 (1993): 395–434; as well as the monographs and essays published in *Untersuchungen zu Handel und Verkehr der vor- und frühgeschichtlichen Zeit in Mittel- und Nordeuropa*, published in Göttingen from 1985, particularly P. Johanek, *Der fränkische Handel der Karolingerzeit im Spiegel der Schriftquellen* (Göttingen, 1987), 4:7–68.

Even the description of the manorial system tends to give greater emphasis to the role of trade, dispelling once and for all the idea that the manorial model necessarily meant a closed economy; apart from the essay by Devroey, "Courants et réseaux d'échange," see in particular P. Toubert, "Le strutture produttive nell'alto medioevo: le grandi proprietà e l'economia curtense," in *La Storia: Il medioevo*, ed. N. Tranfaglia and M. Firpo, 2d ed. (Milan, 1993), 51–90; P. Toubert, "La part du grand domaine dans le décollage économique de l'Occident (VIIIe–Xe siècles)," in *La croissance agricole du haut moyen âge: chronologie, modalités, géographie* (Auch, 1990)—reprinted in P. Toubert, *Dalla terra ai castelli: paesaggio, agricoltura e poteri nell'Italia medievale* (Turin, 1995).

German historiografy, although more prudent, has carried out massive research into what they call *Grundherrschaft;* for a summary and bibliography, see L. Kuchenbuch, "Die Klostergrundherrschaft im Frühmittelalter," in

Herrschaft und Kirche, ed. F. Prinz (Stuttgart, 1988), 297–343; of the specific studies, particularly worthy of note are the examinations of the management of the land by some leading abbeys: L. Kuchenbuch, *Bäuerliche Gesellschaft und Klosterherrschaft im 9. Jahrhundert: Studien zur Sozialstruktur der Familia der Abtei Prüm* (Wiesbaden, 1978), and U. Weidinger, *Untersuchungen zur Wirtschaftsstruktur des Klosters Fulda in der Karolingerzeit* (Stuttgart, 1991); as well as the collection of essays in *Strukturen der Grundherrschaft im frühen Mittelalter*, ed. W. Rösener (Göttingen, 1989).

The destruction of the traditional perception of the manorial system and its replacement by a more flexible and differentiated approach mainly reflect the progress of research into the Mediterranean area and into the economic vitality of the monasteries. On the first point, see P. Toubert, "L'Italie rurale aux VIIe– IXe siècles: essai de typologie domaniale," *Settimane* 20 (1973): 95–132; P. Toubert, "Il sistema curtense: la produzione e lo scambio interno in Italia nei secoli VIII, IX e X," in *Storia d'Italia, Annali* 6 (Turin, 1983), 3–63; V. Fumagalli, *Terra e società nell'Italia padana: i secoli IX e X* (Turin, 1976); B. Andreolli and M. Montanari, *L'azienda curtense in Italia* (Bologna, 1983). On the second point, see J.-P. Devroey, "Les services de transport à l'abbaye de Prüm au IXe siècle," *Revue du Nord* 61 (1979): 543–69; J.-P. Devroey, "Un monastère dans l'économie d'échanges: les services de transport à l'abbaye St-Germain-des-Prés au IXe siècle," *Annales ÉSC* (1984): 570–89; J.-P. Devroey, "'Ad utilitatem monasterii': mobiles et préoccupations de gestion dans l'économie monastique du monde franc (VIIIe–IXe s.)," *Revue bénédictine* 103 (1993): 224–40.

An entirely different interpretation of the *villa* and the *mansus* is put forward by the "fiscalist" or "hyper-Romanist" school; see J. Durliat, "Du caput antique au manse médiéval," *Pallas* 29 (1982): 67–77; J. Durliat, "Le polyptyque d'Irminon et l'impôt sur l'armée," *BEC* 141 (1984): 183–208; J. Durliat, *Les Finances publiques de Dioclétien aux carolingiens (284–889)* (Sigmaringen, 1990); E. Magnou-Nortier, "La gestion publique en Neustrie: les moyens et les hommes (VIIe–IXe siècle)," in *La Neustrie*, 271–320; E. Magnou-Nortier, "Le grand domaine: des maîtres, des doctrines, des questions," *Francia* 15 (1987): 659–700; but see also the critique by J.-P. Devroey, "Polyptyques et fiscalité à l'époque carolingienne: une nouvelle approche?" *RBPH* 63 (1985): 783–94, and C. Wickham, "La chute de Rome n'aura pas lieu," *MÂ* 99 (1993): 107–26. Although it is difficult to agree with the premise, some important insights on the *mansus* can be found in J. Durliat, "Le manse dans le polyptyque d'Irminon: nouvel essai d'histoire quantitative," in *La Neustrie*, 467–504. For the concept of *mansi absi*, see J.-P. Devroey, "Mansi absi: indices de crise ou de croissance de l'économie rurale du haut moyen âge?" *MÂ* 82 (1976): 421–52.

On what probably remains the most important source on Carolingian agriculture, the polyptych of St-Germain-des-Prés, see the new edition of D. Hägermann, *Das Polyptychon von Saint-Germain-des-Prés: Studienausgabe* (Cologne, 1993), and related studies by K. Elmhäuser and A. Hedwig, *Studien zum Polyptychon von Saint-Germain-des-Prés* (Cologne, 1993).

On the cultivation of cereals, the article by J.-P. Devroey, "La céréaliculture dans le monde franc," *Settimane* 37 (1990): 221–53, demonstrates the extraordinary cultural and political implications that can be deduced from an argument that is only superficially of a technical nature. It also makes an equally fundamental contribution on the question of yields. On this point, the traditional interpretation of a universal yield of 2 or 3 to 1 has been challenged on all sides, and effective yields of 5 to 1 or even 7 to 1 have been suggested by several scholars. See, as an example, J. Durliat, "'De conlaboratu': faux rendements et vraie comptabilité publique à l'époque carolingienne," *Revue historique de droit français et étranger* 56 (1978): 445–57.

There is a vast bibliography on plowing up new land and more generally on the role of the forest in the economy of the early Middle Ages; an excellent starting point is C. Wickham, "European forests in the early Middle Ages: landscape and land clearance," *Settimane* 36 (1989): 479–548.

The generally optimistic framework of the Carolingian economy that is generated by today's widespread agreement among scholars also includes a reevaluation of the spread of water mills, previously considered a development of the next millennium. See D. Lohrmann, "Le moulin à eau dans le cadre de l'économie rurale de la Neustrie," in *La Neustrie*, 367–404.

One of the factors contributing to economic recovery, a somewhat obvious one, was the favorable climatic phase, which could be dated from the second half of the eighth century and was to last until the thirteenth century. See M. Pinna, "Il clima nell'alto medioevo. Conoscenze attuali e prospettive di ricerca," *Settimane* 37 (1990): 431–51.

On the reform of weights and measures, J.-P. Devroey, "Units of Measurement in the Early Medieval Economy: The Example of Carolingian Food Rations," *French History* 1 (1987): 68–92. On monetary reform, see the classic work by P. Grierson, "Money and Coinage under Charlemagne," in *KdG*, 1:501–36, and a more recent summary by S. Suchodolski, "La moneta," in *Storia d'Europa*, 3: *Il Medioevo*, ed. by G. Ortalli (Turin 1994), 847–94. For a numis-

matic analysis of Charlemagne's coinage, see J. Lafaurie, "Les monnaies impéri-
ales de Charlemagne," *Comptes-rendus de l'Académie des Inscriptions et Belles-Lettres*
(1978): 154–80. On famine relief, see A. Verhulst, "Karolingische Agrarpolitik.
Das Capitulare de villis und die Hungersnöte von 792/3 und 805/6," *Zeitschrift
für Agrargeschichte und Agrarsoziologie* 13 (1965): 175–89; and K. O. Scherner,
"'Ut propriam familiam nutriat': Zur Frage der sozialen Sicherung in der
karolingischen Grundherrschaft," *Savigny* (Germ.) 111 (1994): 330–62.

The archaeological digs carried out in Villiers-le-Sec from 1981 to 1987 are
the subject of *Un Village au temps de Charlemagne: moines et paysans de l'abbaye de
St-Denis du VIIe siècle à l'an mil* (Paris, 1988), the catalog for the exhibition of the
same name. Another agricultural model, whose results were not substantially
different, was the one in Holland discussed by W. Groenman-van Waateringe
and L. H. van Wijngarden-Bakker, *Farm Life in a Carolingian Village* (Assen-
Maastricht, 1987).

Studies in the early eighties on polyptychs have deepened our understanding
of the peasant demography and family structures: see P. Toubert, "Le moment
carolingien (VIIIe–Xe siècles)," in *Histoire de la famille*, ed. C. Klapisch-Zuber
and F. Zonabend (Paris, 1987), 1:333–59.

On forms of settlement, see F. Schwind, "Beobachtungen zur inneren Struk-
tur des Dorfes in karolingischer Zeit," in *Das Dorf der Eisernzeit und des frühen
Mittelalters* (Göttingen, 1977), 444–93, and other essays in the same volume.

Chapter 13. Patronage and Servitude

Some ideas presented in this chapter are developed and detailed in A. Barbero,
"Liberti, raccomandati, vassalli: le clientele nell'età di Carlo Magno," *Storica* 14
(1999): 7–60.

The historiography of the nobility in the Middle Ages is so vast that it is
impossible to give even a sample of it. See the forty-two pages of bibliography
in K. F. Werner, *Naissance de la noblesse* (Paris, 1998), which is not however a general work, but a highly partisan argument in favor of the theory that the nobility originated from public service in imperial Rome. An equally extensive bibliography can be found in R. Le Jan, *Famille et pouvoir dans le monde franc* (Paris,
1995), which analyzes the wider kinship group typical of nobility in the early
Middle Ages.

On the whole, the field is dominated by German historiography, with its
prosopographic studies and debates on *Stammesadel* and *Reichsadel:* see the criti-

cal review, in every sense of the term, by H. K. Schulze, "Reichsaristokratie, Stammesadel und fränkische Freiheit," *HZ* 227 (1978): 353–73, and for a reliable expression of prevailing opinions, see K. F. Werner, "Bedeutende Adelsfamilien im Reich Karls der Grossen," in *KdG*, 1:83–142, and H.W. Goetz, "Nobilis. Der Adel im Selbstverständnis der karolinger Zeit," *Vierteljahrschrift für Sozial- und Wirtschaftsgeschichte* 70 (1983): 153–91. Although the strictly legalistic perspective has become a thing of the past, much of this historiography has suffered from the theory of a hegemony of noble blood in Germanic society *(Herrschaftstheorie)* and excessive dependence on the techniques of *Personenforschung* and *Namenforschung*. However, there are some local studies that throw light on the way society was organized without preconceptions: see, for example, R. Sprandel, "Grundherrlicher Adel, rechtsständische Freiheit und Königszins," *DA* 19 (1963): 1–29.

For important studies of the *Reichsaristokratie* and the way it operated in a regional context, albeit with occasionally debatable arguments, see W. Störmer, *Früher Adel: Studien zur politischen Führungsschicht im fränkisch-deutschen Reich vom 8. bis 11. Jh.* (Stuttgart, 1973); R. Wenskus, *Sächsischer Stammesadel und fränkischer Reichsadel* (Göttingen, 1976); P. Geary, *Aristocracy in Provence: The Rhône Basin at the Dawn of the Carolingian Age* (Stuttgart, 1985).

The decisive importance of landownership in ensuring the continuation of aristocratic kinship groups, generally underestimated by German historiography, has been demonstrated in a fundamental work, G. Tabacco, "La connessione fra potere e possesso nel regno franco e nel regno longobardo," *Settimane* 20 (1973): 133–68.

There is no satisfactory bibliography on patronage in Carolingian society. More specifically on vassalage, the classical works by Mitteis and Ganshof appear largely to have become obsolete because of their overly legalistic approach (H. Mitteis, *Lehnrecht und Staatsgewalt* [Weimar 1933]; F.-L. Ganshof, "L'origine des rapports féodo-vassaliques: les rapports féodo-vassaliques dans la monarchie franque au nord des Alpes à l'époque carolingienne," *Settimane* 1 [1954]: 27–69; F.-L. Ganshof, *Qu'est-ce que la féodalité?* 5th ed. [Paris, 1982]; F.-L. Ganshof, "Das Lehnwesen im fränkischen Reich. Lehnwesen und Reichsgewalt in karolingischer Zeit," in *Studien zum mittelalterlichen Lehnwesen* [Constance, 1960]), while the provocative work by S. Reynolds, *Fiefs and Vassals* (Oxford, 1994), concentrates too much on economic matters, rather than on patronage. Better then the old but stimulating work by C. Odegaard, *Vassi and fideles in the Carolingian Empire* (Cambridge, Mass., 1945), or the posthumous work by W. Kienast, *Die Fränkische Vasallität: Von den Hausmeiern bis zu Ludwig den Kind und*

Karl dem Einfältigen (Frankfurt am Main, 1990). See also the recent new approach by B. Kasten, "Aspekte des Lehnwesens in Einhards Briefen," in *Einhard: Studien zu Leben und Werk*, ed. H. Schefers (Darmstadt, 1997), 247–267; B. Kasten, "*Beneficium* zwischen Landleihe und Lehen—eine alte Frage, neu gestellt," in *Mönchtum–Kirche–Herrschaft 750–1000* (Sigmaringen, 1998), 243–60.

On the status of slaves and the falling of dependent free men into serfdom, see the systemization of the arguments, including the historiographic ones, recently provided by F. Panero, *Schiavi servi e villani nell'Italia medievale* (Turin, 1999), which, in spite of its title, is also valid for the Frankish region. My few reservations have been argued in my review, published in *Storica* 12 (1998 [*sic*] actually 1999): 133–41. More specifically on the Carolingian age, see H.-W. Goetz, "Serfdom and the beginning of a 'seigneurial system' in the Carolingian period: a survey of the evidence," *Early Medieval Europe* 2 (1993): 29–51. On the slaves of smallholders, see G. Bois, *La Mutation de l'an mil* (Paris, 1989). For an analysis of the mechanisms of subjugation of free men by the power of large landowners, see S. Epperlein, *Herrschaft und Volk im karolingischen Imperium* (Berlin, 1969), and B. Andreolli and M. Montanari, *L'azienda curtense in Italia* (Bologna, 1983). It is always useful to remember that the widespread transformation of rural slaves into *coloni*, which medievalists tend to think occurred in the early Middle Ages, is considered by classical historians to have occurred in late antiquity: see C. Wickham, "Marx, Sherlock Holmes, and late Roman commerce," in *Land & Power: Studies in Italian and European Social History, 400–1200* (London, 1994), 77–98, and D. Vera, "Le forme del lavoro rurale: aspetti della trasformazione dell'Europa rurale fra tarda antichità e alto medioevo," *Settimane* 45 (1999): 293–338. On the improvement of the condition of slaves through the influence of religion, see H. Hoffmann, "Kirche und Sklaverei im frühen Mittelalter," *DA* 42 (1986): 1–24. On the fate of manumitted slaves, see the studies by M. Bloch, *Mélanges historiques* (Paris, 1963), are still fundamental; see also H. Grieser, *Sklaverei im spätantiken und frühmittelalterlichen Gallien (5.-7. Jh.)* (Stuttgart, 1997).

On the concept of *pauperes*, see K. Bosl, "Potens und Pauper," in *Festschrift O. Brunner* (Göttingen, 1963), 60–87. However Bosl adheres to a limited concept of freedom *(Königsfreientheorie)*, which became the dominant theory in the German historiography with the so-called *neue Lehre*. The critical reviews by H. K. Schulze, "Rodungsfreiheit und Königsfreiheit: Zu Genese und Kritik neuerer Verfassungsrechtlicher Theorien," *HZ* 219 (1974): 529–50, and H. K. Schulze, "Reichsaristokratie, Stammesadel und fränkische Freiheit," *HZ* 227

(1978): 353–73, constitute here again a suitable starting point for dealing with this doctrine. More generally, the theory of the *Königsfreien* has been thoroughly refuted by E. Müller-Mertens, *Karl der Grosse, Ludwig der Fromme und die Freien: Wer waren die liberi homines der karolingischen Kapitularien?* (Berlin, 1963); G. Tabacco, "I liberi del re nell'Italia carolingia e postcarolingia," *Settimane* 13 (1966); H. Krause, "Die liberi der Lex Baiuvariorum," in *Festschrift Max Spindler* (Munich, 1969), 41–73; J. Schmitt, *Untersuchungen zu den Liberi Homines der Karolingerzeit* (Frankfurt am Main, 1977). These texts, particularly Schmitt's, are fundamental for reviewing the policy of protecting free men enacted by Charlemagne and Louis the Pious; see also J. Devisse, " 'Pauperes' et 'paupertas' dans le monde carolingien: ce qu'en dit Hincmar de Reims," *Revue du Nord* 48 (1966): 273–87; and E. Magnou-Nortier, "Les *pagenses,* notables et fermiers du fisc durant le haut moyen âge," *RBPH* 65 (1987): 237–56.

Chapter 14. Old Age and Death

The pessimistic interpretation of the latter years of Charlemagne's reign was put forward by F.-L. Ganshof, "L'échec de Charlemagne," *Comptes-rendus de l'Académie des inscriptions et belles-lettres* (1947): 248–54; F.-L. Ganshof, "La fin du regne de Charlemagne: une décomposition," *Zeitschrift für Schweizerische Geschichte* 28 (1948): 533–52. See also, for a more recent study, R.-H. Bautier, "Le poids de la Neustrie ou de la France du nord-ouest dans la monarchie carolingienne d'après les diplômes de la chancellerie royale (751–840)," in *La Neustrie,* ed. H. Atsma (Sigmaringen, 1989), 548–49.

On legislation to improve morals in the later years of his reign, see H. Mordek and G. Schmitz, "Neue Kapitularien und Kapitulariensammlungen," *DA* 43 (1987): 361–439; and W. Hartmann, *Die Synoden der Karolingerzeit im Frankenreich und Italien* (Paderborn, 1989), 128–40.

On the end of Charlemagne's expansionist policy, the fundamental work is T. Reuter, "The End of Carolingian Military Expansion," in *Charlemagne's Heir: New Perspectives on the Reign of Louis the Pious* (Oxford, 1990), 391–405. On the campaigns against the Danes, see H. Jankuhn, "Karl der Grosse und der Norden," in *KdG,* 1:699–707.

Historians have been struggling for a long time with the *Divisio regnorum* of 806 and Louis's coronation of 813, particularly because of the absence of any reference to the title of emperor in the *Divisio.* The classical analysis was by W. Schlesinger, "Kaisertum und Reichsteilung. Zur Divisio Regnorum von 806," in

Forschungen zu Staat und Verfassung: Festgabe F. Hartung (Berlin, 1958), 9–51. For a discussion of the more recent interpretations, see H. H. Anton, "Beobachtungen zum Fränkisch-Byzantinischen Verhältnis im Karolingischer Zeit," in *Beiträge zur Geschichte des Regnum Francorum*, ed. R. Schieffer (Sigmaringen, 1990), 77–119. See also D. Hägermann, "'Quae ad profectum et utilitatem pertinent': Normen und maximen zur Innen- und Aussenpolitik in der *Divisio Regnorum* von 806," in *Peasants and Townsmen in Medieval Europe*, ed. J.-M. Duvosquel and E. Thoen (Ghent, 1995), 605–17.

Specifically on the decision to retain the *regnum Francorum* for the eldest legitimate son, Charles, and set up separate kingdoms of Italy and Aquitaine for Pepin and Louis, see P. Classen, "Karl der Grosse und die Thronfolge im Frankenreich," in *Festschrift H. Heimpel* (Göttingen, 1972), 3:109–34. Classen argues that the principal inheritance was originally to be divided between Charles and the real firstborn, Pepin the Hunchback; see however W. Goffart, "Paul the Deacon's Gesta episcoporum Mettensium and the early design of Charlemagne's succession," *Traditio* 42 (1986): 59–93. Agreeing with Classen are also E. Ewig, "Überlegungen zu den merowingischen und karolingischen Teilungen," *Settimane* 28 (1981): 225–53, and H. Beumann, "Unitas Ecclesiae— Unitas Imperii—Unitas Regni: Von der imperialen Reichseinheitsidee zur Einheit der Regna," *Settimane* 28 (1981): 531–71. The traditional position, which perceived the *Divisio* of 806 essentially as a submission to the egalitarian rules of Frankish law and a temporary sidelining of the *nomen imperatoris*, clearly in contrast with Louis the Pious's *Ordinatio imperii* of 817, has been resurrected by D. Hägermann in "Reichseinheit und Reichsteilung: Bemerkungen zur Divisio regnorum von 806 und zur Ordinatio imperii von 817," *HJ* 95 (1975): 278–307.

On the Romano-Byzantine origin of the ceremony of 813 and its implications, see P. Delogu, "Consors regni: un problema carolingio," *BISIMeAM* 76 (1964): 47–98; and W. Wendling, "Die Erhebung Ludwigs des Frommen zum Mitkaiser im Jahre 813 und ihre Bedeutung für die Verfassungsgeschichte des Frankenreiches," *FMSt* 19 (1985): 201–38.

For some time, historians have been reconsidering the historical figure of Louis the Pious; see P. Godman and R. Collins, eds., *Charlemagne's Heir: New Perspectives on the Reign of Louis the Pious (814–840)* (Oxford, 1990), and E. Boshof, *Ludwig der Fromme* (Darmstadt, 1996).

On Charlemagne's will, see M. Innes, "Charlemagne's will: piety, politics and the imperial succession," *EHR* 112 (1997): 833–55. On the burial, see A. Dierkens, "Autour de la tombe de Charlemagne: considérations sur les sépultures des souverains carolingiens et des membres de leur famille," *Byzantion* 61 (1991): 156–81.

There has been a long debate on whether the title of *Magnus* was habitually associated with the name of Charles by his contemporaries. Prevailing opinion, expressed by, among others, K. F. Werner in *Karl der Grosse oder Charlemagne?* (Munich, 1995), 32–34, is that the appellative was attached to his name only long after his death, commencing from the ninth century, and that in works like Einhard's *Vita Karoli* it was only added in later manuscripts; the form *Karolus, magnus imperator,* which appears on his tombstone and in other places, is protocol and not onomastic. Without challenging this interpretation, we might note that this protocol became standard during Charlemagne's life to a surprising extent: highly official sources, such as the Royal Annals, regularly refer to him as "Carolus magnus rex" (see for example the years 769, 772, 781, and 784). Even more interesting is that the usage was taken up while Charles was still alive by the Italic chancellery in relation to the kings of Italy, Pepin and then Bernard: see C. Manaresi, *I placiti del 'Regnum Italiae,'* Fonti per la storia d'Italia no. 54 (Rome, 1955), vol. 1, nos. 13 (801) and 16 (803): *Pipinus magnus rex;* and no. 26 (813): *Bernardi magni regis.* The same title is applied to Pepin (*magnus . . . rex Pipinus piissimus*) in the contemporary *Ritmo veronese* (*Versus de Verona: Versus de Mediolano civitate,* ed. G. B. Pighi [Bologna, 1960]). This excessive use of the appellative *magnus* is therefore to be considered typical of Charlemagne's age and may therefore be a forerunner of the form *Karolus Magnus* that later prevailed.

INDEX